The Politics of Excellence and Choice in Education

Education Policy Perspectives

General Editor: Professor Ivor Goodson, Faculty of Education, University of Western Ontario, London, Canada N6G 1G7

Education policy analysis has long been a neglected area in the UK and, to an extent, in the USA and Australia. The result has been a profound gap between the study of education and the formulation of education policy. For practitioners, such a lack of analysis of new policy initiatives has worrying implications, particularly at a time of such policy flux and change. Education policy has, in recent years, been a matter for intense political debate – the political and public interest in the working of the system has come at the same time as the breaking of the consensus on education policy by the New Right. As never before, political parties and pressure groups differ in their articulated policies and prescriptions for the education sector. Critical thinking about these developments is clearly imperative.

All those working within the system also need information on policy-making, policy implementation and effective day-to-day operation. Pressure on schools from government, education authorities and parents has generated an enormous need for knowledge amongst those on the receiving end of educational policies.

This series aims to fill the academic gap, to reflect the politicalization of education, and to provide the practitioners with the analysis for informed implementation of policies that they will need. It offers studies in broad areas of policy studies, with a particular focus on the following areas: school organization and improvement (David Reynolds, University College, Cardiff, UK); social analysis (Professor Philip Wexler, University of Rochester, USA); and policy studies and evaluation (Professor Ernest House, University of Colorado at Boulder, USA).

The Politics of Excellence and Choice in Education

1987 Yearbook of the Politics of Education Association

Edited by

William Lowe Boyd

The Pennsylvania State University

and

Charles Taylor Kerchner

The Claremont Graduate School

 **The Falmer Press**

(A member of the Taylor & Francis Group)

New York, Philadelphia, and London

UK   The Falmer Press, Falmer House, Barcombe, Lewes, East Sussex, BN8 5DL

USA   The Falmer Press, Taylor & Francis Inc., 242 Cherry Street, Philadelphia, PA 19106–1906

First published as a special issue of the *Journal of Education Policy*, 2(5), 1987
Reprinted 1989

Library of Congress Cataloging in Publication Data available on request

ISBN 1 85000 397 1
ISBN 1 85000 398 X (pbk)

Jacket design by Caroline Archer

Typeset in 11/12pt Bembo by Chapterhouse Typesetting Ltd, Formby, Lancs.

Printed in Great Britain by Taylor & Francis (Printers) Ltd, Basingstoke, Hants.

Contents

The **Politics of Education Association (PEA)** promotes the development and dissemination of research and debate on educational policy and politics. **PEA** brings together scholars, practitioners, and policy-makers interested in educational governance and politics; is affiliated as a Special Interest Group with the American Educational Research Association (AERA); and meets each spring in conjunction with AERA's annual meeting. The annual membership dues for **PEA** are $US20.00. Members receive the *Politics of Education Bulletin* (published three times a year) and a copy of the annual Yearbook. Membership dues should be sent to Robert Wimpelberg, **PEA** Treasurer, Department of Educational Leadership, University of New Orleans, New Orleans, LA 70148, USA.

About the Editors and Contributors

William Lowe Boyd is Professor of Education in the College of Education at the Pennsylvania State University, University Park, Pennsylvania. His specialty in research and teaching is educational policy and politics. He has been a Visiting Fulbright Scholar in Australia and is co-editor of *Problem-Finding in Educational Administration* and two forthcoming volumes: *Educational Policy in Australia and America*, and *Private Schools and Public Policy*. Prior to going to Penn State in 1980, Dr Boyd taught at the University of Rochester. His PHD is from the University of Chicago. In the summers, he serves as Assistant Director of the National Music Camp at the Interlochen Center for the Arts in Michigan.

Charles Taylor Kerchner is Associate Professor of Education and Public Policy at The Claremont Graduate School in Southern California. his research has focused on the development of teacher unions and the public policy dimensions of education. He is co-author of the forthcoming volume *The Changing Idea of a Teachers' Union*. Prior to going to Claremont, Dr Kerchner was at Northwestern University, where he received his PHD; at the Illinois Board of Higher Education, where he was associate director for academic programs; and with *The St Petersburg Times* in Florida, in a variety of editorial and management positions.

Eric Bredo is a professor in the Curry School of Education at the University of Virginia.

John E. Chubb is a policy analyst with the Brookings Institution in Washington, DC.

Bruce S. Cooper is a professor in the School of Education at Fordham University in New York and visiting professor at the University of London.

Denis P. Doyle is a policy analyst with the Hudson Institute in Washington, DC.

Richard F. Elmore is a professor in the School of Education at Michigan State University.

Frances C. Fowler teaches 6th grade in Oliver Springs, Tennessee, and is on the Board of Directors of the Tennessee Education Association.

James W. Guthrie is a professor in the School of Education at the University of California, Berkeley.

Laurence Iannaccone is a professor in the Department of Education at the University of California, Santa Barbara.

Thomas H. Jones is a professor in the School of Education at the University of Connecticut.

Julia Koppich is a policy analyst with PACE (Policy Analysis for California Education), Berkeley, California.

Tim L. Mazzoni is a professor in the College of Education at the University of Minnesota.

Linda M. McNeil is Chair of the Department of Education at Rice University.

Terry M. Moe is a professor in the Department of Political Science at Stanford University.

David N. Plank is a professor in the School of Education at the University of Pittsburgh.

Joseph G. Weeres is Chair of the Education Faculty at The Claremont Graduate School.

1 Introduction and overview: education and the politics of excellence and choice

William Lowe Boyd and Charles Taylor Kerchner
Pennsylvania State University and Claremont Graduate School

Worldwide developments, particularly in the economic sphere, have produced far-flung consequences for educational policy and politics. Beginning with the OPEC oil embargo and the subsequent worldwide economic recession, and continuing down through the increasingly severe economic competition between industrialized nations, economic and political trends have intersected, producing ripple effects that have affected national social policy, including education (Wirt and Harman 1986). Demands for greater efficiency, productivity, and quality, and sometimes even for privatization of public services have become commonplace. Social and demographic trends frequently are adding to pressures in this direction by eroding middle and upper-middle class support for public services. In the English-speaking world, an early consequence of this was the rise of neo-conservative sentiment and political power, with 'Thatcherism' in the UK, echoed by 'Fraserism' in Australia and 'Reaganism' in the USA (Smart 1987). This volume examines the consequences of these broad trends in the United States, which is now experiencing one of the most sustained educational reform movements in its history.

Indeed, the landscape of American educational politics has been transformed since 1980 when President Reagan took office. The federal role in education has been sharply redefined and reduced and, as a consequence, the state role has been greatly increased. Partly because of federal exhortations (Jung and Kirst 1986), and even more because they perceive a linkage between high quality schooling and economic growth and competitiveness, state governors and their legislatures now are involved in educational policy-making in an unprecedented way. One notable consequence is that the already circumscribed policy-making power of local school districts has been further eroded, as power and control shift ever more to the state capital.

Not only have roles and relationships changed, but there has been a marked shift in the fundamental values guiding American education policy (Clark and Astuto 1986). The pursuit of excellence has replaced equity as the leading goal of American schooling. Although some policy-makers and analysts claim equity need not be sacrificed in the pursuit of excellence, many critics feel that beneath the rhetoric of excellence there is an over-riding concern for economic efficiency and productivity. This concern, they believe, is driving out attention to equity and social justice. At the same time debate mounts about this issue, another facet of the 'excellence' movement has reopened other quite sensitive policy questions. This facet is the concern for choice and diversity in schooling that goes along with many conceptions of what is required for educational excellence. This concern raises several questions. How much client choice of educational programs *within* and *between* public schools is desirable? Should government policies be altered to foster choice between public and private schools? Are choice and excellence indeed always compatible goals in education?

The current reform movement was launched in 1983 by the release of *A Nation at Risk:*

The Imperative for Educational Reform, the report of the federally-sponsored National
Commission of Excellence in Education. In the early days of the reform movement, which
were characterized by a deluge of similar commissions and reports, there was concern that
education reform efforts would have to be carried out rapidly, before policy-makers and the
public once again relegated schooling to a peripheral area of importance. However, the
'window of opportunity' for reform has stayed open much longer than anticipated. The
reasons for this are not hard to find. American political leaders, especially state governors, are
truly convinced that there is a linkage between good schooling and economic prosperity.
Thus, at the July 1987 meeting of the National Governors Association (NGA), Governor
Thomas Kean, of New Jersey, opened the session reporting on progress in school reform by
commenting that, 'Educational reform is intensely competitive. States that succeed will do
better economically.' Similarly, the governor of Indiana recounted how his school reform
effort gained political support through use of a 'television ad to scare people about
competition from overseas where they do believe in eduction'.

     This session at the NGA meeting marked the release of *Results in Education: 1987*
(National Governors' Association 1987), the first of five yearly reports scheduled to follow-
up on the agenda set out in the NGA's '1991 Report on Education', *Time for Results*
(National Governors' Association 1986). This impressive commitment by the governors to
keep the reform movement alive is also paralleled by the efforts of other major agencies and
institutions. Most notable, perhaps, are the reports and long-range plans of the Carnegie and
Holmes groups, both of which are seeking a fundamental restructuring of the schools and of
the nature of teaching as a profession (see Carnegie Task Force 1986, Holmes Group 1986).

     Altogether, the dramatic developments and issues outlined above, and the staying
power of the present reform movement four years after it began, demand a comprehensive
reappraisal of the character of American educational politics. This first Yearbook of the
Politics of Education Association focuses on the political and policy implications of the far-
reaching school reform movement ongoing in the United States.

Background

The emphasis on excellence has reconfigured the politics of American education. As Laurence
Iannaccone argues in his chapter in this book, there is evidence that the political cleavages in
American education have been redrawn with 'excellence' as the dominant belief. Among the
forces producing this development are significant demographic shifts which are transforming
both the character of the national electorate and the constituency of the public schools. In
light of these trends, there is a real danger that support for American public education could
be jeopardized if the current reform movement ultimately should be judged a failure.[1]

     Of course, many may feel there is no real danger. Even if current reform efforts prove
disappointing, aren't most Americans firmly committed to support of public schools? After
all, we've been reforming the public schools with modest results for generations and the
public has remained loyal all along. Why should the present situation be any more precarious
than the past?

     What is new today are the serious implications of current social and demographic trends
in the United States. Taken together, these trends indicate that American public schools will
find it increasingly difficult to retain broad-based public support.[2] To begin with, there is the
growth in the proportion of senior citizens in the population and the decline in the
proportion of families with children in the public schools. Added to this is evidence that
strongly suggests that public schools may have trouble retaining the support of middle and

upper-middle class parents. One factor at work here is the increasing level of education in the populace generally and among the middle and upper-middle class in particular. As the educational level of families rises they tend to become more sophisticated, discerning, and demanding consumers of educational services. Schools are thus under pressure in part because of their very successes. Each generation tends to demand more from the schools than their predecessors. This makes the public, and especially the very highly educated upper-middle class, increasingly quality conscious and unwilling to accept mediocre schooling services.

Another far-reaching development is that the public school population, particularly in urban areas, is composed increasingly of racial, ethnic, and language minority groups. These groups tend to have low political activity and influence, a high incidence of single-parent families, and often suffer learning and physical disabilities. As minority groups increasingly characterize the population of public schools, majority groups may become less willing to send their children to them and, consequently, to finance them. This pattern already has been painfully clear for some time in many of our large city school systems. But added to this now is accumulating evidence that the affluent segment of the Baby-Boom generation is less committed to the support of the public schools than were their counterparts in earlier generations (Odden 1985).

A number of analysts (e.g., Boaz 1986, and his associates) argue that the maturation of the Baby-Boom generation has much to do with the dramatic reconfiguration of American politics since 1970. They stress that, unlike earlier generations influenced by the Great Depression and federal interventions to combat it, the 'boomers' grew up with affluence and a sense that big government causes problems. With their basic materialistic needs satisfied, 'boomers' seek self-actualization and inner directedness. According to Lee Atwater (in Boaz 1986: 34), one way this manifests itself is with a concern for quality: 'Bigger is not better anymore – better is better.' Consequently, 'boomers' desire excellence and choice in schooling and may be skeptical of the ability of bureaucratized, government schools to deliver these qualities. Moreover, affluent 'boomers' or 'yuppies' (i.e., young urban professionals) generally can pay to get what they want since they tend toward double-wage earner families with few children. As a result, they contribute significantly to the growing constituency in favor of excellence, choice, and privatization in education. A curb on this trend which should be noted, however, is the fact that a substantial portion of the 'boomer' population is not only not affluent, but actually facing a decline in their standard of living.

Assessing all of these trends and more, Paul Peterson (1985a) concludes that the adaptive qualities and vast inertia of public schools as well-established institutions should carry them through these difficult times. He notes also that private school costs and fees are likely to soar, pricing out many families and removing the threat of a large shift of enrollment from the public sector. Nevertheless, research on the Australian experience with private schools (Boyd 1987a) underscores the vulnerability of public schools to private school competition. The experience Down Under shows clearly that you don't have to have a large private school enrollment (ours is now about 11%) to create and maintain a dual school system, with all of the associated problems of elitist private schools and demoralized government schools. What is critical is *who* goes to private schools. In Australia, three-quaters of the students still go to government schools. But the prestige and career advantages of attending the elite private schools (which charge substantial fees despite receiving state aid) foster a creaming-off process that drains government high schools of most of their *upper-middle class* students. With the exodus of these students, the academic ethos and reputation of most government high schools decline sharply. Once set in motion this 'creaming-off' dynamic creates a vicious circle that ensures its own maintenance.[3]

Significantly, a major conclusion of Peterson's (1985b) own important historical research is that the strength of American public schools over time has depended on the support of the middle class and an ability to stave off competing institutions. Yet, as Peterson recognizes, the public schools today face increasing competition, not only from private schools but also from day care and manpower training institutions. Indeed, the public schools now may be facing a more challenging environment than those to which they have responded successfully in the past. There can be little doubt about the enormous inertia of public schools, but their adaptive qualities might not be equal to the extraordinarily 'turbulent' field they face due to a threatening combination of environmental trends over which they have no control (cf., Emery and Trist 1965).

One possible scenario might run as follows. Because of mounting national concern about the need to promote US economic 'competitiveness' – coupled with revelations such as the continuing poor math performance of American students when compared to students from other nations – the view will continue to grow that improved educational achievement is imperative for better economic performance in this technological age. Suppose, then, that the 'excellence' movement falters, public school performance lags, and there is growing acceptance of research claiming to document the inefficiency of public schools as compared to private schools (e.g., Coleman and Hoffer 1987, Chubb and Moe 1987). If this happens, we then could witness the political sea change necessary for the creation of a new balance between public and private schools.

In sum, one does not have to be an alarmist to see that many current trends may sorely tax the adaptiveness and resilience of public schools. In view of the combination of factors eroding public support of public schools, there could be a real danger of public schools falling into a downward spiral of decay and disillusionment if the present reform movement stumbles. This is what Albert Shanker (1983) stresses when he speaks of American schools facing their 'first real crisis'. Already, the sociopolitical climate has been receptive to the remarkable shift that the Reagan administration has achieved in the overarching values guiding American eduational policy. As Clark and Astuto (1986) demonstrate, through a systematic program of policies and pronouncements, there has been a 180-degree shift in emphasis away from the values that guided federal policy in the 1970s: from equity to excellence; from needs and access to ability and selectivity; from regulations and enforcement to deregulation; from the common school to parental choice and institutional competition; and from social and welfare concerns to economic and productivity concerns. Clearly, this shift in values challenges many of the traditional tenets of public education. It is in this context that we need to assess the status and implications of the contemporary school reform movement in America.

Issues

Ironically, policies being pursued in the name of excellence frequently are at odds with both the contemporary implications of educational excellence and the conditions necessary for it (see, e.g., Cuban 1986). In an attempt to 'mandate excellence' and 'legislate learning' (Wise 1979), most states have enacted statewide policies that centralize control and standardize the character of public schooling. Yet, for many people excellence in education requires diversity and choice in schooling arrangements. The contradiction between the ends and means of recent educational policy has been well stated by Iannaccone (1985: 8, emphasis added).

> The state centralization of educational control is setting the stage for the next conflicts in the politics of education . . . The specific nature of the battles ahead is becoming

clear. *The absurd attempts to produce effective schools by state standardization, increased state centralization of education, fiscal controls and regulations requiring the imposition from the top of effective school characteristics may be the greatest policy contradiction we have seen in public education in two decades.* That contradiction could even lead to a new public education system. To illustrate using California: were the recentralizers to win the battles ahead in my state, they would lose the war given the continuation of present, well established, ideological drift among the voters. The success of centralist officials in Sacramento would, I predict, finally place the educational voucher on the state ballot.

In general, there has been a widespread failure, in the educational establishment, to appreciate how the politics of excellence tends to promote demands for choice that will reconfigure educational politics and management (Kerchner 1985). Terrel Bell has warned that parental demands for choice among schools and teachers will grow. He notes that schools 'are the last bastion of regulated and controlled services' and predicts that the trend toward deregulation in many industries will reach education in the next three to five years (as quoted in Evangelauf 1986). Although the National Governors Association report, *Time for Results*, endorses greater choice in schooling, most school administrators appear insensitive to this trend or reluctant to acknowledge it. Instead, they cling to the administrative tradition and convenience of the norm of 'universalism' and the 'one best system' approach to the provision of schooling (Tyack 1974).

However, if the politics of education are fundamentally ruled by 'excellence' criteria, then the politics of choice takes on a new character. Vouchers and tax credits may be judged not according to equity criteria, where their claims are weak, but according to 'satisfaction' criteria, where the proponents of broader choice can connect their support for market and quasi-market mechanisms to both consumer preference and higher educational achievement. When viewed this way, client choice is not an abandonment of public education – an exit instead of a voice. Rather, client choice becomes viewed as the provision of alternative means of looking for excellence.

The new emphasis on excellence not only redefines the politics of public choice, but also sets in motion a politics of quality assurance by undermining the old 'logic of confidence' (Meyer and Rowan 1978) that use to be substituted for actual examination of the outcomes of schooling. The politics of excellence and choice – even if confined to the public school sector, as the National Governors' Association report, *Time for Results*, advocates – also creates new pressures for the reform of school administration and related pressures for the reform of teacher unionism.

Nevertheless, although proposals to enhance choice via tuition tax credits or vouchers have attracted much attention, the strong opposition they have elicited generally has blocked the expansion of choice or confined it to public sector ventures, such as magnet schools. Moreover, the major thrust of the statewide 'excellence' reform movement clearly has b. ·n on state mandated measures that typically have the effect of standardizing and centralizing educational policy. Thus, rather than increasing choice and diversity in schooling, these policies reduce what variety exists, albeit in the name of raising standards in pursuit of excellence. Consequently, one of the concerns in this Yearbook is the tension between the competing approaches to educational excellence embodied in the efforts of centralizers and diversifiers. The implications of these efforts for equity and social justice, as well as for excellence and choice, are a major issue. Although some observers believe the United States now is entering into a more sophisticated 'second wave' of the reform effort – concerned with more fundamental change and the restructuring of schools and teaching – it is unclear whether this new wave will temper the thrust toward standardization and centralization.

Overview of the Yearbook

Part 1 of this Yearbook, 'Understanding the politics of excellence and choice', is concerned with the philosophical and policy issues and the political and economic dynamics associated with the current reform movement. In the opening essay, Denis Doyle reminds us that, despite the heavy emphasis on economic reasons for the excellence movement, there are compelling intellectual, social, and moral arguments for the present reform effort. Increasingly, Doyle notes, these concerns push us toward the fundamental educational and political problems of schooling. What should the character of the curriculum be? Should there be a national core curriculum? What standards of performance should be demanded? Who should decide the answers to these questions? Doyle's perceptive essay takes us on an illuminating course through these and other related questions germane to the excellence and choice debate, including what is meant by civic virtue and how schools can foster it. He concludes that, in the best American tradition, 'we are backing into a national curriculum . . . we will not choose a national curriculum so much as a national curriculum will choose us'.

The power of the present reform movement probably arises from the confluence of pressing economic, social, intellectual, and moral reasons for school improvement. But the necessary and sufficient causes of major educational reform efforts are not well understood. In chapter 3, James Guthrie and Julia Koppich explore the history and political dynamics of recent educational reform movements in the USA. They compare four cases of major reform efforts: the National Defense Education Act of 1958, the Elementary and Secondary Education Act of 1965, the Education for All Handicapped Children Act of 1975, and the 1980s' 'Excellence in Education' movement. Their chapter assesses three propositions about reform – the impact of secular economic trends, participation by education professionals, and the influence of exernal events – and appraises the probable outcomes of the current reform effort. They conclude with speculations about the 'primordial policy ooze out of which a catalytic event can trigger a national education reform movement'.

Implicit in the foregoing discussion, and in the background of much of the current debate, is the following question: is economics more important than politics? This issue is addressed in interesting ways by several authors in this Yearbook. In particular, Laurence Iannaccone and Joseph Weeres agree with Ho Chi Minh (see Weeres' chapter) that the answer is 'No'. Thus, in chapter 4, Iannaccone analyzes the political shift from equity to excellence, focusing on the turning point election of 1980 that brought Ronald Reagan to the White House. As Iannaccone sees it, 'the excellence slogan is a symbol of productivity in industrial and economic terms, with application to meritocratic values in education. Education is the caboose, not the locomotive on this train'. Iannaccone concludes that the shift in political values has been such that if a Democrat were to succeed Reagan as president s/he would be pushed in policy directions similar to Reagan. Significantly, Iannaccone's conclusion is supported in a dramatic way by a recent study of Australian and American educational policy that highlights some worldwide conservative trends. In a comparison of Reagan's education policy with that of Bob Hawke's socialist government in Australia, Don Smart (1987) found that, despite the socialist commitment to reverse the conservative education policies of Hawke's predecessor, Malcolm Fraser, Hawke's policies actually have resembled Fraser's.

In chapter 5, Eric Bredo highlights the defects of approaches to educational policy that rely solely on the logic of either bureaucracies or markets. He sees the current debate as one that particularly raises the question of the proper balance of choice and constraint in educational governance. Bredo concludes that 'neither the market nor the bureaucratic metaphor suggests flexible enough strategies for coping with the non-linear, multi-level problems of educational governance'. Rather, he argues, 'the metaphor of community seems better adapted to suggesting ways to handle the interplay of several goals, both public and private, short and long run'. Thus, as a remedy he advocates an approach based upon John Dewey's conception of democratic community.

Richard Elmore's thoughtful analysis of options for choice in public education, in chapter 6, suggests additional ways to avoid the problems highlighted by Bredo's analysis. Among the numerous important points that emerge from Elmore's analysis is that 'policies affecting choice must be evaluated from both the demand and supply sides'. Thus, 'providing consumers with greater educational choice, while at the same time constraining the ability of educators to respond to consumer preferences will only increase dissatisfaction with schools'. One of the most valuable contributions of this chapter is its systematic discussion of the large variety of possible ways of organizing public education. These various combinations provide a wide range of options for enhancing or constraining choice.

In chapter 7, Charles Kerchner and William Boyd examine the dynamics of market and bureaucratic failures in education, particularly in their relationships to the values of choice, excellence, equity, and efficiency. Their discussion highlights four 'policy choice frontiers' relevant to themes developed by Bredo and Elmore: (1) demand-side choice vs. supply-side choice; (2) excellence via 'brand name' structures or via professional market structures; (3) equity via hybrid structures or via public supply; and (4) the efficiency costs of market regulation vs. the cost of managing bureaucratic monopolies. Three policy options emerge from their analysis: *market professionalism, bureaucratic intrapreneurship*, and *community democracy*. Each of these options uses a mixture of market and bureaucratic tools and, together, they illustrate that markets and bureaucracies are not incompatible: both historically and conceptually each has evolved around the failure characteristics of the other. Thus, the authors conclude that 'what doesn't work is as good a guide to policy as what does'.

In chapter 8, Joseph Weeres presents a provocative analysis that challenges much of the mainstream interpretation of American school politics and government. His perceptive discussion not only contributes to the debate about the advantages of increasing choice in public schooling, but makes an important theoretical statement delineating significant limitations of economic and public choice approaches to understanding school politics. Contrary to the view of public choice theorists, who argue that privatization of education would improve the quality and efficiency of schooling, Weeres contends that school districts already behave as markets, with the consequence that, when growth inescapably ends, they inevitably begin a spiral of political as well as economic decline. The answer to their difficulties, Weeres argues, 'lies not in the market but in the concept of civic behavior, the very existence of which the public choice economists bring into question'.

Part 2 of the Yearbook focuses on the problems encountered in implementing plans designed to foster excellence and choice in education. Among these plans, some have been concerned with identifying and replicating the features of outstanding or unusually effective public schools. For example, the 'effective schools' movement promotes a set of core attributes believed to characterize public schools that are unusually effective in eliciting student academic achievement. For some, however, the best models of excellence and choice in schooling are epitomized by outstanding private schools. Consequently, part of the current debate revolves around the question of whether public schools can easily adopt successful features of private schools, or whether fundamental characteristics of public schools must be altered before such features can be transplanted successfully. Chapter 9 presents provocative data from a major survey of public and private school teachers and

administrators that support the latter view. Reporting on a major research project underway, John Chubb and Terry Moe contend that private schools more often possess the
qualities associated with instructionally effective schools than public schools do because the
control structure of private schools frees them from the complex politics and bureaucracy
that impede organizational effectiveness in public schools. Consequently, they conclude –
contrary to Weeres' analysis – that real improvement of public schools will require that
control over them essentially be transferred from government to the marketplace.

Even without the revolutionary change that Chubb and Moe advocate (and that Weeres
would dispute), the quality of many public schools is being substantially improved through
the wide array of reforms currently being pursued across the United States. However, in
chapter 10, David Plank concludes that although clear improvements are occurring among
laggard categories of schools – i.e., in the South and in rural and small towns – the trend is
toward increased homogenization of American schooling, rather than toward diversity and
innovation. Moreover, in concert with an increasing number of observers, Plank questions
how much real change has been occurring in the statewide educational reform movement.
He classifies the current reforms into four categories – ranging from more superficial to more
fundamental reforms – and presents both a political and an organizational analysis to explain
why the more fundamental structural reforms occur less frequently. While features of both
of his explanations intersect with Chubb and Moe's analysis of the problems of public
schools, they also apply more generically to educational organizations, public or private.

The advocates of increased choice in education seemed to face a very favorable environment for advancement in the 1980's. They had a President and administration that favored
increased choice and advocated voucher and tuition tax credit plans, the *Mueller* v. *Allen*
Supreme Court decision in 1983 established a precedent in their favor and, more recently, the
recommendations of the National Governors' Association report, *Time for Results*,
supported increased choice within the public sector. Nevertheless, the next two chapters
vividly document how the political situation has deteriorated for private and parochial school
interests.

First, in chapter 11, Thomas Jones presents an incisive analysis of why the choice movement has made so little progress despite the apparent advantages it seemed to enjoy for a
while. Above all, Jones emphasizes the changes that have made vouchers and tax credits a real
threat, galvanizing the opposition of public educators. The consequence of this has been an
inability to pass the kind of bills that used to succeed and provide at least modest levels of aid
for parochial schools.

Second, in chapter 12, Bruce Cooper describes the consequences of the historic *Aguilar*
v. *Felton* decision in 1984. In this decision, the Supreme Court ruled that public school
teachers no longer could go onto the premises of parochial schools to offer remedial services,
because such involvement violated the First Amendment by causing unacceptable
government entanglement in religion. The fallout from this decision has been far-reaching.
It has completely disrupted the co-operative *modus operandi* established between public and
parochial school groups by passage of the Elementary and Secondary Education Act of 1965.
'What had been a joint belief in *equity* for all underprivileged, low achieving students under
the concepts of 'entitlement' and 'child benefit' has now been transformed', Cooper notes,
'to a battle over *choice* and vouchers'. Cooper analyzes the policy options available for the
resolution of this impasse and, in so doing, throws light on the inability to date to obtain
adoption of policies restoring some degree of pre-Felton federal services for parochial school
students.

The Yearbook concludes with reports on developments in three of the most interesting
school reform states: Tennessee, Texas, and Minnesota. The first two are representative of

Sunbelt states, in which educational reforms have been pushed very hard by energetic governors, sometimes over rather strong protests from teachers' organizations. Minnesota is a unique case in that educational choice proposals have been pursued more successfully there than in any other state. From each of the three states some very useful lessons about educational reform can be learned.

In Frances Fowler's chapter, we have a vivid, first-hand account of the conflict that occurred in Tennessee over Governor Lamar Alexander's ambitious school reform agenda. As she notes, in her perceptive 'view from the classroom', the experience in Tennessee raises an important and fundamental question: 'Is it politically feasible to implement the current conception of educational excellence in a situation where neither adequacy nor equity has been achieved?' The answer, in Tennessee, Fowler says, is negative because the foundation conditions necessary for excellence in schools are absent. She concludes that, rather than being contradictory goals, equity and excellence are complimentary because 'equity and adequacy provide the indispensable foundation for educational excellence'.

Like Tennessee, the school reform experience in Texas is full of color and conflict. Linda McNeil provides an insightful account of the controversies and contradictions so dramatically evident in the Texas experience. As she emphasizes, however, 'school reform in Texas, despite its theatrics, is not an aberrant case'. Rather, the issues and policies evident there are prototypical of the logic and rhetoric being pursued in state education reform across the nation. First, there is 'the idea that public education should somehow be responsible for economic recovery'. Here, McNeil illuminates the irony that 'behind the economic improvement rhetoric were built models of accountability anachronistic to the economic future the reformers articulate'. Second, she calls attention to the irony of the enormous shift to the state education department of authority and control over details of the process of schooling. The result, she contends, is a profound 'deskilling' of teachers that undercuts their professionalism and morale and that is inconsistent with the quality of teaching that is required for excellence in education.

Tim Mazzoni's analysis of Minnesota's experience underscores the unusual combination of factors that seems necessary to bring choice proposals into practice. Mazzoni analyzes policy-making on four choice issues that have been dealt with in Minnesota: tuition tax deductions and post-secondary options, which have produced legislation, and education vouchers and open enrollment, which have not. His analysis examines the four issues in terms of six propositions drawn from relevant theory and research. Mazzoni concludes by showing the way in which three kinds of politics – the politics of confrontation, finesse, and collaboration – influence the policy-making process and the chances for policy innovation.

In sum, the contents of this Yearbook range broadly across the politics of excellence and choice, from discussions of civic virtue and a national curriculum (Doyle), to the shift from equity to excellence (Iannaccone), to options for choice (Elmore) and 'what doesn't work' (Kerchner and Boyd), to the 'deskilling of teachers' (McNeil) and the prerequisites for implementing excellence in education (Fowler). Together, these papers help illuminate facets of the complex developments characteristic of today's 'excellence' movement in the United States. Typical of the analyst and academic, the emphasis in these papers is mainly upon the problems and inconsistencies of the excellence movement, rather than on its accomplishments. As this story is continuing to unfold across fifty states, however, the full significance and lasting impacts of the movement can only be assessed sometime in the future.[4]

Notes

1. This section is drawn from Boyd (1987b).
2. See, especially, Kirst and Garms (1980), Hodgkinson (1985), and Peterson (1985a).
3. Historically, the bulk of American private school enrollment has come from the ranks of working class Catholics. If the upper-middle class component of our private school enrollment had been larger, private schools would have constituted more of a threat to our public schools.
4. For two useful assessments now available, see Chance (1986) and Mueller and McKeown (1985).

References

BOAZ, D., (ed.) (1986) *Left, Right and Babyboom: America's New Politics* (Washington, DC: CATO Institute).

BOYD, W.L. (1987a) 'Balancing public and private schools: the Australian approach and American implications', *Educational Evaluation and Policy Analysis*, 9 (Fall).

BOYD, W.L. (1987b) 'Public education's last hurrah? Schizophrenia, amnesia, and ignorance in school politics', *Educational Evaluation and Policy Analysis*, 9 (Summer).

CARNEGIE TASK FORCE ON TEACHING AS A PROFESSION (1986) *A Nation Prepared? Teachers for the 21st Century* (New York: Carnegie Forum on Education and the Economy).

CHANCE, W. (1986) *The Best of Educations: Reforming America's Public Schools in the 1980s* (John D. and Catherine T. MacArthur Foundation; Denver: Education Commission of the States)

CHUBB, J.E., and MOE, T.M. (1987) *Politics, Markets, and School Performance* (Washington, DC: The Brookings Institution), in press.

CLARK, D.L. and ASTUTO, T.A. (1986) 'The significance an permanence of changes in federal education policy', *Educational Researcher*, October. pp. 4–13;

COLEMAN, J.S. and HOFFER, T. (1987) *Public and Private High Schools: The Impact of Communities* (New York: Basic Books).

CUBAN, L. (1986) 'Persistent instruction: another look at constancy in the classroom', *Phi Delta Kappan*, September, pp. 7–11.

EMERY, F.E., and TRIST, E.L. (1965) 'The causal texture of organizational environments', *Human Relations*, 18, pp. 21–32.

EVANGELAUF, J. (1986) 'School-reform movement said to be moving from capitols to classrooms', *Chronicle of Higher Education*, 7 May, p. 22.

HODGKINSON, H.L. (1985) *All One System: Demographics of Education – Kindergarten through Graduate School* (Washington, DC: Institute for Educational Leadership, Inc).

HOLMES GROUP, INC. (1986) *Tomorrow's Teachers: A Report of the Holmes Group* (East Lansing, MI: Holmes Group).

IANNACCONE, L. (1985), 'Excellence: an emergent educational issue', *Politics of Education Bulletin*, 12, pp. 1, 3–8.

JUNG, R.K. and KIRST, M.W. (1986) 'Beyond mutual adaptation, into the bully pulpit: recent research on the federal role in education'. *Educational Administration Quarterly*, 22 (3), pp. 80–109.

KERCHNER, C.T. (1985) 'At issue: fallout from the politics of school excellence', *Politics of Education Bulletin*, 12 (3), pp. 2, 15.

KIRST, M.W. and GARMS, W.I. (1980) 'The political environment of school finance policy in the 1980s', In J.W. Guthrie (ed.), *School finance Policies and Practices – The 1980s: A Decade of Conflict* (Cambridge, MA: Ballinger).

MEYER, J.W. and ROWAN, B. (1978) 'The structure of educational organizations', in M.W. Meyer, *et al.*, *Environments and Organizations* (San Francisco: Jossey-Bass).

MUELLER, Van D. and MCKEOWN, M.P. (eds) (1985) *The Fiscal, Legal, and Political Aspects of State Reform of Elementary and Secondary Education*. Sixth Annual Yearbook of the American Education Finance Association (Cambridge, MA: Ballinger Publishing Co.).

NATIONAL COMMISSION ON EXCELLENCE IN EDUCATION (1983) *A Nation at Risk: The Imperative for Educational Reform* (Washington, DC: US Government Printing Office).

NATIONAL GOVERNORS' ASSOCIATION (1986) *Time for Results: The 1991 Report on Education* (Washington, DC: NGA).

NATIONAL GOVERNORS' ASSOCIATION (1987) *Results in Education: 1987* (Washington, DC: NGA).

ODDEN, A. (1985) 'Education finance 1985: A rising tide or steady fiscal state?' *Educational Evaluation and Policy Analysis*, 7 (4), pp. 395–407.

PETERSON, P.E. (1985a) 'Economic and political trends affecting education', unpublished paper (Washington, DC: The Brookings Institution).

PETERSON, P.E. (1985b) *The Politics of School Reform, 1870–1940* (Chicago: University of Chicago Press).

SHANKER, A. (1983) 'The first real crisis', in L.S. Shulman and G. Sykes (Eds), *Handbook of Teaching and Policy* (New York: Longman).

SMART, D. (1987) 'Reagan conservatism and Hawke socialism: whither the differences in the education policies of the US and Australian federal governments?' in W.L. Boyd and D. Smart (Eds), *Educational Policy in Australia and America; Comparative Perspectives* (London: Falmer Press), in press.

TYACK, D. (1974) *The One Best System* (Cambridge, MA: Harvard University Press).

WIRT, F.M., and HARMAN, G. (Eds) (1986) *Education, Recession, and the World Village* (London: Falmer Press).

WISE, A.E. (1979) *Legislated Learning: The Bureaucratization of the American Classroom* (Berkeley: University of California Press).

2   *The excellence movement, academic standards, a core curriculum and choice: how do they connect?*

Denis P. Doyle
The Hudson Institute

To paraphrase Mr Justice Stewart, the excellence movement may be hard to define but we know it when we see it. Although it is a diffuse movement, loosely mobilized around issues of student performance – or lack thereof – its emphasis is academic standards, intellectual and moral values, and the public purposes to be served by education. First implicit, now increasingly explicit, is the central issue of curriculum: what should be taught?

In all of this is woven the thread of public funding; were all schooling private, interest in the issue, while no less important, would certainly be less intense. For what is at stake here is the distribution of scarce public resources – first money and time, but also public energy and enthusiasm, and finally, in this secular age, the value of democratic captialism.

Although critics of the Left and the Right accuse the schools of being soft on the issues that are important to them, in terms of democratic theory what is at stake is civic virtue, for no people may be free if they are not educated. Most important, a people may not govern themselves wisely and prudently if they are not *well* educated. The stakes are high and they are real.

Such observations, of course, would hardly surprise the Founders. To them civic virtue was the *sine qua non* of a democratic republic, and it was in some large measure imparted by the formal institutions of society, among them schools. Indeed, without such norms, civilazation itself is unimaginable. Born naked, ignorant and full of appetites, each child must learn the facts and values of the culture anew. It is no surprise that formal schooling plays a major role in that process. Schooling and civic virtue cannot be separated. But there is the inculcation of civic virtue and there is the inculcation of civic virtue.

It may be done from the center out or the top down, or it may percolate up from the bottom or it may radiate from interest groups, or if you will, 'factions'. Whatever its source, it is essential. But if it is both good and necessary to a functioning democracy, that knowledge gives little guidance as to how the object might be achieved. Should there be a common curriculum for every student, or should each one be free to go his or her own way? That will continue to be one of the central questions of the excellence movement.

It cannot be ignored and is very much on the minds of policy leaders in the field. It has attracted the attention and interest of such figures as Assistant Secretary of Education Chester E. Finn, Jr and Stanford Professor (and former Chairman of the California State Board of Education) Michael Kirst. It is hardly a new issue, however, and its present novelty is due to the fact that it has reappeared after two decades of virtual silence on the content of schooling.

Long before the 'excellence movement' there were two broad schools of thought on such matters. One is the vision of school as agent of the state, familiar enough to anyone who cares to peer beyond the Iron Curtain. John Stuart Mill, who was spared the excesses of modern totalitarian and authoritarian regimes, thought that no other objective could characterize government schooling. Government education, whether the dominant power be a priesthood, monarchy, or majority of the exiting generation is

> a mere contrivance for moulding people to be exactly like one another: and as the mould in which it casts them is that which pleases the predominant power in the government . . . it establishes a despotism over the mind . . .

By way of contrast there is the perspective of a supporter of government as the instrument of civic virtue, Simon Bolivar. Addressing the Congress of Angostura, he solemnly observed:

> Let us give to our republic a fourth power with authority over the youth, the hearts of men . . . Let us establish this Areopagus to watch over the education of the children . . . to purify whatever may be corrupt in the republic . . .

There is, however, a less extreme way to think about education and civic virtue in a democracy. How should a free people inculcate those values and attitudes essential to public welfare, domestic tranquility, and the pursuit of happiness? How can order and freedom be reconciled? The task, while not easy, is not impossible. And the American experience of the past century and one half with public education – or the education of the public – is instructive.

There emerged on these shores a notion that education is somehow neutral, technical and value free. Or if it contained any values at all, they were ecumenical values, values that we all shared. Indeed, values that all right thinking people quite naturally shared: the pursuit of truth, loyalty, honesty. In any case, the purpose of school was not to overtly transmit values except the most general Christian ones. The home and church would see to the details: the purpose of school was to learn to read and write, to count. Education was training. Education meant learning 'skills'.

This conception was not without power. The knowledge explosion of the nineteenth century, on the heels of the Enlightenment, gave great plausibility to the notion that education could be pursued without reference to particularistic values. And the Christian Pietism of the time, the ascendance of Unitarian-Universalist thought, made it both possible and convincing to think and talk about a sort of 'generic' Christian education that would be light on dogma but would still get the idea across.

It would be education for the community as a whole, treating all students as recipients of a common body of knowledge and information, within a Christian tradition. Indeed, the religious divisions that had characterized so much of European experience must have made such a view comforting. The age was becoming hightly secular but was still active in devotional pursuits. That Catholics and Jews (not to mention other small sects) might not find Protestant ecumenism as much to their liking as the power structure did, could escape most public notice.

Not to put too fine a point on the matter, it was precisely the refusal of the larger Protestant society to honor the devotional preferences of Catholics that led to the creation of America's system of Catholic schools. The common curriculum of the Protestant was not as appealing to the Catholic as Horace Mann and Henry Barnard would have liked it to be.

If curricular divisions and differences led to different systems of education in the United States in the nineteeth century, what of other nations as they began to create large systems of public education? The pattern is both consistent and revealing. In those countries where cultural and religious homogeneity was total or great, a single school system, with a single curriculum, appeared. In those where cultural and religious variety was substantial, and no 'ecumenical' compromise was possible, tension, even strife, ensued. Among the most enlightened nations – Denmark and Holland, for example – parallel systems were either established or permitted to grow. The reason was straightforward enough; all schools, almost without exception, required devotional exercises. Members of the school community who were not co-religionists almost without exception found this situation offensive, even intolerable. Among other things, to pray in another's faith is either oxymoronic or blasphemous; it is by definition unsatisfying.

In addition to devotional exercises, there was, as a matter of course, a Christian curriculum in which it was assumed that we each pray to the same God. (Apparently the wonderful colloquy attributed to Cardinal Newman had not reached the New World. Newman was approached by a Protestant who was in an ecumenical frame of mind: 'Cardinal', he said 'we each pray to the same God, do we not?' Newman rejoined 'Why yes; you in your way and I in His.') The issue of a curriculum fully imbued with religious values is still very much with us. And while no one seems much concerned about Trinitarian or Unitarian mathematics, there is heated debate on such matter as 'Creation Science' and the role of religion in the curriculum.

What has this introduction to do with the excellence movement? A good deal, I think, because we are simply rediscovering anew a set of old and important issues. We are what we value, and schools cannot escape this simple truth. And at the heart of the excellence movement – if indeed it has a heart – lies the conviction that what children are taught and what they learn makes a difference. Education is not mindless skills, a substantive crap-shoot in which people acquire the 'skill' of reading but care not what they read. (That, indeed, may explain the low esteem reading now enjoys with the young: who pursues empty skills that produce no pleasure or satisfaction?)

The life of the school, then, is defined by the curriculum, what is taught, and the life of the student is defined by what is learned. Members of devout religious comunities have always known this; so too have intense ideologues. So long as the demand is simply for freedom to pursue one's own belief domestic tranquility is possible, as it is in Holland where religious tolerance is as hightly prized as freedom or worship. But in communities in which different belief systems are seen to be irreconcilable, as in Northern Ireland, strife ensues.

In any case, the connection between the school and the larger community – the parents, teachers, administrators, students and friends of the school – is determined by what it is the school stands for, what it teaches. As James Coleman points out, the effective school and community reinforce each other, they resonate to one another. But the issue is more than a published syllabus, a list of textboks and lesson plans.

The 'true' curriculum of any school has two dimensions, one visible, the other invisible. The visible curriculum is books, courses of study, required drill and practice, homework, direct classroom instruction, informal teacher – student colloquies, tests and measures. It is the explicit activities that go on in the school, the kinds of things that can be described in a course catalog. This is the area in which the state has the greatest control, in both public and private school. Curriculum guidelines can be set, tests can be mandated, study plans required, textbooks adopted or proscribed. But state control is by no means complete – it can be, and often is, subverted by the ingenious, inventive or contentious student. In the late 1950s, for example, the Chicago public schools used expurgated Shakespeare, the original too racy for tender minds. No better stimulus to get students to read the full text can be imagined. But this is part of the 'invisible' curriculum, the signals sent by adults to students.

More important, in some respects, than the visible curriculum, then, is the 'invisible'. What is it the school really stands for? what does it represent? Is it a home for inquiring minds, or is it fundamentally anti-intellectual? Does it stand for discipline, hard work, high standards, intellectual integrity? Or does it stand for sloth, and disdain intellectual standards? Is the school authoritarian or libertarian, or does it fall somwhere in between? Does it purport to develop independent thinking ability or simply transmit 'skills'? The differences are real and have meaning.

Having said this, it is worth remembering that while the visible and 'invisible' curricula may be analytically distinct, in the real world they are inextricably bound together. Disciplined inquiry is not an abstract concept; it exists in a context of inquiry into a specific subject for a purpose.

If curriculum, then, is all important, who should choose which curriculum is offered? Or perhaps more to the point, who should decide which curriculum is *required*? Government? In the liberal democracies, the answer, as we have seen, has been guarded. The Dutch require all children to learn Dutch language and history (as well as to study English) but they may do so within a denominational context at state expense. At home, the state may require a 'pledge' of allegiance to the flag, under God. That it may be objectionable suggests that it has pedagogical impact, even if the observance is rote. (It is always possible that insofar as it is objectionable it may produce precisely the opposite effect intended.)

There are powerful historic and political, even philosophical, reasons for inculcating civic virtue as well. The Ancient Greeks, from whom we inherit our intellectual and educational traditions, knew that there was one purpose for education – to prepare people to live in the *polis*, to inculcate civic virtue. Without civic virtue the *polis* itself, the state, would founder. Civic virtue to the Greeks was neither form nor content but both together, knowldge and presence, rhetoric and substance. Neither alone would suffice, and polished presentation was important as was the substance of what was presented.

It was also their insight to know how one acquired civic virtue. The lesson is as true today as it was then. There are three ways: first is 'study', knowledge acquired didactically. Teachers teach and students learn. Students submit to the discipline of learning. Indeed, it is from the word discipline that the term disciple is derived. Second, virtue is acquired by 'example'. Virtuous men and women communicate virtue to the young and to their fellows by example. Third, and perhaps most important, virtue is acquired by 'practice'. Virtue is acquired by behaving virtuously.

And what is civic virtue? It is explicit knowledge – mastered almost to the point of habit – about the rights and responsibilities of citizenship, the opportunities and obligations imposed and offered by a constitutional republic. It is knowing, as Morris Janowitz observes, that the corollary of the right to trial by jury is the obligation to serve on a jury when you are called. It is knowing that my freedom ends where yours begins. It is knowing that rights are earned and must be protected if they are to survive. It is knowing that Oliver Wendell Holmes was right when he observed that 'taxes are what we pay for civilized society'.

Having made these general points, what is it our public schools should do to teach civic virtue? What knowledge and attitudes must children acquire – through study, example and practice – to make them virtous citizens? Let me turn first to 'example', then to 'study', and thence to "practice".

The most striking example in all of history was offered by Socrates: he accepted the hemlock cup, not because he believed himself guilty of corrupting the youth of Athens, but to demonstrate the supremacy of law. His wisdom, if not his courage, is captured in two quotes which are the essence of my point.

The first is by Thomas Henry Huxley:

> Perhaps the most valuable result of all education is the ability to make yourself do the thing you have to do when it ought to be done, whether you like it or not; it is the first lesson that ought to be learned; and however early a man's [sic] training begins, it is probably the last lesson that he ever learns thoroughly.

The second is by Ruskin:

> Education does not mean teaching people what they do not know . . . It is a painful, continual and difficult work to be done by kindness, by watching, by warning, by precept, and by praise, but above all – by example.

As a practical matter this means that our schools must be staffed by moral men and women, adults who care about their calling and their craft, and by the pure force of personality communicate their sense of commitment to their students. There is, of course, no mystery as to who these people are. They are the teachers you each remember, they are the teachers who made a difference in your own life. The problem is not identifying them after the fact but before the fact. Who are they when you hire them? They are teachers who are connected to their disciplinary traditions, who are broadly and deeply educated, who believe in the life of the mind.

These are not empty homilies – there is an internal dynamic to study and scholarship, there are standards to master and cannons of the profession that themselves embody the principles of civic virtue. They include honesty, fidelity, accuracy, fairness, tolerance for diversity, flexibility, and a willingness to change when new evidence is presented. Indeed, what we expect of the well educated adult, what we expect of our better teachers, is precisely the set of traits that we associate with civic virtue.

It is in the interaction between the content of what is taught and the people who teach that the impact of the 'invisible' curriculum is most powerful. It is the messages sent by teachers to students, adults to young people, about what is right and what is wrong, what is acceptable and what is not. A school, for example that sets low standards sends a powerful message – nothing much matters. Get by. It is a dangerous message to give a young person in the late twentieth century because it programs him or her for failure.

The invisible curriculum, of course, undergirds and reinforces the visible curriculum, what it is that is taught, which books are used, and how a student's program of study is organized. It is in this area that education is most problematic and least understood. It has become fashionable in certain circles to think that education is a process, a set of skills divorced from their substantive context.

Nothing could be further from the truth. Education is contextual – it is part and parcel of a substantive experience, of learning about the great works of citizenship. At a minimum it includes knowledge of the great documents of citizenship – Aristotle's *Politics and Ethics* Plato's *Republic*, The Magna Carta, Machiavelli's *Prince*, Locke's *An Essay Concerning Human Understanding*, The Declaration of Independence, the Tenth Federalist Paper, the United States Constitution. John Stuart Mill's *On Liberty*, The Gettysburg Address, Lincoln's Second Inaugural and Martin Luther King's Letter From Birmingham Jail. Education is an empty concept if it is stripped of the content these documents provide.

There is, then, in real education, a body of knowledge, facts, myth, history, anecdote, story that must be mastered. But they are not to be mastered as an exercise in memory alone – they are to be mastered as an exercise in understanding, an exercise in critical thought. Think of the centerpiece of the Fifth Amendment as simply a phrase to be recapitualted without an understanding of its underlying meaning:

> nor shall be compelled in any criminal case to be a witness against himself

Without understanding its purpose and its historical context it is truly non-sense. Why should a suspected criminal not have to testify against him or herself? Protecting all of us from testifying against ourselves emerged from a long and bitter history of the rack and thumbscrew – if a person may be compelled to testify against him or herself, who is to say No to the torturer? Certainly not the victim. Freedom from self-incrimination is no more and no less than freedom from the Inquisition and their tools of trade. It is a strange thing in a century so convulsed by violence of every kind that this simple truth is frequently overlooked when people 'take the Fifth'. It may be the single most important protection a free people enjoy.

But if history and context are important to education, there is an additional aspect that is even more important. It is knowing how to think. And people learn to think by thinking, and thinking hard. That is the essence of the Socratic dialogue, the most enduring and important teaching 'technique' ever devised. The Socratic dialogue is mirrored in one other learning activity, and that is when a student reads a demanding book, one that challenges and stretches.

This is so because books, if they are to mean anything, must embody the value system of which formal education should be a most conspicuous part. Selecting books for children, no less than for oneself, involves the exercise of judgment. And that judgment is informed by values, about what is good and bad, right and wrong.

It is the value system I stress, because values are that part of our world that is not scientifically derived. They include such humane but unscientific attributes as love, loyalty, courage, devotion, piety, and compassion. It is precisely these attributes that give dimension, scope, and meaning to being human.

And it is precisely with these attributes that great literature concerns itself. Think of the *Iliad, Oedipus Tyrannus, The Divine Comedy*, Shakespeare's Tragedies.

Having made these assertions let me draw upon a particularly telling and approporaite example. It is Mark Twain's *Huckleberry Finn*, published 102 years ago. It is arguably the greatest American novel – it is without question among the greatest. It is a book of such importance that no American who has not read it can be considered educated. And no observer or student of America could hope to understand this country without reading it. It is a book that is so faithful to the American experience that it has become a part of it. It both embodies and shapes the nation of which it is a part.

What makes this book important? Its scope and sweep, certainly, but above all, its values. In shape it is a book for the masses – like the Bible or the *Iliad* it tells a story accessible to all. Regardless of the reader's sophistication, there are elements to the story that can be apprehended by the humblest amongst us. And the corollary of this observation is that there is something for the most discerning and demanding reader. And just as it contains much with which to agree, it contains much that shocks, provokes, and even offends. As a consequence, reading the book – and discussing it in class – requires sensitivity and discretion. It is not a book to be taken lightly.

In scope the book traces the human condition – the Mississippi is the River of Life, Huck the child of nature, Jim the victim of an oppressive and merciless society.

The values it embodies are best captured in Huck's monologue after he saves Jim from bounty hunters. About to board the raft to look for a runaway slave, the bounty hunters are led to believe – through dissimulation raised to an art form – that the tent on Huck's raft houses his father smitten by smallpox.

Successful, Huck is not elated:

> They got off and I got aboard the raft, feeling bad and low, because I knowed very well I done wrong, and I see it warn't no use for me to try to do right . . .

Huck continues in this vein and then says,

> S'pose you'd 'a' done right and give Jim up, would you feel any better than you do now? No says I, I'd feel bad –I'd feel just the way I do now.

Huckleberry Finn is specially interesting more than a century after its publication because Huck is attacked today as he was when it was first released. The Far Right believes he is venal at best, hostile to religion at worst: his language is abominable, his behaviour unacceptable. In sum, he is a poor example. The Left is even more outspoken in its hostility to Huck. They level against him the worst of modern epithets – racist.

If one is patient it is possible to retrace the logic that shapes such views, but it is not necessary, because I will stipulate to this: Twain's purpose was to subvert the state, undermine the morals of the young, and challenge the smugness and complacency of the American *haute bourgeoise*. To this accusation I plead Twain guilty. How else can the quoted passages be understood? *Huckleberry Finn* glorifies the commission of a crime, and the power of the book lies in its capacity to continue to confront the conventional wisdom. Twain railed against the organized religion of the day, sanctimonious piety and hypocrisy; indeed, he found organized society – and particularly the state – the cause rather than the cure for social ills. Huck and Jim, children of nature, could escape the corrupting forces of contemporary life only by physical escape.

So far as we can tell, Twain really believed that society was a sentence; the only hope was escape and the development of this idea in *Huckleberry Finn* is the best known of Twain's repeated efforts to deal with it. Its most complete expression was not fully developed until late in life and did not appear in didactic form until the release of the *Mysterious Stranger* (which was published posthumously at Twain's instruction). But the ideas appear in nascent form in *Huckleberry Finn*. If this interpretation of Twain is correct – as I believe it to be – he is far more dangerous than the conventional Left and Right wings know. He is an enemy of the state. Whether or not he should be read by callow youths, then, becomes a question with meaning.

Without dwelling on Twain, it is useful to consider great literature in general to see if the example is idiosyncratic. Are there common threads? The direction assumed by great literature across the ages is the same. While its first purpose is to entertain, its more important purpose is to instruct. It provides examples of courage, strength, and love. It shows the effects of *hubris*, greed, and the will to power. It reveals transcendent accomplishment and abject failure. Such literature is almost never the servant of the state or the advocate of the *status quo*. Great literature challenges assumptions, it breaks with the conventional wisdom.

Du Buffet, champion of l'art brut, in a splendid twist on Plato, asserted that art was subversive, that the state should attempt to suppress it, and that the artist worked best and most effectively when he or she was disdained by the prevailing culture. That is a rather exaggerated version of the idea being developed in this essay – suffice it to say that the artist should at minimum question the conventional wisdom and make the bourgeoise uncomfortable.

Not all great books are offensive, or irreverent, or hostile to the state, but they challenge the conventional wisdom, they provoke the reader, they insist upon engagement with the subject. This is even true of science, particularlly in its early stages when it is concerned with breakthroughs in basic knowledge. Galileo, Kepler and Darwin are only the best known examples.

The controversial nature of a work, then, is a product of its power and authenticity, and it is for this reason that the inexperienced reader will frequently find the great book difficult – it is often very tough sledding. It is tough sledding because it raises fundamental questions about right and wrong. For the inquiring mind, it induces an interior Socratic dialogue.

At issue here is the error to which I allude in the opening pages of this essay. It has caused much of the mischief that continues to plague our schools. An assumption was made – in all good faith – that our schools could be value-free, neurtral, objective; this would defuse the potentially explosive question of which values to teach and how to teach them.

As I have tried to suggest, this version of American education is an old one. In the nineteenth century, what was described as value-free education was really non-sectarian Protestantism, not quite ecumenism, but a robust Unitarianism. Indeed, it is no accident that the early public school reformers were visionary and romantic Unitarians, builders who would use the public schools to uplift and transform each generation. As Horace Mann said, with a striking sense of modernity, in his Annual Report to the Board of Education in 1848:

> If all children in the community from the age of four to that of seventeen could be brought within the reformatory and elevating influence of good schools, crimes . . . might . . . be banished from the world.

When it came to education, Mann, and his supporters and colleagues, had little problem identifying what schools should do. They knew that most teachers were only poorly trained, but they were the inheritors of a classical tradition that brooked little interference. In essence, the curriculum chose itself. So it was in the late nineteenth century that the *McGuffy Eclectic Reader* enjoyed unparalleled success – full of pious homilies and entreaties to civic and religious virtue, its values were widely shared by the community that patronized the public schools. In this context it is important to remember who those patrons were in the nineteenth century; they were almost exclusively white Protestants.

It is still the case that about some values we can be unself-conscious and unembarrassed – honesty, loyalty, perseverance, compassion, bravery. But it is difficult to slip beneath these pious generalizations. The sanctity of human life means different things to different people – abortion, capital punishment, just and unjust wars, the moral dilemmas raised by modern medical technology pose ethical 'either-or's' that do not submit to a uniform, widely-held set of values.

The emergence of modern society – highly diverse, pluralist – means that we can no longer rely on either the classical curriculum of the past or the Protestant consensus of the nineteenth century. In theory, the loss of these traditions could have been replaced with disciplinary traditions, in which knowledge and schooling would be are organized 'vertically', from kindergarten to postgraduate work. In such an existential view of education, the curriculum, teaching styles, and textbooks are joined together in an interlocking, coherent, and continous disciplinary spiral. No matter whether the subject is mathematics, science, the arts, or humanities, a disciplinary tradition provides organization, purpose and depth.

In an attenuated way this disciplinary tradition does exist in the best public and private college preparatory schools. In these institutions, for example, teachers are free to choose Dryden or Donne, Spencer or Marlowe, Shakespeare or Cervantes, Twain or Hawthorne – but the freedom to choose is nearly ephemeral, because the educated person, the student, must eventually read all of them.

What has happened in American education, of course, is the virtual abandonment of the disciplinary tradition. Instead of vertical integration, elementary and secondary schools are organized horizontally. They are not only characterized by self-contained classrooms, they are self-contained organizations with few links to the outside world. Great bands of children are grouped by age and they are given 'problem areas' to study. Communications skills replace English, social studies replaces history and geography; is it any surprise that bachelor living and power volleyball enter the curriculum?

Is it any wonder that there are periodic attempts to purge *Huckleberry Finn* from the classroom? With no intellectual and disciplinary anchor, the school is subject to the fads and vicissitudes of the moment. It has no capacity to fend off the ill-founded accusations of the Babbits of the Right and the ideologues of the Left. When the watchwords of the school become value neutrality, relevance,and relativity anything goes. Nothing is imposed on anyone, except the notion that there are two sides to every question; the great revealed religions and the philosophy of the ancient Greeks, which believe in right and wrong, moral absolutes, no longer provide answers. Not even the existential answer, that teachers know more than students, can be offered with conviction.

It is for this reason that the disciplinary tradition is essential. Having written at greater length than I should on the queestion of study and example let me turn briefly to my final point: practice. 'Happiness', Aristotle tells us, 'is activity of the soul in accord with perfect virtue.' And we achieve this state by practice. Ironically, it is not so much in the exercise of our rights that we learn this, but in meeting our obligations. And it is through submission to a higher principle that we learn to appreciate the importance of our hard-won rights.

At the level of friend and family it means satisfying the reciprocal demands that loyalty and filial responsibility place upon us. At the level of the community it means meeting minimal standards of civility and good conduct. It means not just obeying the law – though that is important – it means accommodation to unspoken standards of behaviour. At the level of the state it means honoring the full and explicit demands of citizenship – at its most mundane it means honesty in paying taxes, at a more elevated level it means voting and citizen participation, and in time of mortal danger it may mean the ultimate sacrifice for a higher good. But these examples lie outside the school.

At the level of the school 'practice' means just what it suggests – doing what is expected of you and doing it well. But it should and could mean much more. It could and should mean service, both to the school and to the community. An old idea in private education, it is just now being taken seriously in the public sector.

By way of illustration, let me mention one of the most important education reforms of the past decade, and one little noted element of it. In the late 1970s Governor Jim Hunt created the North Carolina School of Science and Mathematics (NCSSM). It is known across the country as one of the nation's only public boarding schools. It is devoted – as its name suggests – to demanding study, and enrolls some of the best and brightest youngsters in North Carolina.

It is distinguished academically and socially, for its admissions criteria – there are eight – produce a student body that is representative geographically, ethnically, and racially. And it is among the nation's leading schools in the production of Merit Scholars. But what attracts me to the school is a special graduation requirement; no student may graduate without performing three hours a week of school service and four hours a week of community service. Students from NCSSM spend time in old people's homes, orphanages, day-care centres and hospitals. They work with the elderly, the infirm, the disabled and the dispossessed. And they do so week in and week out. It is a far cry from some of our crumbling inner-city schools, so obscured by graffiti as to be unrecognizable, or wealthy suburban schools, distinguished by the size of the parking lot rather than intellectual accomplishment.

Every high school student in America could be expected to perform community service as a condition of graduation. No one is so poor or elevated as not to profit from it. The 'service' these young people might provide, while important, would be the least of what they did. They would be learning – through practice – habits of service, the very foundation of civic virtue and the personal satisfaction it can provide.

If this is an accurate description of the reality of schooling in contemporary America, then the future of 'choice' is either very bleak or very bright. On the one hand are those who would impose from the center a state or even national curriculum. The idea has much to recommend itself, and cannot be dismissed as frivolous. There is a body of knowledge that all Americans should possess, from Superman to Sophocles, as E.D. Hirsh so eloquently argues in his book *Cultural Literacy*. Indeed, few thoughtful people would argue with the concept. Adults do know more than children; there is a body of thought in each of the scholarly disciplines that should be imparted to all our citizens; knowledge is power; know the truth and the truth shall make you free.

But as we have seen and know from experience, there is another, wholly different tradition in education which exerts a competing claim on our loyalty, and that is the particularistic claim of special knowledge, intellectal values that pertain to the sub-group not the larger group. This includes moral and religious values which cannot in good conscience be submerged in the larger society. The Amish, the Quakers, Orthodox Jews, the devout Catholic, yes , even the atheist, should be free to go his or her own way. At issue is the right of the individual, the dissenting minority, to spiritual and intelectual integrity.

There is, then, real tension in the excellence movement. On the one hand it suggests that we seriously consider a national, core curriculum; What is it we need to know as Americans, both to have a shared sense of community and a shared destiny? At the same time, we need the support, solace and integrity of the smaller, organic communities of which we are naturally a part. No one can be a member of a 'family' of 240 million people. We can be citizens, and owe obligations and expect rights to flow from this larger body politic, but the kinds of association that most of us find deeply satisfying flow from smaller units of organizations.

On the other hand, 'excellence' in any endeavor is often a solitary pursuit, requiring self-discipline and commitment that is special and particularistic. Excellence also assumes many forms – music, art, the quantitative disciplines, languages and the humanities. Over the life of a student the pursuit of excellence calls for progressively greater specialization and more complete immersion in the peculiarities of a given discipline.

This is not to say that some 'core' curriculum cannot co-exist with specialization: it can. It is just more difficult to pull it off successfully. But there is one final concern that the excellence movement has with the idea of a core curriculum that must be addressed: who will chose and of what will the core consist? If it is chosen by the wise and judicious, the penetrating and the discerning, the discriminating and the disciplined – in short, by you and me – the core curriculum will be a wonder to behold. But if is chosen by the ideologues of the Left or Right, the Babbits and Buffoons of American itellectual life, a core curriculum will be a disaster. The fear of the latter is a real one, as anyone who has read Francis FirzGerald's study of American history texts must admit. Anti-intellectualism in America is an old, powerful and even honored tradition, and it is not at all clear that the excellence movement will, even over the long haul, change that.

Lurking beneath the surface of any discussion about the quality of American education is the nagging suspicion that we already have the schools that we both want and deserve. We do have citizen control; we do have a voice in what our schools do and how they do it, however attenuated it may be. Perhaps, after all is said and done, Americans prefer football to the life of the mind. In that case, the excellence movement will simply sink to a lowest common denominator; in which case, the only hope for the discerning parent or student is choice.

As America is the home of happy endings, let me supply one. The Committee for Economic Development's policy statement, Investing in Our Children: Business and the Public Schools (1985) is the only education reform document that I know of that deals with this issue explicitly. The trustees, whose numbers include Fortune Five Hundred CEOs and the Presidents of several distinguished universities, labored long and hard, first on the issue of a core curriculum, than on the issue of a national core curriculum. Their final report recommended that each state identify and promulgate a core curriculum, but that the national government not do so.

This device would honor regional and local differences, it would preserve historical continuity, but best of all would accomplish the same objective as a national curriculum with none of the fuss. The trustees were convinced – rightly, I think – that there is a national consensus, a sort of intellectual center of gravity that binds the nation together – that would spontaneously lead the Boards of Education in Florida and Maine, California and Minnesota, South Carolina and Oregon to adopt a core curriculum that in all important respects would be identical to those of the other states.

By relying on the 'invisible hand' of a shared culture, no bitter political battle would be fought at the national level over the issue of a national curriculum. Indeed, lest the idea seem fanciful, we should remind ourselves that in important areas we already have a *de facto* national curriculum. As the colleges and universities have been the gatekeepers of high school quallity, the Education Testing Service, through its achievement examinations and Advanced Placement examinations, is easing us slowly and painlessly into one. As the SATs fall into ever greater disrepute, the need for a broadened and strengthened battery of achievement tests will increase. And if there are national achievement tests, can a national curriculum be far behind? Indeed, in this scheme of things, we are backing into a national curriculum. And in the best American tradition, we will not choose a national curriculum so much as a national curriculum will choose us.

3   Exploring the political economy of national education reform

James W. Guthrie and Julia Koppich
University of California and PACE, Berkeley

Background

Through good times and bad, the American people have flattered themselves that they alone had mastered the art of mass education. Everyone was aware that classes were overcrowded, school finance wobbly and standards lamentably low.[1]

If we are complacent about our educational achievements, if we allow ourselves to fall behind, we may find ourselves outwitted, out-maneuvered, out-thought and out-built throughout the world.[2]

Quotations such as the above are familiar to virtually everyone informed about contemporary American education. Excellence, academic rigor, higher standards of achievement, greater professionalization of teaching, and fear of international subjugation are common rhetorical accompaniment for the 1980s education reform movement. What may be a surprise is that the above quotations are from the 1950s. Such was the nature of the public pronouncements immediately surrounding the Soviets' 1957 launching of the world's first space capsule.

Lest anyone doubt the intensity of the nation's distress, note the following statement by a famous physicist of the Sputnik period:

Few predictions seem more certain than this: Russia is going to surpass us in mathematics and the social sciences . . . In short, unless we depart utterly from our present behavior, it is reasonable to expect that by no later than 1975 the United States will be a member of the Union of Soviet Socialist Republics.[3]

Sputnik launched more than the space age. It also triggered another episode in the cyclic American effort to reshape public education. Following a year of legislative hearings during which public schools and professional educators were castigated for having diluted the academic purposes of education and accused of all but abetting a Soviet takeover of the nation, Congress enacted the 1958 National Defense Education Act (NDEA). This legislation provided federal matching funds to states and local districts to enhance instruction in science, mathematics, and foreign language. Greater rigor in these areas was intended to restore the United States to worldwide scientific preeminence and technological prowess.

In the early 1980s, the United States again entered a period of education reform. Widely used code words and political symbols employed by reform advocates, the media, and public officials stressed academic excellence, scholarly rigor, and high intellectual standards. United States economic subordination to Japan's growing technological and trade hegemony was a frequently invoked threat. The reform implorations of federal government officials, particularly the Secretary of Education and the President, were fulsome and intense. The response was sweeping. National organizations, states, and local school districts pursued extensive revisions on dimensions such as secondary school graduation requirements, curricula, textbooks, and testing programs. The ostensible objective for this massive reshaping was to render the American labor force more productive, technologically and scientifically more literate, and better able to surmount the international trade threat.

The similarity between the current reform rhetoric and that of an earlier era is striking. Is there nothing educationally new under the sun? Are reformers doomed repeatedly to re-invent the schooling wheel? When reform waves recede do they leave behind them any structural or procedural residue upon which others can build? Are there fundamental differences which separate one national reform era from another? If so, what are they? Are there significant political and economic similarities among national education reform cycles? These questions constitute the focus of this exploratory essay.

The next section describes four post-Second World War instances of national education reform efforts. These descriptions are followed by a discussion of national education reform correlates and indicators. A subsequent section analyzes the similarities between the contemporary reform movement and its predecessors. The final section offers several propositions regarding the antecedents to and causes of national reform movements.

Four cases of national education reform

National Defense Education Act[4]

The Soviet Union launched the first orbiting space capsule, Sputnik, on 4 October, 1957. That event sent shock waves through the American community. The United States' failure to be the first in space was widely attributed to deficient science education in the nation's public schools. In January 1958, then-President Dwight D. Eisenhower delivered a message to Congress in which he stressed the significance of education as a key to national defense. If the United States better prepared its topmost science and mathematics students, the reasoning went, then the nation would produce scientists capable of surpassing the Russians.

Thus, the National Defense Education Act was born. Created by the 85th congress, it was signed into law by the President on 2 September 1958. With the enactment of NDEA, Congress appropriated $40 million for the fiscal year ending 30 June 1959. The money was intended to strengthen math, science, and foreign language programs in the nation's public schools.

The National Defense Education Act appeared to be truly landmark legislation. It was the first major post-Second World War, education legislation. Other bills had been proposed, but none had been passed. However, the road to its enactment was pitted with political potholes. Congressional debate about the proposed law sparked heated discussions, first about the wisdom of federal aid to education at all. Would federal grants to state and local jurisdictions do irreparable harm to the autonomy of state and local educational decision making? Was the federal government simply opening a Pandora's box of intergovernmental problems? Debate then revolved around the direction federal aid, if approved, should take. If federal money was appropriated (discussions were always couched in 'ifs'), should the money be given in the form of block grants or categorical aid? Should federal dollars be earmarked for construction costs or operating expenses? Should states, local school districts, and institutions of higher education be required to apply for the federal money, or should the government simply dole it out?

Ultimately, popular concern with national defense and the spectre of Sputnik forced Congress to act. Federal money was allocated to improve instruction in the areas previously cited – mathematics, science, and foreign language. NDEA was Congress' attempt to lighten the burden of educational improvement by providing money, but not by mandating curriculum. The government would make high quality math, science, and foreign language financially feasible without attaching curriculum-specific strings. The federal government bent over backwards *not* to interfere with state and local programs.

Enactment of the NDEA took place in an intense anti-education atmosphere. Major education interest groups supported the bill, but faith in professional educators was at such a low ebb, that their advocacy of the measure counted for little. Critics of public education were outspoken in expressing the view that the oppressive mediocrity of America's schools was strangling talented students. Leading science policy officials in government, the military, and higher education testified on behalf of the bill and against professional educators. They asserted that US world leadership and the nation's long term survival depended upon creating and sustaining an expanded corps of elite scientists. In that the United States had bested its Second World War Axis power enemies in large measure through scientific breakthroughs, such as harnessing atomic energy, the argument from international competition was persuasive, and the NDEA was enacted.

Elementary and Secondary Education Act[5]

President Lyndon Baines Johnson signed the Elementary and Secondary Education Act into law on 11 April 1965 outside the one-room Texas schoolhouse he had attended as a child. The new law, part of Johnson's heavily publicized 'War on Poverty', authorized federal financial support to school districts for educational programs designed to meet the needs of educationally deprived students in low income areas. The aim of the legislation was to broaden and strengthen the education of children of poverty. The government appropriated $1.3 billion for the program's initial year of operation. The law specified that ESEA funds could be used for preschool and preventive services, remedial instruction, health care, parent education, and teacher training.

Hailed by many as an equal opportunity law, the ESEA was seen as a major step toward bringing children growing up in poverty into the mainstream of American life. Money was to be allocated to states and thereafter to school districts based on a poverty index, not on the basis of educational achievement. The 'given' was that low income children needed special and remedial assistance.

Title I of ESEA received five-sixths of the federal money and nearly all of the publicity. Local school districts were required to develop specific educational programs to meet the needs of their educationally deprived students. It was initially left to local districts to establish objective measures of educational deprivation.

Other components of ESEA received less attention than did Title I, but were significant nonetheless. They constituted what was seen at the time as a reform continuum. Title II provided money for texts, library books, and other instructional materials. Title III authorized funds designed to encourage 'educational innovation' in local school districts. Title IV of ESEA supplied grants for educational research and training. These funds were supposed to develop a deeper scientific base for education. Title V provided federal funds to strengthen state education departments.

Initially the ESEA lacked grassroots constituent support. It marked a rare form of political altruism. The bill catered to the needs of the poor, and those in poverty seldom have significant political influence. However, Johnson administration proponents realized, following his massive 1964 electoral triumph over Arizona senator Barry Goldwater, that the overwhelmingly Democratic Congress would enact virtually any presidential proposal. As if more momentum was needed, the ESEA was couched in the conventional rhetoric of 'manpower development', the time-honored justification for federal education support since the

Land Survey Ordinance of 1785. What little opposition existed was finessed by cleverly designed church-state compromises. Passage in 1964 of a Civil Rights Act had removed racial segregation as a major North-South political impediment to ESEA enactment, and adroit executive branch lobbying enlisted the united support of all major education organizations.

PL 94-142: the Education For All Handicapped Children Act[6]

The Education for All Handicapped Children Act (Public Law 94-142) was signed into law by President Gerald Ford on 29 November 1975. This law, hailed as a 'Bill of Rights for the Handicapped', was based on the premise that handicapped children had a constitutional right to a free and suitable publicly-supported education, regardless of the nature or degree of their limitations. The law stated:

> It is the purpose of this Act to assure that all handicapped children have available to them . . . a free appropriate public education which emphasizes special education and related services designed to meet their unique needs, to assure that the rights of handicapped children and their parents or guardians are protected, to assist the States and localities to provide for the education of all handicapped children, and to assure the effectiveness of efforts to educate handicapped children. (Section 601[c] of the Act)

Congress appropriated $100 million in PL 94-142 entitlement grants for fiscal year 1976. A decade later appropriations were in excess of $1 billion. Money was to be distributed to state education agencies, then to local school districts.

Although the federal government would provide a proportion of the funds necessary to implement this new program, it was understood at the outset that federal funds would only cover approximately 30% of anticipated costs of the new congressional mandates. State and local education agencies would have to support remaining costs. The law specifically required school districts to implement 94-142 requirements, *whether or not* they received federal funds. (In fact, 94-142 was never fully funded; even the federal government's promise of 30% failed to materialize.)

Implementing regulations for PL 94-142 were approved in early 1976, prompting some advocates to label the law 'revolutionary legislation for the bicentennial year'. The law required local school districts to provide 'free, appropriate public education' for all handicapped children, ages 3 to 21, in the 'least restrictive environment'. Districts were to maximize the efforts to 'mainstream' handicapped students by placing them, to the extent possible, in regular education classes with non-handicapped students. In cases in which severity of the handicap made regular educational placement impossible, districts were to break through the isolation of handicapped students by at least housing them in the same buildings as non-handicapped students.

Public Law 94-142 was rife with legal protections and procedural safeguards previously unknown to education bills. Parents who objected to their child's educational placement were to be entitled to a 'fair hearing'. This hearing was to be an administrative procedure, but one with all the courtroom trappings – right to counsel, right to present evidence, right to cross-examine witnesses, and right to a written decision. Parents displeased with an administrative hearing outcome were reserved the right to file a civil suit against the school district.

As with the ESEA, PL 94-142 did not initially have a broad base of popular support. The traditional political 'iron triangle' of a few legislative branch advocates for the handicapped, when teamed with executive branch officials who would administer the new program and handicapped parent special interest groups, was sufficient to gain enactment.[7] The bill was given added momentum by several court decisions which expanded equal rights protections and required that states provide schooling to unserved handicapped students.

Education organizations such as the NEA and AFT supported the bill, but it did not contain major benefits for their memberships. Moreover, these organizations were uncomfortable with the anti-educator ethos which infused the bill and the rhetoric of many of its handicapped interest group proponents. Their opposition was of little consequence, however, as the bill passed easily. Congressional passage was by no means the end of conflict however. Because of the unique adversarial strategy involved, implementation of the bill's provisions was cumbersome and controversial.

The 1980s education excellence movement[8]

Tracing any current political event to its historic roots may involve an infinite regress. Nevertheless, it is reasonable to assert that the 1983 issuance of the National Commission on Educational Excellence report, *A Nation At Risk*, was a primary catalyst for the contemporary United States education reform effort. The report was written in a riveting style, invoked the spectre of foreign domination, and was released in a manner cleverly calculated to capture the attention of the news media. Public scrutiny immediately was concentrated upon the sorry state of American education portrayed in the report. Probably as a consequence, literally hundreds of task forces, blue ribbon panels, and reform commissions were convened to tailor the report's general reform suggestions to the specific settings of states and local school districts.

For the first time in any significant way since the days of Theodore Roosevelt, the nation experienced effective use of the Presidential 'bully pulpit'. President Reagan was quick to recognize the significance of *A Nation At Risk* and the intense public concern it had awakened. He made repeated statements regarding the importance of renewed educational rigor to the nation's future. He admonished state and local officials, as well as parents and educators, to make the changes necessary to restore America's schools to their past levels of prominence. He was careful to specify, however, that the financial burden of reform, if there was any, should be borne by states and localities. In fact, he made clear his view that the dilution of academic and disciplinary standards was in substantial measure a consequence of prior intervention and overly intense regulatory efforts by federal officials. Reform, 'yes', but, in the President's view, federal financial support, 'no'.

States particularly responded to the President's challenge. Numerous legislative bodies enacted omnibus education reform bills. These statutory packages often contained literally dozens of provisions. California, South Carolina, and Texas, for example, enacted bills averaging 40 different reform dimensions. California's reform vehicle, Senate Bill 813, contained more than 80 provisions all by itself.

Despite the variety of political bodies by which such statutes were crafted, the laws bore remarkable similarity. This probably testifies to the widespread and uniform network of ideas that had been fostered by *A Nation At Risk* and national-level advocates of reform. Regardless of the idea's ultimate origin, many states intensified high school graduation rules and college entrance standards, required more statewide achievement testing, extended the length of the school day and school year, legislated higher state standards for becoming and remaining a teacher, ratcheted up the content and vocabulary levels of textbooks, and expanded evaluation procedures and performance incentives for educators.

Unlike the three previously-described reform predecessors, this educational excellence movement was not aimed at a narrow audience of elite or disadvantaged students. Rather, state-initiated change efforts were intended to elevate the academic performance of average and below-average students. It was widely speculated that the entire United States workforce had to achieve at a higher rate in order to enhance economic productivity and to render the nation internationally more competitive.

At least in part, this broadly defined student audience accounts for the fact that educational excellence reforms were not aimed at a particular segment of the school curriculum nor did they depend upon a few newly developed special purpose educational programs. Instead of adding something new to the periphery of the curriculum, as was the case with the NDEA, ESEA, and EHCA, state officials were aiming directly at changing the academic core of schooling: what is taught, what one is expected to learn, who teaches, and how evaluations will be performed.

The contemporary reform movement certainly had its highly visible proponents, e.g. the President, Secretary of Education, an assortment of national commissions and study groups, and a variety of other academic and public luminaries. It is notable, however, for three additional groups of reform advocates: state governors, professional educators themselves, and the business community.

An indicator of the initial seriousness with which the public took the need for school change is perhaps reflected in the intensity with which state governors began to campaign on education issues. In state after state, gubernatorial candidates staked political aspirations on their education reform platform. The prestigious National Governors Association (NGA) even devoted an entire annual report exclusively to the need for education reform.

Also, the National Education Association (NEA) and, particularly, the American Federation of Teachers (AFT) were generally in support of state-initiated reforms. Albert Shanker, national president of the AFT, was among the most outspoken proponents of education reform. Indeed, his ideas were frequently so far reaching and visionary that supporters often feared his views would estrange him from his union's rank-and-file membership.

Business and industrial associations, both nationally and at the state level, supported reform proposals, even on occasions when omnibus bills raised state taxes to assist schools. Highly visible business leaders such as H. Ross Perot of Texas computer fame, led the charge for change in their respective states. Similarly, national business organizations, such as the nationally prestigious Committee for Economic Development (CED), issued reports specifying reform agendas. This marked the first time in more than a quarter century that America's business community was a major participant in the educational policy arena.

Implementation proceded state by state, and it remains too soon to assess the long run significance of the proposed changes. However, regardless of the eventual assessment of the 'educational excellence' reforms, the intensity of mid-1980s national concern for school change was remarkable.

What constitutes a national reform movement?

This is not a rhetorical question. American education is exceedingly vulnerable to short-lived faddish movements. Historical hindsight assists in knowing whether or not an effort at change actually succeeded. For example, it is easy, but only in retrospect, to identify as reforms the establishment of comprehensive high schools and Progressive Era changes in school governance, e.g. the elimination of ward-based boards of education and other structural changes intended to insulate schools from partisan politics. Similarly, the effects of the 'scientific management' movement on American education are evident in the turn of the century growth of professional school administrators. More recently, the unionization of teachers, beginning in the 1960s, appears as a clear and long lasting change in direction for American education.

However, as poignant as such past reforms may be, for every clearcut dramatic change in direction, a good historian can probably list twenty other ephemeral efforts at change which, regardless of the amount of attention generated at their outset, have vanished leaving few if any practical consequences for today's schools.

Even during the professional life of many reading this chapter, numerous reform proposals have been launched only to achieve an inglorious end. Whatever happened to team teaching, Competency Based Teacher Education (CBTE), flexible scheduling, modular school construction, micro teaching, Management by Objectives (MBO), Program Performance Budgeting Systems (PPBS), Learner Verified Materials, and Program Evaluation Review Techniques (PERT)? Each of these may have represented a useful idea. Each certainly received substantial attention in popular education publications. Perhaps one or more of these ideas will resurface and may even make a difference the next time around. However, for the present, these ideas, and hundreds like them, have been consigned to a reform graveyard. They are education's Edsels.

How then can one distinguish a true national education reform movement? What criteria need be applied in order to reduce the prospect of analyzing a non-event? One possible litmus test for reform is financing. Does a reform movement result in added resources for schools? Another potential indicator of reform is to inquire of structural and functional changes within schools. Is anything truly different after a reform movement? Is there any 'residue' of reform?

School revenues and education reform

School spending might be taken as either a cause or consequence of reform. Regardless, of direction, might school spending at least be a correlate of reform? Insufficient resources, particularly diminished resources, might disrupt political homeostatis and trigger reform. Conversely, a reform period might provoke an added outpouring of funding for schools resulting in a resource residue, a kind of economic benchmark after which school spending is elevated. In any event, school spending should be associated, either before or after, with reform movements.

In fact, school spending data lend little help in identifying a reform period. School resources seemingly always increase in the United States, reform or no reform. This comes as little surprise to those who believe Americans are irrationally enamored of education. This view contends that schooling is a secular religion, the more of which individuals attain, the more probable is personal success and societal salvation. This assertion further holds that there is seldom an identifiable phenomenon such as an education reform period so much as there is a continual national search for new justifications to spend added amounts of money on schooling.

It follows from this education-as-secular-religion theory that, other than in the most uncertain of economic times or during periods of intense warfare, American public officials will allocate added resources for schools even if they always have to invent a kaleidoscopically shifting set of popularly acceptable reasons for doing so. Through this set of lenses, education reform is not an end, but only an instrument or conduit through which to convey added money for the nation's insatiable schooling appetite.

This notion appears particularly naive to professional educators, who often view themselves as engaged in a Sisyphus-like challenge of continually badgering the political system for the minimum resources they believe their institution must have simply to maintain itself. Nevertheless, correlational evidence exists to support the idea. Figure 1 displays United States mean per pupil spending and Gross National Product (GNP) for the post-Second World War years from 1945 to 1985. Here can be seen the steady growth in United States GNP and the seeming inexorable increases in per pupil spending. Indeed, except for an economically stagnant four year period of inflation and recession in the late 1970s and early 1980s, per pupil spending has actually escalated faster than the rate of GNP growth. Even when inflation is taken into account, per pupil spending has increased 500% since 1945.

Figure 1. Mean per pupil spending and GNP in the USA, 1945–85.

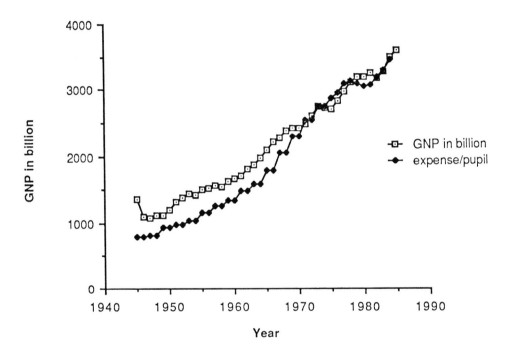

Moreover, there is no stunted statistical pattern characterized by revenue reversals and spending spikes. The upward sweeping curve is unusually smooth, despite the fact that the time period involved encompasses two major international wars, sustained conflict and tension with Soviet Bloc nations, revolutionary technological developments, alterations in fundamental social arrangements, gyrations in the nation's economy, and altering national political party dominance.

NDEA and EHCA federal appropriations were miniscule iceberg tips when compared with the submerged hulk of state and local school spending. Moreover, even the NDEA's explicit matching grant provisions simply did not elicit large levels of new local revenues. The EHCA was accused of the opposite effect. By specifying local school district compliance, but not bearing full program costs, the EHCA added 'encroachment' to the school finance lexicon. It was alleged that PL 94–142 compliance usurped revenues which previously were allocated for the schooling of 'normal' students. The EHCA is said to have resulted in a reallocation of local and state fiscal resources, but few added resources overall.

Similarly, as rich as the ESEA was for its time, referred to as 'Education's Billion Dollar Baby' by Elizabeth Benner Drew,[9] it initially represented only three cents out of every public school dollar and counts for even less than that today. Either slightly before or after enactment of the ESEA, a few states passed their own compensatory education legislation. Seldom, however, were these bills funded on a magnitude even closely proportional to federal appropriations.

The 1980s 'Educational Excellence' reforms follow a period of particularly intense national economic distress. The final years of the Carter Administration were plagued by a foreign cartel's (OPEC) efforts to dominate world oil prices, and United States inflation soared as a consequence. Initial years of the Reagan Administration were dominated by inflation dampening policies which contributed to a recession and high rates of unemployment. The upshot of such economic uncertainty was brutal for schools. Between 1978 and 1983, US schools lost $7000 per classroom in spending power. Educators felt the pain of inflation, in lowered purchasing power, more severely than any comparable occupational category.

By the third quarter of 1983, however, the American economy was experiencing a surging recovery, and school spending began to recapture previously lost purchasing ground. All of this coincided with the 'Educational Excellence' movement, and it is difficult to separate cause and coincidence. This is particularly the case since federal funds are of little consequence in this reform effort. States are not only the initiators of much reform, but also are paying the bill. Moreover, in that they are generally not dependent upon a categorical program reform strategy, it is difficult to trace state reform dollars. They are not 'radioactive', and they often appear to support the core instructional program of local schools. Analysis is rendered more difficult yet by virtue of the fact that enrollments have begun to grow simultaneously. Separating reform from growth and growth from inflation recovery is difficult.

Even experts differ in their views regarding the possible 'fiscal dividend' resulting from current reforms. Debra Inman contends that excellence reforms did not result in significant added resources for schools. Allan Odden asserts that school spending increased more between 1983 and 1987 than would be needed to match inflation.[10] If teachers' salaries are to be a criterion taken into consideration, then reform has not resulted in added resources. Mean national teacher salaries for 1986–87 had not regained their purchasing power position from 1970.[11]

In fact, given the confounding nature of the setting, it is risky to assert any position other than that America's financial commitment to funding education has persisted and grown. It is difficult to assign the credit to national education reform, either now or in the past. In short, school spending, at least by itself, should not be taken as evidence of reform.

The 'residue' of education reform

Resource levels are not, however, the only way, and may not even be the best way, of measuring the incidence of school reform. Tyack, Kirst, and Hansot, after having examined the 'residue' of past school reform efforts, conclude that the changes that persist are those that: (1) alter the structure of schooling; (2) create a new constituency or at least strengthen and expand an already existing constituency; or (3) are easily monitored by outside parties.[12] They offer as examples phenomena such as 'Carnegie Units' used to measure schooling increments, vocational training programs, teacher aides, preschool and after school childcare programs, and counselors. Colleges were strongly attracted to the Carnegie Unit approach to measuring students' secondary schooling because it provided a tangible means for enforcing admission standards and comparing applicants. Teacher aides, which expanded greatly with ESEA funding, were an easy accounting object on which federal officials could depend to ensure that Title I funds were not being used for regular school program purposes.

What kinds of reforms appear not to last? The converse of Tyack, Kirst, and Hansot's prescriptions are those innovations and changes which build no constituency, or perhaps even anger existing school supporters, are difficult to measure or monitor, and do not significantly alter the structure or procedures of schooling. Examples here are the 1960s fashionable reforms of 'flexible scheduling' for schools, so-called 'team teaching' for teachers, and Program Performance Budgeting systems for schools and school districts. Flexible scheduling is a particularly good illustration. It may be that a few secondary schools continue to rotate the sequence of classes depending upon the day of the week. However, it is an idea which generally has disappeared. Whatever its advantages, it had few supporters and was seen by many parents as contributing to lax discipline and wasting students' time.

How do NDEA, ESEA, EHCA, and the education excellence movement rank as reforms when subjected to the 'residue' test? Is there sufficient remaining today to justify a judgment of valid 'reform'?

NDEA: By the 'residue' standard, the NDEA ranks poorly. For example, federal matching funds for local school districts to purchase equipment have long since faded as have the forgiveable loans for prospective science, mathematics, and foreign language teachers, A few National Science Foundation (NSF)-trained teachers still perform in classrooms, but they are rapidly disappearing from age and federal government neglect. The NDEA fits few of Tyack, Kirst, and Hansot's criteria for persistence. It created only a small dependent constituency, teachers in training, textbook publishers, and equipment manufacturers. Each of these owed only transient allegience to the federal funds involved. The NDEA at the time of its enactment was publicly popular but did not attract intense special interest group support. Indeed, one should remember that the debate surrounding its passage was punctuated by widespread criticism of professional educators. Little wonder that when other budget priorities emerged, there were insufficient NDEA defenders. The absence of any lasting effects comes as little surprise. The NDEA qualifies as a reform only in terms of publicity, not in terms of persistence.

ESEA: The 1965 Elementary and Secondary Education Act clearly qualifies as a significant reform when judged by the persistence standard. Several components of the original legislation have disappeared or been consolidated into other legislative authorities, e.g. funding for instructional materials and the original Title III supporting innovative and exemplary educational endeavors. However, the centerpiece of the bill, Title I, containing federal funding for compensatory education, has persisted and grown. It is the largest single annual federal appropriation for public education and it probably is the most visible federal education program to both the public and professional educators.

ESEA, particularly Title I, created large new constituencies, comprised both of those who receive expanded services and those who deliver them. The compensatory education network is large, organized, and influential. It consists of compensatory education program administrators and coordinators from local, state, and federal levels, teachers, and teacher aides, parents and relatives of compensatory education students, and civil rights organizations and advocates. Because the American Federation of Teachers represents many compensatory education teacher aides and has close ties with civil rights organizations, that organization is also a major advocate for the program.

Compensatory education funds quickly became part of the 'budget base' for thousands of local school districts. The fiscal dependency of districts upon these funds and the large network of compensatory education supporters renders it unlikely that this program will be eliminated. Efforts by the Reagan Administration in 1981 to include ESEA Title I in a Block Grant consolidation were quickly abandoned in light of massive congressional and interest group opposition to such a proposal. Suggestions continue to be made for integrating compensatory education services more fully into the core instructional activities of schools, and such suggestions may eventually alter federal compensatory education regulations. However, elimination of the program itself is virtually unthinkable. The ESEA's added attention to students from low income households stands the test and must be considered a 'true' national education reform.

ESEA: The Education for All Handicapped Children Act was less visible with the public, less controversial politically, and less complicated than the ESEA. Nevertheless, it also meets the criterion of persistence. The inclusion of handicapped children into public schooling is now widespread and virtually irreversible. Federal funds do not cover the full costs of the program for most school districts. Nevertheless, districts have become highly dependent upon the added resources. Also, the tightly knit networks of organizations of handicapped students' parents and special education teachers and administrators, when coupled with the cadre of attorneys who benefit from the legal-adversarial nature of the program, renders its continuance assured.

Major education interest groups have little choice but to defend the PL 94–142 program and protect its federal funding base. This fact is all the more interesting given the anti-educator aura accompanying EHCA enactment. However, handicapped children constitute a politically sanctified classification which is subject to attack only by electoral campaign kamikazes and those who would denigrate motherhood and apple pie. As with the ESEA, the Education for All Handicapped Children Act qualifies as a national education reform. School districts behave differently since its enactment and they are not likely to change.

Educational Excellence: What of the contemporary reform movement? Is it likely to leave a 'residue'? One can only speculate in this regard; it is too early to reach a definitive conclusion. Reform proposals about performance incentives, such as merit pay and merit schools, create few supportive constituencies and frequently generate professional educator opposition. Longer school days and a longer school year have proven to be but marginal changes. No proponents have seriously considered lengthening United States schooling to the 240 days a year utilized by Japan. These current reforms do not appear as candidates for persistence.

Intensified high school graduation standards, elevated college admission criteria, and more rigorous textbooks are also reform proposals for which it is difficult to anticipate permanence. Educational performance standards have proved cyclical in the past, and it is difficult to predict what would render them permanent today. Perhaps if the United States came to view itself as engaged in a long term fundamental economic or military competition with the remainder of the world, a competition for which schooling was a crucial component, then high standards might persist. However, despite the likelihood that the nation is indeed embroiled in such a competition, there is little evidence to support the view that the general public will long sustain an allegiance to education reform and intensified schooling standards.

There may be at least two dimensions on which the education excellence movement might achieve lasting consequence: expansion of state-imposed performance indicators and the creation of career ladders for teachers. The contemporary concern for excellence overlaps a secular trend, increasing state responsibility for school policy making and financing. As state officials assume greater fiscal and program responsibility for local schools, they are anxious to have a better developed 'feedback loop' regarding pupil performance and use of state resources. By expanding statewide testing and proposing the imposition of other school performance indicators, the contemporary excellence movement is satisfying this desire for performance measurement. Such testing and indicator provisions might persist.

Several states which have undertaken educational excellence reforms are experimenting with so-called 'career ladders'. This generally is a personnel system restructuring whereby teachers judged to be superior are accorded greater responsibility, different titles, and generally higher pay. These systems are far from being widespread, politically accepted, or administratively stable at present. However, they are potentially quite easy to measure, they do alter the structure of at least one major schooling component, the teacher salary schedule, and they may succeed in building a constituency, teachers who view themselves as benefitting from, or at least as potential benefactors of, a career ladder. Some career ladder plans actually envision restructuring delivery of educational services to students. These plans are in their earliest formative stages.

It is still too early to assess the educational excellence movement's claim on reform immortality. Critics argue that many of the reforms are symbolic but not substantive; that they are cosmetic changes that will not stand the test of time. Advocates of current reform efforts assert that the duration and scope of this wave of education reform give evidence of significant impending structural changes in schools. To be sure, hopeful signs exist. Many local school districts have begun to implement innovative programs which challenge conventional notions of teaching and learning. A number of these programs directly echo the recommendations of national and state level reform reports. It is premature, however, to speculate about whether these experiments with change, if proven successful, will be replicated and institutionalized.

Does the excellence movement differ substantively from its predecessors?

What, if anything, distinguishes the contemporary education reform movement from the NDEA, ESEA, and EHCA? Figure 2 contains a tabular display of the four selected national education reform efforts. The movements are compared on nine variable dimensions. From these comparisons, the excellence movement appears relatively unique among post-Second World War nationwide efforts to alter American education.

Only on two of the nine dimensions, the vibrant nature of the economy and existence of one or a set of catalytic events preceding enactment, do all four cases display similarities. Conversely, contemporary reform appears to differ from all three of the past efforts on at least five dimensions, and it differs from two of the past reform periods on at least one and possibly two other dimensions. Each variable dimension is discussed in detail below.

Figure 2. Exploring the political economy of educational reform.
Comparing Reform

VARIABLE DIMENSION	NDEA	ESEA	EHCA	CONTEMPORARY
Value orientation	Efficiency	Equality	Equality	Efficiency
Economy	Up	Up	Up	Up
Outside catalyst	Yes	Yes	Yes	Yes
Government level	Federal	Federal	Federal	State
Proponents	Scientists	Executive branch	Civil rights	Governors/business
Educators	Anti	Co-operative	Anti	Co-operative
Target population	Special (elite)	Special (poverty)	Special (handicap)	General
Strategy	Categorical	Categorical	Categorical	Multiple
Residue	None	Special programs	Special programs	?

Value orientation

Public policy is shaped substantially by the interplay of three values, *equality, efficiency,* and *liberty.* Belief in these values is deeply embedded in the American ethos. They are represented repeatedly in public pronouncements and evoke deference during ceremonial displays. Each of these abstract conditions is held by proponents to be an end that governments should seek. They are also taken as criteria against which to assess the validity or utility of a government proposal or activity.

The three values are manifested practically in a wide variety of public policies and programs. Public concern for the values shifts periodically, and the balance among the three flows in a fluid fashion with one or two values ascending in significance only later to be subordinated to the interest and political influence of one or both of the others. One of the functions of government is to undertake the policy alterations necessary to maintain a dynamic balance among proponents of the three values.

Education is no exception to this pattern of influence. For example, from time to time, advocates of equality will dominate educational policy issues, only later to give way to proponents of efficiency or liberty. The kaleidoscopic nature of this interaction is made more complex by virtue of the fact that two, or on occasion, three values can share a common expression. For example, proponents of education vouchers, an expression of liberty or choice, frequency contend that such a reform would enhance efficiency and equality as well.

Two of the four reform movements under consideration here are clearly oriented toward the value of equality and two toward the value of efficiency. The NDEA and the contemporary educational excellence movement were each motivated by a different rationale and are distinguishable by a host of other factors. Nevertheless, both are directed at enhancing the productivity of United States' schooling, an efficiency objective.

On the other hand, both the ESEA and the EHCA are aligned principally with the value of equality. Both are intended to expand the range of school services available to a previously underserved or excluded pupil population. Both of these acts had and retain benefits from strong backing the civil rights organizations.

It may be that the reforms occur in value cycles. That is, the exclusive concentration of policy makers upon educational changes catering to one value stream may create a political demand to redress the imbalance from proponents of another value. Thus, equality reforms may lead to a concern for efficiency or liberty or vice versa. The next section of this chapter explores the role that political disequilibrium plays in promoting reform. Suffice it to say here, however, that the educational excellence movement is similar to the NDEA, but differs from its two most immediate predecessors, in its value orientation.

Economic conditions

An upbeat economy undergirds enactment or initiation of all four reform efforts. The Eisenhower years, during the latter stages of which the NDEA was enacted, were particularly notable for their lengthy period of sustained growth in GNP. Similarly, the ESEA was enacted early during President Lyndon Baines Johnson's first complete term in office. The economy was soon to have to support the full burden of the Vietnam War. However, at the time of the ESEA's passage, the American economic engine was in high gear and there was a growing portion of the nation's resources which could be allocated to domestic programs. The Education for All Handicapped Children Act was proposed and passed during the attenuated Ford administration. The economy was characterized by inflation and uncertainty, though nowhere as intensely as would prevail during the subsequent Carter administration. Still, there was sufficient national economic growth, citizen optimism, and revenue resiliency to expand federal education appropriation to include the EHCA. The educational excellence movement was launched during an economic surge. The United States recovered from the early 1980s recession with an unpredicted forcefulness. States enjoyed a fiscal surplus which they could and did allocate to education.

It is difficult to assert that a growing economy triggers education reform. There have been periods of economic growth which did not necessarily lead to national education reform efforts. However, it may well be that economic buoyancy is a precondition of widespread change. Without sufficient resources and popular optimism regarding the nation's future policy-makers may be too preoccupied with other issues to generate added concern for education.

External conditions

Whereas the nation has enacted major education reform legislation in *anticipation* of a war, e.g. the 1917 Smith-Hughes Vocational Education Act, it is unlikely that national energy can be focused on changing education, or any fundamental part of the school system, during a major war. Hence, peace, or at least the absence of widespread armed conflict, may also be a national precondition for a major education reform movement.

However, a war threat or other kinds of international challenge, may well serve as a catalyst, perhaps the most important catalyst, for education reform. Two of the four cases compared here, NDEA and the current education excellence movement, were stimulated strongly by external threats to the nation. The NDEA was a federal government response to a Soviet threat to United States technological dominance. The educational excellence movement is a nationally motivated state-by-state response to an external economic threat. This challenge is based primarily on technology, labor productivity, and the ability to compete with other nations in manufacturing and international trade. Whatever its nature, however, this economic challenge has prompted Americans to be intensely conscious of and concerned about schooling.

Enactment of the ESEA was partially aided by testimony to the effect that the United States economy would benefit from more productive manpower. However, the overwhelming case for enactment was based on education's ability to 'break the cycle of poverty' for youngsters from low income households. The external environment for the ESEA was characterized far more by the need to redress domestic social imbalances than to meet international military or economic challenges.

The EHCA simply was not the product of a widespread or popularly based political dynamic. It was far more a consequence of conventional interest group politics. The 'external' force was the presence of judicial decisions which exerted great fiscal pressure upon states to expand the range of services offered to handicapped students. State officials were willing to trade federal government regulation for financial assistance to meet new court imposed standards. In a sense, state government and local school districts acquiesced to added levels of federal authority in order to mitigate a fiscal threat. There was a new balance to be achieved, but the political disequilibrium involved was domestic not international.

Policy initiation

Here the current reform movement is readily distinguishable from the three comparison cases. The educational excellence movement depends for its policy expression upon legislative enactments and executive proposals of state level officials. This is by no means the first time that states have played a prime role. One need only remember the renowned nineteenth-century education reform activities of Massachusetts' chief state school officer, Horace Mann. Moreover, recent reforms have certainly been undertaken in individual instances by state officials, governors, legislators, superintendents of instruction, and prominent citizens. However, the contemporary excellence movement stands in dramatic contrast to the other major post-Second World War education initiatives in the degree to which it is propelled by state agents.

A contrast with the Education for All Handicapped Children Act is instructive. This legislation had its roots in state level court decisions[13]. However, the policy fruition of reform depended upon federal statutes. Much of the motivation for the current education excellence movement stemmed from a federal government initiative, publication of *A Nation at Risk*. However, the policy expression rests with states.

Why is this the case? In the 1960s or '70s the kind of public attention spurred by *A Nation at Risk* might well have resulted in federal legislation. Why in the 1980s was the federal government's role restricted to agenda-setting and 'bully-pulpit' activities and not policy-setting and program administration? The answer to this question probably lies in the political realm. Many of the contemporary reform proposals are controversial and require government action to be initiated. In the absence of one party dominating both the executive and legislative branches, or broad bipartisan agreement on an issue, it is difficult to gain enactment.

Neither political party dominated both executive and legislative branches of government during enactment of the NDEA or the EHCA. However, these proposals were not politically as controversial as either the ESEA or the component parts of educational excellence reforms. The ESEA was controversial and there were wide partisan differences of opinion regarding the bill. Enactment occurred, nevertheless, by virtue of the Democratic Party's overwhelming dominance of both houses of Congress and the Presidency. Indeed, because of the speedy partisan manner in which the bill was rammed through to passage, one Republican Congressman referred to the ESEA on the House floor as the 'Great Railroad Act of 1965'.

Since 1980, the Presidency and both houses of Congress have not been politically aligned. Moreover, enactment of a federal national educational excellence agenda has been impeded by President Reagan's clearly stated personal view that education is primarily a function of the family, locality, and the state, and the federal government does not have a major role to play.[14] In the face of such conditions, state policy actors rose to comply with the public demand for reform catalyzed by *A Nation at Risk*.

Reform proponents

Leading proponents of all four reform movements are remarkably different. The NDEA was primarily the brainchild of a slender number of nationally prominent science policy experts who had been influential in major Second World War science and technology developments such as the Manhattan Project. They had first-hand knowledge of science and an intense belief in the important role science and technology were to play in the nation's military and economic future. They had the attention of the President, Dwight D. Eisenhower, in the same personal manner they had had his ear during the Second World War when he was a commanding military figure and national hero. They were comfortable with the widespread public respect they had garnered and were used to wielding influence in high government circles. These conditions, when coupled with public anxiety over Sputnik, were sufficient to gain enactment.

The ESEA was primarily an executive branch bill. Major proponents, John Gardner, Wilbur Cohen, Francis Keppel, Samuel Halperin, etc., were Johnson administration officials. They conceived of the bill's components, fashioned a cohesive coalition of interest groups to support it, resolved fundamental political differences before the bill was submitted to Congress, and shepherded it through the enactment process. To be sure, they acted as the President's authorized agents, and they were comforted by huge Democratic Party majorities in both houses of Congress. Nevertheless, this was an unusual executive branch effort at legislative leadership.

In contrast to either the NDEA or ESEA, the Education for All Handicapped Children Act was born out of the support of interest groups and their congressional staff allies. A coalition of special interest groups representing parents of handicapped students, in conjunction with experienced civil liberties attorneys, fashioned the EHCA and guided it through Congress.

The current educational excellence movement has had an unusual set of leaders and proponents. It certainly has had symbolic federal level leaders in President Reagan and high ranking members of his administration. However, it has been state-by-state initiatives on the part of governors, chief state school officers, and business executives which have imparted the most energy to actual policy enactment. This probably marks the first time in United States history that large numbers of state governors have been proponents of education reform. Similarly, the excellence movement marks the first time in at least a quarter of a century that business and industry has played a significant role in shaping and advocating education change.

Educator involvement

There are two apparent models on this variable dimension. Both the NDEA and EHCA were enacted in the absence of widespread support from large groups of professional educators. Indeed, in the case of the NDEA, educator 'bashing' was a popular rhetorical sport of the day. The EHCA was also distrustful of educators, but in that enactment was not widely noted outside the immediate communities of educators and parents of handicapped children, the conflict between professional educators and EHCA proponents was not nearly so protracted as with the NDEA.

Johnson administration officials went to great effort to enlist the endorsements of professional educators during the planning stages for the ESEA. They succeeded masterfully in adding teachers, administrators, and school board organizations to their coalition of supporters. The involvement of educators in the current   excellence movement varies by state. In some states, teacher and administrator organizations have been positively involved in designing and advocating reforms. In other states they have only been passively engaged. In a few states, primarily those considering widespread competency testing of teachers, educators have been vocally opposed. However, the current reform effort, while not always solicitous of educators, cannot easily be characterized as anti-educator.

Target populations

The contemporary educational excellence movement is unique on this dimension. The NDEA was aimed at enhancing the science and foreign language capability of the nation's topmost students. No argument was made that the United States would be submerged beneath the Soviet economy. Rather, it was the Russian scientific establishment which would bury America. The way to overcome this threat was by catering to an intellectual elite and rendering it scientifically sophisticated.

Similarly, both the ESEA and EHCA acts were aimed at special populations, the economically disadvantaged and handicapped children. In contrast, the educational excellence movement is aimed at the vast middle of America's public school student body. The contention is that economic productivity will depend upon elevating the technical capability and economic awareness of the citizenry in general and the labor force in particular, not simply in enhancing the sophistication of elite scientists.

Program strategies

The initial three reform efforts considered here were all 'categorical aid' programs. Categorical aid refers technically to intergovernmental fiscal grants which can be used by a lower level of government to promote specified programs, personnel, products, or places. That is the funds can be deployed to assist a particular target population of pupils, employ added numbers of specified personnel categories, e.g. teacher aides, purchase authorized kinds of equipment, e.g. language laboratories, or spent in a certain geographic area, e.g. small rural schools or big cities.

An assumption in a categorical grant program is that the federal or state government must specify use of resources or local school districts and schools will use the funds for their own priorities. Frequently, categorical programs direct local school districts to add a particular service to the already existing core of the school program. NDEA approved federal funds for local districts to buy science and language related services and materials. The ESEA primarily concentrated federal funds on added services for youngsters from low income households. The ECHA specified added services to handicapped students. In this manner, each of these was a categorical program.

The excellence movement certainly utilizes, depending upon the state involved, categorical strategies. However, excellence funds are generally targeted at the core of schooling itself. Accountability, to the extent to which it occurs, is through statewide testing and index measures, not simply through fiscal accounting, the usual categorical program monitoring approach.

'Residue'

What do these reform movements leave behind? This was described in an earlier section, and no effort will be made here to repeat the analysis. Suffice it to say that there is little current trace of the NDEA, whereas the ESEA and EHCA both fit the Tyack, Kirst, Hansot mold of leaving a 'footprint'. They each altered the structure of schooling by adding services and changing the rules, specified changes which could easily be monitored, and constructed a constituency for the new services. This is the stuff of which reform residue is made.

It continues to be too early to judge the excellence movement on this dimension. The most hopeful signs of reform persistence reside with career ladders for teachers and expanded statewide testing and progress indicator movements. Here the structure is changed, a constituency is created, and monitoring is visible.

Why do reform movements occur? politics, economics, and propositions

Why do national education reform movements occur? What forces or events trigger them? Are there evolving domestic political and economic conditions which alter public attitudes toward schooling and promulgate education change through conventional political channels? Or, are national education reform efforts always stimulated by international events? Alternatively, do professional educators and their national organizations cynically manipulate public opinion and take advantage of whatever conditions are blowing in the policy wind in order to justify constantly increasing resources for education and better working conditions for themselves? This section addresses these questions

There are three conventional explanations for widescale or nationwide efforts to reorient public schooling. One theory, probably with its roots in a social systems view of the world, contends that reform results from political disequilibrium. Another theory adheres to the view that employees control the budgets of 'bureaus' and education reform is but a cover for professional self-aggrandizement by educators. A third theory invokes the spectre of international conflict and competition as the major explanation for national education reform. We explain each in sequence.

Restoring equilibrium

One theoretical contention is that government-initiated reforms generally, and nationwide education reform particularly, result from political disequilibrium. The view here is that a kind of political plate tectonics is constantly occurring wherein the practical manifestions of the values of equality, efficiency, and liberty are like large continents floating on a molten core of political magma. Where these continental shelves abut, where values conflict, there is the potential for much grating about government and intense social friction. This theory holds that one role of government is to relieve such tensions and establish a new equilibrium.

Equilibrium proponents explain that the strong policy emphasis on educational 'equality' during the 1960s and '70s contained the seeds for its own subsequent dilution. They argue that, over time, an unmitigated social concern for equality inevitably diminishes performance standards. Those concerned with high standards, justifiably or not, fear that added efforts at inclusion, such as bilingual education, special education, and compensatory education, will damage overall performance. For them, the only question is when a countervailing movement will gain ascendance and whether it will be oriented toward enhancing choice or efficiency.

Unlike the scientific debate over continental drift theory, the 'geologic record' regarding an equilibrium explanation is neither easy to construct nor consistent. It leads to only the most imprecise research propositions. One can deduce that reform will follow reform. However, when will another reform movement be initiated, what value orientation will it adopt, what will be its practical manifestations? These questions are not answerable simply from a notion of disequilibrium. This theoretical approach appears useful retrospectively but not predictively.

Self-serving professionals

Another school of thought adheres to the view that public policy is heavily influenced by public employees. Arguably, by virtue of their positions and control over information, those who actually work in the 'bureaus' have an unusual opportunity to define the needs of a public institution and shape the agenda for altering or adding to government. Many public officials, particularly at the local and state levels, are part-time elected representatives. The tradition is that they will be laypersons, unsophisticated in the particulars of government programs. Presumably, they are elected by their citizen peers to exercise judgments in the public's best interest and to enact policies consistent with their own campaign platforms.

Conversely, so the argument goes, government employees at almost all levels have an intense interest in protecting and expanding their professional or programmatic domains. They are capable of accumulating enormous knowledge and expertise within their particular realms of employment. Rarely can even full time elected or appointed officials, such as US Senators or Representatives, challenge them. Such officials generally are responsible for a wide span of public issues and do not have the time and energy to become intensely expert in a particular policy or program niche. It is from conditions such as these, far more than from whatever unionized or other collective activity may exist, that the potential political power of government employees flows, or so the argument goes.[15]

It follows from this line of reasoning that professional educators and other school employees may simply manipulate popular concerns to their own policy and personal ends. Under such a proposition, the only education reforms that actually occur are the periodic tradeoffs imposed by policy makers wherein added resources for education are exchanged for some alteration in schooling. Otherwise, what travels for 'educational reform' is only a public justification for added employment of educators, higher pay for teachers, and, perhaps, smaller class sizes.

Unlike the previously described political equilibrium notion, professional self-aggrandizement an opportunity for predictive propositions. For example, if bureaus shape policy, then we should expect proposals, from whatever quarter, to expand schooling when-ever a domestic or international threat challenges the United States. In some ways this is true. The American school curriculum is replete with the instructional residue of past, and some present, national crises, e.g. alcohol and drug education, sex education, AIDS education, added science and foreign language classes, and instruction about the virtues of capitalism and the evils of communism.

However, it is not evident immediately that such expansions of the school curriculum advantage educators. On many occasions additional expectations fail to be accompanied by any added resources, i.e.. more money or more teachers. The existing workforce is expected simply to incorporate one more subject or activity into a school day which is often already overcrowded and illogically fashioned.

The resource evidence in support of the self-aggrandizement notion is mixed. Teacher salaries, as can be seen from table 1, have not increased in purchasing power since the early 1970s. This means that two major national reforms have taken place, ECHA and the educational excellence movement, without teachers gaining in purchasing power. It is true that teacher salaries have been increasing since 1983, the year *A Nation at Risk* was issued. However, these pay gains have only begun to restore remunerative levels badly eroded by the prior five years of inflation and recession. In fact, there is a far greater correlate of educator salaries than reform cycles, namely, supply and demand. When teachers are in short supply, as in the post-Second World War period from 1955 to 1971, salaries increase. During periods of enrollment stability or decline, as from 1972 to 1982, salaries slump. Now that enroll-ments are again growing and states are eager to employ teachers, salaries and other incentives are increasing. The marketplace appears to shape remuneration more than do reforms.

Table 1. Instructional staff* Salaries, 1939–84, in 1983–84 dollars.

Year	Salary p.a. ($)
1939–40	10, 495
1941–42	9, 846
1943–44	10, 103
1945–46	11, 139
1947–48	11, 524
1949–50	12, 932
1951–52	13, 357
1953–54	14, 472
1955–56	15, 735
1957–58	16, 744
1959–60	17, 924
1961–62	19, 295
1963–64	20, 582
1965–66	22, 105
1967–68	22, 829
1969–70	23, 823
1971–72	24, 983
1973–74	24, 409
1975–76	24, 074
1977–78	23, 886
1979–80	21, 917
1980–81	21, 628
1981–82	21, 983
1982–83	22, 012
1983–84	22, 903

*Teachers and principals.

Source: US DEPARTMENT OF EDUCATION (1985–86)
Digest of Education Statistics, Center for Statistics
(Washington, DC: Department of Education).

Evidence regarding the instructional utility of smaller classes is mixed, though the weight of the argument may have shifted modestly to favor correlations between small classes and higher student achievement. Nevertheless, the debate about class size is most often cast in 'either-or' terms: lower class sizes are either an educational advantage to students or a reward to teachers. When class size is set on the teachers' benefit side of the ledger, and teachers are forced to choose lower class sizes or higher pay, they almost always choose increased salaries even if the result is bigger classes. This suggests that lower class size is not teachers' first choice as means to improve their individual situations. Yet, as can be seen from table 2, the United States has experienced reductions in class size every bit as steadily as the increases in per pupil spending displayed previously in figure 1.

An additional observation is warranted about the idea of professional self-aggrandizement. It should be remembered that two of the four national education reform movements considered here were undertaken in the face of at least partial opposition by professional educators. Some might dismiss the NDEA's teacher bashing atmosphere on grounds that it turns out not to be a long-lasting reform. However, the Education for All Handicapped Children Act appears to meet many of the criteria for a valid reform and it certainly has anti-educator components to it.

In sum, the evidence in support of reforms being a result of professional manipulation is insufficient. There is simply too much counter evidence. A more parsimonious and persuasive theory is needed.

Table 2. Pupil–teacher ratios, 1955–81

Year	Elementary	Secondary
1955	30·2	20·9
1956	29·6	21·2
1957	29·1	21·3
1958	28·7	21·7
1959	28·7	21·5
1960	28·4	21·7
1961	28·3	21·7
1962	28·5	21·7
1963	28·4	21·5
1964	27·9	21·5
1965	27·6	20·8
1966	27·0	20·4
1967	26·3	20·3
1968	25·4	20·5
1969	24·8	20·0
1970	24·3	19·8
1971	24·3	19·9
1972	24·0	19·7
1973	23·7	19·6
1974	23·5	19·5
1975	23·2	19·4
1976	23·0	19·3
1977	22·8	19·2
1978	22·7	19·1
1979	22·5	19·0
1980	22·3	18·9
1981	22·2	18·8

Source: US DEPARTMENT OF EDUCATION (1981–82) *Projection of Education Statistics* and (1985–86) *Digest of Education Statistics*. Center for Statistics (Washingtom, DC: Department of Education).

International challenge

Two of the education reforms with which this chapter deals are clearly associated with international events, NDEA and Sputnik and the educational excellence movement and international economic competition. The other two cases, ESEA and EHCA, appear only to be associated with domestic events. What then can be said in the face of such a mixed situation? Asserting that education reform is a function of both international and internal events borders on sophistry. However, if international threats are taken as a possible stimulant of domestic political disequilibrium, then perhaps one gains an increment of explanatory power.

It is altogether conceivable that international conditions can trigger events internally to bring about a rebalancing between equality, efficiency, and liberty. This seems to be particularly true in a modern context when the flow of ideas, technology, and capital is less and less restricted to national boundaries. Through this set of glasses, international conditions need be assessed not so much for their inherent characteristics, but, rather, for their potential effect upon United States internal perceptions, economic and political.

Having reduced 'international threat' to but an explanatory variant of disequilibrium theory adds little to the predictive capacity of the latter. Whatever weaknesses adhered to disequilibrium explanations still hold, even when supplemented with the spectre of overseas challenges. What then can be said regarding the causes or stimulants of education reform?

Preconditions of reform

Several preconditions appear necessary for reform to occur. By themselves, these phenomena are insufficient to trigger significant change. However, in their absence, reform is unlikely to occur.

A rising economic base: First among these preconditions is the availabilty of an acceptable economic base or fiscal dividend upon which reform proponents can capitalize. It may be possible to promote and implement national education reform on a declining economic base, but the United States appears to have no modern models for such a case.

Stable conditions: It may be that significant reform waves cannot occur too frequently. That is, the education system may need a period of stability following a preceding reform effort in order to accept the challenge of another change. Perhaps it is no accident that the four national education reform efforts considered here occurred roughly a decade apart. There were certainly attempts during the intervening years to alter the system; for example, PPBS was proposed as an efficiency innovation following on the heels of ESEA enactment. However, such intervening proposals never persisted. In part this may be because the education system is sufficiently fragile that it can tolerate or accommodate to but a limited number of changes at any one time.

Precursors: A series of preconditions may be necessary for reform, and among them may be a set of precursor ideas. A complete history of the four reforms under consideration in this chapter reveals that each of them was discussed and written about in advance of their embodiment in statute. For example, the National Science Foundation was sponsoring publications and meetings regarding school science reform in advance of Sputnik. Senator Wayne Morse of Oregon had proposed ideas similar to the ESEA in advance of Lyndon Johnson's election or the formation of the Presidential task force which designed the ESEA. Public Law 94-142 proponents had an opportunity to hone many of the ideas embodied in that legislation during their prior state level legal challenges of special education. Several states, for example, California and Florida, had pioneered many of the proposals contained in *A Nation at Risk* prior to its publication. New ideas, or even previously ignored old ideas, by themselves are probably insufficient to trigger reform. However, it may be necessary that they exist before reform can occur.

Prospective proponents: Leadership may well be a function of individual characteristics and an appropriate setting in which to exhibit them. However, for educational reform to occur, there needs to be a major proponent or set of proponents who can act as informed champions for change proposals. Such champions can come from a variety of settings, federal, state, academic, scientific, industrial, etc. They need not be prominent outside their field prior to the reform being catalyzed. However, they must be sufficiently informed and professionally positioned so as to be acceptable as legitimate reform leaders once a catalytic set of events transpires.

Catalytic event: Previously described preconditions may establish a primordial policy ooze out of which a catalytic event can trigger a national education reform movement. The catalyst may well be political imbalance among proponents of equality, efficiency, and liberty. The imbalance may itself be a function of either domestic or international events. However, in the same manner as one can specify that environmental conditions are right for a forest fire, one can specify that the environment is right for educational change. It is virtually impossible to predict precisely from where the 'spark' will come which ignites the change or in which direction the change will move. The 'spark' must occur in a receptive environment, one in which resources and other conditions are acceptable to change. Nevertheless, be it an event or a person, it is difficult to imagine a national reform movement in the absence of a catalytic event.

Acknowledgement

The authors wish to express their appreciation to Michael W. Kirst and Allan R. Odden for assistance with this chapter.

References

1. LASNER, K. ed. (1958) *Our Schools, Colleges, Laboratories are Turning Out Second Rate Brains*, (New York: Doubleday), p. 3.
2. BENTON, W. (1958) *This is the Challenge* (New York: Associated College Presses), p. 5.
3. PRICE, G.R. as quoted in *Life* magazine, 18 November 1957.
4. A history of this bill is provided by MARSH, P.E. and GORTNER, R.A. (1963) *Federal Aid to Science Education: Two Programs* (Syracuse: Syracuse University Press).
5. More has been written about the 1965 ESEA than about any other federal education aid bill. The act, by virtue of its dollar magnitude and sweeping focus, was the most significant federal education reform effort ever enacted. Among the useful background descriptions and analyses are MUNGER, F.J. and FENNO, R., (1961) *National Politics and Federal Aid to Education* (Syracuse: Syracuse University Press); BAILEY, S.K. and MOSHER, M. (1967) *The ESEA: The Office of Education Administers an Act*, (Syracuse: Syracuse University Press); MERANTO, P.G. (1967) *The Politics of Federal Aid to Education in 1965: A Study in Political Innovation.* (Syracuse: Syracuse University Press); EIDENBERG, E. and MOREY, R.D. (1969) *An Act of Congress: The Legislative Process and the Making of Education Policy* (New York: W.W. Norton); GUTHRIE, J.W. (1968) 'A political case history: passage of the ESEA', *Phi Delta Kappan*, 44(6), pp. 302–306; and DAVIS GRAHAM, H. (1984) *The Uncertain Triumph* (Chapel Hill: University of North Carolina Press).
6. Enactment of this bill is described in GUTHRIE, J.W. (1982) 'The future of federal education policy', *Education and Urban Society*, 14(4), pp. 511–530.
7. KIRST, M. and MEISTER, G. (1983) 'The role of issue networks in state agenda setting', Project Report 83–80A1, Institute for Research in Educational Finance and Governance, School of Education, Stanford University.
8. CHANCE, W. (1986) *'The Best of Educations', Reforming America's Public Schools in the 1980s* (Chicago: John D. and Catherine T. MacArthur Foundation).
9. DREW, E.B. (1966) 'Education's billion dollar baby,' *The Atlantic Monthly*, 218 (July), pp. 37–42.
10. INMAN, D. (1987) 'The fiscal import of education reform' and ODDEN, A.R. (1987) 'K–12 public school funding changes in the 1980s', papers presented to the American Educational Research Association annual conference, Washington, DC.
11. US Department of Education (1985–86) *Digest of Education Statistics* Center for Statistics (Washington, DC: Department of Education).
12. TYACK, D.B. KIRST, M.W. and HANSOT, E. (1980) 'Education reform: retrospect and prospect', *Teachers College Record*, 8 (3), pp. 253–269.
13. *Mills* v. *Board of Education*, 348F. Supp. 866 (D. Dist. of Col. 1972): *Pennsylvania Association for Retarded Children* v. *Commonwealth*, 343F. Supp. 279 (E.D.Pa. 1972).
14. WHITE, E.J., CLARK, D.L., and ASTUTO, T. (1986) *An Analysis of Public Support for the Educational Policy Preferences of the Reagan Administration*, University Council for Educational Administration (Charlottesville: University of Virginia).
15. This school of thought is represented by NISKANEN, W. (1971) *Beaureaucracy and Representative Government* (Chicago: Aldine Atherton, Inc.).

4   *From equity to excellence: political context and dynamics*

Laurence Iannaccone
University of California, Santa Barbara

The politics of education, along with its parent discipline, political science, displays a range of disparate topics, methodologies and, less obviously, value commitments; variation is seen apparent in the attention particular researchers give to different units and levels of government. Different schools of thought may be discerned by their own characteristic approaches to the subject, with their respective emphases seen especially in their chosen conceptual points of departure. Some years ago I touched upon what I see as the largest such distinction among researchers in educational policy and politics: that which exists between most of the researchers in the educational policy school and those in the politics of education group (Iannaccone 1980). Other ways of drawing finer distinctions of schools of thought among the politics of education scholars may also be noted (Iannaccone 1975, Iannaccone and Cistone 1974, Iannaccone and Lutz 1978). In a similar way I have argued that when a third-level politics of education change is underway – not the small, on-going incrementalism of routine LEA governance processes, nor the intermediate type of school-district system realignment through abrupt incumbent board member defeat after a significant period of relative quiescience – then scholars must pay major attention to the ideological approach in order to understand what is happening (Iannaccone 1977). This is consistent with the point taken by E.E. Schattschneider in his explanation of why generational change is often the correlate of major change in the issues at issue, in the shaping of the political agenda and his answer to his question, 'Why is a generation the proper period of time for the study of politics?' (1969: ch. 5). A similar point is made by Strickland *et al.* (1968) who define political science as 'the study of who says what the issues are, what is to be done about them, and by whom' (p. 1).

Chapter assertions

The theoretical assertion of this chapter is that ideas operate as the proximate driving force in American politics, in particular in domestic affairs and consequently in the politics of education at every level of American government: state, local and national. Cognitions and aspirations among voters, their views of the 'is' and the 'ought', shaping expectations are seen as the driving influences to predispose voters voting for change and those voting to maintain the *status quo*. Policy is thus viewed as resting upon value-laden public beliefs – interpretations of the American creed or dream – as you will. These are the products of past political conflicts. Having been forged in the furnace of previous major political controversies, they operate as premises of present policy and provide the criterion platform for incremental elaboration of future policy, until they are themselves challenged by enough voices raised to question their accuracy and appropriateness. This orientation is quite different from a marketplace paradigm of self-interest.

In a recent article Steven Kelman (1987) makes a point all too often neglected in the post Second World War efforts to make the study of politics *scientific*. We, academics and the overtrained media experts, all too easily become seduced by our own specializations into displaying an instance of Veblen's 'trained incapacity'. We succumb to a cognitive, rational man model to explain political behaviour. When it does not work, which is most of the time, we fall into the petulant, 'voters are dumb' alternative. While Kelman, commenting on the 1986 Nobel Prize awarded to James Buchanan for his work on public choice, views its recipient as richly deserving, he also views the award as a 'sad event' (1987: 80). Sad, because it reinforces the assumption that there is no difference between economic man and political man; because it applauds the extension of the marketplace paradigm into areas where it is 'inapposite and pernicious' (p.80). Finally, sad, because its cynical descriptive assumptions are not only inaccurate but play a significant part in undermining the norm of public spirit, which shares the fragile character of social norms but is also crucial to our democratic society.

Carroll Foster (1984) reports research testing the rational model hypothesis that voter turnout will tend to be higher in close election contest polities than in others, since in such elections each vote carries greater weight to influence the outcome. The reported research finding 'is that the perceived probability of a tied election at the state level is not a powerful or reliable factor in explaining across-state variation in voter participation rates in presidential elections' (Foster 1984: 688). Several different rational voter models were used in the analysis. Nonetheless, the empirical findings 'suggest that the relationship between closeness and turnout is weak, unstable, or non-existent in all of the models tested' (p. 678). In contrast, the findings of another recent study suggest that political competitiveness is especially affected by the strength and aggessiveness of local party organizations (Patterson and Caldeira 1984). The rational model assumes perceived self-interest as its independent variable. However, Ladd's (1985) examination of national polls about the 1984 Election finds support for Reagan from those who reported liking Reagan personally even in conflict with their not liking his policies. These amounted to some 35% of those surveyed. He further noted some 36% of a lower income group (below $10,000) reported support for Reagan's policies and personality, and support from another 40% of the same lower economic population because of his personal characteristics, and in spite of their not liking his policies. These findings fly in the face of the perceived self-interest independent variable of the rational model. Also, given the rational model's cognitive bias, we should expect that better educated individuals would be less influenced by candidate personal attributes than the less educated. But Glass (1985) found that policies and personal attributes were reported by voters as having about equal effect. Further he reports:

> Better educated individuals do not relegate personal attributes to the back burners in evaluating presidential candidates. Instead, these attributes are every bit as central to the evaluations of the highly educated as to the less educated. (p. 532)

Ladd points to three bases of voter support for Reagan in 1984: personal trust, voter mood of positive expectation in 1983, and affirmation of decentralization and domestic policies in general. These are clearly less cognitive, more emotional and far more global than what is assumed as the key independent variable by rational models and the marketplace paradigm.

My own view is that Kelman is right in his major argument that there are significant differences between the economic man construct and what is needed for a functionally equivalent political man construct. Similarly, my view agrees with his on the lack of appropriate fit between the marketplace paradigm and the choices people make in the political realm, especially in the American voting booth. However, I do not share his fear for the death of the public spirit norm as a consequence of a misleading paradigm and an inappropriate construct for several reasons. First, Machiavelli's political man construct long preceded Adam Smith's economic man; its self-interest drive was at least as powerful as economic man viewed by the public choice model; that view has been common in western society for centuries, especially among the masses, and yet we produced our democratic societies. Second, while not proving that 'ideas rule the world of politics' (Schattschneider 1969: 91), Kelman does provide enough illustrations to indicate that even in our cynical day there is much evidence of 'the ability of ideas to overcome interest in determining political outcomes' (85). Third, and most important, it is precisely because of the ways in which self-interest works in our mass democracy differently from the marketplace that explains why I do not worry about the fragility of the public spirit norm nor fear for its demise.

The following interrelated assertions are the basic statement of this chapter. They also sumarize its major conclusions: First, excellence in education is one of a number of indicators, which have as their referent the predominant value premise guiding American domestic policy since the 1980 election. Second, as illustrated by the sales record of the Peters and Waterman's *In Search of Excellence: Lessons from America's Best Companies* (1982), the excellence slogan is a symbol of productivity in industrial and economic terms, with application to meritocratic values in education. Education is the caboose, not the locomotive on this train. Other indicators correlated with excellence are achievement, merit, productivity, quality and more recently international economic competitiveness. Third, educational excellence as a slogan in the post-1980 politics of education is a symbolic indicator of a broader, more powerful, political shift in ideological emphases guiding general American domestic policy, not just today but for years to come. Fourth, given the high connotation, low denotation quality of effective ideologies, one should expect excellence to be ill-defined leaving the meaning of it open to public respondents. The terms merit, achievement, and productivity are connotatively more powerful in their twin political functions of uniting and dividing new coalitions, creating and refashioning constituencies, and generating support and opposition, precisely because they leave their definition to the responding public audience. Fifth, American belief in equality is not rejected by this shift toward excellence. Instead, what happens is an adjustment among elements of the American creed, a new ranking of democratic values, which in the present case places the concern for equality within the commitment to excellence.

Implicit in these assertions is the need to attempt to explain some political and policy-making processes. Also needed is some discussion of the relationship between American education policy of the national government and general domestic policy values, the political significance and functions of symbolic politics, the relationship of these to ideology and especially the dynamics of relatively rapid, if not sudden, shifts in underpinning values and related political ideologies with their influence on guiding policy premises. Much of the foregoing is either illustrated by or sufficiently interwoven with the meaning and longer term significance of the 1980 election. And, in fact, if the 1980 election and the eight years of the Reagan Republican regime in the White House is – as many Democrats still appear to believe – a deviant case, a sort of aberration, in the normal incrementalism of policy change, then the other assertions also fail. If, instead, the 1980 election is, as I have argued (1981,1982a, 1983a), the key event in a national realignment election era, then it is important for serious students in the politics of education to know more than we seem to know about the laws of relatively rapid or abrupt political change and their effect upon policy.

Meaning and significance of the 1980 Election

The theoretical frame of reference for this discussion is derived from two sources. One is the pre-1980 critical election era political scientists, (Burnham 1970, Key 1955, and MacRae and

Meldrum 1960). The other source is that developed from about twenty years of research on critical elections eras in the much smaller American polity, the local school district. This combination gains from: first the number of such polities experiencing critical election eras resulting in a much greater frequency of opportunities for the researcher to study the dynamics of critical election eras; second the research body on critical election eras in school districts consisting of over a thousand elections in a few hundred districts – admittedly only a small proportion of the nations's school districts, but nevertheless a vastly greater body of empirical data than the few national critical elections eras; and third the comparability of the dynamics of national and local district critical election era processes. The virtues of the first and second are obvious: their utility for the present purpose, however, depends on how well the national and local district critical election era processes fit together.

Briefly stated at a high enough level of abstraction to encompass most if not the entire corpus of research on critical elections in local districts, the progressive unfolding of a critical election period may be seen in the development of a sequence of five themes. Like the movements of a symphony, each of these themes is partly developed under the dominance of preceding ones. Similarly, as each succesive theme rises to become the dominant strain, it subsumes and modulates its precursors without extinguishing them. It recorders the relationship among those which emerged earlier. These themes are: (a) an ascension of voter discontent; (b) a triggering election; (c) the realignemnt of the policy-making subsystem; (d) the articulation of a new policy mandate; and (e) a final test election of the new mandate (Iannaccone 1982b, 1983a).

From the viewpoint of the significance of the 1980 election, it is the fourth theme, the articulation of a new policy mandate which explicates the redirection of domestic policy premises, especially as applied to education, which most concerns us. However, the meaning of the 1980 Election in terms of the third theme, the realignment of the policy-making subsystem, is the first issue to be addressed. Specifically, was the Reagan Election of 1980 a realignment election? The most visible feature in a critical election period is the rejection of the polity's incumbent chief policy-making official, e.g., the school district superintendent, or president of the USA. This is the clearest signal that the political system is undergoing one of its more fundamental changes; it is the point of no return for the predominant policy premises which have held sway for years guiding the polity's policy and the choices of program implementations of that. However, to focus on a single election, even the defeat of a sitting president, may be precise, but it tends to obscure the social, economic and political processes leading to that momentous event and those flowing from it, resulting, not only from it, but in some senses even more from its antecedent processes.

It is, instead, the periodicity of critical election eras in American national politics that appears more significant in the long run than the dramatic defeat of a sitting president. National critical election eras appear to be separated in time by about a generation. Research on the periodicity of school district critical elections likewise displays a roughly generational pattern, some 36 years (Criswell and Mitchell 1980). At the national level, note the 36 years between the realignment of 1932 and the previous one in 1896. The Lincoln Election in 1860, 36 years earlier, was a classic policy turning point election that failed to produce the necessary balance between political and socio-economic systems except through the Civil War. The year 1824 saw the break-up of the Democratic Party, which was realigned in 1828 with the establishment of Jacksonian Party dominance. So, too, adding 36 years to the 1932 realignment election brings us to 1968. The technical event characteristic of national realignments was not present, since Johnson decided not to run, but other characteristic features of previous national realignments were.

Why one generation? Because political philosophy articulated into policy premises and formulae of governance rules the world of politics. This is why the real prize at stake in a critical realignment election and its aftermath, especially the second term test, is the power to define the issues at issue for the voting public. This prize, not the presidency, nor the Congress – the power to state the issues which catch the attention of the general public around which it divides and unites, and about which policy alternatives are defined, is the supreme instrument of power (Schattschneider 1975: 60–75). Why then these particular generational years? Because, 36 yeas before that fateful 1824 election was 1788, when the policy system we still live under was being established.

Most of the time incrementalism, often obscured by routine decision-making, characterizes the normal change processes of American governments. Sometimes various governmental units within the American federal system, working with their own time clocks, exhibit the abrupt and cyclical, as well as deeper reaching policy shifts we have studied in local school districts. As with national critical election eras, these local critical election periods are the chief tension management process of American polities. These shorter periods are preceded by a growing imbalance between political and socioeconomic systems. Critical election periods display the primary processes through which the political system is recurrently brought back into a more balanced relationship with the changing socioeconomic system. Such periods are also characterized by increased conflicts around ideological issues resulting from competing philosophies of government and its service mission.

The ascension of discontent, the first theme of the present period, appeared around the mid-1960s in the 1964 Republican Party's Convention. Most clearly revealing that ascension theme, was the division within the Democrats in the 1968 nomination campaign of ideological clashes taken literally into the streets of Chicago. An early indicator of critical election eras is a significant increase of ideological polarizations within the major parties. An abnormally high intensity of intraparty political conflict spills over into the party's presidential nomination process and platform writing at its national convention. Even Watergate did not suppress the continued ideological polarization of the Democratic Party, as seen in the 1972 McGovern nomination. Domestic policy-making generally, and educational policy-making too in the years between 1968 and 1980, clearly reflected these continuing and growing ideological polarizations. In contrast to the large complex coalition of interests which combined with compromises to produce ESEA in 1965, the major national education policies since 1968 have been distinctively differentiated responses to strong, but nonetheless narrow, single-issue, interest groups. These more recent policies include: PL 92–142; affirmative action, especially in higher education; bilingual education; women's equity; and the creation of the Department of Education. However worthwhile in themselves, these have been responses to distinguishably different organized education lobbies, rather than policy reflecting a widespread consensus of voters. The same character of response to polarized strong interests marked much of the rest of federal policies and legislation during the last years of the Democratic Party's leadership. More important, during the 1970s, while the American voters may not have agreed with Ronald Reagan that the growth of government is the problem, not the solution, they no longer agreed with the Democratic Party's belief in the opposite (Ladd 1984).

The political characteristics of the 1970s suggests that the 1968 election is more akin to a pattern found in a small proportion of our school district cases than to the majority in its incompleteness (Iannaccone 1985). These are districts in which the first incumbent school board member defeat, after years of gradually increasing voter discontent, is followed by the involuntary turnover of the executive, but that event is not in turn followed immediately by the fourth theme, the articulation of a new policy mandate (Chase 1981). The third of the five characteristic themes of school district critical election processes is only partially complete. This in turn suppresses the emergence of the fourth theme for a time. Naturally in such cases the fifth theme in the normal school district critical election processes, the final test election, does not emerge until even later. Instead, a continuing series of chief executive displacements appears for a time, a condition of 'Overturn, Overturn, Overturn It' (Iannaccone and Lutz, 1970: 219–222). The policy doldrums of the 1970s and the survival rates of Ford and Carter are similar to this overturn pattern. In terms of single national realignment elections specifically, and critical election periods more generally, the present national critical election era has been longer than any previous one, twelve years between the triggering election of 1968 and the Reagan election of 1980.

The corpus of local district defeated incumbent board member research does provide at least one carefully analyzed case of incumbent school board member defeat, after a lengthy period of political quiescence, which did not lead to chief executive involuntary turnover. More significant is the fact that it also did not lead to rapid or abrupt policy redirection (Zimering 1986). The evidence in this case led to the conclusion that the issues used by the challengers and supporting the initial incumbent defeat election of two members from a five-member board were based on misinformation. The subsequent behavior of the new board members and the evidence that cleared up the earlier misinformation led to elections supporting the old board and the superintendent. More significant, the previous established policy continued rather than becoming redirected. A simlar finding was reported by Danis (1981) in her study of 50 years of Santa Barbara elections. She compared incumbent defeat elections, leading to chief executive turnover of both Superintendents and the City Mayor, with incumbent defeats which did not replace a sitting chief executive. Her analysis revealed a lack of ideological issues in the latter sort of incumbent defeat elections, ones which neither replaced a chief executive nor redirected policy (Danis 1981: 150–159). Mitchell's (1978) reanalysis of a large number of incumbent defeats and executive turnover, as reported during the decade of 1966–1976, suggests that it is the continued voter support of successful challenges subsequent to the first such defeat that produce chief executive turnover.

In sum, our studies of incumbent defeat elections in local school districts indicate some three types. The most common one is similar to the classic national realignment elections. These lead to the abrupt (within three years) involuntary turnover of the chief school officer and a redirection of educational policy. Indeed, a recent case study of one of these details the processes from election to changes within the classrooms, inside of five years (Pepple 1986). A second sort involves incumbent defeats when educational ideology and related policy issues are not at stake. While many fewer in number, these do provide evidence of a different type of incumbent defeat, one in which long term policy redirection does not follow the election except imcrementally, perhaps a little more rapid than usual. Similar to these in consequences is a third type, where ideological issues are central to incumbent defeat but these issues do not sustain continued opposition even long enough to confirm the challengers in the next election. Finally, within the major pattern of incumbent defeats about policy issues, following an extended period of rising citizen discontent, and subsequently followed by executive involuntary turnover an policy redirection, there exist some instances of what was noted above as 'Overturn, Overturn, Overturn It'. These also lead to policy redirection, but somewhat more slowly through a succession of two or more involuntary chief executive turnovers. The pattern provided by this last subset within the model, produced by the vast majority of incumbent school bard member defeat, most closely approximates the national elections between 1968 to 1980. Applying the five theme model of school district critical election periods to the national level from the mid-1960s up to 1980, one first notes the ascension of discontent and then a triggering election in 1968 without the reconfiguration of public values leading to a redirection of policy. To repeat, it appears akin to the overturn subset of cases within the major pattern. The stage was set, however, for the articualation of a new mandate. The accuracy of this statement is more significant for an assessment of the long-term policy issues than is the technical question of whether 1980 is a realignment election. However, that question deserves attention.

Realignment issues

Discussions of 1980 as a national realignment election turn on questions of definition first. 'If realignment means that the weaker of two parties suddenly becomes the stronger for some time to come by decisively winning in a crucial election at all levels of government, as the Democrats did in 1932, then obviously this hasn't happened since then' (Wrong 1985: 144). Similarly, also noting the example of 1932 tends to obscure the present substantial changes. Ladd (1985) points out, 'For two decades now, political scientists and other commentators have stumbled and sloshed around a conceptual swamp called realignment that we have created for ourselves' (p. 11). He pointed out that he had posed a false dichotomy four years earlier in suggesting that something more like a 'dealignment', a loosening of party affiliations, rather than a realignment had taken place in 1980. In any case something substantial has happened in mass voter behavior.

First, there is a new majority party in presidential voting. This may be seen in the 1972, 1980 and 1984 landslides. The 1968 Republican presidential win may have been more of a rejection of the Democrats in power than a vote for Nixon. But the Republicans have won six of the nine presidential elections since 1952. By 1984 voter identification had grown 'to the point where the plurality of Democrats over Republicans reached its lowest level since 1952' (Wattenberg 1987: 58). The Carter win, Ladd (1985) says, 'is in a sense the most graphic confirmation of the GOP's ascendancy: Jimmy Carter and the Democrats managed only the narrowest win in 1976 even though the Republican Party had been decimated by the Watergate scandals' (p. 17). And I hasten to add, they won narrowly with a Southerner as their 1976 standard bearer, helping to offset the voter shift in that region in which the largest voter mass changes have been seen. As I write these words, my attention is repeatedly diverted by the Iran-Contra hearings. What if the post-Watergate politics were to be repeated? This would only add strength to the argument, for 'how low the Democrats have fallen when their prospects depend upon what happens within the Republican Party. It used to be the other way around' (Wrong, 1985: 145).

Second, post-industrial developments have essentially wiped out the former New Deal coalition. Discussing the Southeast, Wrong (1985) writes, 'There one can speak of a realignment as having already partially taken place' (p. 145). Given the context of many years, Strom Thurmond's 1948 split-off with four states from the Democratic Party can be seen as a very early indicator of our current critical election era. Examining the most recent 1986 Southeastern voting evidence, Petrocik (1987) concludes that it shows the realignment to be programatically significant even were the Democratic Party to retain its numerical edge. He states, 'the similarity between 1986 and previous elections is undeniable. There is no evidence that Southern Whites have returned to their Democratic partisanship of an earlier era. As a group they were at least as Republican as WASPs, the traditional Republican core constituency' (pp. 369–371). Martin Wattenberg (1987) makes essentially the same point: 'the once solid Democratic South is no longer solid at all' (p. 65). Further, his analyses demonstrate a less frequently noted, but no less significant change in another regional distribution of party affiliation. The Western Mountain States, once second only to the South, have given more votes to Republicans than any other region.

Third, the mix of policy issues differs greatly from the New Deal era. Setting aside for later discussion the question of how persistent the new mix is, whether it will continue to shape the presidential campaigns of the next decade or not, it is clear that a different mix of issues from previous ones held sway in the 1980 and 1984 elections. Its domestic policy orientation was clearly focused upon decentralization and increased dependence on the private sector. Groups, organizations, individuals of all sorts have stakes in long-term policy. Understandably, their interpretations of elections are influenced by these personal stakes. Even when their judgment is not impaired by their perceived interests, it may be tactically useful for them to place their desirable interpretations upon election outcomes. Academic researchers are not invulnerable in these areas. The debate over what is or is not a mandate: who has one to do what is endless. We should not therefore be surprised to find politics of education scholars disagreeing about the meaning of the 1980 election.

The research would permit an application of the term mandate to the explicit campaign issues of the first incumbent school board member defeat (Chase 1981, Danis 1981). Nonetheless, given the emotional commitments involved, I have chosen to confine the word to the post-election ideas produced by the winners verbally and behaviorally (Iannaccone 1982a, 1983b). Thus while I have argued that the 1980 election provided a new and different mandate, it is 1984 that provided a real test of the Reagan 1980 Election (Iannaccone 1981, 1982a, 1984). As Ladd (1985) carefully noted, the 1984 Election was a referendum on the President and his administration. And it went for him. This conclusion leads him to the next. 'The proper question seems not whether a realignment has occurred, but rather where it is being pushed by the experiences of the Reagan era' (p. 12). Martin Wattenberg states it most sharply, (1987: 73):

> What made the 1984 election different in my view was the clear contrast between the performance of the incumbent Republican administration and the Democratic administration it replaced. For once the choice was not between the President and an uncertain alternative future. Rather the Reagan-Mondale contest was between the recent past and a present which had seen major changes.

Commenting on the southern voting patterns of the 1986 election, Petrocik (1987) concludes that 'it shows the realignment to be programatically significant even if the Democratic party retains its numerical dominance' (p. 347). A different issue mix has great significance for election outcomes. 'In a conflict, the person who can control ... the definition of the conflict, controls its outcome' (Strickland *et al.* 1968: 5). 'In politics the most catastrophic force in the world is *the power of irrelevance which transmutes one conflict into another and turns all existing alignments inside out* (Schattschneider 1975: 72). A somewhat different research approach by Jo Freeman (1986) yields a similar conclusion. Her comparative study of two major parties found the area of political culture most revealing. She says,

> I would argue that the Republican party is *not* a poor imitation of a normal coalition-building party, but a different type of political organization that does things in different ways. The differences in its political culture have put the Republican Party at a disadvantage in its competition with the Democratic Party for most of the New Deal era. However, the roads to political success have been changing rather rapidly in the last 15 years, and the new roads are ones that the Republican Party is well equipped to travel. (p. 352).

Despite this, her advice to the Democratic Party is that it not change to become more like the Republican Party. However, it is the new mix of issues salient to voters that accounts for the increasing conservatism of elected Democrats in Congress. 'The national trend toward the GOP in the past six to eight years is probably having as much effect on the Democratic party as it is on the Republican Party' (Wattenberg and Ladd 1985: 3). This was in response to a question about Democrats acting like Republicans. The New Deal issues no longer command the attention of most voters.

Fourth, a dealignment, the weakening of voter ties to the parties, is a major feature of the present critical election era. 'The current realignment differs greatly from its predecessors . . . voter ties to political parties are much weaker than in earlier eras' (Ladd 1984: 25). One consequence of this feature is that the Reagan realignment is fragile, although it is real. What has developed is a combination of: (a) candidate-centered rather than party-centered voters; (b) 'incumbents are immune to all but the most massive shortterm surges' (Petrocik 1987: 348); and (c) a two-tier electoral system with Republicans in control of the Presidency and Democrats of the Congress.

These dealignment features may reflect changes in the values and behavioral patterns of voters. They may result from technological changes, especially media ones, of our day. They may even more reflect the increased centralized control of the parties by central committees combined with expanded legal forms and rules about the parties resulting in a slower rate of adjustment to the changes in voter attitudes and public philosophy. In any case, the present critical election era has seen both a significant weakening of the hold of partisanship on voters and a shift of party affiliations. This shift is especially clear in the Western Mountain Region and within the traditional solid South. Martin Wattenberg (1987) concluded that a candidate-centered political age will be with us for a long time regardless of which party wins the next elections. He suggests the public use of the term 'Reaganomics rather than Republican economics' is an indicator of this candidate-centered voter view (p. 71). Petrocik (1987) drew a similar conclusion from his research on voting in the Southeast. Whether the recent voter trends in affiliation yield a Republican majority or not is for him not the chief answer to the realignment question. 'The wait for a realignment should end because one has occurred and is continuing' (p. 373). The Democratic solid South has been one of the most influential aspects of national politics throughout this century. Whatever term is used to describe this change in voter commitments, without the solid South, the American game of national politics is a new and different one.

Political ideology

Mitchell and I have argued that legislatures could be seen as having three tools at their disposal: (1) allocating resources; (2) making rules (both to control behavior and about the rule-making process including allocating status); and (3) exporting ideas by which citizen behavior might be influenced (Mitchell and Iannaccone 1980). Specialist in education and other fields pay attetion to the allocation of resources and the making of rules. Both have considerable impact on our interests and work. Least attended and less understood is the third type of governmental mechanism: the formulation, articulation and enunciation of ideas in expressions of concept, sentiments, beliefs and attitudes to influence policy through the reorientation of public ideology. It is given least attention and underestimated for many reasons: (i) its essential character is more general and less concrete than are the other mechanisms; (ii) they are, also, more subtle, pervasively spreading through the entire range of electoral politics, law making and the formulation of resulting administrative regulation and implementation, and (iii) the processes by which ideological beliefs become articulated as policy premises to guide action are very complex.

The pervasive character of public ideology is evident from its major components consisting simultaneously of conceptual schema, beliefs and emotional commitments. Too, a statement of civic or political ideology may stand apart from the other two typical mechanisms of government as, e.g., Lincoln's Gettysburg Address, Kennedy's Berlin Wall sentence, or the preamble of a statute. Conversely, resource allocations and rules never exist without some explication of implied conceptual schema with value connotations, which are their evaluative component or aspect. Edelman (1977) similarly distinguishes between 'politics as a spectator sport and political activity as utilized by organized groups to get quite specific, tangible benefits for themselves' (p. 5). On the latter sort there is feedback; resource allocations; behavioral regulations; and changes in status have immediately observable consequences. Political professionals, public employees and others expecting immediate concrete benefits from government pay attention to such of these as touch upon their private interest. In contrast, for most voters 'most of the time politics is a series of pictures in the mind . . . a moving panorama' (p.5). Following Edelman's use of the theater analogy, without denying the importance of the craftsmanship of a good playwright and the artistic skill of the actors, the social/psychological responses of the audience determine the successful run of the play. 'It is the needs, and hopes, and the anxieties of men that determine the meanings' (Edelman 1977: 2). It is no accident that the word *catharsis*, the purging of the audience's emotions, has been used at least since Aristotle in descriptions of great plays. It is also used to describe the impact of charismatic leaders. The impact, the cathartic effect, of even the greatest dramas varies over time and place. In politics too, the response of the audience is a key element often neglected by the political professionals and others.

Political ideology has many different functions. One function of ideology is in aiding or in preventing the acceptance and implementation of new policies. This function is most important in the complex, interwoven family of governments of the American federal system, with its mutually dependent policy formation processes. The existence over time of its ideological underpinnings explains the consistency of policy premises and its usual incremental changes. A second functon is in creating conflict and consensus among the society's diverse groups. This is the policy value or issue aspect of the political process of uniting and dividing by means of the predominace of given political issue agendas, which lies at the core of American voter constituency formation. The refashioning of constituencies by a shift in the predominant issue agenda is the most powerful strategy in American politics, because it substitutes a new mix of issues as the basis of political conflict, making the previously predominant mix irrelevant. As noted above, the new conflict '*turns all existing alignments inside out*' (Schattschneider 1975: 72). This is why Schattschneider describes such a switch in conflicts as 'the most devastating kind of political strategy' (p. 71). 'All politics involves group conflicts, but not all conflict escalates' (Edelman 1971: 21). Obviously it does not happen often. An issue, and even more important a new configuration of value-laden issues, does not become the core of a new set of political controversies and the basis for a reshuffling of alliances, voter allegiancies, and the restructuring of a great political party just because some leader says so.

The pervasive qualities and the depth of a political conflict capable of setting a new winning agenda nationally are the reasons I have elsewhere argued that conflicts which escalate into realignment of coalitions and a redirection of policies, are reflections of 'intrinsically unresolvable issues about . . . fundamental tensions inherent in American society' (Iannaccone 1977: 277). Because continued political conflicts about such issues are likely to destroy a society, a substitution of conflicts takes place around a different mix of issues which promises a future solution to the problems posed by irreconcilable tensions. But precisely because these are irreconcilable, at least within the limits of their current circumstances and technology, the new mix of issues and related ideas provides an illusion of solving the old conflicts. But instead it displaces these. A successful effort at such displacement requires an adequate illusion.

> An adequate illusion is the capacity of a dominant political ideology to conceal fundamental irreconcilable contradictions in a society's core values by offering a hope of their reconciliation through the logical development of that ideology's implied techniques (Iannaccone 1984: 23).

Ideology, though rooted in past-oriented myth, is future oriented. It projects the future through a logical extension of proposed solutions to perceived problems. Political ideology is, however, defective because of the limitations inherent in its basic components. These are 'a critique of the going order, a concept of a superior order, and a program for getting there' (Lane 1962: 456). The effective articulation of public ideology depends on three elements of public perception and belief at least: (1) an evaluative description of present circumstances; (2) a picture of the society's aspirations; and (3) a definition of the social project by which things can be changed to make future circumstances more closely approximate those aspirations. In brief, it describes the 'is', the 'ought' and, implicitly, it diagnostically expains the gap between them. It also provides the core idea of a basic plan for how the 'is' can become more like the 'ought'. In turn, this core idea provides the value-laden premise for public policy and implementation programs. Symbols of government function powerfully when 'they reflect people's ideas, their perception of the world, and sometimes their innermost thoughts' (Rotunda 1986: 6). At one and the same time, effective political ideologies 'inform and give direction to subordinate ideas and opinions and keep them consistent one with another; that is, they have an organizing and a consistency funtion' (Lane 1962: 424). Political ideologies operate in the realm of ideas and emotions to maintain boundaries both of inclusion and exclusion among civic participants. They thus reduce anomie and anxiety; they provide a basis for personal identity and so, co-ordinate activities for common effort. Finally, they legitimate political authority and governmental policy.

But most important, the effectiveness of ideas – whether articulated by governmental units officially and in campaign rhetoric by incumbents or by challengers – depends upon their success at stimulating an influenctial and supportive response from a broad range of diverse persons of differing backgrounds, peronalities and interests. The essence of an effective articulation of ideology lies in its social/psychological nature. The articulation of beliefs which influence policy must be high in connotation and low in denotation. It can be effective only when it makes room for a broad continuum of dissimilar, often conflicing interpretations. It must allow for many diverse identifications by quite different persons.

Even the sophisticated modern public opinion polls fail to adequately capture the essential meaning of this cathartic process. In fact, they may mislead their users by their pinpointed specificity. Responses to specific programs, issues and events independently, and even the arithmetic sum of these may and often have indicated less than majority agreement with a president's position on them. This was the case on most of Reagan's specific positions in the months before the 1984 election. In contrast a more ambiguous and all encompassing gestalt of support for Reagan, especially in domestic affairs, has been a hallmark of his presidency including the period before that election. This social/psychological essence of the articulation of policy and public response has been the reality upon which the media's 'Teflon presidency' is grounded. It is also one reason effective ideologies are usually encapsulated in brief slogans, phrases and even sometimes in one word. Take as examples the words, equity, accountability, bureaucracy, or excellence. Their usefulness lies in the fact that they are capable of a wide range of operational definitions so that people with very different purposes can attach their different definitions to them.

Predominant ideas especially must be capable of widely disparate operational definition in order for them to operate so as to carry out their organizing and consistency function. Otherwise they could not be the core idea of a superordinating coalition of coalitions, the necessary belief and slogan dimension of each of the major parties. However, a major party, a grand coalition, inevitably lives on the knife edge of the tensions among its component coalitions. They must be important to rank and file voters or they will not fly. 'When people argue about "mere words", they are talking about fundamentals, infrastructure, not superstructure' (Rotunda 1986: 98). Moreover, in the words of Schattschneider (1975), 'A victorious alignment accumulates a tremendous body of hangers on', (p. 72). One consequence of this is that the predominant coalition is held together by the alignment around which it was formed and its expression of political ideology. But its inferior coalitions, while accepting the core concepts of that alignment's political ideology, inevitably have a stake in operationally redefining it to suit them better. The political system's dynamic results from the single fact of its complexity and size. No alignment and no ideology can satisfy all of its component subsystems equally. The predominance of one basic value underpinning a core ideology in any policy system is achieved partly by subsuming other essentially held values beneath it, usually through implicit rather than explicit rankings by means of their redefinition to be consistent with the dominant idea. The struggles within a grand coalition tend to be operational redefinitions of core ideology. These intraparty conflicts are usually surpressed above all by the larger interparty conflicts in which the opposition seeks to establish a different predominant value expressed through its political ideology. A critical election era in America substitutes a new political ideology consisting of a significantly different mix of ideas, almost none of which are new ones.

From equity to excellence

During the 1970s national policies for equality took another, extended and different form. Once again the operational meaning of equality took on a different flavor. What had once been an effort to provide relief from legal segregation and fiscal inequality had spawned a variety of equity programs. The different slogan reflected an operational difference. This policy metempsychosis by the late 1970 revealed the internal chaos of the dominant Democratic Party's component coalitions. Its programs became viewed by many voters as specific interest give-aways. The policy rhetoric of equity was edging toward quotas based on racial, ethnic or gender discriminations. Whether intended or not, the operational definitions moved in the direction of a zero sum contest. Policies so defined leave only one question to the political arena: 'Whose ox shall be gored?' Worse, the changed economic conditions, including a decline in productivity, meant that the era of carrot inducements had given way to a punitive era of regulatory whips by the 1970s; the articulation of eliminating legal barriers to equality and fiscal inducements had given way to a perceived legalized inequality and increased regulation to produce equity. This late stage came on the eve of the 1980 election. It was characterized by a proactive stance of increasingly centralized national agency interventions to solve social problems in states, local districts and higher education campuses. The voter perception, accurate or not, that Democrats suported bureaucratic interference and special interests was one unintended consequence of the journey that began in 1932. That perception is ironic. This was precisely how voters perceived the Republicans after 1929. Those governmental actions of the 1970s also reveal the characteristic late decisions of established policy systems near the end of their lease on power. They go beyond the zone of voter tolerance in the years shortly before a realignment.

Part of the preceding argument can be illustrated by noting changes in the operational meanings of equality in national education policy. Beginning with the 1954 decision the first road traveled was the elimination of legal, *de jure* barriers. This had relatively wide consensual support, except in the Southeast. The next road was that of *de facto* segregation. It produced a clear, but still not dominant, political backlash by the 1968 triggering Election. During this same period a significant operational redefinition of fiscal and educational equality was taking place. The shift from equality of input to outcome – never actually achieved – produced no small amount of political conflict. What Mosher and Wagoner (1978) noted about education policy could have been said as accurately about American domestic policy generally. 'Tensions are mounting between those who see the need for increased regulation, centralization, and accountability, and those who fear a continuing erosion of institutional and professional autonomy and who thus are encouraging decentralization and adherence to informal or negotiated arrangements' (p. xi). Most important for the meaning of 1968 and 1980 elections, much of this conflict was within the dominant Democratic Party of the 1960s. It emerged increasingly in the 1970s.

However, the process of dealignment had already been underway for years prior to the 1980 election. So was the growth of the Republic Party. This is in part rooted in the eternal and paradoxical love affair Americans have with business, often a love-hate relationship. Schattschneider (1975) views the dualism in America of government and business as one of the greatest modern unresolved conflicts (pp. 116–125). It is also one of the central dynamics of democracy. 'In some ways *the public interest resides in the no man's land between government and business'* (p. 120). Lane (1962) too, in his analysis of American voters, points out that, regardless of changes in the specific view of the government and business relationship, it was and is a critical element in the political ideology of American voters (pp. 261–267). Whatever the New Left might wishfully have thought in the 1960s, the New Deal was not a revolution against the private sector. Instead, the political realignment of 1932 is better understood as a rebellion against what was seen as bad and cruel business.

In discussing the question of why there is no socialism in the United Stares, Lowi (1985) offers two major explanations. One of these he sees as the influence of American federalism. The other is the American tradition of violence, i.e., rebellion, in contrast to the European tradition of revolution. The impact of federalism in supporting the two party stytem, and in preventing this country's politics from adopting either Far Left or Right ideologies, is often underestimated. Implicit in this restraining function is a tendency of the federal system to check the predominant ideological drift from carrying its overarching value – whether it be freedom or equality – to its logical extremes.

Aaron Wildavsky (1985), in a recent analysis of American society and federalism, distinguishes some three sorts of political cultures: hierarchical collectivism, market individualism, and egalitarian sectarianism (p. 46). He argues that all of these American political cultures believe in equality. They differ in its operational definition. For the egalitarian sectarians, it means equality of results; for competitive market individualism, it means equality of opportunity (p. 48). All these various political cultures also believe in decentralization but have different operational definitions of it. However, he describes as 'a compelling truth: federalism and equality of result cannot coexist' (Wildavsky 1985: 49). More fully he says,

> Uniformity is antithetical to federalism . . . were there to be a change in values toward equality of conditions, the political culture which undergirds federalism would fall apart. You can have a belief in equality of opportunity to be different, but you cannot have a belief in equality of results to be the same and still have a federal system (p. 43).

Lowi's second explanatory variable is America's rebel character. Unlike a revolution, which seeks to establish a different form of government based upon a different set of fundamental beliefs about authority, rebellion seeks to reform and improve the existing system. The purpose of rebellion, like evangelical conversion, is not to destroy the present order but to redeem it.

Louis Hartz (1955) suggests the sources of American political ideology lie in the presence of Lockian liberalism and the absence of feudalism against which to create a revolution (p. 20). Hence 'America which has uniquely lacked a feudal tradition lacked also a socialist tradition' (Hartz 1955: 6). He earlier describes America as, a society which begins with Locke . . . stays with Locke, by virtue of an absolute and irrational attachment it develops for him, and becomes as indifferent to the challenge of socialism in the later era as it was unfamiliar with the heritage of feudalism in the earlier one. (Hartz 1955: 6).

Hartz goes on to describe the predominance of the commitment to democratic capitalism as the new Whig ideology, which became successful, 'when it gave up the aristocratic frustration of Hamilton and catered openly to the acquisitive dreams of the American democrat, uncovered by a strategic accident the historic ethos of American life' (pp. 205–206). In effect it united Hamiltonian means to Jeffersonian goals and shaped the municipal reform in both major parties. 'Unfurling the golden banner of Horatio Alger, American Whiggery marched into the Promised Land after the Civil War and did not really leave it until the Crash of 1929' (p. 203). Even the New Deal did not disturb the American democrat in his or her 'Lockian Americanism' (p. 270). Truman's second administration speeches are seen by Hartz as a

blend of the fighting Roosevelt and the complacent capitalist oratory of Herbert Hoover. Surely such a synthesis would have been impossible if the New Deal had been defined in anticapitalist ideological terms (p. 272).

This is similar to the major theme in David Vogel's (1980) discussion of American support of the New Deal. It represented an effective alternative for restoring the viability of the American private sector. The American love affair with business has not ended. The 1980 Election, but much more significant the voter drift into dealignment, the increased numbers of Republican voters, the regional shifts in voter partisanship, and the rising status of conservative Democrats within their party are reflections of a massive undertow of voter commitment to a ideological restatement of the relationship between freedom and equality. Lane (1962) has called these values 'democracy's two greatest ideals' in his research report on American political ideology (p. 81).

Since the French Revolution, a slogan of three words, *liberté, fraternité* and *egalité*, has powerfully articulated and symbolized the meaning of western middle-class democracy. It has proven useful guidance for students of comparative western democracies. The predominance of either freedom or equality is also useful in examining the changing policy emphases of different policy eras in America, especially domestic policy emphases including education. The predominance of one basic value in any policy system is achieved by subsuming other values beneath it, usually through implicit rather than explicit rankings by their redefinitions. Thus the values of liberty and human kinship were redefined through most of this century, certainly since 1932. They have been viewed as dependent upon equality. Social and economic equalization has been viewed as a precondition for liberty. This view is significantly different from the Lockian nineteenth century view of liberty. Liberty was then seen as necessary to produce equality. When political ideology changes its emphasis from one to the other it is, in part at least, a reaction against the previous era's emphasis.

The 1932 emphasis was upon equality achieved through the major social project or policy premise commitment to centralized national government intervention in state and local domestic matters. The year 1980 was a critical realignment election ending a policy era which began in 1932. It set the stage for a different emphasis on the operational meaning of *liberté, egalité* and *fratenité* in the American public creed. *Egalité* was the predominant ideological emphasis underpinning the social project policy premises from the New Deal through its last omnibus expression in Johnson's Great society, and its piecemeal expressions in the 1970s. *Liberté* is the predominant policy value of the present policy era. It is the expression of the competitive market individualist political culture.

Excellence in education is its educational policy slogan. Its basic voter support has been developing for some years. The concern for educational achievement like the American voter's love affair with business has been with us all along. In preparation for this chapter the saliency in the public media of the two topics, achievement and equality, in education was examined in a small unpublished study. We used content analysis of the education columns in the June and September issues of *Time Magazine* from 1954 through 1985 inclusive. Rather than create a bipolar measure, each of these topics, equality and achievement, was scored for separately. A negative relationship between the two was not an automatic artifact of the content analysis scoring rules. Two findings appear significant. In general, over the 32 years involved there is a pattern of negative relationship between the achievement and equality curves. For example, the years with the highest equality scores, 1955, 1956, 1959 and 1972 are among the lowest achievement score years. The converse is especially pronounced in 1960, 1964, 1965, 1983 and 1984. The six years of 1967 through 1972, and the 1954, 1955 pair are the only consecutive years in which the equality topic scores are systematically above the achievement topic scores. Overall, however, the topic, achievement, tends to dominate about twice as many years as that of equality. There are only a few issues in which neither of these topics was discussed. This finding is consistent with the belief that achievement and equality are salient long-term underpinning values in American educational polciy – indeed in domestic policy generally. The finding of a negative relationship between their pre-dominance in the *Time* education sections is another hint suggesting that when either predominates in American domestic policy, the other is subsumed beneath it, but not erased. Its presence is still felt. Educational achievement topics predominated in our data more often than equality during these last three decades, when concern for equity policies many have been higher than any decade in this century with the possible exception of the 1930s.

Finally, in the words of Dennis Wrong (1985), Reaganism 'is far from being a peculiarly American manifestation but is consistent with political and economic trends at work in other major Western democracies with advanced industrial mixed economics' (p. 148). So too, the predominance of excellence in education is not a uniquely American phenomenon. It is a broad ranging – if not worldwide – international development affecting education in many diverse countries (Iannaccone 1983b). Studies of education politics and policy development in 11 nations reveal that the same policy value predominates in different nations with different forms of government and economic circumstances, i.e., post-industrial, smokestack industrial and underdeveloped countries, as well as in left-wing revolutionary, neo-fascist totalitarian governments, and more democratic ones alike. A number of nations preceded the United States in their commitments to productivity as the predominant policy value.

In sum, the educational policy shift from equity to excellence is a component of the larger similar national domestic policy shift. These changes are worldwide in breath. In depth, they reach to the long existing roots of American Lockian liberalism and America's commitment to capitalism. To some extent, at least, this political ideological change in emphasis has been underway for a long time, as may be seen in regional mass voter shifts. So, I have argued that even were the Democratic Party to regain dominance in Presidential elections, the 1980 election has resulted in a redirection of American policy toward a new mix of political issues and ideas. Most prominent among these is the commitment to freedom, with its correlates of increased reliance on the private sector, concern for industrial productivity, toleration for some degree of inequality, and support for competitiveness in the world, with correlates of merit and achievement in education. The political symbolism of excellence in education is not only contextually held in place by the present dominant political ideology, but is also in organic union with powerful and historic values likely to continue for many years to shape educational policy-making and education.

References

BURNHAM, W.D. (1970), *Critical Elections and the Mainsprings of American Politics* (New York: W.W. Norton Co. Inc.).

CHASE, W.M. (1981), 'Superintendent turnover: antecedent conditions and subsequent organizational changes', PH D dissertation, University of California, at Santa Barbara.

CRISWELL, L.W. and MITCHELL, D.E. (1980) 'Episodic instability in school district elections', *Urban Education*, 15, pp.189–213.

DANIS, R. (1981) 'Policy changes in local governance', PH D dissertation, Univesity of California at Santa Barbara.

EDELMAN, M. (1971). *Politics as Symbolic Action* (Chicago: Markham Publishing Co.).

EDELMAN, M. (1977). *The Symbolic Uses of Politics* (Urbana: University of Illinois Press).

FOSTER, C.B. (1984), 'The performance of rational voter models in recent presidential elections', *The American Political Science Review*, 78, pp. 678–690.

FREEMAN, J. (1986) 'The political culture of the Democratic and Republican parties', *Political Science Quarterly*, 101, pp. 327–356.

GLASS, D.P. (1985) Evaluating presidential candidates: who focuses on their personal attributes? *Public Opinion Quarterly*, 49, pp. 517–534.

HARTZ, L. 1955. *The Liberal Tradition in America*. New York: Harcourt, Brace and World, Inc.

IANNACCONE, L. (1975) *educational Policy Systems: A Study Guide for Educational Administrators* (Fort Lauderdale, FL: Nova University Press).

IANNACCONE, L. (1977) 'Three views of change in educational politics', in J.D. Scribner (ed.) *The Politics of Education*. (Chicago: University of Chicago Press).

IANNACCONE, L. (1980) 'Emerging philosophical and ideological issues in the politics of educational', in H.D.G. Gideonse *et al*,. (eds.) *Values, Inquiry, and Education* (Los Angeles: University of California, Center for the Study of Evaluation).

IANNACCONE, L. (1981) The Reagan presidency, *Journal of Learning Disabilities*, 14, pp. 55–59.

IANNACCONE, L (1982a) 'Turning point election periods in the politics of education', in N.H. McCabe and A. Odden (eds.) *The Changing Politics of School Finance* (Cambridge, MA: Ballinger Publishing Co.).

IANNACCONE, L. (1982b) 'Changing political patterns and governmental regulations', in R.B. Everhart (ed.) *The Public School Monopoly* (Cambridge, MA: Ballinger Co.).

IANNACCONE, L. (1983a) 'Community education and turning point election periods (TPEPs)', in D.H. Schoeny and L.E. Decker (eds), *Community, educational, and Social Impact Perspectives* (Charlottesville, VA: Mid – Atlantic Center for Community Education).

IANNACCONE, L. (1983b) 'Lessons from the eleven nations', in R. Murray Thomas (ed.) *Politics and Education: Cases from Eleven Nations* (Oxford: Pergamon Press).

IANNACCONE, L. (1984) *Political Legitimacy and The Administration of Education* (Victoria, Australia; Deakin University Press).

IANNACCONE, L. (1985) 'excellence: an emergent educational issue', *Politics of Education Bulletin*, 12, pp.1–8, 12.

IANNACCONE L. and CISTONE, P.J. (1974) *The Politics of Education* (Eugene, OR: ERIC Clearinghouse on Educational Management).

IANNACCONE, L. and LUTZ, F.W. (1970) *Politics, Power and Policy*: The Governing of Local School Districts (Columbus, OH: Charles E. Merrill Publishing Co.).

IANNACCONE, L. and LUTZ, F.W. (1978). 'The dissatisfaction theory of governance, in F.W. Lutz and L. Iannaccone (eds.) *Public Participation in Local School Districts* (Lexington, MA: D.C. Heath and Co.).

KELMAN, S. (1987) ' ''Public choice'' and public spirit', *The Public Interest*, 87, pp. 80–94.

KERCHNER,C.T. (1985) 'At issue: fall-out from the politics of school excellence', *Politics of Education Bulletin*, 12, pp. 2–15.

KEY, V.O. Jr. (1955) 'A theory of critical elections', *Journal of Politics*, 17, pp.3–18.

LADD, E.C. (1985) 'On mandates, realignments, and the 1984 preseidential election', *Political Science Quarterly*, 100, pp. 1–25.

LANE, R.E. (1962) *Political Ideology* (New York: The Free Press of Glencoe).

LOWI, T.J. (1985) 'Why is there no socialism in the United States?' *Society*, 22, pp. 34–42.

MACRAE, D. Jr. and Meldrum, J.A. (1960) 'Critical elections in Illinois, 1888 – 1958', *The American Political Science Review*, 54, pp. 669–683.

MITCHELL, D.E. (1978) 'Measurement and methodological issues related to incumbent defeat and superintendent turnover', in F.W. Lutz and L. Iannaccone (eds.) *Public Participation in Local School Districts* (Lexington, MA: D.C. Heath and Co.).

MITCHELL, D.E. and IANNACCONE, L. (1980). *The Impact of Legislative Policy on the Performance of Public School Organization*. (Berkeley: University of California Institute of Governmental Studies).

MOSHER, E.K. and WAGONER, J.L. Jr., (1978) *The Changing Politics of Education: Prospects for the 1980s*. (Berkeley, McCutchan Publishing Corporation).

PATTERSON, S.C. and CALDEIRA, G.A., (1984) 'The etiology of partisan competition', *The American Political Science Review*, 78, pp. 691–707

PEPPLE, M.J. (1986) 'Educational Excellence: A Function of School Board and Executive Succesion' PH D. dissertation, University of California at Santa Barbara.

PETERS, T.J. and WATERMAN, R.H. *In Search of Excellence: Lessons from America's Best Run Companies* (New York: Harper & Row).

PETROCIK, J.R. (1987) 'Realignment: new part coalitions and the nationalization of the south', *The Journal of Politics*, 49, pp. 347–375.

ROTUNDA, R.D. (1986). *The Politics of Language* (Iowa City: University of Iowa Press).

SCHATTSCHNEIDER, E.E. (1969) *Two Hundred Million Americans in Search of a Government* (New York: Rinehart & Winston).

SCHATTSCHNEIDER, E.E. (1975) *The Semisovereign People: A Realists View of Democracy in America* (Hinsdale, IL: The Dryden Press).

STRICKLAND, D.A., Wade, L.L. and Johnston, R.E., (1968) *A Primer of Political Analysis*. (Chicago: Markham Publishing Co.).

VOGEL, D. (1980) 'The inadequacy of contemporary opposition to business', *Daedalus*, 109, pp. 47–57.

WATTENBERG, B. and LADD, C.E. (1985) 'Politics: 1986 and beyond. An interview with William Hamilton and Robert Teeter', *Public Opinion*. 8, pp. 2–7, 17.

WATTENBERG, M.P. (1987) 'The hollow realignment: partisan change in a candidate-centered era', *Public Opinion Quarterly*, 51, pp. 58–74.

WILDAVSKY, A. (1985) 'Federalism means inequality', *Society*, 22, pp. 42–49.

WIRT, F. and KIRST, M.W. (1982) *Schools in Conflict* (Berkeley, CA: McCutchan Publishing Corporation).

WRONG, D. (1985) 'The end of ideology?' *Dissent*, 32, pp 144–149.

ZIMERING, D.M. (1986) 'Factors in disruption of a turning point election process', PH D. Dissertation, University of California at Santa Barbara.

5   Choice, constraint, and community

Eric Bredo
University of Virginia

As a society we are once again considering how to invest schooling with renewed social purpose. After being ignored and left in a policy vacuum, schools have again become subjects of popular and governmental attention. However, this renewed attention also raises some thorny issues, such as the proper balance of choice and constraint in educational governance.[1] Can we reinvigorate educational institutions without constraining them to such a degree that they become merely an arm of the state, or loosening them so much that they dissolve into a babel of privatized concerns?[2]

When an institution appears to have lost direction, a frequent response is to call for a change in its form of control. Many of the current educational reform initiatives have suggested such changes, usually emphasizing either sterner direction from the helm, or *Sauve qui peut*. For instance, recent state level educational reforms have mostly increased centralized control by narrowing educational objectives, increasing the time students must spend in school, and increasing graduation requirements and teacher certification standards (Boyer 1986: 43). On the other hand, proponents of educational vouchers and home schooling have renewed their efforts for decentralized control and educational 'choice', principally by shifting control to the family and widening the range of tax-supported alternatives available beyond the current public shcools.

In this chapter I will contrast these two general approaches to educational reform. In other words, I will consider the choice versus constraint, or markets versus bureaucracies issue, as it arises in education (March and Simon 1958). My aim will be to introduce some skepticism about either approach as a general solution to current problems. Specifically, I will argue that both are onesided, linear approaches that oversimplify the relation between public and private, and short-run and long-run interests. If we see these different interests as interacting, then it will become clear that a strictly linear approach to dealing with them creates as many problems as it solves. I will conclude by contrasting bureaucratic and market metaphors with a community metaphor, suggesting that the latter highlights some considerations missing in the former two.

While my focus will be on choice versus constraint in education, there are clear parallels between this topic and related issues in other fields, such as the relative desirability of global versus incremental decision-making in political science, central plans versus markets in economics, or rationalism versus empiricism in philosophy. At a general level, then, the issue concerns the adequacy of linear strategies, of either a top-down or bottom-up variety, for solving non-linear, multi-level problems.

Markets and education

Arguments for changing the way an institution is controlled tend to suggest that such a change will either improve the attainment of a specific goal, such as standardized scholastic achievement scores, or will result in some more general improvement. The narrower argument tends to be made on empirical grounds by citing studies showing the relationship between changes in control and achievement, while the broader argument tends to be made on more theoretical grounds. Both sorts of arguments deserve scrutiny.

Markets and achievement

Taking the narrower argument for educational 'choice' first, will markets increase achievement scores? The history of past claims for educational innovations as achievement boosters can be characterized as one of early euphoria when only a select clientele participated, followed by later sobriety as a broader spectrum of students was involved. The fact that selection effects are relatively strong makes it easy to be fooled into believing that a new program produces higher achievement when it simply attracts an educationally more advantaged group of students (and teachers).

Research on desegregated schools in the mid-1960s, for example, suggested that desegregation boosted the achievement scores of some of the children attending desegregated schools (Campbell and Coleman 1982). This finding became important in educational policy circles, serving to justify efforts towards desegregation. Nonetheless the results of later reseach on desegregation can be summarized as finding weak and inconsistent results (St. John 1975). It now appears that racial mixing *per se* has had few systematic effects on achievement.

As another example, some of those supporting open education in the 1960s and 1970s (a change in control which involved increased *student* choice) argued that it would increase achievement scores. After the initial enthusiasm died down, more careful research on its effects showed little or no difference from traditional classroom settings (McPartland and Epstein 1975). If anything, the two sorts of settings seemed to be good for different objectives and suited to different sorts of students (Peterson 1979).

The research that is most relevant to the issue of educational choice is that on the effects of private schooling on achievement. A relatively recent study comparing achievement in public, parochial, and other private schools suggested that private schools, in particular parochial schools, produced higher achievement scores for comparable students than public schools (Coleman *et al.* 1982). However, this study has provoked considerable criticism for the adequacy of its controls on selection bias. Follow-up studies that better match student backgrounds find fewer differences. In fact, a recent reanalysis of the same data found that the apparent advantage of parochial schools drops from five points on the achievement test used to less than half a point when student body composition is controlled (Raudenbush and Bryk 1986). In short, the differences appear to be trivial.

In each of these cases it has been all too easy to believe that there are programmatic effects when there are simply differences in the sorts of students enrolled. While we cannot accurately separate these two sorts of influences without an impossible level of experimental randomization or control, I nonetheless would suggest considerable skepticism regarding the 'it will boost achievement scores' argument when applied to this change. It would be nice if valued learning were so easily achieved. However, there is no compelling reason why achievement scores should be affected in a uniform way by a change in the degree of control.

Markets and responsiveness

This brings me to the broader argument that markets will increase efficiency and responsiveness to educational 'consumers' just as they help increase efficiency and responsiveness in the private sector. Under certain conditions competitive markets are known to be good mechanisms for ensuring that goods that people demand are efficiently produced in the right quantities to satisfy that demand. In a competitive market firms that do not produce what people want, or are inefficient in doing so, will go out of business while responsive and efficient ones will survive. Applying the same argument to schools, it is asserted that in a competitive educational market schools that are efficient in producing what people want will stay in business while others will go out of business. Thus a market approach is seen as a way of ensuring the efficient supply of the educational services parents desire.

While the 'markets are responsive' argument may have ideological appeal, how applicable is it to education? For markets to be efficient, conditions must be such that consumers can learn from their mistakes and producers can learn from theirs.[3] Or, if individuals cannot learn, then there must be collective learning through turnover among individuals or firms. However, a market approach emphasizes local learning or problem-solving, assuming that the pursuit of local marginal advantage will result in global success. But under certain conditions local problem-solving may not be globally optimal. For instance, in an environment in which there are many small sharp peaks of value dotting a more gradually changing landscape of larger mountains, the pursuit of marginal local advantage will likely result in being trapped on a local spire far from the top of the larger peaks. This is a well-known problem with 'hill-climbing' problem-solving strategies in which choices are based on local knowledge and marginal advantage.

More specifically, local learning or problem-solving is likely to fail when a choice has distinct and/or certain short run outcomes that distract attention from more diffuse and/or uncertain long run outcomes. Addictive choices, as in cigarette smoking, are an example where short-run pleasure is counterbalanced by less clear or pressing long-run chances of getting cancer. In choice situations like this people often attend to the short run rather than the long-run consequences because the long-run lessons are really collective lessons about the *average* chance of getting cancer. Such long-run lessons are then invisible to the individual even though they may be quite clear from a collective standpoint (as in epidemiological data). The individual who is not aware of this collective experience is then 'too soon old and too late smart'. Needless to say the tobacco industry is very pro choice.

Many educational decisions have a similar character in that one only gradually discovers their long run import. As the French sociologist Raymond Boudon (1978: 54) puts it:

> the gradual character of the discovery of roles . . . is a dictum of general importance. This gradual character has, generally, the consequence of inflating the costs of exit . . . This is why, even in the case of non-total institutions, social actors can have the feeling of being *caught in a trap*. This situation is often characteristic of schooling processes.

Boudon mentions the case of a person who is attracted to the external features of a career but does not realize until too late what it actually involves. By the time the career is found to be less desirable than it seemed, the cost of changing to another major is prohibitively high.

Paul Willis (1981: 107) makes a similar point in an ethnography of the oppositional peer culture of British working class youths:

> For a specific period of their lives 'the lads' believe that they dwell in towers where grief can never come. That this period of impregnable confidence corresponds with the period when all the major decisions of their lives are settled to their disadvantage is one of the central contradictions of working class culture and social reproduction, and one in which the state school, and its processes, is deeply implicated . . . By the time the answers are known it is too late to apply them. The obvious and the alluring achieve their opposite underneath.

The potentially entrapping character of educational decisions is important despite the rhetoric that parents know best, because many parents do not in fact know how to use schooling to their children's best long-run advantage. They may pick a school that is attractive or culturally comfortable in the present but has hidden long-run disadvantages. While some families may not face this issue since their family culture is consistent with the cosmopolitan culture likely to be rewarded in the broader society, others face a genuine (if unrecognized) dilemma in choosing between their childrens' short and long run interests.

This analysis suggests that educational choices are very different from those idealized in the economic theory of pure competition. Schooling is as much a preparation for the future as for the present. Because of ignorance of its long run consequences, choosing a school may be more like choosing a spouse or choosing to have a child than like choosing a loaf of bread. In choices of this sort some of the most important information is only available long after you have made the choice. A theory based on the rational consumer, which uses the 'markets are responsive' argument, will then be misleading in educational situations because of this uncertainty and because short and long-run preferences may well be contradictory in practice. Market-oriented approaches are then likely to trade short- for long-run responsiveness, rather than being responsive in a more inclusive sense that considers both.

A second condition that violates the assumptions of pure markets is when perople's choices have side-effects on one another. If one person's smoking affects another's chance of getting cancer then individual choice will result in the undesirable consequence of more people getting cancer than chose to do so.[4] If one assumes that people have a much livelier awareness of their own interests than those of others, then such ignoring of the collective consequences of individual choice is quite likely.

Education is by its very nature a social activity involving significant side-effects. It does not merely change individuals: it also changes the relationships among them (Meyer 1977). Schooling unifies or divides people just as it elevates or subordinates them. It highlights some languages, customs and historical viewpoints and downplays others. It creates 'expert' elites and lay 'citizens'. It even affects those who do not get it since they will be considered relatively more 'ignorant' as more people become 'educated'. Thus, when parents choose one sort of schooling or another, they are in part choosing among the forms of social life they hope to reinforce or bring into being. For instance, in a society in which race and class are major bases for social discrimination they may try to keep their children relatively blind to such discrimination in the hope of not contributing to it. Similarly, they may school their children in a way that emphasizes cultural and religious variety, or one that emphasizes a single sectarian view. These social side-effects of educational choices are not taken into account by the market model which is efficient and responsive only when such effects do not exist.

When the issues of short- versus long-run or individual versus collective outcomes are considered, one can see that there are collective lessons which independently choosing individuals are unlikely to learn from their own experiences. Thus, the market argument for family choice is based on an analogy which applies only imperfectly to schooling. Like all analogies, its appropriateness needs to be evaluated rather than assumed.

To conclude with respect to the claimed benefits of 'choice' or markets, both the argument that choice will boost standardized achievement scores and that market mechanisms will assure educational efficiency and responsiveness should be viewed skeptically. While we do not know exactly about achievement scores, neither past experience nor present data are terribly encouraging. More generally, the market model is evocative but has limited applicability to education. When one faces dilemmas involving potential conflict between short and long run interests or individual and collective interests, the issue is not resolved by merely saying 'let the market decide'.

Bureaucracy and education

Arguments for increased constraint and bureaucracy mirror the arguments for markets. Here too there is the narrow argument that constraint will increase achievement scores and the broader argument that it will facilitate the attainment of more general goals such as that of educational 'effectiveness'. However, the argument for bureaucracy is the opposite of that for markets, in that it emphasizes the virtues of global as opposed to local rationality. I will first consider the narrower argument that constraint will increase achievement scores, and then the broader argument that constraint will increase school effectiveness in general.

Bureaucracy and achievement

Current bureaucratic and regulative reforms have recently been cited as responsible for increasing achievement scores, which is ironic since markets are also seen as ways of increasing achievement scores. One should consider this conclusion with respect to bureaucracy every bit as cautiously as the conclusion that markets will have such an effect, and for similar reasons.

Public school achievement scores are just as subject to selection bias as are scores for those in private schools. Scores may be going up, but so are drop-out rates among those students least likely to do well on the tests. When some urban school systems have drop-out rates of 40, 50, or 60%, selection effects may be overwhelming, increasing the possibility that score increases are due to selection bias among those surviving to take the tests rather than to overall improvement in the age cohort. With increased pressure to 'look good' it is also not unusual for schools to fiddle with the groups of students that take the tests. In many schools those considered 'learning disabled', 'emotionally disturbed', or 'mentally retarded' do not take the tests, thus providing an additional incentive for placing students in these categories. Some districts appear to be attempting to maintain district achievement scores while desegregating by placing many of their Black students into such special programs. In one district I have been studying, the rate at which elementary school students were held back and not promoted to the next grade has gone up 100 times, or 10,000% in the last ten years. This has the effect of ensuring that the students in any particular grade are older, on the average, when they do take the tests.

Selection bias also figures in recent comparisons between scores for students in the US and those in other countries, although here it operates in the opposite direction. The US is generally seen as lagging in such comparisons. However, if one corrects for the fact that a larger group of students survive to graduate from high school in the US than in many other industrialized countries – Japan being an important exception – then US achievement scores appear to be in the same ballpark as those of comparable industrial countries (Husen 1976). Of course we can raise our averages by weeding out more students, but it is only the average score of the survivors that is then increased, not the scores of the whole age cohort.[5]

It is also clear that many of our schools are teaching to the test, if not directly coaching on it. Some schools I know of pass out a sample of Scholastic Aptitude Test items to teachers every week with the instruction that they be sure to teach those items (with slight changes in wording) to their students. At the district level, many curriculum specialists spend their time selecting curricular materials on the basis of their consistency with achievement test items rather than on the basis of their broader intellectual or instructional quality. Even some state level curricula appear to be being designed with as much an eye to the tests as to other criteria. It is no wonder that test scores are going up, but far from clear that the increase signals a meaningful educational improvement.

Bureaucracy and effectiveness

Increased bureaucracy has also been seen as a means towards the attainment of more global social and individual goals. *A Nation at Risk* emphasized the need to narrow the curriculum and raise educational standards in order to maintain national economic competitiveness (National Commission on Excellence in Education 1983). Others have seen the need for a core curriculum for purposes of national social integration, or for a common, quality education for purposes of educational equality and life-long learning (Butts 1980, Adler 1982).

The search for bureaucratic solutions to global problems is particularly clear in the 'school effectiveness movement'. This modern attempt to define the 'one best system' is similar to the centralization movement promoted by the administrative progressives at the turn of the century, however this time primarily at the state rather than city level (Tyack 1974). The contemporary effort is to find policies and practices which will increase the general effectiveness of schools in attaining educational goals. However, virtually all of the prescribed remedies have involved more control through stronger administrative leadership, narrowed goals, reduced curricular choice, and tightened evaluation.

The theory behind this effort, which has not been well developed thus far, seems to be an implicit theory of bureaucracy based on global problem-solving. In this view, institutional structures, with their particular division of labor, are global solutions to social problems. Their structures are means to social ends. If one assumes that current institutions are basically well-designed, but being run in too loose, undisciplined, and unco-ordinated a fashion, then the basic problem is how to ensure conformity to institutional norms so that the institution can better function. The school effectiveness movement seems to be primarily addressed to this problem.

In considering the value of such global rationality, it is again useful to focus on potential linkages between short- and long-run goals, and individual and social goals. As an example of the former, Mortimer Adler (1982) argues in his *Paideia Proposal* that public schooling often focuses on short-run goals. In contrast to this Adler suggests that schools should help people become lifelong learners, giving them a broad education applicable to life's universals. This is to be accomplished by offering the same great books-style curriculum to everyone. By offering everyone the same education Adler believes one simultaneously solves the problem of educational quality and educational equality. As Adler puts it, quoting Robert Hutchins, 'The best education for the best is the best education for all'.

This proposal addresses the problem of potential short-sightedness that was raised when considering market proposals. It focuses on long-run aims and the good curriculum, as designed by Adler. However, in doing so it neglects the connection with peoples' short-run circumstances. There may be no connection between their present circumstances, capabilities, and aspirations, and the long-run aims to which Adler's program is adapted. While Adler recognizes that some will need 'remedial' programs to bring them up to speed, such remediation assumes that everyone shares, or should share, the same long-run objectives whatever the cost. Some may experience no difficulty with this, but others will find an incompatability between their present circumstances and desires and Adler's long-run objectives for them. In other words, the problem here is just the opposite of what it was in the case of markets. Here, setting long-run objectives without regard to present circumstances invites contradiction just as much as giving sway to short-run interests without regard to long-run consequences. If the former is opportunism, the latter is utopianism.

Others emphasize the value of schooling for attaining social goals such as economic growth or social integration. For instance, human capital theory argues that there are positive economic side-effects of people gaining more education primarily due to increased economic productivity. Since these benefits are not gained soley by the individual being educated, but spill over to others, there is justification for public support of schooling to artificially lower its price, so that people will invest in enough of it to fully profit from its positive side-effects. For others it is the side-effects of social integration which justify compulsory, publicly-supported schooling. If one side-effect of schooling is that it enables socially diverse people to get along with one another better, then there is a public interest in supporting such schooling over and above the individual's private interest in getting it.

Both of these arguments seem to me to be correct, in that the justification for public support of schooling must be based on its enhancement of such positive social side effects. However, it is all too easy to slide from the potential for such benefits to the conclusion that the current public schools actually provide them. There is now considerably more skepticism about the generality of such social benefits than there used to be. The links between schooling and productivity, and schooling and economic growth are seen as uncertain and contingent (Berg 1970). Schooling may only make people more productive if the jobs in question resemble school tasks. And schooling may only facilitate economic growth if it is consonant with the job market, rather than producing more graduates who are educated but unemployed.

There also is some doubt about the generality of the notion that schools promote social integration by teaching common values. While some see schools as teaching a virtually consensual 'modern' culture based on individualism, hard work, rationalism and tolerance, among other values (Dreeben 1968), others argue they teach the values of a particular status culture, principally that of a WASP middle class (Collins 1971) or that they teach obedience and docility as required by a class stratified system (Bowles and Gintis 1976). Finally, others question whether they teach any broad social values at all, seeing schools as teaching only the narrow institutional values of being patient, waiting in line, and coping with boredom and bureaucracy (Jackson 1968).

These different interpretations actually may not be so inconsistent as they seem since common experiences may have different effects. Schooling may have different meaning for different groups of pupils. To oversimplify somewhat, those for whom school is culturally familiar and instrumental in the long run are likely to see it as offering rational socialization for modern life. Those for whom schooling is culturally alien, but who share its ends are likely to see it as a status culture, a set of hurdles that they must overcome to advance them-selves. Finally, students who share neither immediate culture nor long run aims are likely to experience schooling as the imposition of an alien culture. Given these differences in response, the principal attitudes and values learned at school are likely to be different for different groups of children, suggesting that we will not get common effects out of common schooling unless the school occupies a similar place in people's lives. Once again the potential contradictions between individual and collective interests are not resolved with a simple nostrum.

To summarize these comments on arguments in favor of bureaucracy and uniformity in education, I have suggested, first, that we need to be skeptical about claims that bureaucratic reforms have increased achievement both because of selection bias and because there is more teaching *to* if not teaching *of* the test. Second, I have also suggested that arguments favoring bureaucracy omit full consideration of possible contradictions between such global rationality and local interests. It is all very fine to make a global peaks your goal, but to do so without regard to the costs of getting there, or to whether it is possible to get there at all, invites disappointment.

Markets, bureaucracies, and communities

Despite the evident differences between an incremental market approach and a planful bureaucratic one, the two also have much in common. Each is a narrowly rational approach, although at different social levels. The market approach is based on assumptions of individual rationality, while the bureaucratic approach is based on assumptions of collective rationality. However, both are subject to the limitations of traditional rational models arising from the fact that they do not take into account pragmatic aspects of choice that affect real (as opposed to idealized) problem-solvers (Simon 1982).

One of the assumptions of traditional rational models is that decision-makers have consistent preferences. Yet if the previous analysis is correct, some of the most important educational choices involve interacting and sometimes contradictory goals. An analogous situation is bicycle riding, where one must maintain short-run balance while continuing to go in the right direction. Since these two goals are dynamically interrelated one cannot be solved independently of the other. In other cases the coupling between goals may be less tight, and co-ordination in the solving of them less urgent. However, when options are constrained it may be difficult or impossible to attain multiple goals adequately, resulting in a dilemma. The educational examples discussed earlier, in which short-run interests may conflict with long-run interests, or individual with collective interests, are similar cases in which interdependent goals may become dilemmas.

Both traditional rational models and many of the newer information-processing models are ill equipped to deal with multiple interacting goals:

> most traditional problem-solving research has been concerned with finding the solution to a single, difficult problem (e.g., finding the winning chess move). By contrast, most everyday problem solving consists of synthesizing solutions to individually simple, but complexly interacting, problems. (Wilensky 1983: 14).

When faced with inconsistent preferences a linear-rational model is either paralyzed, since it cannot find any viable solutions, or it finds a solution to one goal and ignores the fact that attaining that goal will undo attainment of the other.

The way one approaches a problem has much to do with whether it remains solvable or becomes a dilemma. One way to create a crisis is to adopt a linear approach to a nonlinear problem. A neophyte bike rider, for example, who attempts to solve separately the problem of balance or direction, is likely either to stay upright but run into something, or to be pointed in the right direction but fall over. This is particularly true when optimal solutions are sought, for then the potential solution to one problem will even more dramatically constrain possible solutions to the other, with the result that no solution may be found to either.

This is precisely what both market and bureaucratic approaches attempt to do. A market approach, for instance, focuses attention on individual interests, while ignoring collective interests. It looks at how individuals pursue their private interests and assumes that this private pursuit will also advance the public interest. However, this happy conclusion depends on there being no side-effects of people's outcomes on one another, as noted earlier. Those who have experienced an arms race, theater fire, or the effects of gasoline hoarding will attest that the selfish pursuit of individual interest may sometimes result in everyone being worse off. When people's actions have side effects the collective interest may be quite different from an aggregate or resultant of individual interests (Schelling 1978).

A bureaucratic approach adopts the opposite view, focusing on collective interests while leaving individual interests in the background. It seeks the best plan for attaining collective, organizational goals. Here it is implicitly assumed that the optimal solution to a collective problem will leave individuals better off, but this need not be the case. The collective solution may be so draconian, so limiting of individuals' options, as to create many more problems for them than it solves. Trying to create equality by treating everyone precisely the same, regardless of circumstance, is an example. Bureaucratic incentives may also add to local costs by distorting local priorities, such as by providing incentives to 'test well', regardless of the value of what one has learned. Such costs to the individual are not considered in the bureaucratic approach.

Both market and bureaucratic approaches, then, adopt a one-sided or linear strategy which attends to one facet of the overall problem while neglecting the other, thereby likely producing undesirable unanitcipated consequences. It is just this sort of one-sidedness that is bothersome about some of the recent reform proposals. Market-oriented choice proposals are only too often thinly veiled attempts by some to 'get theirs' regardless of the impact on others. On the other hand, bureaucratic proposals all too often appear to be aimed at shoring up existing insititutions and practices regardless of their worth for those they are supposed to serve. What is missing from both approaches is a concern for the mutual accommodation of public and private interests rather than naively assuming that the two interests are colinear.

A contrasting metaphor that seems better attuned to such accommodation is that of community, a democratic community in particular (Dewey 1966a). The concept of community has been a central one in our educational history, from the common school to the comprehensive school to the racially integrated school. It is centrally concerned with the facilitative interplay of private and public interests, since responsible community members look out for the welfare of others and of the generalized community, just as responsible communities look out for the welfare of their members.

Consider, for example, a parent's choice between sending a child to a public or a private school. The parents who are sensitive to both public and private aspects of the issue must consider both which school is best for their child and the effect of leaving a school on those who remain. As Albert Hirschman points out, leaving an organization ('exit') may enhance or undermine the influence ('voice') of those remaining, depending on circumstances such as the commitment of the remaining members to the institution (Hirschman 1970). This would imply that socially responsible people need to take both private and public considerations into account in making their decisions. Two sets of goals enter into their decisions: the welfare of their child, and their part in the welfare of the community. Thus a particular choice may have to be justified as much for what it does for those who do *not* exercise it as for those who do.

The same principle also applies at the institutional level. While the principal justification for collective decisions is likely to be their protection of the public interest, fruitful institutional decisions in fact may be those that provide the infrastructure enabling individuals to be as independently efficacious as possible. Thus one important justification for institutional choices is that the constraints they impose help to empower rather than limit the members of the community. In other words, good leaders help set the conditions enabling groups to make sensible decisions themselves, just as most parents seek to establish the sort of environment which enables their children to grow to become effective, autonomous individuals.

There are various ways in which interacting problems may be practically managed. One aspect of this issue concerns which steps to take towards attaining each goal, the other which goals to entertain. As Herbert Simon (1979: 32) suggests, 'There are at least two ways in which multiple goals can be introduced into such a [serial processing] system . . . The first is by queuing – attending to several goals in sequence. The second involves generalizing the notion of goal to encompass multifaced criteria against which possible problem solutions are tested.'

Dewey (1966b: 122) proposed a variant of the first as a way of handling the interplay of individual and social goals when he asked:

> Why then should it be thought that one must take his choice between sacrificing himself to doing useful things for others, or sacrificing them to pursuit of his own exclusive ends . . . ? What happens is that since neither of these things is persistently possible, we get a compromise and an alternation. One tries each course by turns.

Trying 'each course by turns' allows each goal to be approached in the light of constraints derived from a partial solution of the other. People act one moment as private individuals, the next as a public citizens. Or they consider the different sides of the problem at different moments. Such sequencing of attention works relatively well as long as one does not confuse the occasions on which each set of concerns is relevant, or overly constrain one set of goals by choices made in light of the other.

The other aspect of this problem concerns considering which goals to entertain. Sometimes it may be necessary to drop or modify some goals so as not to become paralyzed by goal conflict. In effect, one considers one's goals in the light of second order goals such as 'achieve as many goals as possible' or 'achieve the set of goals with the highest value' or 'avoid impossible and redundant goals' (Wilensky, 1983). An interesting example concerns goals that are by definition contradictory. For instance, if success in school is defined as getting ahead of others, such as being in a certain percentile ranking, then there are obvious conflicts between individual and collective success. Similarly, if some groups believe that for a school to serve them means that it must cater to their unique identity, which is what makes them different from others, then the school cannot serve both them and others. In both of these cases, such goals need to be reconceptualized in a more sensible light that considers their interaction with other goals.

In the end, a fuller exploration of the metaphor of community, with its emphasis on a Janus-faced concern for both public and private, may provide a salutory corrective to the unilateral stance of the market and bureaucracy metaphors. Such a metaphor does not eliminate concern for a sphere of private autonomous action, or one of public planning and constraint. However, it does place both of these in a different light, making neither an end unto itself. While a one-sided rationalism of either sort can seem hard-edged and defensible, when viewed more broadly they may be merely narrow and rigid.

Conclusion

I have suggested that neither the market nor the bureaucratic metaphor suggests flexible enough strategies for coping with the non-linear, multi-level problems of educational governance. Neither strategy which they suggest, either choice or constraint, offers an adequate general approach to coping with problems which have multiple, interacting goals. The metaphor of community seems better adapted to suggesting ways to handle the interplay of several goals, both public and private, short and long run. It too has limits of appropriate usage, like any metaphor, but it nonetheless can serve as a useful corrective to the excesses of both the market and bureaucratic models and the linear-rational model that underlies them.

Notes

1. For an historical view of the 'order' versus 'liberty' issue see 'Forming the national character: paradox in the educational thought of the revolutionary generation' in Tyack (1967).

2. Ernest L. Boyer (1968, p. 42) recently noted 'This is our central dilemma historically, Americans have wanted local control of education but national results ... In the end we do the worst of all things ... ' The 'worst of all things' to which Boyer refers is the attempt to get national results through the use of rigid standards and SAT scores as yardsticks.

3. In microeconomic theory the optimality of competitive markets depends upon a number of conditions which are not always fully spelled out. For instance, it must be easy for suppliers to enter the market, there must be variety of suppliers in a locale, consumers must be well informed of the merits of the different products, it must be possible to substitute one product for another, and there must be no externalities (side effects) of one person's purchases on the utility of the outcomes of others. For the sake of simplicity and educational relevance I have emphasized only some of these conditions here.

4. I am assuming that interdependencies are not included within the market where, for example, those who smoke might compensate those who do not. In the cases of interest here I believe it is unlikely that interdependencies could be 'untangled' in this way.

5. Japan is a particularly interesting exception to this rough comparability between systems, but for reasons that are the opposite of those usually cited. The usual lesson taken from the Japanese case seems to be that the competitiveness of their system is principally responsible for its producing higher achievement scores for a larger percentage of the age cohort. Actually, these outcomes may be due in part to their system being, in *some* ways, so co-operative. As Thomas Rohlen (1983: 308–309) puts it in an ethnography of education in Japan, 'Within each school, a general egalitarianism prevails. No tracking occurs, and the homeroom system encourages a sense of togetherness ... Entrance competition is basically impersonal. It occurs among large numbers. Within schools, direct competition and differentiation among students is limited and not encouraged by teachers. This contrasts with our own case where local competitiveness is intense, but global competition rather diffuse (Goldman and McDermott 1986). Thus the lesson we seem to be taking from the Japanese is a peculiarly American interpretaion of their situation, just as they gave a peculiarly Japanese interpretation to our type of education when they adopted it after the war.

References

ADLER, M.J. (1982) *The Paideia Proposal* (New York: MacMillan).

BERG, I. (1970) *Education and Jobs: The Great Training Robbery* (New York: Praeger).

BOUDON, R. (1978) *The Logic of Social Action* (London: Routledge and Kegan Paul).

BOYER, E.L. (1986) 'How not to fix the schools', *Harpers*, February, p. 42.

BOWLES, S. and Gintis, H. (1976) *Schooling in Capitalist America* (New York: Basic Books).

BUTTS, R.F. (1980) *The Revival of Civic Learning* (Bloomington, IN: Phi Delta Kappa).

CAMPBELL, E.Q., and COLEMAN, J.S. (1982) 'Inequalities in educational opportunities in the United States', in E. Bredo and W. Feinberg, (eds) *Knowledge and Values in Social and Educational Research* (Philadelphia: Temple University Press) pp. 85–98.

COLEMAN, J.S., HOFFER, T. and KILGORE, S.B. (1982). *High School Achievement: Public, Catholic, and Other Private Schools Compared* (New York: Basic Books).

COLLINS, R. (1971) 'Functional and conflict theories of educational stratification', *American Sociological Review*, (36), pp. 1002–1019.

DEWEY, J. (1966a) 'The democratic conception in education', in J. Dewey, *Democracy and Education* (New York: Free Press), pp. 81–99.

DEWEY, J. (1966b) 'Natural development and social efficiency as aims', in J. Dewey, *Democracy and Education* (New York: Free Press).

DREEBEN, R. (1968) *On What is Learned in School* (Reading, MA: Addison-Wesley).

GOLDMAN, S.V. and McDERMOTT, R.P. (1986). 'The culture of competition in American schools', in G.D. Spindler, (ed.) *Education and Cultural Process*, second edition (New York: Holt, Rinehart and Winston).

HIRSCHMAN, A.O. (1970) *Exit, Voice, and Loyalty* (Cambridge, MA: Harvard University Press).

HUSEN, T. (1976) 'Academic performance in selective and comprehensive schools', in J. Karabel and A.H. Halsey. (eds.) *Power and Ideology in Education* (New York: Oxford University Press).

JACKSON, P.W. (1968) *Life in Classrooms* (New York: Holt, Rinehart and Winston).

KOWALSKI, R. (1979) 'Global problem-solving strategies', in R. Kowalski, (ed.) *Logic for Problem-Solving* (New York: North Holland).

MARCH, J.G., and SIMON, H.A. (1958). 'Plan or no plan: the great debate', in J.G. March and H.A. Simon (eds.) *Organizations* (New York: Wiley), pp. 200–210.

McPartland, J. and Epstein, J. (1975) 'The effects of open school organization on student outcomes'. The Center for Social Organization of Schools, Report No. 195, The Johns Hopkins University.

Meyer, J.W. (1977) 'The effects of education as an institution', *American Journal of Sociology*, 83, (1), pp. 55–77.

National Commission on Excellence in Education (1983) *A Nation at Risk: The Imperative for Educational Reform* (Washington, DC: US Government Printer).

Peterson, P.L. (1979) 'Direct instruction reconsidered', in P.L. Peterson and H.J. Walberg, (eds.) *Research on Teaching* (Berkeley: McCutchan).

Raudenbush, S. and Bryk, A.S. (1986).'A hierarchical model for studying school effects', *Sociology of Education*, 59, p. 10.

Rohlen, T.P. (1983) *Japan's High Schools* (Berkeley: University of California Press).

Schelling, T.C. (1978) *Micromotives and Macrobehaviour* (New York: W.W. Norton).

Simon, H. ed., (1979) *Models of Thought* (New Haven: Yale University Press).

Simon, H.A. (1982). *Models of Bounded Rationality*, Vol. 2 (Cambridge, MA:MIT Press).

St John, N. (1975), *School Desegregation* (New York: Wiley).

Tyack, D.B. ed. (1967) *Turning Points in American Educational History* (Waltham, MA: Ginn and Co.).

Tyack, D. (1974) *The One Best System* (Cambridge, MA: Harvard University Press).

Wilensky, R. (1983) *Planning and Understanding* (Reading, MA, Addision-Wesley).

Willis, P. (1981) *Learning to Labor* (New York: Columbia University Press).

6   *Choice in public education*

Richard F. Elmore
Michigan State University

Should parents and students be empowered to choose among schools, or among programs within schools? Should educators be empowered to organize and manage schools, to design educational programs, to recruit and select students, and to receive public funds for providing education to those students? These are the two fundamental questions of educational choice.

The first might be called the 'demand side' question. It poses the issue of whether the consumers of education should be given the central role in deciding what kind of education is appropriate for them. The second is the 'supply side' question. It poses the issue of whether the providers of education should be given the autonomy and flexibility to respond to differences in the judgements of consumers about what is appropriate education.

These questions go to the very roots of the finance, organization, and political control of American public education. Education policy in the US is, for the most part, based on the premise that the individual interests of parents, students, and educators should be subordinated to broader public policy objectives. Among these objectives are a broadly educated citizenry, an understanding in the citizenry of the basic principles of democracy, fairness in the distribution of the opportunities and rewards of education, an understanding of and tolerance for others unlike ourselves, and preparation for an economically productive adulthood. These objectives have been expressed in laws, institutions, and processes that set the basic structure and content of American public education.

While there is some variation in the finer details of structure, from state to state, and from community to community, two features cut across all locations and levels. First, the money to pay for education flows from taxpayers to local school boards and to adminstrators who decide how it will be spent. Consumers do not directly 'purchase' public education, either with their own money or with their share of public revenue. Second, decisions about who attends which school, who teaches in which school, and what is taught in schools are formally lodged with local boards and administrators, operating within a framework of state and federal policy. In other words, finance, attendance, staffing, and curriculum content are locally centralized political and administrative decisions, not private consensual decisions between consumers and providers.

Of course, states have made major inroads into local authority over finance, personnel and content, through tax and revenue equalization, labor relations laws, certification requirements, and content mandates. In this sense, there is a significant degree of state centralization in certain key areas. But at the level of what might be called 'allocation decisions' – that is, deciding who will do what in which setting – local boards and administrators still play the dominant role. In this chapter, finance, staffing, attendance, and content refer to allocation decisions in these areas.

The organizing principle of this system, then, is local centralization. From the national or state level, education appears to be highly decentralized enterprise, since most detailed decisions about the conduct of education are delegated to the 15000 or so local school districts. But from the client's or teacher's point of view, the system appears to be highly centralized and bureaucratic. Decisions about who gets access to what kind of eduction are determined by centrally administered rules and structures, rather than by the preferences of clients and providers.

To raise the supply side and demand side questions of educational choice, then, is to challenge this basic structure of locally centralized administration and to suggest that if parents, students, and school-level educators were given more choice the system would perform better. The current debate on educational choice is about this proposition.

This chapter is designed to inform that debate in three ways: first, by reviewing the research and the policy issues that lie behind the debate; second, by defining the range of possible options that state and local policy makers might pursue in responding to the issue of choice in public education; and third, by assessing the risks and benefits of experiments with enhanced choice for clients and providers of education.

This analysis of policy options illustrates how policy-makers, by examining a range of solutions to the problem of school organization, can alter the relationship between clients and providers. The main points of the analysis can be summarized briefly as follows:

- Policies affecting choice must be evaluated from both the demand and supply sides. Providing consumers with greater educational choice, while at the same time constraining the ability of educators to respond to consumer preferences will only increase dissatisfaction with schools.
- Policies affecting choice must take account of the broader public aims of education, in addition to the individual preferences of consumers and providers. These aims include providing a strong basic education for every school-aged person.
- Policies affecting educational choice can be broken into four discrete categories: finance, attendance, staffing, and content. Within these four categories, policy-makers have a wide range of options for enhancing and constraining choice. Various combinations of finance, attendance, staffing, and content correspond to distinctive forms of organization. The current system of local bureaucratic centralization represents only one of a large number of possible ways of organizing public education.
- There is little evidence that greater choice for consumers and providers of education will, by itself, dramatically change the performance of schools. But there are still substantial reasons why policy-makers might want to initiate experiments in enhanced choice.

The problem: accommodating diversity in locally centralized systems

The case for choice

Consider the following hypothetical case:[1]

> Ann Orlov is eleven. She and her younger brother Larry live in the city with their parents Harry and Jean. Harry earns $14,000 as a policeman; Jean adds $3000 as a part-time secretary. Ann attends Willis Elementary, the neighborhood public school. She is not unusually bright but has shown a strong interest in art and in the lives and work of artists. She dislikes Willis, in part because so little time is devoted to her special interest. She studies art in a community program on Saturdays, but otherwise – apart from a 45-minute once-a-week art class taught by a specialist – she regards her formal

education as a waste of time. She would be delighted to spend her days following the art teacher around, but that is out of the question in view of all the other children to be served. Ann's regular teacher finds it inconsistent both with his own role and with Ann's needs for her to be allowed to sit alone in the back of the classroom all day and draw. The Orlovs have asked the principal at Willis, a sympathetic woman, for aid or advice. Unfortunately she sees no way to help Ann, short of enrollment in another school.

Ann has begged to go to school elsewhere. She would prefer a school that emphasizes art, but would be happy even to be assigned to a teacher whose regular class routine responded to her interests. Her parents want to help, but there are problems. The Orlovs cannot afford Bellwood, the arty but expensive private school that Ann thinks she would like. The modestly priced local Catholic school might serve, but the Orlovs oppose this solution on religious grounds. They might discover a public school in the city with an attractive art program or teacher, one located within reasonable traveling distance; but the school authorities would have to approve Ann's transfer from Willis, and this is not likely. Of course, the Orlovs could move to the attendance area of the other school. They could even move to a different school district. A number of their former neighbors have done so, and some are pleased with the outcome.

For the Orlovs, however, there are limiting conditions. Policemen are supposed to live in the city, so a change of districts for Harry might mean finding a new job. And for many reasons – the park, the neighbors, shopping, the church, the cost of moving – the Orlovs prefer their present neighborhood and would find it painful and expensive to move. Their gravest concern is for Larry, who loves Willis's strong music program, including a boy's chorus in which he solos. Harry and Jean feel any move would be risky. If the student body in the new school is separated into ability groups, thy might assign Ann to the wrong program. More important, the Orlovs are worried that, even if the family moves, subsequent shifts in teaching personnel or official policy might leave the whole family even worse off than before.

Armin Schroeder is a young art teacher in the public schools of a blue-collar suburb adjoining the city. He has developed a proposal for a comprehensive elementary curriculum in the symbols and materials of the artist's world. Schroeder has tried to persuade his school authorities to give him an experimental school, but, though sympathetic to experimentation, they are already committed in other directions. In any event, Schroeder's success in his own district would probably be of little help to Ann Orlov; even if there were spaces available, she is not likely to be granted a special transfer outside her district. Schroeder does not have the capital to start such a school on a private basis. Even if he could raise the money, he would probably have to charge more than $1400 a year tuition; he might be able to attract a rich clientele and survive, but he prefers not to run an elitist school. Possibly enough families like the Orlovs would try his school to make it viable – if they could afford it. Most of them could not. The Orlov's savings are insignificant and their responsibilities weighty; family resources are already diminished by $700 paid yearly in various taxes that support education, and the public school is 'free'. Under these circumstances even wealthier people often forego the private alternative they might prefer.

Ann Orlov's case represents what many critics regard as a basic pathology of American public education. 'The state is content to trust the Orlovs with sophisticated decisions regarding food, hours of rest, and other important matters affecting the child', Coons and Sugarman argue. 'Only when it comes to education has the state . . . virtually emasculated the family's options' (Coons and Sugerman 1978: 10).

The central control exercised by local school systems, Coons and Sugarman continue, is a formula for stagnation, unresponsiveness, and mediocrity. 'Public schools today are rarely permitted to die of unpopularity', they argue. 'Thus, their incentive to innovate is meager, and their capacity to terminate unsuccessful programs is as bad or worse' (Coons and Sugarman 1978: 154).

Furthermore, they argue, the absence of choice and competition works against the very ideals of equal opportunity that the public schools are supposed to embody. 'The poorer the family, the less its ability to furnish home remedies for educational ailments; . . . the more difficult it is to escape an underfinanced or mismanaged public school system by changing residence; and . . . the less its ability to induce the public system to provide the alternative classroom or program it prefers' (Coons and Sugarman 1978: 26).

These convictions are shared by others representing widely divergent political view-points. Stephen Aarons argues that the existing organization of schooling 'provides free choice for the rich and compulsory socialization for everyone else'; it 'confronts the dissenting family with a choice between giving up its basic values . . . as the price of gaining a free education in a government school or paying twice in order to preserve its . . . rights' (Quoted in US Department of Education 1985). 'Government-operated schools', argues Joel Spring (1982: 33), 'are destructive to the political culture of a democratic society and are one of the major obstacles to the free development and expression of ideas.'

James Coleman (1985) adds, 'public schools have become increasingly distant from the families of the children they serve, increasingly impersonal agents of a larger society.' Schools have lost their capacity 'to support and sustain the family in its task of raising children'; they have lost their claim to a community of interest with families. The restoration of schools, Coleman concludes, requires 'abandoning the assumption of the school as an agent of the state and substituting an assumption [that] the school is properly an extension of the family and the social community . . . of which the family is part.'

The intellectual roots of the current debate on educational choice can be traced from Thomas Paine and Adam Smith in the eighteenth century, through John Stuart Mill in the nineteenth century, to a variety of conservatives, liberals, and radicals in the twentieth century (Coons and Sugarman 1978: 18–19). In 1962, conservative Milton Friedman (1962: 85–107) proposed a system of publicly financed educational vouchers. In the late 1960s, the idea was picked up by a liberal Democratic administration and elaborated, with financial support from the US Office of Economic Opportunity (OEO), into a proposal for a regulated educational voucher system (Center for the Study of Public Policy 1970), which was in turn elaborated into a demonstration project in Alum Rock, California (Rand Corporation 1978).[2] In 1985, the Reagan administration proposed that the federal government's largest education program, Chapter 1 of the Educational Consolidation and Improvement Act, be changed to an individual voucher program for disadvantaged children (US Department of Education 1985). And in 1986, the National Governors' Association (1986) endorsed greater parental choice in education as one of its main educational priorities.

The common thread in these ideologically divergent views is a profound disillusionment with what David Tyack (1974) has called 'the one best system' (see also Tyack and Hansot 1982). This system of localy centralized political and bureaucratic control, Tyack argues, is an outgrowth of the municipal reform movement of the nineteenth century, which tried to substitute enlightened lay leadership and scientific management for political patronage as the organizing principle of public education. The basic structure that grew out of this period – a locally elected lay board of education, a large and functionally specialized central administration, and schools run by principals reporting to the central administration – persists to this day and has a resilience, Tyack argues, that far surpasses its educational effectiveness.

Local centralization of administrative functions in public schools, the argument goes, creates a self-interested bureaucracy with strong incentives to maximize its budget, control its clientele and subordinates, and expand its domain of influence, but only very weak incentives to attend to the essential processes of teaching and learning (see Michaelson 1981).

Choice in the existing system

An enlightened public school administrator, confronted with these arguments, would probably reply that they represent a gross caricature of the typical public school system and a complete misunderstanding of the role that parent and student choice play in that system. Many school systems offer a considerable array of choices within and among schools. Parents and students play an active role in the choice of these programs. In fact, our enlightened administrator might continue, community sentiment seems to be running strongly against greater choice and toward clearer, more uniform academic standards for all students, regardless of students' and parents' personal tastes or preferences. The public doesn't always value choice above other possible objectives, the administrator might conclude.

There is considerable empirical and theoretical support for the enlightened administrator's viewpoint. Consider the array of choices confronting students and parents in the existing system. Some choices, like place of residence and public versus private schooling, are time-consuming, costly to make, and costly to reverse once they are made. These might be called 'lumpy' choices.

Many parents and students, however, make smaller, more manageable educational choices. These require smaller expenditures of money and time, and are easier to reverse. They can have significant consequences for parents, students, and schools. These are somewhat 'smoother' choices. Public school systems frequently offer a range of programs within and among schools, for the academically talented, for the handicapped, for students with specific learning problems, for the artistically, vocationally, or scientifically inclined, and many more.[3] The availability of these options allows parents to exercise educational choice by influencing the assignment of their children to teachers, classes, schools, and special programs within schools or school systems. In some instances – special education, for example – school officials are required by federal and state policy to include parents in choices affecting the assignment of their children.

Some significant proportion of parents actively exploit these opportunities; other parents accept the assignments they are dealt, either because they are unaware that they have choices or because they willingly delegate those choices to others. In some instances, parents and students are 'active choosers',[4] in the sense that they exploit their options; in others, they are 'inactive choosers',[5] in the sense that they defer to the decisions of professionals, they don't acknowledge or understand their options, or they are simply satisfied with what they have. Some parents and students may be consistently more active than others. Some, by virtue of their background or economic circumstances, may be less able to assert their preferences.

The existence of choice, and of active choosers, within public school systems doesn't mean that those systems are necessarily responsive to all clients. The array of choices in a given system, in fact, may be predicated on the assumption that few parents are active choosers. A high proportion of active choosers might disrupt the central determination of attendance, staffing, and content. Indeed, teachers and administrators may intentionally discourage active choice for the majority of their clients to prevent the disruption of central administration.

Students also exercise considerable choice in determining their education, mainly at the secondary level. Some student choices are 'programmed' by the rules and structures of their schools. College prep courses, advanced placement courses, vocational and career courses, so-called general education courses, and electives are all part of the standard menu of options in the typical comprehensive high school. As with parental choice, some significant proportion of students (often with the guidance of a parent or another influential adult) actively exploit these choices, while others more or less accept what the system deals them.

Some choices that students make are not programmed by the rules or structures of their schools. One important unprogrammed choice, which is not ordinarily thought of as educational, but has enormous educational implications, is the choice that students make about how much time to spend on education, leisure, and work. About half the teenage population is actively involved in the labor force, which means that they are either employed or are looking for work. Employment appears to have significant effects – both positive and negative – on school performance.[6] Anyone who has ever lived with a teenager can recount the struggles that occur over how much time will be spent on homework, athletics, earning, and hanging-out.

Of far greater educational consequence is the choice made by one-fifth to one-half of the nation's teenagers not to go to school at all.[7] Some of these young people take advantage of education and employment-training opportunities outside the public schools. Some never return to any form of education.

To summarize, while the critics of the 'one best system' have a point about its relative unresponsiveness to the preferences of individual clients, the system presents a variety of choices to its clients. Some of the choices (changes of residence, for example) are lumpy, in that they entail large costs and risks, while some are relatively smooth (changing teachers, for example), in that they require small costs and risks. Some choices are programmed by the existing system (special schools and programs within schools), while some are unpro-grammed and lie in the hands of consumers (work, study, leisure). Some clients take an active posture toward their choices; others take an inactive posture. Critics can argue about the appropriateness of the constraints that the system of local centralization places on choice, or about the differential impact of choices on different types of clients, but they cannot argue that the system offers no choice. Likewise, supporters can argue that the system offers a variety of choices, but they cannot argue that those choices are equitably distributed or that they necessarily contribute to the best outcome for all clients.

Before we move further in this discussion and into the analysis, we might ask what results we could expect if parents, students, and educators had more choice.

The collective consequences of individual choice

Underlying the argument for increased choice in education is a set of assumptions about the effect of individual choice on the responsiveness and performance of schools. These assump-tions might be summarized as follows:

- Parents are more likely to be satisfied with a school they have chosen, and to support their childrens' learning in such a school.
- Students are more likely to engage in the work of schooling more seriously when they (and their parents) have chosen the kind of school that they find appropriate to their needs.

- Teachers are more likely to enjoy their work and make the commitment necessary to successful teaching when they have chosen the setting in which they work and take an active hand in the construction of their school program.

When parents, students, and educators choose the setting in which education occurs, the argument goes, we should expect better results – in school achievement, attendance, and attainment. The notion of 'community' often figures prominently in these arguments. Enhanced choice, the argument goes, creates communities of shared values that command the loyalty of participants, that set clear expectations, and that are more likely to succeed in accomplishing common goals.

The empirical evidence on these assumptions is suggestive, but hardly definitive. Comparisons of public, private, and Catholic high school achievement seem to show that Catholic schools exceed public schools, controlling for student composition. Furthermore, the Catholic school effects seem greater for minority and low income students. Private schools also show greater achievement than public schools, again controlling for student composition, but the private school advantage is on the order of half as large as the Catholic school advantage. The size of these differences and their statistical and educational significance are matters of considerable debate in the social science community, but the direction of the comparisons is consistent across analyses (Coleman *et al.* 1982, Goldberger and Cain 1982, Murnane 1981).

One important finding of the research on public and non-public schools, which has not been given the same visibility as the public/non-public comparisons, is that 'even the largest estimates of a private school advantage are small relative to the variation in quality among different public schools, among different Catholic schools, and among different non-Catholic private schools. Consequently, in predicting the quality of a student's education, it is less important to know whether the student attended a public school or a private school, than it is to know which school within a particular sector the student attended' (Murnane 1984: 270).

A related survey (Chubb and Moe 1985) of the attitudes of public and non-public school educators reveals that public school educators perceive more external control over their work, are more likely to stress bureaucratic and public relations aspects of their jobs, and more likely to complain about lacking the essential resources to do their jobs than non-public educators. Non-public educators, on the other hand, are more likely to perceive positive parent and student expectations and are more likely to perceive their schools' goals as clearly communicated than public school educators. Non-public teachers are more likely to perceive their principals as playing a constructive role, and are more likely to know what their colleagues are teaching and to co-ordinate content decisions. Non-public schools are more likely to have school-wide standards on such subjects as homework than public schools. It is important to remember that these results come from a survey of attitudes, rather than practice, and that they conceal wide variation on both the public and non-public sides.

A final piece of evidence comes from the Alum Rock voucher experiment (Bridge & Blackman 1978: 82ff, Rasmussen 1981: 58ff). Parents who participated in the voucher experiment expressed a high degree of satisfaction with their schools, although consistently less satisfaction than non-voucher parents. Teachers in voucher schools expressed a high degree of satisfaction with the system at the outset, but their support declined sharply with time. While there is some evidence that voucher programs differed across schools, there is no evidence that they produced differences in student achievement. Geographical proximity, rather than curriculum content, was the major determinant of parental choice.

In principle, it is difficult to disagree with the argument that enhanced choice creates communities of shared values that command the loyalty of participants, that set clear expectations, and that are more likely to succeed in accomplishing common goals. It is plaus-ible to predict that organizations with captive clientele have weaker incentives to respond to their clients' needs and preferences than organizations that have to compete for their clients. Organizations that receive their budgets from centralized political and bureaucratic autho-rities, rather than directly from clients, have weaker incentives to respond to those clients. Organizations that receive their clients and staff from centralized assignment systems, and have the nature of their work determined by rules set elsewhere, are more likely to be respon-sive to central administrators and rulemakers than to clients (Wolf 1979).

So, other things being equal, unrestricted client choice should make all consumers of education better off. But other things are never equal.

If all the significant costs and benefits of education could be represented in the price that consumers were willing to pay, as with toothpaste or breakfast cereal, then there would be no reason, in principle, why consumers shouldn't choose and pay for whatever quantity or type of education they prefer, without any public involvement whatever. But this is not the case for at least three reasons. First, your educational choices have significant effects on my welfare, and *vice versa*. Much of the beneficial effect of schooling derives from association (with other students, with teachers, with communities), rather than from individual consumption. Hence, your decision to leave my school affects my opportunity to learn in ways that are not adequately accounted for in the price of your tuition. Second, we can realize certain collective benefits only if we agree to limit our individual choices, for example, by requiring everyone to have a certain minimum amount of education. These collective benefits include, for example, life in a stable democracy populated by literate voters and the availability of a highly skilled, mobile labor force in the event of a national emergency. Third, we may agree that we value certain things, such as racial equality or access to a decent stand-ard of living for all members of society, because these things are good in themselves, regardless of the material benefits they provides to us. So we may insist that a certain amount of education be provided all members of society to prevent social consequences we regard as bad in and of themselves.

All of these are reasons why we might choose rationally to have the government involved in the provision of education, why government might be empowered to limit individuals' educational choices, and why government involvement in education might promote society's welfare in ways that a purely private market in education might not (see Musgrave and Musgrave 1973: 52–64, 80–81 and Garms *et al.* 1978: 46–60).[8] Even Milton Friedman, who concedes few legitimate governmental constraints on individual choice of any kind, acknowledges the duty of the government 'to require that each child receive a minimum amount of schooling of a specified kind' (Friedman 1962: 86).

But one cannot parlay a rationale for goverment *involvement* in education into a rationale for a government *monopoly* over education. For all the reasons argued by the advocates of increased educational choice, a public monopoly would probably increase the problems of responsiveness and performance associated with the current system of limited competition. Perhaps more importantly, some citizens assert a right to choose non-public education for religious or personal reasons that would make a public monopoly impossible to sustain. Indeed, since the US Supreme Court's 1925 decision *Pierce v. Society of Sisters*, the dominant consistitutional doctrine in the US has been that states cannot prohibit children from attend-ing non-public schools, though states may regulate non-public schools to assure that they serve the broader public interest.

To summarize, there are plausible reasons to believe that the existing system of local centralization creates serious problems for the performance and responsiveness of schools. Yet neither of the two extreme alternatives to this system – a private market for education or a complete public monopoly – is defensible in theory or practice. There, is however, a great deal of latitude for enhancing choice in the existing system.

A useful approach to understanding the role choice in public education, then, is to focus on ways in which the elements of school organization – finance, attendance, staffing, and content can be changed to affect the relationship between clients and providers. We now turn our attention to this approach.

Policy options: choice by design

The central problem, defined earlier, is how to use the elements of school organization to affect the relationship between clients and providers in ways that are likely to enhance the responsiveness and performance of schools. Three sets of actors are central to this enterprise: clients, providers and policy-makers. Each brings a distinctive set of interests and resources, to the common task of schooling.

Clients (parents and students) provide the raw material for schools and, by their choices, they deliver important signals about their preferences for what is learned in school. Providers (teachers and administrators) bring the expert knowledge of content and pedagogy necessary to capitalize on the talents and preferences of consumers. Policy-makers (board members and legislators) hold the proxy for the public at large, providing the money and authority necessary to make the enterprise work. Policies are more likely to work when they complement and reinforce the distinctive interests and resources of these actors.

Table 1 suggests some ways in which the elements of school organization can be brought together differently by policy-makers in order to change the relationship between clients and providers. The point of this analysis is to illustrate how, by examining a range of solutions to the problem of school organization, we can alter the relationship between clients and providers. The exact options discussed in the analysis are less important than the underlying message that (1) the existing system of local centralization represents a very limited view of the relationship between clients and providers; and (2) there are many ways of altering this relationship, while at the same time representing the broader public interest in the organization of schools.[9]

Table 1.   Illustrative choice options.

	School Organization			
Element	Local centralization	School-site decentralization	Co-operative contracting	Regulated market
Finance	Payment to districts; centralized budgeting	Lump-sum payment to schools; decentralized budgeting	Contracting with consumer or producer co-operatives	Payment to clients
Attendance/ staffing	Central assignment with centrally administered exceptions	Centrally administered matching	School-level selection; minimum regulation	School-level selection; minimum regulation
Content	Central rulemaking; decentralized implementation	School-level planning; decentralized rulemaking and implementation	Examination-driven	Consumer-driven

Finance

Finance determines the flow of money through the system. Most analyses of educational choice treat finance as a dichotomous variable: either we allocate money to schools through centralized administrative systems, or we give money directly to parents, in the form of vouchers or tax credits, for the purchase of education. This dichotomy sharpens the politcal debate, but it considerably understates the range of forms that financing can take and the range of ways finance can influence the relationship between consumers and providers.

Between the poles of payment to districts and payment to individual consumers are at least two other financing arrangements, each with a different set of incentives attached. These alternatives are lump-sum allocations to schools and contracting. Lump-sum allocations are a form of administrative decentralization. Schools are treated as 'revenue centers', receiving a budget based on a per-pupil allocation, presumably adjusted for special students. Schools are responsible for allocating those funds among various activities, with minimum guidance from central administrators. A school might, for example, choose to reduce the number of full-time teachers, and increase part-time aides, in order to free teacher time for special instructional activities, individual tutorials, or part-time administration. Decentralization would require some degree of flexibility on part of central administration in defining what constituted a school, in order for schools to have the flexibility to design their internal structures along different lines. Some schools would choose the traditional structure with a full-time building administrator; others might choose a completely different structure, like one in which teachers assume administrative responsibility or hire a business manager. The tighter the restrictions on what constitutes a school, the more lump-sum allocations look like centralized financing.

Contracting could take a number of forms, but it is mainly distinguished from centralized or lump-sum allocation by the fact that the contractor is not necessarily a subordinate unit of the contracting agency. Contracting arrangements might be made with producer co-operatives (e.g., groups of teachers wishing to form a school) or consumer co-operatives (e.g., groups of parents who organize a school and hire people to staff it) or neighborhood groups who might wish to take over the operation of their neighborhood school. Under these arrangements, the contracting agency, which would probably be a local school board, could stipulate conditions for contractors, such as adult-student ratios, staff qualifications, minimum hours, performance expectations, etc. The tighter these stipulations, however, the more contracting begins to look like central control. Contracting is a common form of financing for public human services other than education – day care, community mental health, employment training, etc.

Lump-sum allocations and contracting represent the use of finance to shift the locus of allocation decisions from central administrators to providers. Vouchers and tax credits represent a shift to consumers. The financing of consumer co-operatives is a hybrid, a mechanism for funding consumers in an organized capacity.

Attendance and staffing

Attendance and staffing determine the allocation of people to classrooms and schools, and consequently the fit between consumers and providers. Under centralized attendance and staffiing systems, as they operate in practice, students and teachers are centrally assigned to schools, but the system accommodates exceptions for certain purposes, such as racial balance or faculty seniority. At the opposite extreme from central assignment is the regulated market model envisioned by voucher advocates, in which students and teachers choose schools based on their preferences. In the regulated market model, only selected constraints are set on these choices, designed to limit the possibility of outright discrimination or monopoly (see Coons and Sugarman 1978: 148–152, 194–211).

Between these extremes lie a number of possibilities. Richard Murnane (1987) observes that consumer and producer choice in education actually entail three distinct components: *matching* student interests and capabilities with programs, *choosing*, or the process of students and parents selecting among alternative programs and *being chosen* from a pool of applicants to participate in a competitive program. One alternative might stress centrally administered matching as a mechanism for establishing the fit between students and staff. Board members and central administrators could set a broad menu of themes within which parents, students, and teachers would be expected to find some common ground. Any group of consumers or providers could propose an academic program organized around one of the themes, or central administrators could assign groups of educators to develop academic programs around themes and offer parents, teachers, and students the option of affiliating with one or more programs. This kind of centrally administered matching maintains central control over the specification of content options and provides some means of justifying attendance and staffing decisions on the basis of educationally relevant criteria, but it allows for a sorting of educators and students according to mutual interests. It also allows for the definition of options in ways that cut across racial, ethnic, and neighborhood lines, increasing the likelihood that choice will result diversity of student populations. Everyone – students and staff – would be required to choose and the central theme would be making the closest possible match between the interests and capabilities of students and educators. Significant changes in district student and teacher assignment practices would be necessary, as would some preference-ordering system, since not everyone would get their first choice. These changes could be made either on a district-wide basis or by designating 'free zones' within or across established attendance areas. Many desegregating districts have already moved significantly in this direction by liberalizing transfer policies, establishing magnet schools, and allowing students to move among schools during the school day.

Another alternative might stress selection at the school level, rather than centrally mandated matching. Staff and student assignment could simply be delegated to the school level, in much the same way as these functions are performed currently within universities, by charging the chief administrator or the corporate board of the school with the responsibility for selecting staff and students within certain broad personnel procedures and a budget constraint. Parents and students would apply to schools, and would be allowed to switch affiliations between application periods. Likewise, teachers, after some initial sorting process based on voluntary affiliation or central matching, could apply to any school on a space-available basis. New teachers entering the system would have to be hired by a school before they could be hired by the system at large – the reverse of centralized hiring. Because of the universalistic nature of elementary and secondary schools, any system of school-level selection would have to include either centrally mandated enrollment quotas or generous financial incentives to assure attention to the needs of difficult-to-teach students.

Centrally mandated matching and school-level selection represent alternative ways of shifting the locus of responsibility for attendance and staffing from central administrators to parents, students, and educators. They constitute ways of removing these key decisions from impersonal, standardized systems to structures in which real people are required to make and justify choices. Because of this attribute, they are not likely to be popular, at least initially, with those established school administrators and teachers who are the beneficiaries of centralized assignment. The idea behind the shift toward school-level selection is that the act of affiliating with a group is, in itself, an important source of motivation for doing well in that group.

Content

Content determines what is taught and, indirectly, how it is taught. Existing policies and practices toward content are not easily captured by a simple formula. There are a multititude of state and district level prescriptions that bear in one way or another on content – subject matter requirements, graduation standards, textbook adoptions, and the like. But there is also considerable evidence that these prescriptions have mixed and complicated effects on what is taught. The reasons are twofold. First, content requirements can be complied with in *pro forma* ways at the district and school level. A district or school may teach Algebra I, but do so in a watered-down or souped-up way; it may use the prescribed textbook, but only finish half of it or supplement it with more advanced materials. There is virtually no direct inspection of compliance with content requirements. Second, content requirements interact heavily with classroom teaching to produce distinctively different experiences for different students in a nominally standardized curriculum. Teacher A may require students to work in groups on projects designed around standard topics, while teacher B may lecture and pass out ditto sheets. The existing system, then, is characterized by centralized rule-making with highly decentralized implementation.

At the opposite extreme from this system is the one envisioned by voucher advocates, in which content decisions are market-demined, with minimal or no central regulation. In the regulated market model, every centrally mandated content requirement is seen as com-promising the essential principle of consensual choice between consumers and providers (see Coons and Sugarman 1978: 167ff).

In one sense, the locus of content determination could be seen as the most basic issue of choice, since changes in finance, attendance, and staffing practices would have little effect on the array of actual choices for consumers and providers if everyone were teaching the same thing in the same way. But even in the existing system there is little central control over the implementation of content requirements, and considerable variation in what is actually taught. Hence, it is far from clear that central rule-making on content results in uniform practice. A more realistic assumption would be that the environment surrounding content decisions can be modified in certain ways, but that many of the key content decisions under any arrangement of finance, staffing, and attendance will occur at the school and classroom level.

One alternative to the existing system would be to decentralize rule-making as well as implementation. Since many key content decisions are already made at the school and classroom level, one could simply formalize that practice and make it more visible. A school might be required, as a conditon for public support, to prepare a statement of content and learning objectives and to submit to periodic reviews of their plan and performance by an external review panel composed of other educators, citizens, and state or local policy-makers. State and local policy-makers could describe the minimum elements of a plan, but the actual formulation of content and pedagogy would be left to the school, in its corporate capacity, defined to include parents and students, as well as educators. State and local policy-makers could exert influence or leverage over content in much the same way as they do now – by 'jawboning', or calling attention to exemplary programs and deficiencies in the proposals and practices of schools.

Another option is to influence content by measuring performance. That is, all content decisions could be nominally left to consumers and providers, but state or local government would stipulate that in order to advance to certain levels, and ultimately to receive a diploma, a student would have to pass a series of examinations in specified content areas. In order to receive continued public financial support, a school would have to maintain a certain success rate on the examination. Exams could be administered by a central agency and evaluated by teachers from other schools against a template provided by the examining agency.

The amount of variability in content from one school to another would depend on the frequency, breadth, and detail of the examination stystem. A system that tested only for basic mastery of academic subjects – writing, mathematics, science, history – would permit wide latitude in both pedagogy content. A system that tested for levels of proficiency, rather than only for basic mastery, would allow some schools to focus exclusively on rigorous training for the highest level of proficiency in academic subjects, while others might aim for basic mastery supplemented by training in the arts, technology, or vocational skills.

An exam-driven system might also allow for mobility among schools and programs. At the secondary level, some students might formally 'test out' of certain subjects and move on to more advanced courses at the post-secondary level. Other students requiring remedial help might focus exclusively for some period of time on a single academic subject in which they are having trouble. At the elementary level, parents might choose, for example, to enroll their children in intensive summer sessions in a given subject in order to free up time during the school year for extra instruction in art or music.

The problems with exam-driven systems are fairly well known. Without more restraint than most policy-makers are willing to exercise, examinations can quickly become at least as obtrusive as centralized rule-making in specifying content. Under pressure to justify the rigor and fairness of the exams, the examining agency would probably graft more and more specific content areas onto the exam, resulting in less and less flexibility for the design of school programs. Under pressure from diverse educational interests, examiners might adjust the content of the exam to reflect the emphases of certain types of schools. Regardless of how careful the examining agency was in limiting the exam to only basic subject matter, some schools would still compete by selecting students with high aptitudes for the exam, by allowing the content of the exam to dominate their curriculum, and by advertising their success rates to prospective applicants. Exams that discriminate on the basis of proficiency in subject matter knowledge can also discriminate on the basis of other attributes, including race and sex, raising questions of equity. Any uniform exam system carries the implicit assumption that children follow more or less uniform stages of development, which is not an accurate reflection of the diversity of childrens' intellectual growth.

Decentralized rule-making and examinations both entail many practical problems, but they could result in a significant shift in the incentives under which consumers and providers operate. Both force the locus of responsibility for content decsions ot the school level. Decentralized rule-making uses process – planning and politics – as the main mechanism for generating engagement and commitment. Examinations use performance. Both provide a significant degree of central influence over content, though by indirect means. Decentralized rule-making exerts influence through central review and approval. Examinations use exam content and collegial norms. Both forms of influence are hightly susceptible to recentralization, if policy-makers are not committed to shifting the locus of responsibility, because both involve the creation of new bureaucratic structures with their own interests.

Organization

The options described in table 1 are grouped by school organization. In local centralization, the classroom is the central focus of the system, and each successively broad organizational level above that – the school, the district, the state, and the federal levels – makes some claim on classroom activity. Different levels make different, often overlapping or competing, claims. But the dominant theme is centralization of administrative functions at the district level. The district, in its corporate capacity, is the main administrative unit; the classroom, nested within the school, is the basic provider of education.

At the other extreme is the system visualized by advocates of regulated voucher systems, in which schools act as small autonomous firms, operating under the minimum constraints necessary to prevent monopoly or discriminatory practices. Consumers are direct recipients of government financing, which they, in turn, use to purchase education from providers. Staffing, attendance, and content decisions are made by mutual consent among consumers and providers, with no central planning or control, other than the minimum necessary to assure that certain conditions of consumer access and market structure are met. Central influence, insofar as it occurs at all, takes the form of 'market enhancing' activities – such as the consumer information functions performed by the Better Business Bureau, or the market-clearing functions performed by counseling and placement services.

Between these extremes we have defined two of a virtually infinite number of organizational possibilities, for illustrative pruposes. One of these might be caled school-site decentralization, which combines lump-sum financing of schools, centrally mandated matching of students and teachers with programs, and school-level planning for content. Schools, rather than individual consumers, are the recipients of government funding. District-level administration consists of setting the menu of content options through a combination of consultation with the community and central decision-making, making lump-sum allocations to schools, and running a district-wide matching system that pairs students and educators with the program options that most closely approximate their preferences. This option contains a considerably stronger central role for district administrators than the one envisioned by the regulated market model, but a considerably less centralized one than the nested hierarchy.

Another possible option might be called co-operative contracting. This model combines a contracting model of finance, in which funding is delivered to schools by contracts with consumer or producer co-operatives, based on *per capita* reimbursements for services. As in the regulated voucher model, schools are free-standing organizations, run by their owners, that select staff and students themselves within a structure of public regulations designed to provide protection against monopoly and discriminatory practices. The main difference between the co-operative contracting model and the regulated voucher model, at the provider level, is that the form of organization allowed to participate in public financing would be restricted to consumer or producer co-operatives. This mechanism would be much like the preferential financing currently offered by the federal government for health maintenance organizations, which are consumer or producer owned providers offering health care on a flat-fee, rather than a fee-for-service, basis. The content taught in the co-operative contracting model could be centrally influenced by a centrally administered examination system, which would provide direction for curriculum content without prescribing the actual subjects and materials to be taught.

There are many other possibilities. The important point is not to present an exhaustive analysis of options, but to illustrate the way in which alterations of policies affecting finance, attendance, staffing, and content change the form of organization and the relationship between clients and provides of education. With the movement of finance from individual consumers, to consumer cooperatives, to producer cooperatives, to schools in a decentralized system, to school districts, the locus of fiscal leverage shifts among key actors. With the movement of attendance and staffing decisions from individual clients, to cooperatives, to matching systems, to centralized bureaucracy the conditions of affiliation between educators and their clients change. With the movement of content decisions from consumer-driven, to exam-driven, to school-site planning, to central rule making, the locus of decisions about what is taught shifts. Any of these shifts would have important implications for the distribution of power and authority in the provision of public schooling.

Should policy-makers experiment with choice?

This analysis has attempted to array a range of options for enhancing and constraining client and provider choices on several dimensions, and hence to break the large, dichotomous choices proposed by voucher and tax credit advocates down into smaller, bite-sized pieces that policy-makers can digest and experiment with on a smaller scale. One of the chief complaints by critics of the existing system has been that its structure imposes prohibitively large and unequal costs on clients who are dissatisfied with the quality of the schooling they received. Changes of residence and enrollment in private schools, we saw, were extraordinarily 'lumpy' choices, entailing large costs in money and time to make and reverse. The effect of breaking key dimensions of choice into smaller, more manageable pieces is to 'smooth out' client choices, reducing costs and potentially making them more manageable for all consumers.

This analysis also underscores why it is important to frame experiments around the problem of choice in both supply-side and demand-side terms.[10] Loosening up choice on the consumer side, through changes in attendance policies, for example, while leaving constraints on the provider side, in the form of limits on staff assignment and content decisions, will result in increasingly diverse client demands being placed on a narrow and rigid structure. Loosening up choice on the producer side, in the form of increased school-level responsibility for staffing content, while leaving constraints on the consumer side, in the form of centralized attendance policies, results in more school-level control, but not necessarily more responsiveness to client demand. Whatever the array of options, reducing central control on one side, without also reducing it on the other, will defeat the purpose of enhanced choice by putting one or the other side at a disadvantage.

Is there any firm evidence upon which to base a judgement that these structural options, or any others we might develop along similar lines, will improve the academic achievement of students? The short answer is no. The evidence, examined earlier, suggests that there is no simple causal relationship between choice, as we have discussed it here, and students' academic performance. Saying there is no direct causal relationship, however, is not the same as saying that there are no grounds for experimentation with choice.

In the absence of such evidence, there are many reasons why it might be useful to experiment deliberately with options of the sort outlined above. First, the limits of local centralization have been clearly established. The centralization of finance, attendance, staffing, and content exact a relatively high cost in administrative overhead, and in the diversion of energy and commitment from the central tasks of teaching and learning. Even the greatest alleged strength of the system – its ability to deliver a relatively standard product to a relatively broad clientele – is undermined, first, by the fact that it is hemorrhaging one-fifth to one-half of its clientele during their adolescent years, and second, that the education of those who remain is, at its best, highly variable in quality, and at its worst, dismal.

A second reason for experimenting is that consumer and producer choice may be values worth recognizing in their own right, regardless of their instrumental relationship to student performance. A basic philosophical premise of democratic thought is that government derives its authority from the people, rather than possessing inherent authority. When nominally democratic institutions like the public schools become bureaucracies with interests of their own, they raise serious questions about their relationship to those they are supposed to serve. Loosening up the structure of schools, providing more influence for citizen-consumers and professional providers, is one way of sending signals to the bureaucracy that its interests are not paramount.

A third rationale for experimenting with new forms of consumer and provider choice is that it may be a way of engaging the creative energy of paretns and educators in the solution of serious educational problems, independent of whether choice by itself is a good or effective thing to do. Hierarchies, of the type represented by local centralization, condition clients and providers to look up for solutions, to higher-level administrators and policymakers, rather than inward at themselves or outward toward their peers. Pushing decisions on finance, staffing, attendance, content, and organization out into the schools may result in more attention at that level to the deliberate design of teaching and learning, rather than to the implementation of plans formulated elsewhere.

These arguments in favor of experimentation with policies directed at educational choice, however, should be approached with several cautions. The first and most obvious is that the existing system has proven extraordinarily resilient in the face of attempts to change it. In the Alum Rock voucher experiment, for example, the information educators made available to parents on their educational options was not useful in descerning differences among programs, and there is substantial evidence that the programs themselves did not represent carefully thought out and implemented options. Teachers and administrators fought and defeated proposals to publicize achievement test scores across programs, on the grounds that they did not provide fair comparisons. And teachers and administrators opposed the introduction of a third-party organization to act as an 'impartial' arbiter on questions of information and administration (Cohen and Farrar 1977).

The results of other experiments with choice have not been much more encouraging. Teachers and administrators tend to adapt client choice systems to ease their effects on established patterns, rather than adapting their behavior to the new incentives introduced by client choice. Small-scale, within-district experiments create divisions between participants and nonparticipants – parents, teachers, and students alike. These divisions result in charges of inequity that create political problems for school administrators and local board members. Alternative programs tend to lose their distinctiveness and their support among teachers and clients over time (Rand Corporation 1981, Cohen and Farrar 1977, Metz 1986, Murnane 1987, Nault and Uchitelle, 1982, Raywid 1985).

A second *caveat* is that recent studies of public secondary schools show that students already are presented with a considerable array of choices among courses and alternative programs within schools, but that the typical student either chooses a program that lacks coherence or defers to a standard program specified by another adult, typically a counselor, which also lacks focus. Only in exceptional instances do highly motivated students choose academically challenging programs. The typical teacher accepts this state of affairs as inevitable, though he or she may find it objectionable in principle (See Powell *et al.* 1985, also Boyer 1985, Sizer 1984). The picture presented by this research is one in which student choice functions to reinforce a mediocre, substandard level of academic content and performance, rather than higher expectations.

On the other hand, there is some evidence that a few public schools are successful at creating environments in which academic learning occurs among students from a variety of backgrounds. These settings are usually described as ones in which educators have clear expectations for academic success, educators provide reinforcement for student achievement, students operate under clear guidelines for behavior and discipline, educators agree on academic objectives, and school leadership supports teachers in instructional and discipline decisions (see Rutter *et al.* 1980: 180ff, Lightfoot 1983: 309ff, Purkey and Smith, 1983, and Rowan, *et at.* 1983). Conspicuously absent from this research, however, is any evidence about the influence of parent, student, or teacher choice in those settings on student achievement.

A third caution is that any experiment with educational choice must come to terms with the problem of active versus inactive choosers. There is some evidence that parents differ by race and social class in the amount of information they have about available options and in their preferences for academic content, discipline, and instructional style (Nault and Uchitelle 1982). One possible consequence of experiments with increased choice for clients and providers is a situation in which nominally neutral mechanisms produce highly segregated school populations. Another possible consequence is one in which active choosers congregate in one set of schools and inactive choosers end up by default in other schools, creating a stratified system which is responsive to the former and ignores the latter (see Hirschman 1969).

Finally, there is no guarantee that enhancing client or provider choice will increase the quality of education provided to the average student. Most, if not all, of the power of client choice to improve schooling rests on the ability of clients to make informed choices. High quality information about the content and performance of schools is difficult and costly to get, it must be collected with care, and it must be interpreted with detachment and scepticism after it is collected because it presents a limited picture of what schools are about. Supply-side competition introduces strong incentives for providers to present superficial or inaccurate information on effectiveness, to package information to promote their product, and to protect certain types of information that would be useful in making client choices as proprietary. Since providers control the 'technology' of schooling, they have a significant advantage over consumers in the control of useful information. Demand-side competition introduces strong incentives for active choosers to use their market power (money, time, influence, access) to gather and use information that improves their relative position in the market. In other words, one effect of introducing greater choice may simply be to increase competitiveness without increasing quality, because quality is an ambiguous commodity in education.

In summary, the major argument in favor of experiments with increased choice is that they provide a much needed prod to a system that is increasingly bureaucratic in its relations with its clients. The major problems associated with such experiments are either that they will be coopted by the system they seek to change or that, if they succeed, they will impose the risks of mindless and destructive competitiveness without the benefits of greater attenton to quality.

Acknowledgements

The author is Professor, College of Education, Adjunct Proffessor, Department of Political Science, Michigan State University, and Senior Research Fellow, Center for Policy Research in Education (CPRE). The author benefited from the helpful comments of members of the CPRE seminar on choice and the CPRE research and dissemination advisory committees. Special thanks to David Cohen, Jim Fox, Paul Hill, Helen Ladd, and Lorraine McDonnell, who reviewed an earlier draft and offered many useful comments. The research was supported by the US Department of Education, Office of Educational Research and Improvement, grant number OERI 6–86–0011. The views expressed are those of the author, and do not represent endorsement by sponsoring organizations.

Notes

1. This illustrative case is taken from Coons and Sugerman (1978: 8–9).

2. For a case study of this period, see Cohen and Farrar (1977).

3. Evidence on this point is scanty, but suggestive. Surveys suggest that something like one-third of urban districts have schools that are specifically identified as 'magnet' or 'alternative' schools, but the designers of these surveys suggest that they seriously underestimate the proportion of programs offering choice to parents or students. The surveys do not include within-school alternatives, district-wide transfer schemes, or education and employment-training programs outside the public school system. Nor do they attempt to measure the frequency of active parental or student choice in absence of specific programs designed to offer choice (see Raywid 1984, 1985).

4. In a 1982 survey (Williams *et al.* 1983), about 12% of parents said they had chosen to send at least one child to a non-public shcool and about 20% of parents whose children were enrolled in public school said they had actively considered non-public schools. About 53% of public school parents said they considered the quality of the public schools in making residential choices. Significantly larger proportions of minority and low income people than the general population said they had exercised active choice by these criteria. Overall, though, the non-public school population is more likely to be white, affluent, and well educated than the general population.

5. I am indebted to Mary Metz and Mary Ann Raywid for assistance in framing this distinction, though neither is responsible for the use I have made of it.

6. A study of teenage employment in a Southern California county (Greenberger and Steinberg 1981) showed that young workers gained in self-reliance, punctuality, social interaction skills, and knowledge of practical matters, but that their employment offered them little opportunity to interact with adults or to use cognitive skills. Work did not appreciably affect teenagers' career plans, nor did it deter delinquency. Above 15 to 20 hours per week, the cost of work, in terms of declines in school performance, job-related stress, and negative attitudes toward work, outweigh the benefits.

7. Data from the US Department of Labor's National Longitudinal Survey of Labor Market Experience (NLS) Youth Cohort, show that about one-ahlf of male high school dropouts and about one-third of female dropouts give school-related reasons for their decision to leave school. The dropout rate in vocational programs is higher than for academic programs. Retention in one grade increases the likelihood of dropping out by 50%; retention in two grades increases the likelihood by 90% (see Morgan 1984, as quoted in Mann 1986: 308). Analyses of the US Department of Education's High School and Beyond (HSB) Survey found that school-related factors, including expected academic performance, test performance, and grades, were the most powerful predictors of whether a student will complete high school or drop out (Wehlage and Rutter 1986).

8. For an account that emphasizes the role of education in promoting democratic values, see Levin (1983).

9. This analysis owes much to the influence of my colleague Peter May and his article, 'Hints for crafting alternative policies' (1981).

10. For another discussion of the argument for joining supply-side and demand-side changes, see Nathan (1983).

References

RAND CORPORATION (1978) *A Study of Alternatives in American Education.* R–2170/1–NIE through R–2170/7–NIE (Santa Monica, CA: The Rand Corporation).

BOYER, E. (1985) *High School: A Report on Secondary Education in America.* (New York: Harper).

BRIDGE, R.G. and BLACKMAN, J. (1978) *A Study of Alternatives in American Education, Vol. IV: Family Choice in Schooling* (Santa Monica, CA: The Rand Corporation).

CENTER FOR THE STUDY OF PUBLIC POLICY (1970) *Education Vouchers: A Report on Financing Elementary Education by Grants to Parents.* (Cambridge, MA: CSPP).

CHUBB, J. and MOE, T. (1985) 'Politics, markets, and the organization of schools', unpublished paper delivered to the Annual Meeting of the American Political Science Association, September.

COHEN, D. and FARRAR, E. (1977) 'Power to the parents? The story of education vouchers,' *Public Interest* pp.1–22.

COLEMAN, J.S. (1985) 'Schools, families, and children', Ryerson Lecture, University of Chicago.

COLEMAN, J.S., HOFFER, T. and KILGORE, S. (1982) *High School Achievement: Public, Catholic, and Private Schools Compared* (New York: Basic Books).

COONS, J.E., SUGARMAN, S. (1978) *Education by Choice: The Case for Family Control* (Berkeley, CA: University of California Press).

FRIEDMAN, M. (1962) *Captialism and Freedom* (Chicago, Il: University of Chicago Press).

GARMS, W., GUTHRIE, J. and PIERCE, L. (1978) *School Finance: The Economics and Politics of Public Education* (Englewood Cliffs, NJ: Prentice-Hall).

GOLDBERGER, A. and CAIN, G. (1982) 'The causal analysis of cognitive outcomes in the Coleman, Hoffer, and Kilgore Report', *Sociology of Education*, 55, pp. 103–122.

GREENBERGER, E. and STEINBERG, L. (1981) 'Part-time employment of in-school youth: an assessment of costs and benefits', unpublished research report, University of California, Irvine.

HIRSCHMAN, A. (1969) *Exit, Voice and Loyalty: Responses to Decline in Firms and Organizations* (Cambridge, MA: Harvard University Press).

LEVIN, H.M. (1983). 'Educational choice and the pains of democracy', in T. James and H.M. Levin (Eds.) *Public Dollars for Private Schools: The Case of Tuition Tax Credits*, (Philadelphia: Temple University Press), pp. 17–38.

LIGHTFOOT, S.L. (1983) *The Good High School* (New York: Harper).

MAY, P. (1981) 'Hints for crafting alternative policies', *Policy Analysis*, 7, pp. 227–244.

METZ, M. (1986) *Different by Design: The Context and Character of Three Magnet Schools* (New York: Routledge & Kegan Paul).

MICHAELSON, J. (1981) 'A theory of decision-making in the public schools: a public choice approach' in S. Bacharach (ed) *Organizational Behavior in Schools and School Districts* (New York: Praeger).

MORGAN, W. (1984) 'The high school drop-out in an overeducated society', Center for Human Resource Research, Ohio State Univesity. February; Quoted in D. Mann, 'Can we help dropouts: thinkng about the undoable', *Teachers College Record*, 87, p. 308.

MURNANE, R. (1981) 'Evidence, analysis, and unanswered questions', *Harvard Educational Review*, 51, pp. 483–189.

MURNANE, R. (1984) 'A review essay: comparisons of public and private schools: lessons from the uproar,' *Journal of Human Resources*, 19, pp. 263–277.

MURNANE, R. (1987) 'Family choice in public education: the roles of students, teachers, and system designers', *Teachers College Record* 88, forthcoming.

MUSGRAVE, R. and MUSGRAVE, P. (1973) *Public Finance in Theory and Practice* (New York: McGraw-Hill).

NATHAN, J. (1983) *Free to Teach: Achieving Equity and Excellence in Schools* (New York: Pilgrim Press).

NATIONAL GOVERNORS' ASSOCIATION (1986) *Time for Results: The Governors' 1991 Report on Education* Task Force on Parent Involvement and Choice, Supporting Works.

NAULT, R. and UCHITELLE, S. (1982) 'School choice in the public sector: a case study of parental decision-making', In M. MANLEY—CASIMIR, (ed.) *Family Choice in Schooling: Issues and Dilemmas* (Lexington, MA: Lexington Books).

POWELL, A., FARRAR, E. and COHEN, D. (1985) *The Shopping Mall High School: Winners and Losers in the Educational Marketplace* (Boston, MA: Houghton—Mifflin).

PURKEY, S. and SMITH. M. (1983) 'Effective schools: a review', *Elementary School Journal*, 83, pp. 427–451.

RAND CORPORATION (1978) *A Study of Alternatives in American Education*. R–2170/1–NIE through R–2170/7–NIE (Santa Monica, CA: The Rand Corporation).

RASMUSSEN, R. (1981) *A Study of Alternatives in American Education. Vol. III: Teachers' Responses to Alternatives.* (Santa Monica, CA: The Rand Corporation).

RAYWID, M.A. (1984) 'Synthesis of research on schools of choice', *Educational Leadership*, 42, pp. 70–78.

RAYWID, M.S. (1985) 'Family choice arrangements in public schools', *Review of Educational Research*, 55, pp. 435–467.

ROWAN, B. *et al* (1983) 'Research on effective schools: a cautionary note', *Educational Researcher*, 12, pp. 24–31.

RUTTER, M. *et al.* (1980) *Fifteen Thousand Hours: Secondary Schools and Their Effects on Children* (Cambridge, MA: Harvard University Press).

SIZER, T. (1984) *Horace's Compromise: The Dilemma of the American High School* (Boston, MA: Houghton-Mifflin).

SPRING, J. (1982) 'Dare educators build a new system?', in M. Manley-Casimir, (ed.) *Family Choice in Schooling: Issues and Dilemmas* (Lexington MA: Lexington Books).

TYACK, D. (1974) *The One Best System: A History of American Urban Education* (Cambridge, MA: Harvard University Press).

TYACK, D. and HANSOT, E. (1982) *Managers of Virtue: Public School Leadership in America, 1820–1980* (New York: Basic Books).

US DEPARTMENT OF EDUCATION, (1985) *Justice and Excellence: The Case for Choice in Chapter 1* (November 15) Washington DC: US Department of Education).

WEHLAGE, G. and RUTTER, R. (1986) 'Dropping out: how much do schools contribute to the problem?' *Teachers College Record*, 87, pp 374–392.

WILLIAMS, M.F. HANCHER, K.S. and HUTNER, A. (1983) 'Parents and school choice: a household survey', School finance Working Paper, US Department of Education.

WOLF, C. (1979) 'A theory of non-market failure', *Journal of Law and Economics*, 22, pp. 107–139.

7   *What doesn't work: an analysis of market and bureaucratic failure in schooling*

Charles Taylor Kerchner and William Lowe Boyd
Claremont Graduate School and Pennsylvania State University

Of all the educational reform battles, none is more spirited than that between the advocates of market forces and public bureaucracies. Thick-skinned warhorses join the contest at legislative hearings and university colloquia, each promising superior performance across a broad front of social values: choice, excellence, equity, and efficiency but the cannons of debate frequently shoot past one another.

The reality of public policy in education is the satisfaction of *multiple* values, and the use of a *mixture* of market and bureaucratic educational production. All but the heartiest libertarians have not advanced freedom of choice to the exclusion of mandatory attendance, and the most strident equity searchers recognize differentiation by merit. No proposal has been made for a state monopoly on schooling or for anything that approaches an unregulated free market. The debate is not fought at the poles; proponents each want to embrace part of the opposite value. Just as political conservatives frequently vote for big government, that which David Stockman (1975) called 'the social pork barrel', advocates of higher standards through testing frequently also support client choice through program options such as bilingual or special eduation or options such as magnets or specialty schools.

Whereas our political, system responds to multiple, sometimes contradictory, values, our analysis of alternatives is often much less ingenious. Those who value choice highly are drawn to market or quasi-market policy solutions, and those who value standards are drawn to organizational or bureaucratic solutions. Therefore, with few exceptions (Garms *et al.* 1978; Elmore 1987) we frequently fail to give proper weight to trade-offfs between values or hybrid delivery systems. Second, and most important to this chapter, we frequently ignore the implications of implementation. Implementation analysis, termed the 'missing chapter' (Wolf 1979: p. 133) in policy studies, turns on the ability of any system – public, private or mixed – to produce services that support the intended values. We know that markets sometimes fail to produce some socially desired goal and that compensating for market failure is a substantial topic in the discipline of economics and the practice of public policy. Markets exhibit cycles of boom and bust and have tendencies to seek stability through collusion and monopolistic practices that make them less productive of choices and their products more costly to consumers. Bureaucracies exhibit their own failures. They tend to ossify and to displace client service goals for goals associated with the well-being of employees and managers. Only through analyzing failure tendencies of markets and bureaucracies, can we tentatively describe clusters of policies that are both internally complementary and responsive to implementation problems.

Market and bureaucratic failures

The hidden hand of the market may prove unsteady in its grip; likewise, governments may not succeed when markets fail to turn private vices into public virtues. Some problems may prove intractable in the face of any intervention. However, bureaucracies and markets are each prone to different failures, and examination of the failure pattern paves the way for the discussion of different policy options. The relationship of market and bureaucratic failures to choice, excellence, efficiency and equity is shown in figure 1.

Figure 1.   Market and bureaucratic failures to support four values

	CHOICE	EXCELLENCE	EQUITY	EFFICIENCY
MARKET FAILURE	Too few providers	Undisciplined market	Discriminate by Wealth	High transaction costs
BUREAUCRATIC FAILURE	Inflexibility	Inconsistent or weak standards	Discriminate by Political Influence	Monopoly costs

The value of *choice*, or liberty as it is sometimes put, is threatened when the market fails to provide enough competitors. Certain market conditions, particularly those involving increasing returns and declining marginal costs, have a tendency to result in monopoly (Arrow 1971). In other situations, market imperfections decrease the flow of information or technology necessary to enter competition. Many of these conditions are particularly applicable to education. When these conditions exist, it is common for government to directly regulate a 'natural' monopoly or to provide legal barriers, such as anti-trust laws, to prevent a single firm from exercising too great a hold. A bureaucracy threatens choice through inflexibility, a failure to respond to clients that is rooted in the substitution of internal goals that often have little relationship to the social goals the bureaucracy is supposed to pursue. Wolf (1979: 117) calls this bureaucratic behavior 'internality', meaning that 'private or organizational costs and benefits are included in the calculus of social decision makers'. Arrow (1974) calls it 'an internal version of the price system'.

The value of *excellence* is threatened by markets when the nature of trades allowed in the market is poorly defined or badly enforced. There are virtually no unstructured or unrestricted markets. Curbs are placed on what goods or services may enter into trade and the conditions under which they may be traded. In education, licensure, accreditation and even building codes structure the characteristics of the competitors; and rules, such as attendence area transfer policies, variously inhibit or stimulate choices betwen school districts and students. Market structures reflect quite different meanings of the term excellence. For instance, markets can be estabished around trading commodities in which goods are graded or grouped and traded on the basis of price with no distinction among products within group. Markets can also be established with great variation among goods and services offered, such as is the case with brand-name merchandise that enters the market offering conspicuously different qualities and which is sold at different prices.

Bureaucratic organizations endanger excellence when they fail to produce clear expectations or when their performance deviates so radically from formal expectations that service providers lower expectations for themselves and the public comes to believe that the organization is *incapable* of high quality. Expectations influence outcomes, as the 'excellent schools' reformers have long recognized. However, the greater danger to public-sector organizations occurs when frustrated clients abandon a public service in search of alternatives. This 'exit' option, which Hirschman (1971) first recognized in the flight of customers from the state-owned Nigerian railway system, has also been observed in the movement of middle-class Americans from big city schools. Client abandonment undercuts political support by depriving schools of their most vocal supporters and critics.

Equity in its various meanings can be undercut by illegitimate discrimination in service delivery by either markets or bureaucracies. Markets are particularly vulnerable to allocating services according to economic class. Law and medicine, in particular, face chronic problems in the maldistribution of services according to economic circumstance. As a result, there has been intervention in the form of public health services and publicly-supported insurance plans in order to provide health services to those who otherwise would be unable to afford them. These services, like education, have a public-benefit character in addition to rendering their obvious private benefits.

Bureaucracies face two equity problems. They fail to distribute equitably when they deliver a large proportion of social goods to those who are more influential or more in favor politically. Group interest, particularly that of clients and service providers, has a substantial effect on the supply of services, sufficiently so to distort markets. In addition, bureaucracies almost inevitably centralize service delivery, placing 'power in the hands of the social worker instead of the client' (Wolf 1979: 128).

The value of *efficiency* is threatened in market settings when large transaction costs are required to provide goods or services. Organizations exist as efficient economic units because the costs of co-ordination, control and production are less through employment than through repeated market transactions with independent suppliers of goods and services (Arrow 1974). It has been suggested that transaction costs are particularly high when there is great uncertainty about how inputs are related to outputs and, thus, expensive contingency contracts or monitoring procedures are required (Williamson 1975). These characteristics are precisely those which contemporary organizational theory ascribe to educational institutions. Krashinsky (1986) uses the transaction cost effect to argue against educational vouchers on efficiency grounds: the high costs of monitoring voucher schools and providing information to parents.

Bureaucracies threaten efficiency in well-recognized monopolistic behaviors, paying employees more than the market wage and failing to curb practices that have outlived their usefulness. Comparisons of public and private school teacher salaries universally show that government employed teachers are better paid than their private sector counterparts, frequently as much as 25%.

Four policy frontiers

Understanding the tendency of markets and bureaucracies to fail is particularly important as one discusses specific public policy questions. The four policies analyzed in this section represent choices of how best to support each of the core values in education:

1. The problem of whether to increase client choice in education through using 'demand side' interventions, such as vouchers, tax credits, and independent contractors, or 'supply side' choice through administrative decentralization, magnet schools, and transfer regulations.
2. The problem of whether to define excellence through a single, unified profession of education or whether to support multiple standards, educational 'brand names' that cater to quite different ideas of quality.

3. The problem of whether to promote equity through increasing the ability of individual
   clients to gain access to the education they want or through increasing the ability of the
   political system to respond to group and commonweal demands.
4. The problem of whether efficiency is better advanced by atempting to regulate the market
   or manage the bureaucracy.

Figure 2.   The policy choice frontiers.

	CHOICE	EXCELLENCE	EQUITY	EFFICIENCY
	[1]	[2]	[3]	[4]
MARKETS	Demand side choice	Brand name structures	Hybrid structures	The costs of market regulation
	vs.	vs.	vs.	vs.
BUREAUCRACIES	supply side choice	professional market structures	Public Supply	The costs of managing bureaucratic monopolies

Policy 1: *Demand side vs. supply side choice*

It is erroneous to connect choice solely with market provision of educational services. Public
universities provide very differentiated education, and school systems have long practiced
internal differentiation, so much so that the 'shopping mall' metaphor attached to American
high schools became a target of criticism and an object of reform. When given the
opportunity to choose, most public school students did not pick a particularly challenging
mix of educational experiences (Powell, *et al.* 1985). The policy issue is not so much between
market choice and bureaucratic rigidity as it is between whether the choices, in Richard
Elmore's (1987) terms, should be 'demand side' choices – with consumers empowered with
vouchers or tax credits to pick the services they want – or whether choices should be 'supply
side' choices in which bureaucracies engage in decentralization and deliberate diversification.

Within any given setting, markets are generally conceded to be more rapid to adapt
than bureaucracies. However, without special inducements to potential service providers,
choice would likely be limited in the less attractive segments of the market: poverty-prone
and physically unattractive locations such as inner-cities and isolated rural districts, and
difficult, costly to serve students such as learning handicapped or language minorities.

While we cannot simulate exactly what the choices would be if the market were relied
on more heavily for educational services, we can gain some insights from medicine as a
service subsidized by private insurance for the employed and public insurance for the
unemployed and retired. Clearly, subsidization provides health care for a much greater
segment of the population than was formerly the case. By 1981 the number of hospital visits
per year was actually greater for the poor than for the non-poor. But there are still serious
gaps. 'Findings from recent studies suggest that being poor is no longer a major deterrent to
obtaining adequate health care; being uninsured is. To be uninsured and poor is the most
serious problem of all' (Blendon 1986: 127). Approximately one-third of the poor women of
childbearing years are uninsured, and post-neonatal infant mortality has actualy risen in
recent years (p. 134).

Inducing the medical market to extend its services to the poor has not been without cost
of heavy government involvement. The number of hospital visists by the poor shows a
dramatic upturn at precisely the time when public medical insurance came into force

(p. 127). Overall, the expansion of all forms of insurance has created an explosion in medical costs. Medicine's share of the GNP started to decline in 1984 only after substantial regulation of the market by government and private insurance carriers, and after the expansion of health maintenance organizations as alternatives to private service providers (p. 133).

Magnet schools, administrative decentalization, and the freedom to transfer from one school or district to another would also be productive of increased choices. Given the relatively complex decision systems associated with bureaucratic change, we would expect fewer choices than the market would produce, but that those choices might be better distributed through rich and poor, attractive and unattractive places. Jones (1987) is pessimistic on this point, as are what might be considered the reformist voucher advocates, such as Christopher Jencks (1966).

However, the data on public-school provided choices are not entirely bleak. First, one must realize that choice is not a universally shared value, either among school people or among the public at large, and that for half a century schools marched well to the drumbeat of standardization and control, with the 'one best system' as an organizational motif. Schools carried a service ideal that was much the same as the Bell System's: high quality and reliability without much variation.

Only in the last 20 years has this service ideal been seriously challenged, and during that time we have seen the growth of family or client choice mechanisms, although they are certainly not universal, nor universally applauded. Elmore's (1987) synthesis suggests that about one-third of big city school systems offer some kind of magnet or specialty school program. In some states, such as California, each school district must provide an 'alternative' high school for those students whose behavior or learning style makes them either unwanted or unhappy at the conventional schools. Students in larger numbers make choices within schools about the courses and programs they will take, although not always the choices school reformers would have them make. But the most dramatic student choice has been the one that has drawn the most negative reaction: fully 20% of high school students choose not to go to school at all. Additional choice, it is argued would help solve this problem, but the evidence on this point is mixed. Educational consumers of all ages do actively display a school/leisure utility curve, and college students, who are given the most choices, show a substantial ability to choose leaving school over finishing degrees.

Either markets or bureaucracies can be induced to produce choice. Markets appear more facile than perhaps they actually are because comparisons are frequently made between relatively unstructured, unregulated market choices, such as the environment of independent schools, and the highly structured bureaucratic situation in which public schools are located. If the structures were similar, the difference also would be reduced.

This discussion of client and producer choice yields three policy conclusions.

First, as Elmore (1987) reminds us, there is a wide variety of choice options available, combinations of public and private schools, contracting-out options, and possibilities for diversity ('intrapreneurship' is the word being used in the business literature). Given the scale of existing public school mechanisms, these incremental changes may well be the only feasible ones.

Second, empowering clients to choose *among* schools is a qualitatively different decision than allowing choice *within* a school, and this is the case whether the schools involved are privately or publicly run. A choice of educational philosophies within a school breaks down cohesiveness and institutes shopping based on the student culture and preferences. A choice of schools, however, allows each school to form its own internally coherent culture. This is a characteristic of successful Roman Catholic schools and of public schools that have undergone successful rejuvenation (Murnane 1986: 179).

Third, widening choices only works when the choice abilities are symmetric. Allowing greater student choice and not allowing correspondingly broader choices of students and curriculum by schools immediately deepens the inability of existing schools to solve problems. In such a setting, competent, engaged clients will quickly leave, turning the existing schools, mostly public, into the keepers of the least motivated and least able (Boyd 1987, Hirschman 1970). If choice is to be used as a vehicle for school improvement, rather than as an escape mechanism for the motivated or the wealthy, then schools and teachers will need to be able to make choices that match student choices.

The inescapable question that dogs all discussions of expanded choice is: who provides education of the unchosen? An educational system that mandates attendance ultimately must require some school to take the least attractive students. Governments can increase the relative financial attractiveness of different types of students by differentially supporting them, but less able, less motivated students will be, on the whole, much less attractive. Without a guaranteed placement these students would be unlikely to find a school. Functionally, this means that for many students the neighborhood public school will continue to be the school of last resort.

2: Professional vs. brand-name excellence

Structures and rules *bound* most markets making the metaphor of a free market an attractive illusion (Larson 1977). Governments structure markets through agricultural inspection, pure food and drug laws, and automobile emissions requirements. Buyers and sellers jointly organize markets, such as stock or grain exchanges, and such markets are closely monitored to see that buyers can be found for would-be sellers and that price fluctuations are orderly. Producers hedge against uncertainty and leverage the competition through vertical and horizontal integration. Purchasers and producers both seek standardized products, such as the size of computer disks or photographic film, and evaluate market-produced products and services through such procedures as grading agricultural goods and accrediting schools. Market restrictions color even governmental purchases of goods and services through regulations that restrict what governments can buy (such as teacher credentialing requirements, or special building codes for public buildings) or the purchase process (purchase orders or the requirement for multiple written bids). From the public policy perspective, the question is not whether market forces should be brought to bear on education, but how those forces should structured.

While there are several different types of markets (Mitchell and Kerchner 1981), two types predominate in educational policy discussion: professonal markets and art/craft markets. In professional markets, schools would adhere to a single standard and the choice between them would be made largely on the basis of consumer trust. In markets that offered educational services as a combination of art and craft, there would be quite different educational services associated with different cost characteritics. The consumer would choose that combination of cost and service that represented good value.

Professional control requires a monopoly, a restriction on who may enter a field of practice and who may define that which constitutes legitimate practice – a very constrained market. As Larson (1977: 40) puts it: a condition of a unified profession is 'that there be a group of professionals ready to champion the propagation of one ''paradigm'' and this group have enough persuasive or coercive power to carry the task through'. Everett Hughes (1958) noted that professions have struck a bargain with society: in return for organizing great knowledge and skill, society has granted the professionals social control and autonomy.

Practitioner entry is strictly limited, and the content of good educational practice is structured by the profession rather than by consumers. Not uncommonly, the amount of professional service offered is less than that which would be demanded in a free market. All service occupations face the dilemma of enforcing a single high standard of training and practice and of thereby creating a shortage of practitioners or of allowing entry standards to fall sufficiently to meet demand. Medicine faced this problem even in the mid-nineteenth century, and it has been a perpetual problem for public school teaching (Larson 1977: 131). The extreme financial attractiveness of medicine has brought overall supply and demand into balance, but the distribution of medical care between affluent and poor, cosmopolitan and rural areas, is still out of balance.

Professional services are prone to escalating costs as the monopoly restriction on entering the field becomes associated with status and income protection for professionals. Between the years 1965 and 1978, expenses for publicly provided medical care for children grew at 8.8% a year, a rate nearly 3.5 times greater than the expansion in the GNP (Fuchs 1983: 250). Medical salaries have also increased substantially over the same period.

Professions also can be depicted as severely constricting equity in the sense that professions exist both intellectually and socially under the supposition that the professional's judgement about the right or proper course of action is substituted for that of the client. Starr's (1982) history of medicine suggests that physicians became professionals when the technology of X-rays, electrocardiograms and laboratory tests made it impossible for patients to directly diagnose their own conditions. Much of the community control movement in education rested on a perception that educators had become, in a sense, too professional. As Coons and Sugarman (1978: 51) put it, 'The existing educational regime with its professional garrison is the family's primary competitor for power over the child's school experience and is likely to remain so.' Power may be exercised with competence, care and compassion, and it may be subject to checks and balances, but the essence of profession is that knowledge of the client's condition and of the possible treatments is so complex and subjective that ultimately informed decisions can only be made by the professional (Wolf 1979: 128). Obviously, this opens the possibility for abuse, and creates a gaping inequity between the authority of the professional and that of the patient.

Craft and art markets exist as primary alternatives to organizing around profession. Each is a useful principle of organization for a more deregulated market. Artistic markets are the most deregulated of all, most akin to an educational free market in which consumers could partake of education, or refrain from partaking, strictly on the basis of taste. In craft markets goods and services are regulated according to some external standard, such as accreditation for the school and licensure for teachers, but within the craft context there is substantial competition based on mixtures of price, features, and quality. Schools package the mixture and display it as their image in an effort to attract students, philanthropic support, and programmatic contracts. These programs appeal on the basis of value, rather than price alone, and thus schools are able to talk about the investment value of a prep school education or the returns from a specialized trade school. Because positive images are valuable, craft markets have a tendency to oligopolize around those images. Schools form leagues or associations, and colleges reshape departments to conform to the institution's image of itself.

Brand-name education, combining elements of craft and art, places a floor under excellence. Common standards could well exist, but there also would be substantial deviation. The clients would be expected to be knowledgable about the differences and to be able to distinguish between solid performers and fly-by-nighters, just as consumers of higher education now do. But close-order attempts at standardization, such as statewide curriculum frameworks being initiated in the current reform movement, would be incompatible.

However, schools, as part of their brand-name, might well decide to comply with external standards, just as schools now follow accreditation standards.

Equity problems: Brand-name education is subject to three kinds of social and economic inequity. First, inequity is associated with the provision of education, the likelihood that more choices would be available in more desirable locations. However, this is fundamentally an implementation problem rather than one associated with market structuring, and these problems will be addressed in a subsequent section.

Second, class-based inequity is likely to result from student selection. In order to preserve their distinctive identities, brand-name schools need to involve mutual choices by the school and the client. The kinds of random assignment provisions suggested in some voucher plans would destroy the very premise on which craft and art identity and loyalty rest. While there could be enforcable curbs on overt racial or sexual discrimination, it is highly likely that the student characteristics most favored by schools would be class-biased. Extraordinary care would have to be taken, and financial incentives offered, if children from less wealthy homes were to receive the same range of choices that those from more wealthy homes would receive. If these measures were inadequate, then schools would quickly devolve into a tracked system based on social and economic class, and the poorest would likely receive few, if any, choices at all. Consumer choice of program type may also prove to be class-biased in the sense that middle class parents empirically tend to chose child-centered programs while working class parents pick more highly structured, teacher-centered environments (Murnane 1986: 182).

Third, inequities would probably exist based on information. Knowledge about and awareness of choices and how to assess them is class biased. The evidence so far is that lower class parents are much less knowledgable about available choices for their children than are parents from homes with high incomes (Murnane 1986: 182). However, there is also evidence that parents in districts that provide choices are more knowledgable about school programs than parents from the same backgrounds whose children attended schools that did not provide choice options.

Organizations vs. institutions: The choice between structuring excellence along professional vs. brand-name lines involves choosing between organizational and institutional mechanisms to maintain the desired level of common standards. Structuring education as a profession, which it cannot now sensibly be called, requires constructing an extra-organizational institution to screen and test novices, to oversee professional education, and to maintain standards across organizations. The Holmes Group approach to teacher education standards, elite leadership, and national board exams typify the structures needed to start organizing education along these lines. Organizing by brand-name requires building schools with strong organizational indentities, and consequently it requires a relatively weak extra-organizational institution. If fundamental schools are to thrive alongside of Montessori schools and developmental schools, then each identity must be considered legitimate. If there were societal oversight at all, it would have to be external to school processes. National exams or standard achievement tests would fulfill this function.

The feasibility of professional structuring lies in the ability to create and codify a paradigm of education, which is distinct enough to eliminate heretics and attractive enough to be legitimated by legislatures and universities. National teacher competence exams, *if legitimated as the standard of entry for the field*, would establish *de facto* such a paradigm because a codified practice would soon   be constructed around the examination requirements. Historically, however, legislatures have not been willing to establish such firm entry requirements for public schools because to do so would cause a drastic shortage of teachers. As a result, we see a pattern of very low-order tests, such as those used in Texas and California, combined with a category-oriented certification process.

The feasibility of brand-name structuring lies partly in the ability to establish very broad minimum standards for entry, which are universally enforced. At least for public schools, our current certification standards come close to fulfilling this need. But the more fundamental need of distinctive brand names is the requirement to develop robust 'schools' of educational practice centered around different educational philosophies and teaching pedagogies. Fundamental schools, developmental schools and others would need to develop distinct identities, training and certification procedures and program evaluation techniques. Montessori schools are perhaps the only such current example. Finally, the differences among brand names must be salient to education's clients; brand-name schools must be more valuable and desired than undistinguished, generic, 'plain-wrap' schools or the brand-name structure will collapse.

The choice between structuring educational markets along professional or brand-name lines is a crucial one because the choice involves substantial cost in structuring the country's educational establishment. Failure to make a definitive choice of market structuring is the worst public policy of all. What is likely to result is overstructured, 'sham professionalism' that espouses excellence, but cannot enforce its standards. Pretences of professionalism require all the costly training and self-governance mechanisms associated with real professionalism without allowing those mechanisms to engage in self-control and conspicuous quality demonstration.

Policy 3: *Individual or collective finance equity*

There is substantial disagreement over whether financial equity in education should be achieved by subsidizing the fair purchases of educational services by individual families or through equalizing the distribution of funds to public agencies. A family-based system of educational finance appears, alternately, attractive and hazardous.

The first equity problem is one of sufficiency: the notion that equity should not be about distributing poverty. The current menu of public school reforms implies approximately a 25% increase in educational funding for items such as longer school days and years, smaller classes, and higher teacher salaries. The failure of governments to provide needed social goods is one recognized both in traditional welfare economics (Pigou 1932) and in the economics of public choice (Buchanan and Tulloch 1962). The deteriorating quality of public service, the perception of which has been a driving force in educational reform, is treated by public choice economists as an inevitable failure of bureaucratic production (Buchanan 1972: 31). The problem originates with the joint social-private benefit characteristic of education and the inability of governments to deliver just the package of limited social goods to students excluding them from gaining the private benefits from schooling. Standard economic theory argues that the government cannot successfully give away goods that are individually valued by the recipients. Thus, demand for education which is virtually free to the individual consumer rises to levels greater than the political system is willing to supply, and consequently public brueaucracies face the problem of 'deteriorating quality of service' (Buchanan 1972: 31). This occurs because citizens make different decisions as 'buyers' of education than they do as 'sellers'. The citizen consumer wants a bounty of free services while the citizen seller as taxpayer is sharply constrained and quite willing to be a 'free-rider' consuming benefits, but not paying for them. The solution, it is argued, is to eliminate the artificial separation between consumer and taxpayer, between private demand and public supply.

One solution to this problem is to recognize the dual public good/private good nature of education and to devise ways of encouraging or requiring individuals to make a contribution toward their own education, or that of their children. Traditionally, colleges and universities have done this through charging tuition. We do not find it odd that public colleges charge tuition and fees and that these frequently escalate sharply in graduate professional programs where the student, not the state, is the primary beneficiary of the additional education.

Elementary and secondary public schools have invoked quasi-tuitions, sometimes for books and supplies, and nearly universally for band uniforms, outdoor education expenses, and other so-called options. Recently, there has been a tendency for educational hybrids to appear – mixtures of public and private schools and mixtures of public and private services within a school day.[1] Privately operated day-care centres are found on school sites or in adjacent buildings. Privately run services (often by public school teachers) offer after-school tutoring and summer enrichment and adventure programs. Religious institutions have traditionally offered after school classes in language, culture and dogma. More recently, examples have been noted of students who split their curriculum between church-sponsored and public high schools.

Increasing family inputs to education have highly attractive aspects. Both analytically and in practice it can be shown that allowing a combination of tax-generated funds and individually purchased private benefits will increase the total amount spent on education (Stubblebine 1972). The relationship between family involvement and support and educational outcomes is strongly positive and, as Clark's (1983) study of poor Black families shows, those impacts can be felt across socioeconomic conditions. The logical way to induce families to pay for the education they receive is to publicly support those aspects of education that support the general welfare – literacy and a common core of values that support democratic citizenship – and to require consumers to pay for those things that will be of personal benefit such as technical training and extra-curricular experiences that are enriching or of intrinsic benefit. This is the intent of Friedman's unrestricted voucher plan in which parents would be free to spend the voucher amount plus 'any additional sum on educaional services from an "approved" institution of their own choice' (Friedman 1955: 127). Historically, this and other unrestricted voucher ideas are economically similar to the flat grant state-aid systems that were used to support public schools at the turn of the century, a point not lost on the voucher advocates (Stubblebine 1972: 205). In effect, the local schsligtaxes that supplemented state grants were locally imposed tuitions assessed on a sliding scale according to property wealth.

Unfortunately, the equity problem involved in family provision of education are as obvious as those that occurred with the local tax provision. Because the variation in family income is greater than that of school districts, even more severe equity problems would result. The public policy response to inequality in school district revenue bases has been to require allocations to school districts to be made on the basis of state wealth rather than school district wealth, and there is no technical reason that poor families cannot be subsidized in the way that poor school districts are now subsidized. Indeed, the legal argument ultimately adopted in California's *Serrano* decision, also supported 'family power equalizing', a system of subsidized payments to parents (Coons *et al*. 1971: 200–242). Garms, *et al*. (1978: 241–247) adopt this logic in support of their hybrid school-voucher plan which provides for: a basic public education through grade eight, grants for secondary education that students could use throughout their lifetime, and subsidized, wealth-equalized education coupons, which individuals could purchase and communities could further subsidize. The proposed solution is both distributionally equitable and economically efficient in the sense that the family contributions to tuition coupons would bring into play market forces that would push supply and demand toward equilibrium.

However, two major problems remain. The first is the economic problem of joint supply – the inability to avoid distributing a private good along with a public good. The second problem is the economic tendency to escape paying subsidies when alternate means of service provision are available.

The literature on school finance has long recognized the difficulty of attempting to capture the public good characteristics of education in a finance formula. Dollar-per-student equality appears fair, but the reality of school practice comes closer to 'need equalization' (Garms *et al.* 1978: 201). The bundle of services considered of public benefit varies by the individual's learning ability, social condition and physical location. In response to this perception, finance formulas have become very complex amalgams of grants and categorical funds.

Public and private benefit aspects of education are further intertwined in the actual production of education in public schools. Allocations of space, time, attention, equipment and other school resources are not equally distributed. The loose-coupling literature on educational organizatons postulates that schools distribute resources in a way that approximates a need equilibrium. Attempting to break apart in provision or delivery that which is a public good and that which is a private good would be extremely difficult.

Because the delivery of public and private goods is not feasibly separated, a decision to encourage greater non-public production of education would also have to acknowledge a general shift away from that which is common and public in education and a greater embrace of that which is private.

The second challenge to the feasibility of family contributions in support of education comes in the form of the 'free rider' problem. Essentially the problem is this: what incentive would a rich person have to subsidize the education of the poor? Under the current school finance system, the child of the rich receives the public benefits and private benefits together, by enrolling in a public school. These benefits come in a single lump and they are of substantial value. Because of equalization, part of the rich family's taxes may be distributed to poor schools, but because public and private benefits of schooling are delivered together substantial benefits flow back to the rich family. Equalized revenue distributions to the school districts place the children of the poor and rich in schools which are mutually dependent in the fiscal sense. The rich family retains a political interest in supporting public schools because it has an economic interest in the distribution of public school revenues.

Under an equalized family contribution system, the rich family's contribution for the poor family's private benefit would be politically extracted, but it would receive little return benefit in terms of a coupon – just as rich and upper middle income families now are sharply restricted in the benefits they receive from college tuition grants. Their incentive would be to exit the public system and provide as small a subsidy as possible. The amount of the total education bill covered by the basic public education grant would likely decline over time. Subsidization of coupon vouchers for the less wealthy would be unpopular among taxpayers and would be viewed politically as a pure transfer payment: welfare in the political sense. It is hard to conceive of an educational finance mechanism that would be less popular.

Policy 4: *Minding markets vs. managing bureaucracies*

In pursuit of efficiency, all organizations must balance the cost of market transactions with those costs associated with organizational maintenance (Williamson 1975). Public agencies are particularly at issue because of their seemingly inexorable increases in costs and the difficulty of finding a robust production function that links spending more with better results. When examined over a century, one finds public spending expanding faster than the GNP by 2 to 3% a year (Borcherding 1977: 19). The policy response offered by public choice theorists, and a great many others, is to divorce financing of public services from direct governmental provision (Buchanan 1977: 17). Privatization and contracting for services appear as attractive alternatives to incurring the costs of public monopoly.

But we are also well aware that monopoly costs cannot be reduced without incurring other costs in their stead. These are the costs of market structuring and regulation, which are necessary to nudge the market toward maintaining choice, offering high quality services, or providing equitable treatment. As Okun (1975) reminds us, even transfer payments designed to allow the less affluent to purchase market services are delivered in 'a leaky bucket'.

Public schools as monopolies are generally thought to be economically inefficient in the wage levels paid teachers and in the numbers of administrators and other non-teaching personnel hired. The teacher wage effect is often ascribed to the effects of teacher unionism, although union/non-union comparisons are difficult because there is no large non-union sector among public school teaching, except in those states which forbid collective bargaining. As one might expect, there are large variations in estimates of the union wage effect – from 0 to 27% – but a 5 to 10% effect is probably realistic (Kerchner 1986, Lipsky 1982).

The more pointed comparison is between public and private school teacher salaries, and here the comparisons appear large indeed. However, when one compares the *characteristics* of teachers in the different sectors, then the gap narrows appreciably. Chambers' (1985) study of San Francisco area teachers showed private school teachers would earn more if they taught in public schools, but they would make less than the existing pool of public school teachers because they lacked the experience, education, and credentials for which public school teachers gain salary increments. Conversely, public school teachers would make less if they taught in private schools, but they would make more than the existing cohort of private school teachers. Even in the private school market, the sample of public school teachers had more of the qualifications that the market valued.

Public schools are also more extensively administered than are schools in other sectors, and administrative intensity has increased. The self-aggrandizing tendencies of public employees seeking to create more and better jobs are thought to be a major contributor to the growth in public budgets (Niskanen 1971). And some have suggested that it helps to explain school consolidation (Staaf 1977).

But the specific antecedents of administrative intensity tend to suggest that program structure and school size may be more explanatory of administrative intensity than personal rent seeking. Rowan's (1981) study is significant in this respect because it suggests that there may be bureaucratic causal factors, but that they may well be external to the schools themselves. Much of the increase in administrative activity in schools is associated with the layers of reform that have, over the last 40 years, mandated new programs and services. The administrative structures are frequently imported and grafted on to existing schools.

Recognizing the institutional rather than the organizational sources of administrative growth is important because the same dynamics could occur in private schools which accept contracts. As we recognize in military defense contracting, the structure of the contract, rather than whether the managers are public or private empolyees, has a substantial effect on program cost.

Where bureaucracies incur excessive employee and administrative costs, market distribution systems incur regulation and information costs. James (1986) has examined these effects in the Netherlands, which in effect, has had a voucher plan for years. Private schools receive the same subsidy as government schools and they charge a small tuition in addition, with the result that they are slightly more expensive. In addition, the system imposes costs on the country's transportation system, which students must use to gain access to schools outside their immediate neighborhood. Although James (1986: 126) does not specify the amount, the system also has substantial regulatory costs. Dutch Ministry of Education regulations apply to private schools, inspectors visit the schools, and the Ministry audits financial records.

In addition, most market systems project relatively high regualtion costs. Because most market-oriented proposals have not been implemented, we cannot know with certainty how expensive this aspect of market structuring would be, but the descriptions suggest they would be consequential. Joe Nathen (1987), who co-ordinated the National Governor's Association report on education, lists the features of what he considers a desirable choice plan (1987: 750):

1. a specific list of skills and knowledge expectations;
2. transportation for low-income families;
3. student assignment procedures that advance desegregation, which means that unlimited choice will be unlikely;
4. parent information and counseling;
5. interdistrict transfers;
6. fiscal protection for small districts;
7. equalized funding across districts;
8. planning, training and professional development funds available to teachers;
9. a survey of parent preferences and system assessment;
10. continuing oversight so the system does not experience unexpected results.

The California ballot proposition fostered by Coons and Sugarman's (1977) family choice plan was similary complex, with mechanisms to provide information and assign students without racial bias. The complexity was generally thought to have decreased its political attractiveness.

Conclusion: a centrist approach to policy clusters

The foregoing analysis of educational policy based on the failure characteristics of markets and bureaucracies was designed around the trade-offs involved in different approaches to achieving each of the four social values most frequently associated with educational policy. One goal of policy analysis, however, is to fashion policies and institutions capable of simultaneously supporting multiple values. Indeed, most of the calls for reform are explicit assertions that big gains can be made in one value without costs to other values:

> We propose an idea in the great American tradition: that you can increase excellence by increasing choice.
> (National Governors' Association 1986)

> Private provision of public goods and services: reducing spending (and taxes) without reducing benefits.
> (Buchanan 1977)

> In establishing a framework for progressive alternatives, it is necessary to project a concept of education in which quality and equality are mutually inclusive standards.
> (Bastian et al. 1985)

> Incorporation of elements of choice in systems of [racial] integration eventually should achieve more than the current efforts of courts and legislatures.
> (Coons and Sugarman 1978).

While we know intellectually that there is no 'free lunch' policy analysis drives us to search for low-cost menus. Such options exist in the form of *compatible policies*. Erickson's (1986) research on private schools suggests that at least some of the policies that make schools attractive to parents also help schools become effective: admissions and dismissal policies that keep out disruptive students may make schools simultaneously effective and attractive. Tuition charges may further choice and evoke more parental involvement in their child's education.

Three policy options emerge from the review conducted in this chapter. Although each option involves trade-offs between choice, excellence, efficiency, and equity, each option also acknowledges and promotes each social value. While these are certainly not the only policy clusters possible, they do suggest quite different priorities for educational reform, and, hence, areas of concern that could receive less public attention.

The first policy cluster is *market professionalism*. Under this concept, educational reform centers on establishing a strong and independent teaching profession, and virtually no attention is paid to schools as organizations. In terms of the categorization scheme used in the previous section, this policy cluster combines demand-side choice, professional market structures, hybrid service delivery organizations and the costs of market regulation. Under market professionalism, professional teachers carry an instructional monopoly in publicly subsidized schools. Rigorous training and entrance examinations are enforced, and emergency credentials and other shortcuts are abolished. Professional associations enforce quality standards, and schools which fail professional muster are ineligible to receive public funds. Course content and teaching methods vary, as do the relative emphases of different schools. State or national examinations are given at the end of specified grades, and these allow comparisons among schools. Schools are formed by groups of professionals who want to practice together and who submit approved operational plans to the local school authority. The local school authorities form schools on a combination of geographic and curriculum considerations. They may operate schools or contract with others, but each school is economically dependent on student enrollment for its revenue.

By involving strong professional controls, this system would provide more quality control than would be the case in a less restricted market, yet it would maintain the disciplining effects of the market because of student choice. Schools that were unsuccessful in attracting clients could not survive. These schools would doubtless be stratified by social class, although unless housing patterns change, they probably would not be more stratified than current public schools. However, the schools would also be stratified by talent and ability.

The second policy cluster is *bureaucratic intrapreneurship*, which combines demand-side choice, brand-name market structuring, public supply, and managed bureaucracy. Under this concept, school reform concentrates on establishing internal diversity within existing school districts. Groups of teachers and administrators are allowed to 'contract-in', agreeing with the administration to establish (or transform) schools to particular standards. In return, they are released from large portions of administrative regulation and external control over content and procedure. Schools sites differentiate themselves according to learning style, educational philosophy, and organizational structure. Parents and schools mutually choose each other. School districts streamline operations and place a premium on school site operations. Sites become the focus of budgeting, labor agreements, and most educational policy. The school site is also the locus of employment. Districts would guarantee fulfillment of employment contracts, but permanent employment status would be specific to a school site. Rank, benefits and salary status could be carried to another school, but there would be no employment guarantee in the event a school site declined in attractiveness. Schools have individual admission standards, and the school district may form new schools if portions of the population appear underserved.

This option is in many ways the polar opposite of the first one. School standards and responsiveness to conditions rest on a locally elected body. Parents would have the ability to choose among options, but the public body would have the task of deciding what options to develop. Change would be both politically and market-driven. External professionalism and its enforcement are relatively unimportant, as is most of the current apparatus of teacher certification. Obviously, this policy cluster does not offer the same levels of quality assurance as the professional model. It also does not undertake the monopoly service costs associated with professionalism. The buyer would have to be somewhat more vigilant, although external examinations and voluntary standards inspections are also compatible with this mode of operation. Families would receive social-class equity in their choices, but schools doubtless would attempt to cream-off the most talented students, and thus some students would have more choices than others.

The third policy cluster is *community democracy* involving a mixture of demand and supply-side choice, professional controls, political processes and managed bureaucracy. Under this concept reform concentrates on forming public bodies of manageable size and complexity. These bodies could be geographic or could be based on common lifestyles or educational preferences. Such bodies would operate essentially as membership benefit districts, in similar fashion to community redevelopment districts, mosquito abatement districts, or historical preservation agencies. Fiscal distributions would be the function of the state, but each school and school site council would have virtual autonomy and legal responsibility for its operations. The state would provide central pensions and benefits to facilitate teacher transfer, but the school district would be responsible for continued employment. Teacher professionalism is important, as is the case in the first option, and the profession would have a monopoly on the provision of teachers. Schools could attempt to attract new families, and each new family would become a voting member.

This option trades off a strong social mission for the school in return for strong local determination. Schools become very small governments, much like an owners association in a condominium or co-operative apartment building. Engagement, which comes with the right to associate with a social group of tractable size, is associated with the forces of the market in attracting new participants. Of the three options, this would be the most suspect form a conventional civil rights standpoint, and standards for entry and retention of students would require the most scrutiny. However, of the three options, this one does the most in connecting political and economic interests in a single marketplace, and it distributes both political and economic votes on a one person/one vote basis.

Each of these three options is interesting because, by using a mixture of market and bureaucratic tools, they illustrate that markets and bureaucracies are not incompatible, that both historically and conceptually, each has evolved around the failure characteristics of the other. Thus, what doesn't work is as good a guide to policy as what does.

Note

1. For an interesting discussion of the emergence of such educational hybids in Israel, see Inbar (1988 forthcoming).

References

ARROW, K.J. (1971) 'Political and economic evaluation of social effects and externalities', in *Frontiers of Quantitive Economics*, Michael D. Intriligator (ed.) (Amsterdam: North-Holland).

ARROW, K.J. (1974) *The Limits of Organization* (New York: W.W. Norton).

BASTIAN, A., FRUCHTER, N., GITELL, M., GREER, C. and HASKINS, K. (1985) *Choosing Equality: The Case For Democratic Schooling* (New York: The New World Foundation).

BORCHERDING, T.E. (1977) 'One hundred years of public spending, 1870-1970', in T. Borcherding (ed.) *Budgets and Bureaucrats: The Sources of Governmental Growth* (Durham, NC: Duke University Press).

BLENDON, R.J. (1986) 'The problems of cost, access and distribution of medical care', *Daedalus*, 115 (2), pp. 119–135.

BOYD, W.L. (1987) 'Balancing public and private schools: the Australian experience and American implications', *Educational Evaluation and Policy Analysis*, 3, 2.

BUCHANAN, J.M. (1972) 'The inconsistencies of the national health service', in J.M. Buchanan and R.D. Tollison (eds.) *Theory of Public Choice: Political Applications of Economics* (Ann Arbor: University of Michigan Press).

BUCHANAN, J.M. (1977) 'Why does government grow?' in T. Borcherding (ed.) *Budgets and Bureaucrats: The Sources of Governmental Growth* (Durham, NC: Duke University Press).

BUCHANAN, J.M. and TULLOCH, G. (1962) *The Calculus of Consent* (Ann Arbor: The University of Michigan Press).

CHAMBERS, J. (1985) *Patterns of Compensation of Public and Private School Teachers* (Stanford, CA: Institute For Educational Finance and Governance, Stanford University).

CLARK, R. (1983) *Family Life and School Achievement: Why Poor Black Children Succeed or Fail* (Chicago: University of Chicago Press).

COLTON, D. (1984) 'Desegregation budgets as constructed reality', *Politics of Education Bulletin*, 11, p. 7.

COONS, J.E. and SUGARMAN, S.D. (1978) *Education by Choice: The Case for Family Control* (Berkeley: University of California Press).

ELMORE, R.F. (1987) 'Choice in public education', in W.L. Boyd and C.T. Kerchner (eds.) *The Politics of Education and Choice: PEA Yearbook 1987* (London: Falmer Press), pp. 79–80.

ERICKSON, D. (1986) 'Choice and private schools: dynamics of supply and demand', in D.C. Levy (ed.) *Private Education: Studies in Choice and Public Policy* (New York: Oxford University Press).

FRIEDMAN, M. (1955) 'The role of government in education'. In R.A. Solo (ed.) *Economics and the Public Interest* (New Brunswick, NJ: Rutgers University Press).

FUCHS, V.R. (1983) *How We Live: An Economic Perspective on Americans from Birth to Death.* (Cambridge, MA: Harvard University Press).

GARMS, W.I., GUTHRIE, J.W. and PIERCE, L.C. (1978) *School Finance: The Economics and Politics of Public Education* (Englewood Cliffs, NJ: Prentice-Hall).

HIRSCHMAN, A.O. (1970) *Exit Voice and Loyalty: Responses to Decline in Films. Organizations and States.* (Cambridge, MA: Harvard University Press).

HUGHES, E. (1958). *Men and Their Work* (Glencoe, IL: Free Press).

JAMES, E. (1986) 'Public subsidies for printers and public education: The Dutch case', in D.C. Levy (ed.) *Private Education: Studies in Choice and Public Policy* (New York: Oxford University Press).

JENCKS, C. (1966), 'Is the public school obsolete?' *The Public Interest*, 2, pp. 18–27.

JONES, T.H. (1987) 'Politics against choice: school finance and school reform in the 1980s', in W.L. Boyd and C.T. Kerchner (eds) *The Politics of Education and Choice: PEA Yearbook 1987* (London: Falmer Press), pp. 153–163.

INBAR, D.E. (1988 forthcoming) 'A "back door" process of school privatization: the case of Israel', in W.L. Boyd and J.G. Cibulka (eds) *Private Schools and Public Policy: International Perspectives* (London: Falmer Press).

KERCHNER, C.T. (1986). 'Union-made teaching: the effects of labor relations on teaching work', in E.Z. Rothkopf (ed.) *Review of Research in Education. Vol. 13* (Washington DC: American Eduational Research Association).

KRASHINSKY, M. (1986) 'Why educational vouchers may be bad economics', *Teachers College Record*, 88 (2), pp. 139—151.

LARSON, M.S. (1977) *The Rise of Professionalism: A Sociological Analysis* (Berkeley: University of California Press).

LIPSKY, D. (1982). 'The effect of collective bargaining on teacher pay: a review of the evidence', *Educational Administration Quarterly*, 18, pp. 14-42.

MITCHELL, D. and KERCHNER, C.T. (1983) 'Labor relations and teacher policy', L. Schulman and G. Sykes (eds.) *Handbook of Teaching and Policy* (New York: Longman).

MURNANE, R.J. (1986) 'Family choice in public education: the roles of students, teachers, and system designers'. *Teachers College Record*, 88(2), pp. 169–189.

NATHAN, J. (1987) 'Results and future prospects of state efforts to increase choice among schools', *Phi Delta Kappan*, 68, pp. 746–752.

NATIONAL GOVERNORS ASSOCIATION (1986) *Time for Results: The Governors' 1991 Report on Education* (Washington DC: NGA).

NISKANEN, W.A. (1971) *Bureaucracy and Representative Government* (Chicago: Aldine-Atherton).

OKUN, A. (1975) *Equality and Efficiency* (Washington DC: The Brookings Institution).

PIGOU, A.C. (1932) *The Economics of Welfare*, 4th edn. (London: Macmillan).

POWELL, A., FARRAR, E. and COHEN, D. (1985) *The Shopping Mall High School: Winners and Losers in the Educational Marketplace* (Boston: Houghton–Mifflin).

ROWAN, B. (1981) 'The effects of institutionalized rules on administrators', in S. Bacharach (ed.) *Organizational Behavior in Schools and School Districts* (New York: Praeger).

STAAF, R.J. (1977) 'The public school system in transition: consolidation and parental choice', in T. Borcherding (ed.) *Budgets and Bureaucrats: The Sources of Governmental Growth* (Durham, NC: Duke University Press).

STARR, P. (1982) *The Social Transformation of American Medicine* (New York: Basic Books).

STOCKMAN, D.A. (1975) 'The social pork barrel', *The Public Interest*, 39, pp. 3–31.

STUBBLEBINE, W.C. (1972) 'Institutional elements in the financing of education', in J.M. Buchanan and R.D. Tollison (eds.) *Theory of Public Choice: Political Applications of Economics*. (Ann Arbor: University of Michigan Press).

WILLIAMSON , D.E. (1975) *Markets and Hierarchies* (New York: The Free Press).

WOLF, C. Jr. (1979) 'A theory of nonmarket failure: framework for implementation analysis', *Journal of Law and Economics*, 22(1), pp. 107–139.

8   *Economic choice and the dissolution of community*

Joseph G. Weeres
Claremont Graduate School

Shortly before Ho Chi Minh initiated his rebellion against the French, he told a French general whom he knew well of his intentions. The general tried to dissuade him by conducting what today we would term a cost-benefit analysis: describing, on the one hand, the enormous array of military forces the French could commit to the conflict; on the other hand, detailing the pitiful resources available to the rebels; and concluding that the revolution would fail because this balance of power would make it impossible for the rebels to enlist the active support of the Vietnamese people.

Ho Chi Minh countered by saying that he was going to prove to the French general that politics was more important than economics. The struggle, he argued, would be for the hearts and minds of the Vietnamese people. Their decisions would be predicated, not on individual self-interest and the calculus of personal costs and benefits, but upon identification with the national interest. The French general's estimates of relative military advantage would prove to be illusory in this context because the revolution would mobilize the resources of an entire people against the French army. France was to learn the hard way that Ho Chi Minh's analysis was correct.

It may seem strange that I should begin a chapter on local school district politics with a description about a conversation between Ho Chi Minh and a French general. But I want to establish at the outset the cultural relativity of the analysis of school politics contained in this paper. Throughout much of the world, individual identification with community (family, village, ethnic group, religious sect, etc). is a more powerful determinant of human behavior than individual self-interest. The most significant decision-making units in these societies are not individual persons, but groups or classes of people exercising collective power to achieve societal benefits.

I shall argue, however, that the reverse is true in American urban politics, because local community governance occurs within an environment dominated by individual economic choice. Individual firms, households, and persons can move freely from one locality to the next, and usually are presented with a diverse menu of different types of cities and school districts from which to choose. Local governments, in fact, must compete with one another to attract businesses and individuals to their communities (Tiebout 1956, Peterson 1981).

Furthermore, the municipal reform movement, by pushing political parties out of urban government and separating school and city governing structures, succeeded in getting politics out of education. It made school districts behave like markets rather than makers of collective political decisions, and made individual choice rather than collective political decisions drive the governing system. Indeed, I shall argue that these economic choices exercised by individuals historically overwhelm the capacity of school districts to govern themselves effectively. As a result, state governments increasingly are being pressed to centralize the governance of public education.

In making this argument, I employ the analytical framework of public choice theory, an extension of economic reasoning applied to the study of politics. Central to this approach is the notion that the fundamental unit of analysis is the rational individual seeking to maximize his or her self-interest. From this basic postulate, a rather elegant model can be constructed that accounts for much of the landscape of contemporary American educational politics. Keep in mind, though, the *caveat* of cultural relativism: the rational economic actor at the heart of this model is a hypothetical creature, and doesn't necessarily represent universal human propensities. What we really are studying are historically specific socioeconomic institutions and their influences on the behavior of people within those societies. By transforming urban governments into markets, municipal reformers made economics more important than politics, and individual choice more salient than collective action.

Economic growth and individual choice

The chaotic consequences of the municipal reform movement upon school district politics were masked for decades by the economic growth within most large metropolitan areas. Migration of farmers into the urban areas, and the Baby Boom following the second World War, fueled an unprecedented expansion of the urban area. This growth generated political stability in school politics through homogeneous grouping of individuals by taste and income, and through the convergence of individual self-interest around the economic gains to be accrued through growth.

Homogeneous grouping

Competitive economic markets, with large resource carrying capacities, tend to segment consumers and firms into isomorphic groups. Firms respond to competition by seeking niches in the market. Consumers seek to optimize the realization of their self-interest by identifying firms that sell products most inexpensively that closely match their preferences.

In 1956, Tiebout applied these economic postulates to the political economy of large metropolitan areas. He argued that local governments put together packages of services (e.g., schools, roads, parks, etc.) to attract fiscally secure taxpayers, and consumers shop for governments that offer the most services for the least tax dollars. The convergence of economically rational citizens and local governments results in a distribution within large metropolitan areas of relatively small, internally homogeneous communities, stratified from one another by the median income of residents and the quality of governmental service.

Segmentation of the populace into small, homogeneous communities, each with its own government, creates conditions conducive to political stability. By freely selecting the community in which they reside, residents already have expressed a measure of consensus about the kind of community they want (and are willing to pay for). The similarity of their incomes also reinforces the probability that individual preference orderings will not diverge widely.

Economic self-interest

Both businesspeople and ordinary citizens benefit economically by community growth. For businesspeople with land holdings, growth provides the opportunity to increase substantially the value of that property. Retail merchants stand to gain a larger base of customers. Bankers and owners of financial institutions can make money through mortgages and direct investment in property.

In order to accrue these gains, however, businesspeople must exercise substantial influence on local governments. City planning commissions directly control the use allocation of land within the city. City commissions enact policies that enhance or diminish the capacity of the city to attract additional residents and businesses. School boards determine where school sites will be located. All of these governmental decisions affect the capacity of businesspeople to make money during periods of economic growth. A retail merchant needs to know beforehand where the major roads are going to be built, where property will be zoned for commercial use, where the kinds of clients who will shop in his or her stores will reside. Owners of land need to control zoning regulations so that they will know which parcels to sell and which to hold for appreciation. Whether a parcel of land will be adjacent to the city dump or the site for a shipping mall makes a great deal of difference in the kind of profit a landowner can secure from the economic growth of the city. Assuming that these businesspeople act rationally, they should become deeply involved in local community politics during periods of economic growth.

Ordinary residents also benefit by growth, through the economic rents they accrue as a result of increases in their property values. When cities build better schools, improved roads, sewage treatment facilities and provide wider ranges of governmental services, they enhance the attractiveness of the community to prospective homebuyers. Existing homes increase in value. However, the cost associated with the provision of governmental goods that produced these increased property values is rarely paid for immediately. Instead, local governments issue bonds in the form of long-term debt. Homeowners who reside in the community during the early phase of growth gain the immediate benefit of an increase in the value of their property, but are able to defer the full cost associated with the existing level of governmental services. These costs are transferred in part to homeowners who move into the community later. As growth diminishes, new residents bear the costs of governmental service, but share less in the 'profit' associated with those services. The last homeowner who moves in before growth ceases, earns no economic rent on growth, and pays the remainder of the governmental debt incurred by the previous homeowner.

Growth, thus, enhances consensus in governmental politics because it orders individual economic preferences. Businesspeople and homeowners share a mutal interest in the growth of the city, and the provision of governmental services necessary to secure that growth. Individuals who will benefit significantly from its realization have an incentive to bear some of the costs associated with its political procurement. They are willing to serve on blue-ribbon committees, to shepherd proposals through planning commissions, to help sponsor school board candidates, and to enlist the participation of individuals more altruistically motivated by the prospects of building a better community. Citizens are also willing to support tax and bond referenda, because it is usually in the economic self-interest to do so.

Under these conditions, it is relatively easy for a school board to earn the right to govern. By enacting policies that enhance growth, and thereby advance most residents' individual self-interests, school boards can secure the kind of political distance from the voters that municipal reformers hoped for. Political demands can be measured against the yardstick of growth. Those that don't square can be rejected with the political certainty that most residents, on balance, will continue to support the board. This places the board in a position to legitimate the activities of its school administrators, and to live up to the reformers' credo that the functions of policy-making should be separated from those of administration.[1]

These conditions, however, generally do not persist indefinitely, for the economic growth is subject to the law of diminishing returns. Tiebout aptly named his seminal paper,

'A pure theory of local expenditures', because it makes the theoretically pure, but unrealistic, assumption that these urban markets clear quickly and completely. In its pure state, changes in the mix of governmental service levels and capacity of residents to pay taxes should result in a reshuffling of all the residents in the metropolitan area sufficient to re-establish internal homogeneity within each community. In practice, this rarely occurs either quickly or completely. Individuals cannot move from one location to the next that easily: the costs are too high. For poor people, such moves often are impossible. Local communities also sometimes diversify their economies to protect themselves from unpredictable economic shifts. The result is that communities develop more heterogeneous populations than Tiebout's pure theory predicts.

Empirically, most communities follow a growth pattern similar to the S-shaped curve associated with the law of diminishing returns. Initially, a community experiences internal growth, adding additional housing units and businesses. But eventually, the community runs out of available land for new housing sites, particularly single family dwellings. The total population of the community then tapers off. As the housing stock and the economic infrastructure age, the community finds it increasingly difficult to attract outsiders with similar taxpaying capacity to purchase the older homes. (The more affluent prospective home purchaser usually can find a new residence in a growing community.) As a result, the composition of the community becomes more heterogeous: older, often retired, residents in the oldest homes (individuals who frequently cannot move because they don't have sufficient disposable income to purchase another residence), the residents who comprised the bulk of the community during the growth phase, and the newer residents who are less affluent, frequently from racial or ethnic minorities.

The speed with which a community moves through this growth pattern varies with the physical size of the community, the supply and demand for housing, and the natural resources associated with the community. Physically large cities will take longer to consume the available stock of land. When demand for housing exceeds supply (as has been the case in many regions during the past few years), a reserve pool of affluent homeowners may be available to purchase the older homes. Communities that contain, or are located adjacent to, areas of great natural beauty (e.g., an ocean) may always be able to attract affluent residents. But most cities, particularly the smaller ones, go through the cycle within twenty to thirty years, the amount of time it takes the housing stock to age sufficiently to make it less desirable.

Figure 1 depicts the S-shaped growth pattern, and the type of school politics associated with each segment of the curve. The growth stage, as we already have seen, is characterized by community consensus and the formation of a community power structure (where the community has some form of industrial and commercial development). Stability and decline, however, produce more chaotic political environments, because the elites who participated during growth generally no longer can accrue a sufficient economic benefit for themselves to offset their costs of political participation. Participation by businesspeople, in particular, should decline.

A partial test of the growth and participation hypothesis

To see whether this hypothesis would hold up to empirical scrutiny, I reanalyzed the raw data from the 1967 51 Permanent Community Sample data set. Clark (1968) and his colleagues at the National Opinion Research Center conducted interviews in the 51 cities designed to measure the influence of specific groups in the city on five different policy areas. I

Figure 1.   Community economic growth pattern and type of community politics.

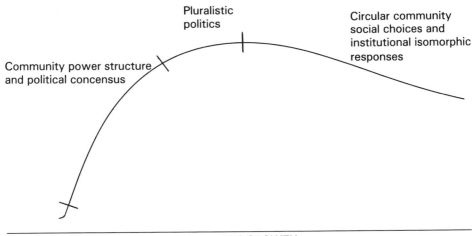

hypothesized that the influence of business groups in these cities would be a function of four variables: (1) economic growth, (2) growth within the SMSA in which the city was located, (3) level of business employment, and (4) the extent to which the city was insulated from business competition within the SMSA. (Appendix B contains a description of the variables and their measurement.)

Table 1 presents the results of the multiple regression models for the influence of specific business groups across an aggregate of five local political arenas: school board elections, municipal bond referenda, mayoral elections, urban renewal, and air pollution. Table 2 presents the results for aggregate influence of four business groups – industrial leaders, financial leaders, retail merchants, other businessmen – on the five specific local political arenas.

Table 1.   Influence of business groups on all five policy arenas.

	Bankers and financial leaders	Industrial leaders	Retail merchants	Other businesspeople	Chamber of commerce
City growth (1950–1980)	0·555***	0·561***	0·378**	0·344**	0·286*
Growth in SMSA (1960–1970)	−0·350**	−0·185	−0·175	−0·034	−0·227
Business employment	−0·018	0·117	0·286**	0·218	−0.023
Business competition	0·077	0·111	0·115	0·178	−0·153
r^2	0·30	0·27	0·16	0·15	0·09

All regression coefficients are standardized

*$P> \cdot 10$
*$P> \cdot 05$
***$P> \cdot 01$

Table 2.   Influence of business groups in specific policy arenas.

	School board elections	Mayoral elections	Municipal bond referenda	Urban renewal	Air pollution	Aggregate of five arenas[†]
City growth (1950–1980)	0·530	0·153	0·538***	0·356**	0·359**	0·519***
Growth in SMSA	−0·314*	−0·253	−0·110	−0·069	−0·082	−0·211**
Business employment	0·156	−0·117	0·080	0·206	0·267*	0·166
Business competition	0·107	−0·132	0·095	0·262*	0·132	0·133
r^2	0·25	0·08	0·26	0·20	0·15	0·24

All regression coefficients are standardized.

*P> ·10
**P> ·05
***P> ·01

[†]includes industrial leaders, bankers, and financial leaders, retail merchants, and other businesspeople, but not the Chamber of Commerce.

As hypothesized, the city growth pattern was connected to business influence. Business groups generally exercised more influence in growth cities than declining ones. This finding held up for all the specific business groups, and across all but one of the political arenas (the mayoral elections). The other three variables did not fare so well. The effect of the growth in the SMSA variable, however, may be underestimated in the equations. Careful inspection of the raw data revealed that growth cities located in SMSAs which weren't growing rapidly had somewhat higher business influence scores than cities in growing SMSAs. The purpose here was to test the opportunity cost of involvement. Collinearity with city growth (Pearson $r = 0.40$) may have masked the effect of SMSA growth. (The signs of the coeffients are all in the hypothesized direction.)

The Permanent Community Sample data provide a severe test of the economic growth and business participation hypothesis, because Clark did not study some of the activities where business groups would be most influential: e.g., city planning commission and urban redevelopment agency. Nevertheless, the results do show that the hypothesis apparently has some empirical applicability to school board politics.

In examining the theoretical argument supporting this hypothesis, I have focused mainly on the effects of growth on economic choice. Growth brought symmetry to the individual preference ordering of most citizens, induced political participation, and provided the foundation for the formation of a political community. Economic decline, however, leads to the dissolution of this sense of community. To see why this occurs, we need to examine the insight that founded public choice theory.

A problem in aggregating individual preferences

One important criterion by which the rationality of individuals is judged is the transitivity of their preference orderings. If an individual has preferences for three goods (A, B, and C), and prefers A to B, and B to C, he or she would, if rational, prefer A to C. An individual who preferred A to B, and B to C, but also preferred C to A, would be revealing that he or she didn't know what he or she wanted. His or her preference ordering would be circular, and thus would violate the criterion of transitivity.

For many years, economists thought that it would be possible to take the preference orderings of individual persons within a group and aggregate them into a preference ordering for the collectivity as a whole. If this could be done, then it would be possible to identify the collective interest or common good for a group, based on the individual preference orderings of its members. On a societal basis, this would make possible the identification of the public interest, while maintaining the integrity of the preference orderings of individual persons.

In 1950, however, Kenneth Arrow, in what now is regarded as the foundation of public choice theory, proved that this quest was impossible given a majority rule principle. While Arrow demonstrated his famous 'impossibility theorem' with mathematical logic, the argument can be presented very simply. Suppose three individuals order their individual preferences for three alternative goods. The first person prefers A to B and B to C. The second prefers B to C and C to A. The third prefers C to A and A to B. Thus we have the following individual preference orderings:

Person No. 1 prefers: A to B to C
Person No. 2 prefers: B to C to A
Person No. 3 prefers: C to A to B

A problem is evident immediately. Although each individual has a transitive preference ordering, the group as a whole, given the majority rule principle, has an intransitive, circular, order to its preferences. The preference ordering of the group follows this pattern:

Individuals 1 and 3 prefer: A to B
Individuals 1 and 2 prefer: B to C
Individuals 2 and 3 prefer: C to A

A majority of the group prefers A to B, B to C, and C to A. The group, in other words, doesn't know what it wants.

Politically, the effect is a voting cycle within the group in which one majority keeps displacing another. The majority that prefers A to B may win initially, but eventually will be removed by the majority that prefers C to A. That majority, in turn, will be pushed out by the majority which prefers B to C. When the majority that prefers A to B reasserts itself, the group will have become ensnarled in an intransitive cycle of majority decisions that leads nowhere.

In the public sector, circular social choice can be mitigated in several ways. Obviously, a dictator can impose either his or her own individual preference ordering on a group, or, in the case of a benevolent leader, install a preference ordering that reduces the probability of a circular choice cycle from developing. In the United States, the two-party system of government traditionally has served a similar function at state and national levels, while still preserving individual freedom of choice. By limiting choice to two final preferences, the two-party system neatly solves the circularity problem under majority rule. (If there are three persons and one prefers A to B, another B to A, and a third A to B, a majority of the group prefers A to B.) The logic of these elections is such that, in order to win, both political parties must appeal to the same set of voters who are clustered around the median on the electoral issues. By impelling candidates to address the same voters, the two-party system assures political stability. (See Appendix A for a more complete description of this process.) Finally, social choice can be based on community norms that mitigate against the pursuit of pure individual self-interest. In a family, for example, individuals may order their preferences, not simply in terms of what they individually want, but on the basis of what other family members want. Children, for example, may to be taught to share. These norms may shape individual preference orderings enough to avoid circular social choice.

The municipal reform movement, however, pushed the political machines out of local government, and the economy of metropolitan areas mitigates against the formation of community norms. The lives of individuals are functionally divided among many communities: they may work in one city, reside in another, and spend their leisure time in several others. The average American moves every seven years. Under these conditions, it becomes very difficult to forge among residents some sort of local community identification that would produce norms strong enough to channel individual preference (see Katznelson and Weir 1985). Economic growth encouraged individuals to invest in city government because it enhanced their own individual economic self-interests. But in the absence of growth, school districts function as markets in which efforts to aggegrate individual preference orderings result in unstable social choices.

The politics of economic decline

After economic growth ceases, many of the individuals who participated earlier no longer have much incentive to contribute to the maintenance of the political system. Significant business leaders, for example, rarely participate in school board politics in economically declining cities. Because economic growth had provided a foundation for pluralistic politics by ensuring that most exchanges involved non-zero sum transactions, the norms of mutual accommodation and trustee boardsmanship may continue for some time after growth flattens out. School superintendents may find that they must 'work' the board more, but consensus on major issues often can still be achieved.

Eventually, however, the cleavages that were created in the community through economic development begin to overwhelm the capacity of community leaders to sustain the norms of pluralistic exchange. The problem often first manifests itself in the incapacity of the board to pass tax and bond referenda. Residents vote their self-interest in turning down additional increases in governmental expenditure when those services no longer will enhance the value of their property. These rejections at the ballot box begin to sever the connection between the electorate and the school board. Admission to the board, which under conditions of economic growth often was controlled by an informal community power structure, now increasingly becomes subject to direct electoral politics. Sponsored candidates find themselves being effectively challenged by representatives from special interest groups. Circular voting cycles emerge as the cleavages engendered by growth become more salient: old residents against new homeowners, the fiscally less well off against the more affluent, businesspeople against homeowners.[2]

Boards often initially try to shield themselves from these conflicts by avoiding controversial issues. They may even strike a deal among themselves only to discuss publicly matters upon which they have already unanimously agreed. Community members, however, counter by taking their demands directly to the superintendent and his or her administrative staff. When some issue arises that the board cannot sidestep (e.g., court-imposed racial integration, school closure), trustee government comes unglued.

The structural weaknesses municipal reform engendered in school district government now become apparent. Trustee boards dissolve into individuals who represent narrow constituencies intensively committed to a single or narrow range of issues. Electoral politics often resembles that associated with multiple-candidate elections: the process yields victories to candidates who cannot retain office. Recall elections ensue, and the electoral process begins to approximate the circularity in Arrow's (1951) social choice paradox.

These intransitivities carry over into the board's efforts at policy-making. The board often is incapable of formulating and maintaining a coherent educational program. Moreover, because board members individually represent narrow interests with intense preference, they feel pressured to cross the boundary that the municipal reformers had set between policy and administration. One symptom is that board members begin going directly to site administrators for information or to give advice or to inspect the school program without first going through the superintendent.

Some economists suggest that under these conditions school administrators become rent-seekers: that they exploit the inability of the board to govern by shaping policy to suit their own self-interests (e.g., to inflate their salaries).

That argument is based on the assumption of bureaucratic failure: that the appointed managers, almost always called bureaucrats in the public choice literature, can, indeed, find the important economic rents they seek. The classic example, noted both by political scientists and economists, is of the pressure to expand public bureaus and augment personal spans of control because advancement in government civil service rankings is related to the number of employees under one's supervision rather than to the quality of one's output (Buchanan and Tullock 1962, Niskanen 1971). However, conditions conducive to self-aggrandizement are particularly absent from the social environment of public schools. Fiscal or status rewards are not closely tied to program or school district size. Relative to the complexity of their jobs, most big city superintendents are badly underpaid in comparison with their rural and suburban counterparts. Most are virtually powerless to make their fiefdoms expand programmatically, and virtually all have lost the fiscal pursestrings to external sources.

More typically, administrators respond by trying to couple themselves to the institutional environment. Professional norms, state and federal regulations, court decisions – all provide a more secure justification for decisions in an unstable political environment than the administrator's own personal judgement. By making local administrative decisions isomorphic with the requirements of the institutional environment, administrators try to secure a measure of stability for local school governments (Meyer and Scott 1983).

Citizen groups also by-pass the local political processes to seek state and federal intervention. For many groups in declining communities, it is economically rational to turn outside for help. By trying to shift the fiscal burden to state and federal government, they can avoid funding programs out of regressive local property taxes that burden citizens in economically declining cities. Politically, it also makes sense because the channeling of external funds enhances their local political clout (Pfeffer 1981).

In the early 1960's, urban decay and population loss was confined mainly to the large central cities. Since then is has engulfed many of the inner ring suburbs. As the scope of decay has spread, federal and state governments have been drawn inextricably into local socio-economic and political conditions. The public policies that have emerged are not driven solely by either local or state/national definitions of need (Thomas 1986). The compromises, however, have produced a confusing pattern of functional responsibilities, making it increasingly difficult for citizens to feel in control of public education. The demands for privatization are likely to get louder.

Conclusion

The capacity of public education to meet the educational needs of our society increasingly is being questioned. Public choice theorists contend that the privatization of education would improve the quality of services and the efficiency of the delivery system. In advancing these proposals they claim that public education is ensnarled in social choice circularities intrinsic to democracy.

This diagnosis, I have argued, is deficient, because school districts already behave as markets, not systems of collective political decision-making. The coincidence of urban growth and decline with individual choice about where to live and do business has created its own cycle of circularity, chaotic and unstable majorities on local school boards, and waves of reform and short issue-attention spans in state legislatures as education competes for issue salience with welfare, highways, prisons, and water projects.

The answer to voting circularities lies not in the market but in the concept of civic behavior, the very existence of which the public choice economists bring into question. Ho Chi Minh recognized the difference between civic interest and self-interest when he realized that the Vietnamese people would rather endure great hardships of their own making than relative ease under French rule. The civic mind considers not only the desirability of the commodity involved, but also the connection between that commodity and others. Without denying the existence of self-interest on the part of elected officials and public employees, the record of major public policy changes over the last generation strongly suggests that something other than individual rent-seeking was taking place. As Kelman (1987: 86–90) argues, legislative votes to support the war on poverty, environmental protection, tax reform, and deregulation in trucking, airline travel, and telephone service were almost all cast *against* the expressed wishes of powerful lobbies. Moreover, there is evidence that individual voters distinguish between the civic good when they vote to support or oppose incumbent candidates. While all voters tended to support incumbent candidates in good times, their votes were virtually unconnected to whether they *personally* had experienced good or bad economic fortune.

Privatization of educational services robs the individual of a vehicle for expressing a public interest. Creating an individual client choice will not allow the one out of five children now being raised in poverty in the United States to alter their circumstances very much, because the economic vote for education which they would receive through a voucher would not materially affect their other surroundings. Only through an ability to aggregate preferences regarding fair distribution can that voice be effective counted.

Notes

1. Districts comprised of affluent, well-educated professionals often generate more turbulent politics than that usually associated with districts experiencing economic growth. The reason is that these residents tend to think of education as a luxury good. As with most luxury goods, individual tastes vary, and the probability increases that conflict will ensue. In the main, though, an interest in growth underlies the turbulence at the surface. While the conflictual politics are troublesome to boards and school administrators, the discord rarely reaches the point where the district's capacity to provide a coherent educational program is imperiled.

2. Stone (1976) describes the conflict within the city of Atlanta between businessmen who wanted to redevelop the downtown area and homeowners who wanted city resources expended in the neighborhoods, thereby enhancing residential property values.

References

ARROW, K. (1950) 'A difficulty in the concept of social welfare', *Journal of Political Economy*, 58, p. 4.
ARROW, K. (1951) *Social Choice and Individual Values* (New York: Wiley).
BUCHANAN, J.M. and TULLOCK, G. (1962) *The Calculus of Consent: Logical Foundations of Constitutional Democracy* (Ann Arbor: University of Michigan Press).

CLARK, T. (1968) 'Community structure, decision-making, budget expenditures, and urban renewal in 51 American communities', *American Sociological Review*, 33, pp. 576–593.

KATZNELSON, I. and WEIR, M. (1985) *Schooling for All: Class, Race and the Decline of the Democratic Ideal* (New York: Basic Books).

KELMAN, S. (1987) 'Public choice and public spirit', *The Public Interest*, 87, pp. 80–94.

MEYER, J. and SCOTT, R.W. (1983). *Organizations and Environments* (Beverly Hills, CA: Sage).

NISKANEN, W. (1971) *Bureaucracy and Representative Government* (Chicago: Aldine Atherton).

PETERSON, P. (1981) *City Limits* (Chicago: University of Chicago Press).

PFEFFER, J. (1981) *Power In Organizations* (Boston: Pitman).

STONE, C. (1976) *Economic Growth and Neighborhood Discontent* (Chapel Hill: University of North Carolina Press).

THOMAS, R. (1986) 'Cities as partners in the federal system', *Political Science Quarterly*, 101, p. 1.

TIEBOUT, C. (1956) 'A pure theory of local expenditures', *Journal of Political Economy* 64, pp. 416–424.

Appendix A.

The logic of two-party elections

To simplify our discussion, let us assume that an election has only one issue (e.g., governmental spending as a percentage of GNP) and that the preferences of voters are evenly distributed along a continuum ranging from zero governmental spending to 100% (with M designating the median voter). Assume further that each voter will favor the candidate who comes closest to his or her position on the continuum. What are the appropriate electoral strategies for the candidates, given their own personal preferences (designated by an $X1$ and $X2$ on the continuum)?

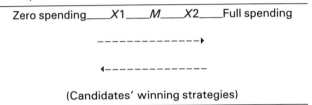

Zero spending____$X1$____M____$X2$____Full spending

(Candidates' winning strategies)

Clearly, the winning strategy for each candidate is to disguise his or her own personal preference, and move towards the center to capture the median voter. If both candidates follow this strategy, they will contest for the narrow range of voters who occupy the center. Elections in two-party systems, in fact, often decided by very small electoral margins (e.g., the Kennedy-Nixon, Humphrey-Nixon, Carter-Ford presidential elections). The politics of 'me-tooism' often characterizes these elections. Candidates agree on most general issues, refuse to offer specific policy proposals (because the opponent could easily adopt a counter winning strategy), and, instead, attempt to woo voters with personality and style. Political consensus and stability mark two-party systems. Voters often find the elections so boring and irrelevant to their personal political preferences that many choose not to vote.

Appendix B.

Measurement of variables from the 51 permanent community sample data set

Data from the PCS consists of interviews with eleven persons in each of the 51 cities: the mayor, the president of the Chamber of Commerce, the head of the largest labor union, the editor of the newpaper with the largest circulation, the chairpersons of the Republican and Democratic parties, the president of the largest bank in the city, the president of the bar association, the health commissioner, the director of urban renewal, and the director of the last major hospital drive. In 1967, each interviewee was asked to judge the influence of a number of different groups and organizations on five different policy arenas: school board elections; municipal bond referenda; mayoral elections; urban renewal; and air pollution. The choice of ratings available to respondents were: (1) support essential; (2) support important, but not essential; and (3) support not important. Included among the groups and organizations the interviewees rated were industrial leaders, bankers and financial leaders, retail merchants, other businessmen, and the Chamber of Commerce.

To measure the influence of each business group on each issue, the ratings of the interviewees were recoded so that 'support essential' was coded as a 2 'support important, but not essential' as a 7, and 'support not important' as a 0. Next, a mean score was calculated for each business group an for each issue area based on the number of interviewees who responded to the question in each of the cities.

The four independent variables were measured as follows:

(1). *City growth*: The total population of each city was plotted from 1950 through 1980. Cities which had had significant and sustained population increases from 1950 through 1970 were coded with a 2. Those whose populations had tapered off or remained stable through 1970 were coded as a 1. Those that had declined during this period were coded as a 0. The cities were divided approximately equally among the three categories. The argument hypothesized a positive relationship between the city growth code and business influence.

(2). *SMSA growth*: the percentage change in total population within the SMSA from 1960 to 1970. A negative relationship supports the hypothesis.

(3). *Business competition*: The total number of manufacturing, retail, wholesale trade, and selective services establishments within the city was divided by the total number of those establishments within the SMSA (US Census of Business Data for 1968). A positive relationship supports the hypothesis.

(4). *Business employment*: The total number of persons employed in manufacturing, wholesale trade, retail trade, and selective services was divided by the city's population (US Census of Business Data for 1968). The hypothesis predicts a positive relationship between business employment and political influence.

9   No school is an island: politics, markets, and education[*]

John E. Chubb and Terry M. Moe
The Brookings Institution and Stanford University

What makes some schools more effective than others? In the view of most educators and policy-makers, it is features of the schools themselves: school autonomy, strong leadership, clear school goals, rigorous academic requirements, an orderly setting, teacher involvement in school decision-making, high parental interest and involvement, and high expectations about student performance. These and related features have been shown in scholarly research to enhance school effectiveness.

State and local policy-makers, under considerable public pressure to do something about the decline in educational quality, are now working earnestly to impose these desirable features on their schools directly. Graduation requirements and homework policies are being made more rigorous. More highly qualified teachers are being sought with the help of better pay and proficiency exams. Principals are being trained to be stronger leaders, teachers exhorted to have higher expectations, and parents encouraged to play a more active role in their childrens' education.

But will these sorts of reforms work? We do not think so. We believe that schools are largely products of their environments and that the fundamental determinants of school effectiveness are to be found in the larger setting or system in which schools operate. Weak leadership, principal-teacher conflict, and other problems do not plague our public schools through inadvertence or misunderstanding or because the people involved are not highly trained or motivated. In most cases, no one is really at fault – the fault lies with the system. Until educational reforms move beyond a narrow focus on schools *per se*, they are doomed to the treatment of symptoms rather than causes.

The public and private environments

The primacy of the environments is well illustrated by a comparison of public and private schools. They obviously have very different environments, offering a rich basis for comparison. In addition, they seem to have different levels of effectiveness: current evidence suggests that private schools are in fact more effiective than public schools at educating comparable students. It is reasonable to expect, then, that private schools already tend to be characterized by precisely those organizational features that reformers have been urging on the public schools – and that it is the environmental differences between the two sectors that largely account for the organizational and performance differences.

In an effort to address these issues, we recently participated in the design of a large-scale survey of public and private schools. Our analysis of the survey will ultimately take the form of a book (Chubb and Moe 1988 forthcoming). This article is a midstream report, summarizing out theoretical arguments and preliminary findings.

Before we turn to the findings, exactly how would we expect public and private schools

[*] This article first appeared in *The Brookings Review*, Fall 1986, © 1986 The Brookings Institution, Washington DC.

to differ? In our view, a good many differences can be anticipated by recognizing that the schools are controlled in fundamentally different ways: one by politics, the other by markets.

Public schools are governed by democratic authority and thus are properly controlled by and responsible to 'the people', particularly local citizens and their representatives on the school board. But this is not the schools' only constituency. State and federal governments also have legitimate roles to play in financing, setting standards, and otherwise bringing their preferences to bear. Citizens everywhere, regardless of whether they have children or even live in the district, have a hand in governing the local school – as do their agents, the politicians and administrators who run the various levels and units of government. Public schools are obliged to respond to all these constituencies, however diverse, difficult to meet, and internally inconsistent their demands might be. Schools are administrative subordinates in a very complex system of political authority and control. About this, they have no real choice.

Private schools are not part of this system of governance. Generally speaking, they are owned and managed. Most have some sort of governing body that at least has the trappings of 'democratic' control, but these are far different from those in the public sector. Private school constituencies are very small and homogeneous by comparison, and the relevant demands and constraints are substantially local. In the typical private setting, it is much clearer who is in charge and what the standards are – and those who disagree are free to seek educational services elsewhere.

The ready availability of the exit option is crucial, for when students and parents are afforded the opportunity to make choices among schools, a second mechanism of social control or governance is at work: the market. Democratic governance is one means by which society can try to shape the nature of its schools, the market is another. It provides direct incentives for private schools to please the immediate consumers of educational services, students and parents. Some of these consumers may place emphasis on academic excellence, others on discipline or work habits, others on religion. However it is segmented, market demand will tend to find its reflection in the supply of services by private schools.

This responsiveness to market demand comes about for two main reasons. First, tuition is a major source of revenue for most private schools. This forges a strong link between financial well-being and school performance, giving the schools important incentives to tailor their policies and programs – and to bolster their effectiveness – in ways that appeal to chosen segments of the market. Second, a natural selection mechanism is operating: even if many schools adapt poorly or unwisely to market demand, those that happen to be providing what people want will succeed and those that do not will fail (or, if subsidized, become small and uneconomical). Adaptation and natural selection combine to ensure that the pool of surviving schools will tend to provide the kinds of services demanded.

Public schools are almost always monopolists in their sectors and are largely sheltered from market forces. Because they are 'free' and accordingly far less expensive than private schools, and because most parents are neither wealthy enough nor obsessed enough with education to change their residence with changes in school quality, public schools have a semi-captive clientele with little choice but to patronize the local monopoly. This is particularly true of low-income citizens. Public schools are sheltered even further by the fact that their funding comes from political authorities via taxation rather than from parents as a fee for services rendered. Parents may complain about the quality of education, but they are not in financial control.

It is of great consequence that our society has chosen to control its schools through politics rather than markets. Because democracy involves many interests, constituencies, and institutional components, and because control is never automatic – requiring rules and regulations, monitoring, and other means of promoting compliance with democratic directives – social control of this sort is implemented through an extensive set of bureaucratic arrangements. The public education system is inherently bureaucratized. It is also very sensitive to the incentives that guide the decisions of politicians and administrators. Ever concerned with re-election and political support, politicians are inevitably responsive to powerful groups – like teacher unions – with strong views about how the system should be structured and operated, views that reflect their own financial and professional stakes. Administrators, for their part, tend to respect, defend, and promote the bureaucratic control mechanisms around which their very jobs are defined. The expressed interests of students and parents are but a small part of all this.

Control in the private sector looks very different. Because the typical school setting is much simpler, the number of participants smaller, and legitimate authority concentrated in the 'owner', the control problem is less onerous and requires a far less imposing bureaucratic apparatus, if any. More importantly, market forces encourage the development of schools that have the kind of policies and organizational characteristics that parents and students find valuable. In this way, the immediate consumers of educational services can 'control' their schools without any administrative apparatus or formal participation at all for directly imposing their preferences.

For reasons that this brief discussion has only begun to suggest, then, there appear to be fundamental differences in the environments of public and private schools due to their orienting structures of politics and markets, and these differences should have pervasive implications for the ways in which schools are organized and operated. In the sections that follow, we will elaborate this line of reasoning in greater detail, and in outlining some preliminary results from the responses to our recent survey, suggest why we think the findings look as they do.

A new survey

Our study builds upon 'High School and Beyond' (HSB), a 1980 survey of more than 1000 public and private schools and some 60,000 of their students. HSB was the basis for *High School Achievement* (Coleman *et al.* 1981). It provides the most detailed as well as the most provocative and influential comparison of public and private schools to date. The central conclusion: private high schools promote substantially more learning – as much as one year's worth – than public high schools do.

HSB was expanded in 1982 by a follow-up survey of 25,000 seniors, whose test score changes from sophomore year to senior year provide direct measures of individual learning. This wealth of information on students, however, was not matched by comparable data on the organization and environments of their schools. If HSB was to be useful in explaining why private shcools seem to perform more effectively, then comprehensive information was required on the schools and their larger settings.

To this end, we participated along with others in a project to supplement HSB with a new survey. Approximately 500 of the original schools were included in this study, with questionnaires administered to the principal and 30 teachers in each. The more than 11,000 responses to this 'Administrator and Teacher Survey' (ATS) permit us to characterize the HSB schools in terms of many of the factors thought to encourage school effectiveness: relationships with parents and outside authorities; leadership; goals; structure; decision-making; and educational practices. If school performance is heavily influenced by environmental and organizational factors, the ATS and HSB surveys taken together will provide the best information ever assembled for explaining how and why – and for developing reforms with real prospects for success.

Below we outline some of our preliminary findings on the organizational and environment of schools. For purposes of comparison, we break down the private sector schools into three types: Catholic, Elite (high performance college prep), and Other Private (a catch-all category). Throughout we suggest why a 'politics and markets' perspective helps explain the pattern of public-private differences. The more complicated task of linking all these characteristics to student performance is tackled in our book (Chubb and Moe 1988 forthcoming).

The findings

External authorities

If the operation of politics and markets suggest anything, it is that public schools should find themselves operating in larger, more complex governing systems and that these governing systems should tend to leave them with less autonomy and control over their own policies, structure, goals, and operation. It is a foregone conclusion that the first proposition is true when it comes to higher levels of political and administrative authority: public schools are part of state and federal governmental systems through various hierarchic and budgetary linkages, and private schools generally are not. But what about immediate outside authorities, those best situated to oversee and constrain the school at the local level?

Not surprisingly, virtually all public school are hierarchically subordinate to school boards and to outside administrative superiors. The private sector is far more diverse. Almost all private schools, regardless of type, have a school board of some sort, but often there is no accompanying administrative apparatus. Such an apparatus is quite rare among the Elite schools and nearly half of the Other Private schools are similarly unencumbered. It is the Catholic schools that most resemble the public schools in this regard; some two-thirds of them have both school boards and administrative superiors.

These are reasonable and not altogether surprising patterns. But they tell us only that private schools are subject to fewer outside authorities; they do not tell us whether the authorities that private schools actually do face are any less demanding than those that public schools face. It turns out that they are less demanding indeed. On five basic policy dimensions – curriculum, instructional methods, discipline, hiring, and firing – school boards in the public sector appear to have more influence over school policy than they do in the private sector, regardless of the type of private school. The differences between public and private are consistently much greater for personnel and disciplinary policy than for matters pertaining to educational practice and content. It is similarly true that private school principals, relative to their school boards, play a more autonomous role in setting policy than public school principals do, and their autonomy is greater over personnel and disciplinary matters than over those concerning curriculum and teaching methods.

When it comes to the influence of administrative superiors, only Catholic schools have a bureaucracy sufficient to justify a comparison to public schools. Here we find that the famed Catholic hierarchy plays, by public sector standards, very little role in setting school policy. On all five dimensions, the influence of administrative superiors is far less in Catholic than in public schools, and Catholic principals have more autonomy in setting school policy than public principals do.

True, these are simple measures of influence. But the patterns they yield are quite uniform and entirely consistent with out expectation that public schools would be subject to greater control by external authorities. The authorities that are so ubiquitous in the democratic context of the public school are often simply absent from private school settings, and even when they are an acknowledged part of the governing apparatus, they are less influential in the actual determination of school policy. Private schools, it would appear, have more control over their own destinies.

Choosing the organization's members

External authorities are by no means the only constraints that limit the ability of a school to structure and operate its organization as it sees fit. Two in particular – tenure and unions – restrict a school's freedom to exercise perhaps its most significant form of control: its ability to recruit the kinds of teachers it wants and to get rid of those who do not live up to its standards. Public schools are much more constrained in these regards.

Our survey shows that 88% of public schools offer tenure while only a minority of the private schools do. Among the schools that do offer tenure, moreover, the proportion of teachers who have actually been awarded it reflects the same asymmetry: 80% of the eligible teachers in public schools have tenure, while the figure is some 10 to 16% lower in the private sector. The differences in unionization are even more substantial. The vast majority of public schools are unionized – some 80% – almost all of them by either the National Education Association or the American Federation of Teachers. In the private sector, by contrast, teachers are rarely represented by unions. Only about 10% of the Catholic schools are unionized; virtually none of the Elites and Other Privates are.

These differences are anticipated by a politics and markets perspective. Tenure systems in public schools are special cases of civil service systems that exist at all levels of government. Historically, these systems arose to prevent politicians from rewarding their supporters with public jobs. Reformers recognized that the widespread use of patronage was inconsistent with the kind of expertise, professionalism, and continuity so necessary to effective government, and – in a halting process that took decades to accomplish – they brought about the pervasive adoption of civil service systems built around objective qualifications and designed to protect employees judged to be meritorious. Tenure is one of the protections.

Public education unions, although initially resisted by politicians wedded to patronage, eventually found political allies of their own. Unions could offer organization, money, manpower, and votes to politicians, and in state and local elections, where voter turnout is typically very low, these are attractive inducements indeed. As education unions thrived, they gained not only economic concessions but contractual guarantees of job security that reinforced the protections of the civil service system and introduced wholly new constraints into personnel decisions affecting the local school.

Although there is nothing to prevent unions from gaining a foothold in private schools nor to keep private schools from adopting tenure and other civil service-like protections, there is nothing comparable to government that drives them in that direction. Whether unions and tenure systems take hold in the private sector is determined to a far greater extent by the market. Schools may choose to offer tenure and other protections as a means of attracting good teachers, particularly given that public schools offer that benefit. But private schools may also decide, especially if the supply of teachers is high, that they can offer a very attractive set of benefits – such as good students, orderly atmosphere, and collegial decision-making – without offering tenure at all. As in any market setting, unions may or may not succeed in organizing teachers. But they cannot count on symbiotic relationships with the authorities, as public unions can, to help their cause.

To assess whether school control over personnel is perceptibly constrained by tenure, unions, and forces outside of the school, we asked principals to evaluate an assortment of potential barriers to hiring and firing teachers. Public school principals are more constrained in both respects. For instance, they face substantially greater obstacles in dismissing a teacher for poor performance than private school principals do. The procedures are far more complex, the tenure rules more restrictive, and the preparation and documentation process roughly three times as long. Their complexity and formality make dismissal procedures the highest barrier to firing cited by public school principals. For private school principals the highest barrier is a personal reluctance to fire. These responses provide a rather poignant statement of the differences between the sectors: while the public school principal is bound most by red tape, the private school principal is bound most by his or her conscience.

Even if superintendents and central offices wanted to delegate greater control over teachers to public school principals – and, in general, there is no reason to think they have incentives to do this – many of these personnel decisions cannot in practice be delegated. In the public sector, tenure protections are usually guaranteed through laws that are written by school boards or state legislatures, and union contracts are typically bargained at the district level. Tenure and unionization tend to settle the question of when and how the basic personnel decisions will be made in the public sector. They will be centralized. In the private sector, schools are largely free of such constraints and have far greater flexibility to choose their own members and chart their own paths.

Parents

In most respects private schools would seem to have ideal parental environments. Parents, after all, have made a positive choice to send their children to a private school, presumably because they care about education and have a high appraisal of the school. And if at any time they change their views, they can exercise their option to exit. This means that the school is likely to enjoy significant gains: they gain children whose family lives encourage education and parents who not only will facilitate school objectives through monitoring and the like, but will be informed and supportive when they take an active interest in school decision-making. Parents who may cause problems are precisely the ones most likely to drop out of the school's environment voluntarily.

Public schools are not so fortunate. Many of their students come from families that put little or no emphasis on education; the students come to school with poor attitudes and orientations, and the parents do little to facilitate the school's efforts. Because private schooling is often not a viable option, many parents who do not support the school's goals, methods, or activities will remain in its environment nevertheless – and some, perhaps many, will use the domocratic mechanisms at their disposal (as well as interactions with principal and staff) to express their discontent and press for change. Far from gaining sustenance from a supportive parental environment, the public school may often find itself dealing as best it can with conflict, disappointment, and apathy.

Not all public and private schools will neatly fit these molds, of course. But it seems clear that characteristics inherent in the two sectors – characteristics anchored in politics and markets – encourage the kinds of environmental differences outlined here. The results from the ATS study are consistent with this line of reasoning. Parents in the private sector, regardless of the type of school, are uniformly more supportive of their schools. They have higher expectations about their children's educational performance, they are more active in monitoring their children's behavior outside of school, and they are more deeply involved with the school as an organization. Private school principals, not surprisingly, also express greater satisfaction with their parental environments. Relationships with parents are more co-operative than in the public sector and less restrained by the kinds of formal rules and norms that, due to democratic governing structures, impinge on the flexibility of public school principals. In short, the operation of politics and markets on parental environments appears to put public schools at a real disadvantage.

The principal

The principal, more than any other single person, is responsible for negotiating successfully with the environment – for dealing somehow with demands and pressures from parents, unions, administrators, and school boards – and is widely regarded as a key to school effectiveness. Excellence in education appears to be promoted by a principal who articulates clear goals, holds high expectations of students and teachers, exercises strong instructional leadership, steers clear of administrative burdens, and effectively extracts resources from the environment.

Less often stressed, however, is that the school environment can have a lot to say about whether the principal is able to practice these precepts of effective leadership – or, for that matter, is even motivated to practice them. Effective leadership does not simply inhere in the individual filling the role; it is unavoidably contingent upon the demands, constraints, and resources that the principal must deal with. Depending on the nature and strength of these forces, even the 'best' principal may have only a marginal effect on school performance.

We found substantial differences between public and private school principals. To begin with, private school principals have considerably more teaching experience – almost four years more for principals in Catholic schools, and over five years more for those in the Elites and Other Privates. Private school principals also come to their jobs with different motivations than their public counterparts. They are more likely to stress control over school policies, while public school principals place geater emphasis on a preference for administrative responsibilities, a desire to further their careers, and an interest in advancing to higher administrative posts.

These differences in experience and motivation appear to shape the principal's performance as a leader. As judged by their own teachers, private school principals are more effective instructional leaders and are more likely to exhibit other basic qualities of leadership – knowledge of school problems, openness with the staff, clarity and strength of purpose, and a willingness to innovate.

From the standpoint of politics and markets, these findings make sense. In the public sector, the administrative hierarchy offers an attractive avenue for career advancement. Public school principals tend to disembark from teaching relatively early, get on an administrative track, and take the job of principal to keep the train rolling. Private principals are scarcely on a track at all. They stay in teaching longer, and their view of the principalship focuses more on its relation to the school than on its relation to their movement up an educational hierarchy.

Of course, these are not the only determinants of leadership. Public school principals are forced to operate in much more complex, conflictual circumstances in which educational success is more difficult to achieve regardless of the principal's (perhaps considerable) abilities. If anything, however, the public school principal's lack of teaching expertise and his or her hierarchic career orientation probably contribute to these leadership problems.

Goals and policies

Given what we know of their environments, there is every reason to expect that public and private schools should adopt very different orientations toward the education of their students. Because public schools must take whoever walks in the door, they do not have the luxury of being able to select the kind of students best suited to organizational goals and structure. In practice this means that the pursuit of educational excellence must compete with much more basic needs – for literacy, for remedial training, for more slowly paced instruction. In addition, the hierarchic structure of democratic control ensures that a range of actors with diverse, often conflicting interests will participate in deciding what the public school ought to pursue and how. Private schools, largely unconstrained by comparison, should find it easier (if they want to do so) to place a high priority on excellence and, whatever their goals, to choose a set that is clear and consistent.

Our results confirmed these expectations. In terms of general goals, public schools place significantly greater emphasis on basic literacy, citizenship, good work habits, and specific occupational skills, while private schools – regardless of type – are more oriented toward academic excellence, personal growth and fulfillment, and human relations skills. These goals are also upheld by specific policies and are clearly discerned by the staff. Private schools have more stringent minimum graduation requirements; their students, regardless of track, must take significantly more English and history, science and math, and foreign language than public school students in order to graduate. In science, math, and foreign language the differences range up to two years. Private schools also have stricter homework policies. Ninety percent of all public schools leave the amount of homework entirely up to teachers. Finally, private teachers uniformly say that school goals are clearer and more clearly communicated by the principal than public teachers report; and they are more in agreement among themselves on school priorites.

All of these characteristics that private schools possess in greater abundance are stereotypical of effective schools. They are also characteristics that, due to the differential operation of politics and markets, would seem extremely difficult for public schools to develop in the same degree.

People, decisions, operation

Politics and markets cannot hope to tell us everything we might want to know about organizational structure and process, but they point us in a clear direction. The critical fact about the public school environment is not just that it is complex, but that it imposes decisions about policy, structure, personnel, and procedure on the school. Nowhere is this more apparent than in the control over the most crucial agent of organizational performance: the teacher.

As we have seen, the public school principal is far less able than his or her private counterpart to staff his or her organization according to his or her best judgment. This, in turn, should promote differences in staff heterogenity and conflict. Public school teachers may reject the principal's leadership, dissent from school goals and policies, get along poorly with their colleagues, or fail to perform acceptably in the classroom – but the principal must somehow learn to live with them. When these teachers are represented by unions, as they normally are, leadership difficulties are magnified. Professionalism takes on new meaning: as a demand that decision-making power be transferred from the principal to the teachers. Private schools are not immune from personnel problems and struggles for power. But the fact that the principal has much greater control over hiring and firing means that he or she can take steps to recruit the kinds of teachers he or she wants and weed out those he or she does not. It also means that teachers have a strong inducement to perform.

By comparison to his or her public school counterpart, the private school principal is better able to create a team of teachers whose values, skills, and willingness to work together tend to mirror those qulifications he or she deems conductive to the pursuit of organizational goals. At the same time, he or she is in a position to make teacher professionalism work for rather than against him or her. Without real threat to his or her own authority or control, he or she can encourage teachers to participate in decision-making, extend them substantial autonomy within their own spheres of expertise and promote a context of interaction, exchange of ideas, and mutual respect.

The data from the ATS survey support this general line of reasoning. Private school principals consistently claim that a larger percentage of their schools' teachers are 'excellent', suggesting that these principals are more confident in the abilities of their own staff members than public school principals are in theirs. Private sector teachers, in turn, have better relationships with their principals. They are consistently more likely to regard the latter as encouraging, supportive, and reinforcing. Private school teachers also feel more involved and efficacious in important areas of school decision-making that bear on their teaching. In particular, they feel more influential over schoolwide policies governing the curriculum, student behavior, teacher in-service programs, and the grouping of students of differing abilities. In their classrooms they believe they have more control over text selection, course content, teaching techniques, and student discipline. Even on matters of hiring and firing, private teachers believe they are more influential, despite the almost complete absence of unions in their sector.

Relative harmony between private school principals and teachers is matched by relative harmony among the private teachers themsleves. On a personal level, relationships are more collegial in the private sector. Stated in the plain terms of the survey, private school teachers are more likely to believe they can count on most staff members to help out anywhere, anytime, even though it may not be part of their official assignment, and that the school seems like a big family. On a professional level, private school teachers give greater evidence of mutual involvement and support. They are more likely to know what their colleagues are teaching, to co-ordinate the content of their courses, and to observe one another's classes. It should come as no surprise, then, that private school teachers also feel more efficacious than public school teachers, are much more satisfied with their jobs, have better attendance records, and tend to work for less money.

In short, private schools do tend to look more like teams. This is what the operation of politics and markets should lead us to expect.

Implications

These results stand to shed light on the puzzle of school performance and the prospects for school improvement. Previous research suggests that private schools outperform public schools and that differences in school performance are associated with differences in school organization. If this research is essentially on target, the results of the ATS survey are, at least in part, to be expected. Private schools turn out to have more of the organizational attributes – such as strong leadership, clear goals, a teamlike atmosphere – that are thought to enhance school performance than do public schools.

We have tried to do more, however, than simply present findings and relate them to existing work. We have also tried to make sense of these differences between public and private schools by arguing the logic of politics and markets. In the most general sense, this argument derives from our belief that environmental context has pervasive consequences for the organization and operation of all schools far more important than most of the literature suggests. More specifically it derives from our belief that the key differences between public and private environments – and thus between public and private schools – are anchored in their characteristic methods of social control.

Public schools are captives of democratic politics. They are subordinates in a hierarchic system of control in which myriad interests and actors use the rules, structures, and processes of democracy to impose their preferences on the local school. It is no accident that public schools are lacking in autonomy, that principals have difficulty leading, and that school goals are heterogeneous, unclear, and undemanding. Nor is it an accident that weak principals and tenured, unionized teachers struggle for power and hold one another in relatively low esteem. These sorts of characteristics constitute an organizational syndrome whose roots are deeply anchored in democratic control as we have come to know it.

Private schools are controlled by society too, but there are few, if any, political or administrative mechanisms to ensure that they respond as they 'should'. They make their own decisions about policy, organization, and personnel subject to market forces that signal how they can best pursue their own goals and prosperity. Given their substantial autonomy, it is not surprising to find that principals are stronger leaders, that they have greater control over hiring and firing, that they and the teachers they choose have greater respect for and interaction with one another, and that teachers – without conflict or formal demands – are more integrally involved in school decision-making. As in the public sector, these sorts of organizational characteristics are bound up with one another, and they jointly arise from the surrounding environment. Different environments promote different organizational syndromes.

If this is essentially correct, the standard proposals for reforming public schools are misconceived. Reformers are quick to say, for instance, that schools should have greater autonomy or that principals should be stronger leaders, but these sorts of reforms cannot simply be imposed on schools in the public sector. In the first place, politicians and administrators have little incentive to support fundamental reform; their careers are tied to their own control over the schools, and they are unavoidably responsive to well-organized interests with stakes in the institutional status quo. To be sure, they have supported certain minor reforms. But these – such as stricter graduation requirements and tougher discipline – leave the basic structure of the system intact.

In the second place, any reform that leaves the basic structure intact will tend to be assimilated and neutralized. In general, the various components of the existing system are so strongly interconnected that any attempt to change one component in isolation will set off a series of compensating adjustments among all the others, mitigating the impact of the reform. While reformers might yearn for a maverick principal who comes on like a strong leader, for example, such a person would quickly tend to get into hot water with political and bureaucratic superiors, teachers, and unions – and find him or herself either looking for a new job or adopting a new leadership style.

While it may seem like heresy, the key to public school improvement may well be to break the bonds of democratic politics. If public schools are to develop the organizational qualities that most research indicates are essential for real improvements in education, it may be necessary to emulate the system of control that governs the private schools, where teaching and professional autonomy flourish. There are various ways in which this might be carried out. But in general terms, effective control over schools would be transferred from government to the market. Government would still set minimum requirements. It also would provide funding, likely in the form of vouchers allocated to parents. But virtually all the important decisions about policy, organization, and personnel would be taken out of the hands of politicians and administrators and given over to schools and their clients: the students and their parents.

In a system requiring competion for students and resources, schools would have incentives to move toward more efficient and effective forms of organization. Schools that cling to costly bureaucratic methods, that do not attract and utilize talented people, that fail to encourage collegial and productive relationships among their members, or that lack strong leadership towards clearly defined educational goals – that is, schools that look like many of today's public schools – would tend to go out of business. Effective schools would tend to prosper.

This is a reform so profound and threatening to established ideas and practices that it may not be taken very seriously. But if schools are largely products of their environments, it may be the only reform that can substantially improve their performance.

References

CHUBB, J.E. and MOE, T.M. (1988 forthcoming) *Politics, Markets, and School Performance* (Washington DC: The Brookings Institution).
COLEMAN, J.S., HOFFER, T. and KILGORE, S. (1981) *High School Achievement.* (New York: Basic Books).

10 Why school reform doesn't change schools: political and organizational perspectives

David N. Plank
University of Pittsburgh

Introduction

The school reform movement has recently played to mixed reviews. Allen Odden has asserted that the movement 'has moved faster than any public policy reform in modern history' (Odden 1986: 335). William Lowe Boyd has called the school reform movement 'the most sustained and far-reaching reform effort in modern times', and has described its accomplishments as 'truly extraordinary' (Boyd 1987: 28).

In the same article, however, Boyd has suggested that the school reform movement has brought about 'less *real* reform . . . than meets the eye' (p. 21). Richard Rossmiller has described the movement as 'more symbolic than substantive', responsible for little in the way of significant change in the schools (Rossmiller 1986). Others, including Albert Shanker and Terrence Deal, have disparaged the effects of recent reforms on schools, teachers, and students, and have begun to call for 'structural' rather than symbolic changes (Rodman 1987, Nienhuis 1987).

Similar disagreements have emerged in evaluations of the financing of school reform. Deborah Inman has argued that the states have not provided sufficient funds to support 'comprehensive school reform', and also that the states have often failed to appropriate sufficient revenues to support specific reform initiatives (Inman 1987). In contrast, Allen Odden has concluded that real increases of between 20 and 25% in total educational revenues between 1983 and 1987 represent a clear and sufficient commitment to translate reform rhetoric into action (Odden 1987).

These assessments are not necessarily contradictory. The school reform movement has had important consequences for school systems in many parts of the country. Widely adopted changes include increases in public expenditures on education; statewide assessment of student achievement; higher standards for high school graduation and teacher recruitment; and extensions in the school day and school year. Many changes have taken place in American education in the past five years, and large real increases in educational revenues have accompanied them (US Department of Education 1984, *Education Week* 1985, Bell 1986, Odden 1987).

At the same time, however, most of the reforms that have been adopted in this period have not significantly altered the traditional structure and functioning of American public school systems. Quantitative analyses of reform commonly measure change in terms of the number of undifferentiated 'reforms' adopted in each of the states, but some reforms entail far more significant consequences for schools and students than others. Nearly all of the reforms that have been adopted in the past five years have left the structure and operation of American schools and school systems largely intact. Moreover, new education revenues have often been used to increase funding for current programs, rather than to support specific reform initiatives.

In this chapter I present a preliminary assessment of the character and consequences of the recent school reform movement. In the first section I present a typology of school reforms, in which recent reforms are grouped in four categories according to the degree of organizational change which they entail.[1] An analysis of published state by state comparisons of reform legislation indicates that the most widely adopted reforms are those that require the smallest organizational changes.

State-by-state comparisons of reform initiatives also indicate that the largest effects of the reform movement have been observed in previously laggard areas, including Southern states and poor and rural school districts within states. In the second section of the chapter I argue that the principal consequence of the reform movement to date has been further homogenization of educational standards and practices across states and across districts, rather than innovation or differentiation.

In the third section I present two complementary explanations for the observed pattern of changes brought about by the school reform movement. The first of these suggests that the bargaining necessary to win approval for educational reform in a pluralist political system serves to blunt radical initiatives and to reduce the likelihood of structural change. The second identifies three sets of internal and environmental factors at work in organizational fields that constrain the growth and development of similar organizations along increasingly similar lines. In the concluding section of the paper I assess the current state of the movement and the prospects for the 'next wave' of school reform.

A typology of school reforms

Figure 1 provides a summary of the major educational reforms adoped in the American states in the years since 1983, categorized into four groups: additive reforms, external reforms, regulatory reforms, and structural reforms. The four categories of reforms are ranked in terms of the magnitude of the organizational changes that they entail, with additive reforms requiring the least change and structural reforms the most.

Additive reforms

Additive reforms are changes that aim to improve the perfomance of the schools by adding new programs and functions or by increasing the resources available to educators. In the most recent period of American school reform such changes have included new revenues for

ADDITIVE	EXTERNAL	REGULATORY	STRUCTURAL
New revenues	Pre-service teacher tests	Longer school day	Career ladders
Increased salaries	Certification changes	Longer school year	Smaller classes
Pre-school initiatives	Education school standards	Fewer extracurricular activities	In-service teacher tests
Mandatory kindergarten	New HS graduation requirements	More basic skills	Vouchers/tax credits
Computer literacy	Exit tests	Statewide assessment	
Aid or prospective teachers	New college admission standards		

Figure 1.   Typology of major school reforms

schools, salary increases for teachers, computer literacy programs, and compensatory efforts of various kinds, including the establishment of mandatory kindergarten and pre-school programs in states which previously lacked them. Additive reforms have relatively small effects on the organizational character of schools, offend no significant interests, and enhance the legitimacy and prestige of educators. Because they generate little opposition and are relatively easy to implement, they are the most widely-observed variety of educational reforms, in the current as in previous reform movements.

External reforms

External reforms are reforms where the costs of change can be imposed on organizational outsiders, including students and prospective teachers. External reforms imposed on students in the current reform movement have included increased high school graduation requirements, 'exit tests' for high school graduation, and increased college admission standards. Those imposed on prospective teachers have included pre-service competency tests, 'fifth-year' teacher training programs, stiffer teacher certification requirements, and so on.

External reforms are based on the assumption that the causes of educational problems lie outside the educational system, and that better inputs to the system (e.g., more effort by students, more highly-qualified recruits to teaching) will result in better outputs (e.g., higher achievement) without changes in the system itself. External reforms may generate protest among affected constituencies: students and parents may dislike 'no pass, no play' rules, and teachers' colleges may resist the imposition of 'fifth-year' teacher education programs. Such reforms confirm the competence and legitimacy of current educators, however, and they leave the structure and operation of schools and school systems unchanged. They are consequently likely to be welcomed by politically powerful groups, including school boards and teachers' unions.

Regulatory reforms

Regulatory reforms commonly entail the intensification of present activities. In this category of reforms are longer school days and school years, smaller class sizes, cutbacks in extra-curricular activities, renewed emphasis on the core curriculum and 'basic skills', statewide achievement testing, and so on. Regulatory reforms acknowledge that some of the causes of educational problems lie within the educational system, and they may require changes in the behavior of some organizational members. At a minimum, they require teachers and administrators to put more time and effort into their jobs. Like additive and external reforms, however, regulatory reforms are based on the assumption that the structure of the educational system is sound, and that more of what the schools are doing now – more time, more effort – is all that is needed to bring about improvement.

Regulatory reforms increase the workload of educators and may result in closer supervision and regulation of schools, administrators, and teachers. They are likely to lead to increased standardization in educational programs across districts and across states, but they do not otherwise require changes in the way schools are structured or in the way they work.

Structural reform

Structural reforms require alterations in the structure and operation of schools and school systems. They disrupt organizational routines, threaten organizational members, and may call into question the school system's legitimacy, efficacy, and claim on public resources. Recent proposals for structural reform include career ladder and 'merit pay' plans, competency tests for present teachers, and educational vouchers and tax credits. Such reforms challenge widely-shared assumptions about the nature and purpose of education by proposing redefinition of (for example) who is entitled and qualified to teach, or of what kinds of institutions are or are not 'schools'. Proposals for structural reform evoke powerful opposition from constituencies with interests in the present educational system, and are only rarely proposed and even more rarely adopted.

The outcomes of the school reform movement

An assessment of state-level reform initiatives in the years between 1983 and 1985 indicates that almost all of the reforms adopted in this period fall into the first three categories[2] (see table 1). Nearly all states have provided additional revenues for public schools as a consequence of the reform movement, and most have also attempted to increase the quality of inputs provided to the educational system by raising standards for students and prospective teachers. Significant numbers have introduced a variety of regulatory reforms, including increases in the length of the school day and the school year and new curriculum standards. In contrast, only a handful have proposed structural changes in the way schools and school systems are organized and operated.

The most striking feature of table 1 is the disproportionate number of external reforms that have been introduced in the current reform period. Virtually all states have approved measures aimed at improving the quality of inputs to the educational system and regulating the environment of the system. High school graduation requirements have been increased in almost every state; stiffer teacher certification requirements and pre-service competency tests for teachers have also been widely adopted. The distinguishing characteristic of these reforms is that they require virtually no changes in the present structure or operation of schools. Instead they seek to change the behavior of students and prospective teachers, in the hope that this will be suficient to improve the performance of the educational system.

The important exception to the general failure to adopt structural reforms in state educational systems is the career ladder for teachers, variations of which have been introduced in 24 states (Bell 1987: 19–20). Career ladders represent a potentially significant change in the way educational systems are organized, insofar as they pay teachers on the basis of what they do (and possibly how they do it) rather than simply on the basis of credentials and years of experience. The extent of the changes that will ultimately be observed remains to be seen, however. In some states the revenues needed to fund career ladders have not been appropriated by the legislature (Inman 1987). In other states, including Texas, revenues appropriated to support career ladders have been distributed as across-the-board salary increases in some districts for lack of an acceptable procedure for determining salary differentials.

Most of the other structural reforms that have been adopted (e.g., 'merit pay' plans in Florida and Tennessee, and parental choice plans in Minnesota and Colorado) are now being abandoned or scaled back to make them more acceptable to educators. The institution of a competency test for present teachers in Texas generated intense political conflict, and was an

Table 1. Approved reforms, by states and categories, 1983–1985.

State	Additive[a]	External[b]	Regulatory[c]	Structural[d]	Total	% Change in Educational Revenues[e]
*AL	1	6	2	0	9	5.21
AK	0	2	1	0	3	33.17
AZ	0	6	2	0	8	−7.15
*AR	1	2	3	0	6	25.16
CA	1	5	2	1	9	29.70
CO	0	0	1	0	1	26.20
CT	0	3	1	0	4	25.30
DE	2	4	4	0	10	16.66
*FL	1	6	4	1	12	31.05
*GA	1	6	1	0	8	22.13
HI	0	1	0	0	1	12.85
ID	1	3	2	1	7	15.22
IL	0	1	0	1	2	6.63
IN	0	4	2	0	6	24.33
IA	0	3	0	0	3	−5.06
KS	1	4	2	1	8	10.43
*KY	1	5	3	0	9	14.54
*LA	2	6	3	0	11	11.09
ME	3	4	1	1	9	20.95
MD	0	4	0	0	4	16.91
MA	0	1	1	0	2	16.94
MI	0	0	2	0	2	−4.24
MN	1	0	1	0	2	12.98
*MS	2	4	2	0	8	26.00
MO	1	6	0	0	7	17.76
MT	0	2	0	0	2	5.70
NE	0	3	1	1	5	7.46
NV	0	4	1	0	5	25.61
NH	0	3	3	0	6	23.79
NJ	1	4	0	1	6	21.23
NM	0	3	0	0	3	3.17
NY	0	5	0	0	5	19.43
*NC	1	7	4	0	12	24.94
ND	0	0	2	0	2	2.91
OH	0	2	2	0	4	10.31
*OK	1	3	1	1	6	−22.52
OR	0	3	1	0	4	1.29
PA	0	4	1	0	5	17.52
RI	0	4	1	0	5	13.14
*SC	3	5	5	1	14	14.28
SD	0	4	1	0	5	6.61
*TN	2	6	3	1	12	20.31
*TX	1	6	2	1	10	32.04
UT	0	3	0	1	4	14.55
VT	0	3	2	0	5	15.74
*VA	1	5	1	1	8	28.59
WA	0	3	1	0	4	22.38
WV	1	3	3	0	7	12.02
WI	0	1	1	0	2	16.77
WY	0	2	1	0	3	34.04
	30	174	77	24	295	17.51

[a]Additive reforms: salary increase, new minimum salary, mandatory kindergarten, pre-school initiatives.
[b]External reforms: pre-service competency tests, revised certification standards, raised education school standards, aid to prospective teachers, raised graduation standards, exit test, raised college admission standards.
[c]Regulatory reforms: Longer school day/school year, limits on extracurricular activities, reduced class size, statewide assessment, promotional gates test.
[d]Structural reforms: career ladder, merit pay.
[e] 1983–1987, constant dollars.
*Southern states.
Sources: Education Week, 11 February 1985; Odden 1987, table 9.

important factor in the electoral defeat of the governor who proposed the test. Despite (or perhaps because of) the controversy, the test that was finally administered was passed by more than 99% of the state's teachers, and plans to administer subject-specialty tests have since been dropped.

Analysis of the state-by-state data presented in table 1 suggests that the main effect of the recent school reform movement will be to increase the similarities among American school systems, both within and across states. At the state level the broadest array of educational reforms has been adopted in the South, where levels of expenditure and educational standards were previously relatively low (Peterson 1984). Reforms in most states outside the South have been less sweeping. The recent reform movement has allowed Southern states to begin to 'catch up' with historically more advanced states, and Southern school systems will look more like Northern school systems as a result.[3]

Similarly, virtually all of the widely-adopted reforms will have their largest effects in poor and rural districts which did not previously meet the new standards. Legislation requiring minimum salaries for teachers, for example, will have small short-run effects in urban and suburban school districts, where salaries already meet or exceed statutory minimums. In rural districts, however, such legislation can bring about large increases in salaries. This is equally true of new curriculum standards and graduation requirements, which will serve primarily to bring poor and rural districts into compliance with standards already in effect in more prosperous districts. The result will be further standardization in the operation of local school districts within states (Plank 1986).

The rhetorical shift from 'equality' to 'excellence' among school reformers has been widely-noted (Iannaconne 1985, Clark and Astuto 1986, Boyd 1986). Despite this shift, however, the substance of many of the reforms adopted durng the current reform movement is in fact similar to that of earlier, ostensibly 'equalizing' reforms, and equity issues have been and remain at or near the top of reform agendas in most states (Strain 1985, Chance 1987). Reform packages in several states have included changes in the school funding formula that shift resources from wealthy to poor and urban school districts. Other reforms raise minimum performance standards for schools and for students, and may be expected to improve the quality of education received by students in previously disadvantaged states and school districts.

Moreover, the reforms that have been widely adopted do not generally offer incentives for innovation and differentiation among schools and school districts, but instead impose futher standardization. Such changes tend to advance an equalizing agenda rather than one dedicated to 'excellence'. The recent shift in rhetoric may be important in itself, or it may portend a more significant shift in policies in the future, but to date the consequences of the new rhetoric have been smaller than has often been asserted.

Educational reform and organizational change

In this section I present two complementary explanations for the failure of the recent school reform movement to bring about significant changes in the structure and functioning of American schools.[4] The first argument suggests that competition and bargaining in a pluralist political system tend to prevent the adoption and implementation of structural educational reforms. The second asserts that identifiable dynamics in 'organizational fields' constrain the development of organizations pursuing similar goals (like public school systems) along increasingly similar lines.

School reform and pluralist politics

In many states, reform proposals were developed by heterogeneous 'blue-ribbon' commissions or in close consultation with affected constituencies. Among the many weaknesses of commissions as engines for reform is the practically mandatory effort to include among commission members representatives of all affected interests, and the common requirement that endorsement of all commission recommendations be unanimous (Peterson 1983). Such practices have the advantage that commission recommendations are widely supported and potentially achievable, but they have the corollary disadvantage that little in the way of significant change is proposed. Data on several of the national reform commissions confirms that the memberships of the panels were nearly identical, with similar representatives on each panel from a variety of key constituencies: large corporations, teachers' unions, colleges of education, state legislatures, and so on (Ginsberg and Plank, n.d.).

'Blue-ribbon' commissions have been a favored strategy for developing reform proposals at the state level as well, with similar consequences. All 50 states appointed commissions to study the problems of their educational systems in the first two years of the reform movement; many appointed more than one. As at the national level, these commissions commonly included representatives from a diverse array of constituencies, and as a result they came forward with relatively innocuous reform proposals. In states which have not relied on reform commissions (e.g., Pennsylvania) reform proposals have nevertheless been developed in close consultation with all affected constituencies, with similar results.

In some states (e.g., Texas, Arkansas, Florida, and Minnesota) education-minded governors have put forward more radical proposals for reform over the opposition of important constituencies, including teachers. Even in states where this strategy was successful and structural reforms were proposed, however, interest groups opposed to reform (e.g., teachers, fundamentalists, advocates of local control) have for the most part been successful in forcing compromises on proposals for structural change, or at least in scaling back major reforms prior to implementaton.

Another factor limiting the scope of the school reform movement has been the cost of reform proposals. Major educational reforms (e.g., career ladders) can cost a lot of money, and political support has not always been forthcoming for the tax increases or cutbacks in existing programs needed to fund reform initiatives. Even in states like Texas where major reforms have been adopted (and tax increases approved) ambitious proposals have been scaled back for lack of the resources to pay for them, and a deteriorating financial situation has required cutbacks in newly-established programs.

According to this argument, then, the exigencies of bargaining in a pluralist political system have tended to limit reform proposals to those that can win the approval of all interested groups, with the consequence that changes in the structure and operation of state educational systems have not been seriously considered. In those states where more radical changes have been proposed the opposition of key constituencies and the lack of adequate funding for ambitious new programs have produced compromises on initial reform proposals, and have limited the implementation of reform initiatives.

School reform and instituational isomorphism

A second argument is based on recent work in organizational therory, and especially on work by DiMaggio and Powell (1983). According to this argument, the growth and development of organizations in common organizational fields (like public school systems) is constrained by the operation of three overlapping sets of environmental and internal factors, which together foster institutional isomorphism. Through these processes organizations pursuing similar goals come increasingly to resemble one another. DiMaggio and Powell identify these processes as 'coercive', 'mimetic', and 'normative'.

Coercive factors include legal and fiscal regulations that limit the changes that can be made in public school systems if they are to retain their legitimacy and claim on public resources. Legal requirements that all children between certain ages be enrolled in school, that teachers be certified by the state, and that curricula include some subjects and exclude others establish a framework for public school systems within which only limited variability is possible (Meyer and Rowan 1977). Many of the relevant legal boundaries to educational reform are defined at the national level, and these impose a common character on school reforms across states. Legislation governing schools at the state level imposes a similar uniformity across districts.

Mimesis is the tendency for organizations to imitate innovations adopted by more successful or more prestigious organizations in their fields, including, for example, educational reforms adopted in wealthier or more industrialized states. Mimesis has been an important factor in the recent school reform movement, as many of the most widely-adopted reforms (e.g., minimum teachers' salaries, increased graduation requirements) have been based on standards established in more advanced states and districts, and as governors have competed to establish their credentials as reformers and to demonstrate their states' commitment to education. Reforms that have proven to be achievable or effective in one state have been enacted in others, and policy networks of governors and state education officials have worked actively to develop a common agenda.

Normative factors include the common training, intellectual networks, and professional journals that govern professional employees' (e.g., teachers') sense of what practices and procedures are legitimate in a particular organizational field. Shared values and common definitions of what is appropriate and effective confine reform proposals to relatively narrow boundaries. In the current reform movement educators have played a central role in defining the reform agenda, even in states where some reforms have been adopted over their objections (Chance 1986: 105–106). Moreover, the implementation of school reforms depends decisively on educators, and in practice teachers and administrators are often able to shape legislative mandates to fit their own beliefs about legitimate educational practice.

In summary, structural reforms in American school systems are hard to imagine and even harder to achieve, because such changes call into question the legitimacy and claim on public resources of the educational system. They disrupt familiar organizational routines that are valued by administrators, teachers, and parents. They often imply large real costs for current employees of educational systems, in return for presumed future benefits which are widely diffused, difficult to specify, and impossible to measure. They challenge common understandings about what educational systems look like and how they work.

Under these circumstances the homogenizing character of most recent reforms is not surprising: such changes reaffirm the value and legitimacy of the present educational system, and require only modest changes in familiar structures and routines. They bring schools and school systems into closer conformity with standards established by more successful models, and confirm the wisdom and probity of those currently in charge of the system, and of those who put them there. Such incremental reforms are unlikely to bring about great improvements in the performance of the educational system, but neither do they impose large costs or undue risks.

Conclusion

In concert, the exigencies of political bargaining and the operation of the organizational dynamics described by DiMaggio and Powell have had two consequeces for the school reform movement. First, they have almost uniformly limited the reforms that have been proposed and adopted in state legislatures to those that reinforce rather than challenge the present structure and functioning of American school systems. Second, they have constrained school reform movements in the 50 states in ways that have ensured that the main consequence of reform has been further homogenization rather than differentiation among school systems, both across and within states.

Current assessments of the school reform movement have begun to reflect some disenchantment with the effects of recent school reforms (Olson 1987). Though the movement has not accomplished all that its supporters promised, however, it has brought about some important changes in American schools, especially in the South and in rural areas. The reform movement has not changed schools in profound ways, but it has raised public awareness of educational issues and has improved the quality of education provided to large numbers of children, especially those who were previously disadvantaged.

Current calls for the 'structural reform' of American schools reflect this disenchant-ment, but there is not yet a very clear sense of what structural reforms would look like, or of how to bring them about (California Commission on the Teaching Profession 1985, Task Force on Teaching as a Profession 1986, National Governors' Association 1986). There is an emergent recognition, though, that 'the next wave' of the reform movement will have to foster local initiatives and differentiation among schools and school districts if significant improvements are to be made in the performance of the American educational system (Education Commission of the States 1987). This is to be welcomed, but in light of the political and organizational obstacles to major changes in the structure or operation of schools and school systems discussed here, there is little reason to be optimistic about the movement's prospects.

Notes

1. Throughout this paper, the term 'reform' refers to changes in educational systems brought about by executive or legislative action at the state level. Local efforts at school improvement (e.g., the 'effective schools' movement) are not directly considered.

2. I am now compiling similar data on reforms adopted in the years since 1985. I do not expect these to require significant changes in the arguments presented here.

3. Between 1983 and 1985 the 37 non-Southern states approved an average of 4.59 reform initiatives, while the 13 Southern states approved an average of 9.61 reforms. The difference in means between the two groups is significant at the 0.001 level. In terms of financial support for reform, the 13 Southern states increased their spending on public schools by an average of 17.91% between 1983 and 1987, while the 37 non-Southern states increased their spending by an average of 14.75%. The difference in the two means is not statistically different from zero, and the southern states are starting from a lower base. The process of catching up thus may be a slow one.

4. For a similar argument from a different historical period see Plank (1987).

References

BELL, T.H. (1987) 'Education in America: is the nation still at risk?' Horace Mann lecture at the University of Pittsburgh, reprinted in the University of Pittsburgh School of Education *Newsletter*, Winter, 1, pp. 18–20.

BOYD, W.L. (1986) 'Public education's last hurrah: schizophrenia, amnesia, and ignorance in school politics', paper presented to the annual meeting of the American Political Science Association, Washington DC.

BOYD, W.L. (1987) 'Rhetoric and symbolic politics: President Reagan's school reform agenda', *Education Week*, 18 March, pp. 21, 28.

CALIFORNIA COMMISSION ON THE TEACHING PROFESSION (1985) *Who Will Teach Our Children?* (Sacramento: CCTP).

CHANCE, W. (1986). '... *The Best of Educations*' (Washington DC: The John D. and Catherine T. MacArthur Foundation).

CLARK, D.L. and ASTUTO, T.A. (1986) 'The significance and permanence of changes in federal education policy', *Educational Researcher*, 15 (8), pp. 4–13.

DIMAGGIO, P.J. and POWELL, W.W. (1983) 'The iron cage revisited: institutional isomorphism and collective rationality in organizational fields', *American Sociological Review*, 48, pp. 147–160.

EDUCATION COMMISSION OF THE STATES (1987) *The Next Wave: A Synopsis of Recent Education Reform Reports* (Denver: ECS).

Education Week (11 February 1985) 'Excellence: a 50 state survey'.

GINSBERG, R. and PLANK, D.N. (n.d.) 'Catch the wave: the structure of educational reform commissions', unpublished manuscript.

IANNACONNE, L. (1986) 'Excellence: an emergent educational issue', *Politics of Education Bulletin*, 12 (3) pp. 1, 3–8.

INMAN, D. (1987) 'The financial impact of educational reform', paper presented to the annual meeting of the American Educational Research Association, Washington DC.

MEYER, J.W. and ROWAN, B. (1977) 'Institutionalized organizations: formal structure as myth and ceremony', *American Journal of Sociology*, 83, pp. 340–363.

NATIONAL GOVERNORS' ASSOCIATION (1986) *Time for Results* (Washington DC: NGA).

NIENHUIS, M. (1987) 'Reformers neglect schools' cultures, author says', *Education Week*, 4 February, p. 15.

ODDEN, A. (1986) 'Sources of funding for education reform', *Phi Delta Kappan*, January, pp. 335–340.

ODDEN, A. (1987) 'The economics of financing education reform', paper presented to the annual meeting of the American Educational Research Association, Washington, DC.

OLSON, L. (1987) 'Less is more: coalition rethinking the basic design of schools', *Education Week*, 18 February, pp. 1, 22–24.

PETERSON, P.E. (1983) 'Did the reform commissions say anything?' *Brookings Review* (Winter), pp. 3–11.

PETERSON, P.E. (1984) 'The politics and economics of school reform', paper presented to the Conference on Educational Policy sponsored by the Center for Legal Studies on Intergovernmental Relations at Tulane Univerity.

PLANK, D.N. (1986) 'The ayes of Texas: rhetoric, reality, and school reform', *Politics of Education Bulletin*, 13, (2), pp. 9–13.

PLANK, D.N. (1987) 'Educational reform and organizational change: Atlanta in the Progressive Era', *Journal of Urban History*, in press.

RODMAN, B. (1987) 'Futrell asks group to work with NCATE; broaden agenda, Shanker urges', *Education Week*, 11 February, p. 16.

ROSSMILLER, R. (1986) 'Some contemporary trends and their implications for the preparation of educational administrators', *UCEA Review*, 27 (1), pp. 2–3.

STRAIN, S. (1985) 'School finance equalization: progress in Texas?' paper presented to the annual meeting of the American Educational Research Association, Chicago.

TASK FORCE ON TEACHING AS A PROFESSION (1986) *A Nation Prepared: Teachers for the 21st Century* (New York: Carnegie Forum on Education and the Economy).

US DEPARTMENT OF EDUCATION (1984) *The Nation Responds: Recent Efforts to Improve Education* (Washington DC: USDE).

11 Politics against choice: school finance and school reform in the 1980s

Thomas H. Jones
University of Connecticut

The German word *zeitgeist* means 'spirit of the age' a distinctive aphorism describing a leading trend of thought within a particular time period. The idea that all pupils, regardless of their family's financial means and place of residence, should choose more freely among schools has been a candidate for *zeitgeist* during the present decade.

School choice finds allies among scholars, practitioners and politicians. The idea has generated a spate of writings advocating choice and considerable scholarly empirical investigation. An incumbent president, extremely popular during much of his term of office, advocates choice. Some governors have given the idea a guarded endorsement. Although the ratings have diminished since, a 1983 Gallup Poll found that 51% of Americans favored allowing parents to choose among government-financed private, parochial and public schools.[1] Financial mechanisms to facilitate choice have been the subject of policy proposals at all levels of government. For all these reasons there has been some expectation that 'school choice' would take its place alongside the 'common school movement', the 'progressive era', and 'equal educational opportunity' as descriptors of historic shifts in American education.

The position put forward here however, is that the choice 'movement' is losing ground. Far from being a 1980s *zeitgeist*, choice will turn out to be an historical footnote to education in the 1980s. The evidence supporting this thesis comes from personal observations and efforts to promote school choice in one state[2], and from nearly any issue of *Education Week*, the *Phi Delta Kappan*, or any education policy journal you care to peruse: as a pervasive national movement choice simply has not caught on. Although it clearly has some appeal as a concept, choice has *not* had much direct influence on political behavior nor is it likely to in the near future. This is so despite the substantial successes of recent reforms of the public schools the 'excellence' movement, teacher salary and qualifications provisions, in-service education for teachers, and so on.

Why choice politics fail

Educational choice is not a sudden controversy. From the time of the common school movement in the early nineteenth century, school choice has been a public issue, although in the early years of the republic, distinctions between private and public schools were not recognized with the same precision as they are today. Schools organized and controlled by religious bodies sometimes received public financing and might be open to all children within a particular community. On the other hand, prayer and religious observances in the public schools were not uncommon.

By the latter decades of this century a critical policy distinction had been built around the broadly social and secular mission of the public schools versus the client-based and frequently religious mission expressed by private schools. Arguably, the most important actor in developing the broad outlines of this policy distinction between school sectors has been the judiciary. Guiding the judiciary in financial as well as other educational matters has been the constitutional principle requiring a 'wall of separation' between church and state.

In delineating this 'wall of separation' as applied to school finance, the general pattern of policy formation had been state legislative enactment followed by subsequent judicial review. The scenario is as follows. Private school interests were sufficiently powerful within particular states at particular times to get one or another form of categorical aid enacted into law – school bus transportation, textbooks, psychological services, etc. Then, citizens opposed to aid challenged it in the courts. Courts upheld or invalidated the particular statute in question, laying down broader legal principles in the process. This set up the next round. The private school interests, emboldened by their most recent judicial success or chastened by their most recent judicial failure, went back to the legislature with a new aid design incorporating the court's most recent Constitutional interpretation (Anderson 1981). If the new aid package passes the legislature, it too subsequently is challenged in court.

The decline of the old politics

In the last decade or so certain events have taken place which may have shattered this historic process. First, the courts have ruled upon just above every conceivable form of government aid directed *expressly* at private schools (*Lemmon* v. *Kurtzman* 1971, *Committee for Public Education And Religious Liberty* v. *Nyquist* 1973, *Meek* v. *Pittenger* 1975, *Wolman* v. *Walter* 1977, *Aguilar* v. *Felton* 1984).[3]. Under current court interpretations most forms of aid are unconstitutional; proponents of private school funding *per se* appear to have few, if any, constitutional avenues open to them. Private school advocates are finding that traditional political lobbying for government aid is useless if the courts subsequently invalidate them.

A second important element disrupting the traditional process emerged when private school aid no longer could be addressed as a discrete political issue. In the old days a financial aid package would be enacted into law with the knowledge that only the private school part of it would be subsequently challenged in court. Legislators could afford to be very friendly to private school interests, but all final decisions would rest with the judiciary. Whatever the courts did would not directly affect public school finance. Private school aid policy was just exactly where private schools themselves were perceived to be off in a box all their own. The advent of tax deductions, credits and vouchers, however, and their subsequent acceptability to federal courts, were to change legislative perceptions fundamentally.

Private school finance to center stage

Given the judicial problems with most of the categorical aids aimed at private schools, vouchers, tax deductions and tax credits seemed an ideal solution. They raise the possibility of distributing very large sums of money in new ways potentially advantageous to private schools. At the same time they avoid many of the legal problems raised by earlier forms of aid.

In 1955 Minnesota enacted a statute permitting state income tax-payers to claim a deduction from gross income for expenses incurred in educating their children. The deductible amount was raised in 1976 and again in 1978. The Minnesota statute differs from legislation in other states because it applies to expenses for *all* children no matter whether they attend a public or private school. As a factual matter, however, most of the children who benefit are enrolled in private schools. In this context the statute was challenged in court. Successive lower court decisions were appealed and in 1983 the United States Supreme Court finally ruled. Child-based funding on the Minnesota model seems to be the one form of aid which apparently does pass judicial muster (Mueller v. *Allen* 1983).

Unlike the public schools, private schools have no wish to educate each and every child within their sector. Voucher and tax credits offer the possibility of much more substantial funding than the categorical aids that private school interests traditionally have sought. For both these reasons private school interests should welcome the voucher/tax credit mechanism. And often they do. The drawback is that, while the judicial principles laid down in *Mueller* would seem to solve one problem for private school interests, that of a constitutionally-permissable aid mechanism, they create a maze of new problems.

The decision in *Mueller* combined private school finance with the potential for significant structural reform of the public schools. This *combination* of policy initiatives causes new and unprecedented challenges for school finance politics generally and private school aid particularly.

At the first level are problems of definition and extent. The least radical alternative would permit pupils to attend a variety of appropriate public schools *within* their school district. This idea is usually coupled with proposals for school site budgeting and other mechanisms which would encourage autonomy for building principals within permissable limits. A second, more radical alternative would permit families selection of public schools *among different* school districts within the same state. Under this conception the state grant-in-aid would follow the child to the public school district of his/her choice. The third and most radical alternative would permit families to choose among public and *publicly-subsidized private* schools. This, of course, is the voucher which nearly everyone thinks of, and either loves or hates as the case may be.

This third alternative is the most radical in part because it appears to subsume the first two. That is, it is apparently impossible to craft a Constitutionally-permissable financing mechanism that provides vouchers/credits useable at private schools only (see *Committee* v. *Nyquist* above). Public schools and school districts necessarily would be included, whether they wanted to be or not.

Such highly controversial policy reforms affecting the private and the public sector make vouchers and tax credits a politically unwieldy bundle. The idea of a 'public schools only' voucher has made some headway with Albert Shanker and with certain state political leaders. In its 1986 report, *Time for Results*, the National Governors Association endorsed the concept of greater parent choice among public schools (Sirkin 1986). Student choice within the public sector has been tried on a very limited basis is a few states. But the experience of the Office of Economic Opportunity in the 1970s suggests that the 'public schools only' voucher is an idea with even less organized constituency than the private schools possess. For example, the Alum Rock voucher demonstration has pretty well dropped from public view.

This does not imply, however, that the 'public schools only' voucher lacks political significance entirely. At the level of political discourse, 'public schools only' vouchers are very significant. 'Threats' of voucher and tax credit legislation serve to mobilize public education forces in a way which the old politics of categorical aid to private schools never could (Malen 1985). No longer is the issue one of just a few textbooks or supplementary services for a few children off in another school sector. Vouchers and tax credits appear to threaten jobs and future livelihoods of thousands of public school teachers: masses of children would 'defect' to the private schools! (Recent surveys suggest this fear is unfounded; see Clark 1987).

Talk of 'public schools only' vouchers does serve to raise hopes, but these are hard to take too seriously. Essentially people at the upper echelons of the public educational system would be telling people at the lower echelons of the same system, 'You must compete, but I shouldn't have to.' Local school superintendents are unlikely to impress their building principals with the virtues of inter-school competition when they limit that competition to the schools which they superintend. Chief state school officers may hurt their own credibility if they extol the virtues of inter-district competition yet limit that competition to the state system of which they are the chiefs. Based on past experience and on this logic, 'public schools only' vouchers are likely to enjoy very limited application. But the idea is significant for rhetorical purposes in that it raises a maze of additional controversies, thereby serving to reinforce the normal inertia in the political process.

Vouchers and tax credits as an aid device move private school finance to the center of the fiscal stage. No longer can legislators view the private schools in the traditional way as a very minor player asking only for small amounts of categorical aid which, likely as not,will be turned down by the courts anyway. With vouchers/tax credits as the mechanism, private school aid necessarily changes public schools too, implying a new and much more complex political dynamic.

A federal government strategy?

A new political environment would not necessarily seem to be a bad thing for proponents of school choice. They did not fare particularly well in the earlier environment. The voucher movement and associated research interest in private schools certainly can claim partial responsibility for bringing new leadership to prominence in education.

A federal strategy is enticing for at least two reasons. Conceptually, federal educational reform holds the possibility of immediate and major national impact. State-by-state reform is a much tougher slog, taking a generation or more to complete (Jones 1981). At a practical level proponents of choice had both a national administration and a widely read research document, the 1982 Coleman Report, to support their cause. That much of the new leadership is located in Washington, DC is understandable for both these reasons.

The problem is that the federal government is much too *far* from the traditional money centers in school finance. School finance policy is mainly made at the state level. Conservative Republican administrations at the national level, with their penchant for parsimony in domestic spending generally and educational spending particularly, rarely making lasting impact on school finance policy.

The Reagan administration seems not unlike its Republican predecessors in this regard. The administration's proposals for tax credits came to prominence just at the time that national attention began to be riveted on massive federal budgetary deficits. The national leadership argued that it was time to reduce both the size of the federal budget and the degree of federal control in public education. They argued that education finance has a state responsibility, yet they endorsed tax credits. On the one hand leadership seemed to be arguing for a federal 'hands-off' policy; on the other hand they were endorsing a new, expensive and controversial federal initiative. It seemed to most observers that private schools would be financd through reducing the federal public education budget. The spectre was raised that needy students in bilingual and Chapter One programs would be adversely affected. In this way the proposed budget reductions provided the most hostile climate possible for consideration of the federal tax credit initiative.

Compounding the adverse fiscal climate, the new Washington leadership had its attention co-opted by the many commission reports focusing national attention on pursuit of 'excellence' in the public schools. Since public schools enroll almost 90% of the nation's children, improvement of that sector was understandably a priority. But the public school reform emphasis may have indirectly thwarted federal choice initiatives. One model of political behavior suggests that people tend to focus on one issue at a time. To the extent that the model obtains in this situation, higher academic standards for the public schools may have replaced choice as a claim on popular and professional attention.

While money was tight at the federal level some states were running large budget surpluses. Evidence suggests that school finance reform is best accomplished at times of fiscal surplus (Hickrod 1986). It would have seemed reasonable therefore that voucher advocacy would be strong in several states besides Minnesota. But, of course, much of the movement's leadership was occupied in Washington, DC where there was no new money.

Leadership depends, however, not only on a few top people but upon substantial numbers of knowledgeable people who find the cause – compelling parent, teacher and administrator organizations, professors, foundation executives, activist lawyers and the like. These people translate into immediate political power because they can be easily and quickly enlisted in the effort.

Private school interests are at a particular disadvantage here. Much smaller and more decentralized operations than the public school organizations, private school organizations usually lack the time, money, personnel, and prior experience to mount effective lobbying and public relations efforts. Traditionally they have not even thought much about public relations except with regard to their own schools. Most of their leaders wish never to become involved in education politics. Although tax credits and vouchers call for spectacularly good political acumen, private school forces simply haven't been up to it. Outside Minnesota the school choice movement has not developed patterns for effective political action.

One interesting source of evidence in this regard is the defeat of school choice at the ballot box in state after state. Catterall's (1984) survey found, according to Gallup polls, that support for vouchers rose from 40% in favor during the late 1970s to 51% in favor at the 1983 peak. But in those states holding referenda, voters opposing tuition tax credit initiatives rose from 59% to 65% during roughly the same time period. A second source of evidence is the large number of reports generated in recent years by state level school study groups and finance commissions formed on a temporary basis to make recommendations to governors and legislatures on education policy. States organized a very large number of such commissions recently in connection with the excellence movement. Yet vouchers and tax credits surfaced in hardly any of their recommendations. The reason is that advocates were not represented among the commission members. Choice advocates do not come from the traditional education interest groups that make up such commissions. Apparently business, which was represented on many commissions, did not press the issue.

It is clear to most students of politics that blue ribbon governmental advisory commissions can play a vital role in state policy-making. These interest group and citizen based task forces are the life blood of traditional school finance reform movements. They mobilize public opinion and create the pressures necessary to enact legislation. Representation may not have been vital in the bygone days of the old politics when private school forces were trying merely to get a few dollars in 'child benefit' categorical aid. But vouchers change the rules, and private school politics has not yet gotten that message.

The 'bully pulpit'

Weaknesses in political organization might be overcome in time with sufficiently compelling intellectual arguments, and proponents do claim an inherent superiority in a system which allows families to choose among different schools (Doyle and Finn 1984). The principal argument, however, advanced in recent years as to why governments should fund private schools is based on student achievement. The very well known study done by Coleman *et al.* (1982) reported, *inter alia*, that private school students do better on standaridzed tests of reading and mathematics than public school students even when differences in students' background are statistically controlled. One possible and often discussed implication of the study was that since private schools are more effective they deserve government aid.

Controversial findings and conclusions such as these always generate subsequent debate. There is considerable dispute as to whether the data justified the findings and conclusions reached by Coleman *et al*. Achievement differences between the sectors may have been due more to peer group differences, home and family background characteristics than to school sector differences (NAEP 1981). More important for present purposes, however, is the funding implication. And in that regard the student achievment controversy may have done more harm than good for the cause of choice. In a different context it has been argued that private schools are good precisely because they are *not* government funded (Erickson 1982). Furthermore, education politics rarely responds to success with more funding; on the contrary, from NDEA in the 1950s to PL 94–142 in the 1970s, it has been pupil or system *inadequacy* which elicits substantial public largesse. To get money in the public sector you have to show need. High test scores won't do it. They show that you *don't* have need.

The final problem with the test score argument has come with the successes of the excellence movement. The Department of Education has reported that their Washington DC 'bully pulpit' has worked well in this regard. Public school students' test scores are now improving yearly. Under these conditions it seems unlikely that the public will find the pupil achievment issue to be a compelling reason for government finance of private schools.

The sabre of government regulation

Even with a weak political power base and a questioning of the pupil achievment argument, choice advocates might expect that they at least had a unified corps of support within the private school community itself. Private schools enroll just over 10% of the nation's children. In terms of sheer size this number compares favorably with other special interest groups. There would seem to be a considerable if largely untapped potential for participation in the policy process.

The problem is that private school interests are themselves divided over the wisdom of soliciting government aid. First, there is an objection on theological grounds. Many fundamentalist and evangelical Christians have a very long history of antipathy toward government, dating back centuries to the time of European absolutism and the original migration of their co-religionists to the new world (Sorauf 1976, Reichley 1985).

For others opposition may be based on a blend of personal religious views and a conception of civic patriotism. None of the mainline Protestant denominations expresses official support for aid to private, religious schools; nor do most Jews. The National Council of Churches and the American Jewish Committee frequently ally with Americans United for the Separation of Church and State in litigation on private school aid questions (Maddox 1986). And Catholics are by no means of one mind on the issue.

For all these reasons there are some private school leaders opposed to government aid within every denomination. The issue is more intra-denominational than inter-denominational. It is often forgotten that separation of church and state is itself a concept rooted in theology, one which today is shared by nearly all Americans, whatever their religious traditions. Because there are such dfferent conceptions of what 'separation' means in context of financing, no church speaks with one voice.

Still other anti-aid rationales are based on purely secular and pragmatic considerations. Some schools are in excellent financial condition without aid; aid might produce new competitors. Very wealthy families (which make up a small minority of all private school families) are considered to be undeserving. Or conversely, if tuition payments hurt the family's living standard, they should. Government aid would limit family fnancial sacrifices and thereby reduce the level of family commitment to the mission of the school. Private schools would become like public schools in this regard. In sum private school leaders display the same range of opinions on this issue that the general public displays, although not in the same proportions.

The one concern shared by every private school leader is government control over their school program. They understand full well that state and federal mandates have burgeoned in the public school sector in recent years. Many of the recent political efforts of private school organizations have been directed towards limiting the application of various governmental regulations to their sector. State-sponsored private school accreditation processes have been established successfully in many states (Lines 1985). Most of these processes, however, still leave private schools broad latitude in such areas as teacher certification, curriculum selection, and pupil testing. Thus in many states private school-governmental relations are calm. When aid is discussed, however, some public officials readily rattle the sabre of government regulation. There is some implication that with government funding added control inevitably would follow.

Private school leaders realize that there is some irony in asking for aid under these circumstances. Although they would like government aid they have a deep-seated fear that with the money state control would come. Their work of the past few years would have gone for naught. The result of all this is an uneasy *modus vivendi*. In return for minimal state regulation many private school leaders are willing to make few, if any, financial demands on the state.

As a result of all these considerations private schools are possibly the only interest group in education which has substantial misgivings about its own support through public finance.

Summary, implications, counter arguments

At the beginning of this decade implementation of educational choice appeared to have a good chance of success. The Reagan election and the Coleman report brought the idea to the political foreground. The Minnesota example and the subsequent Supreme Court decision in *Mueller* v *Allen* was a tremendous boost.

Choice advocates have been unable to take advantage of the situation, however. Unaccustomed to center stage politics, the movement is very poorly organized. Attempts at state level reform through referrenda failed. What leadership there was focused its hopes on Washington DC at precisely the wrong time. The principal issue raised by the Coleman Report, student achievement, redounded to the benefit of the present system of public schooling. As a result of these developments, the political climate for vouchers, tax deductions and credits seems less favorable now than it was six years ago, despite the favorable Supreme Court ruling.

If the educational choice movement is to have continued political significance, its strategies and tactics will have to change. Federal budget deficits imply a return to a state level strategy. In some states there are sufficient surplus revenues to finance both tax credits and a healthy increase in public school aid. A state focus provides 50 chances of success rather than just one.

The Minnesota experience suggests that strong parent organization is vital. That state's Citizens For Educational Freedom association is organized in nearly every private school and has chapters in every legislative district. They have a substantial dues-paying membership and a full time executive director.

Since the choice movement affects public schools also, it must ultimately reach out to progressive leadership in the public sector. One cannot expect every public school leader, or even most leaders, to endorse choice. But the most enlightened ones will.

Basing the case for educational choice primarily on private school student achievment never has been a comfortable strategy. It implies an inherent superiority which most private school leaders did not seek before the Coleman Report and do not claim now. Educational choice needs to be based on a better supporting rationale. There are, of course, many such rationales. Discussion of them is beyond the scope of this paper. The most distinctive features of private education, however, is its emphasis on values and religious faith. The contrast between public schools and private schools in this regard is very sharp and evident to all.

Religion was not much discussed in the era when private schools were asking for 'child benefit' categorical aids. That approach emphasized the secular side of the educational program. Now, however, the voucher/tax credit mechanism with its emphasis on aid to children rather than aid to schools implies new possibilities for changing the nature of the aid argument. Given current trends in politics and society, religion for those who want it may be seen as a legitimizing issue.

It has been observed that during most of American history three broad goals have conditioned educatiinal finance policy *liberty, efficiency* and *equity* (Garms *et al.* 1978). All of these need to be considered for any major new spending plan to succeed politically. School choice advocates have done a good job with liberty and efficiency. The fact that private schooling provides options and is cost-effective is not in much debate.

The area in which choice advocates have failed badly is building their equity case. Nearly every study finds substantial disparities in facilities, teachers salaries and per pupil expenditures between most public and most comparable private schools whatever their location, city suburban or rural. In some private schools inferior educational resources combine with family poverty.

Much of the school finance litigation and legislation of the 1970s was intended to promote equal spending per pupil among public schools within each state. Thus in many states a child attending any public school is guaranteed by statute to have minimum school services and mnimum spending levels. However if that same child attends a private school, even one 'accredited' by the state, spending minimums and most service guarantees do not apply.

For these reasons the equity case for helping children attending private schools is a very strong one indeed. It is entirely possible that that some future generation may look upon failure to address the issue of spending equity for children in private schools as a colossal oversight of contemporary reform movements, one indicative of an anti-religious bias in education in our time.

Finally, one can imagine scenarios which would invalidate the analysis presented here.

Some states are finding that they cannot finance even the public school finance reforms they have recently enacted. It has been suggested that governors and state officials might begin to view vouchers and tax credits as a mechanism to share the costs of education with parents, thereby removing some of the burden from state treasuries. Secondly, most public choice economists argue that theoretically, if given the opportunity, families of all income brackets would make greater contributions to the education of their children. Vouchers and tax credits (no doubt with provisions skewed in favor of lower income groups) might gain conceptual legitimacy as a way to increase the total amount of school spending in an era of severe public spending stringency. Thirdly, if state political leadership did not push for choice, parents might. The Minnesota Citizens for Educational Freedom and the special education lobby provide powerful examples in this regard. Fourth, choice might occur through judicial decisions as an out-growth if interpretations of existing statutes and Constitutional guarantees. Under state-centralized financial plans, it may make little sense to restrict school choice to the district where the child's parents pay property taxes. Students might be permitted to attend schools out-of-district since there would be no taxpayer implications. Finally, if it could ever be detached from religious controversies and attached to the concept of school choice, the goal of values education in the curriculum might become politically persuasive.

From still another viewpoint, however, the Minnesota example now seems threatened as a national model. Governor Perpich, heretofore an advocate, has scheduled elimination of the deduction in his sweeping tax reform plan. It is highly ironic that the model followed by Minnesota's tax reform planners is President Reagan's own 1986 federal tax reform initiative. It is argued that since the new federal law is intended to do away with special tax breaks and special interest loopholes, state income tax laws should conform (Viadero 1987).

Conclusion

The excellence movement has resulted in increased salaries for pubic school teachers in many states. This, in turn, makes survival problematic for many private schools over the next few years. Private school administrators are finding it increasingly difficult to compete for new teachers and retain existing staffs. There will be difficult trade-offs among higher salaries and school fee increases, school closings and decisions to keep schools open at an even lower standards of material resources (Cibulka et al. 1982, Cibulka 1985). These serious internal problems will take time and resources away from public and governmental relations efforts, thereby reducing still further the likelihood of implementing school choice policies through the political process.

Despite the voucher and tax credit hullabaloo, non-government schools receive a smaller proportion of government aid to education today than they did a decade ago.[3] This essay has tried to elaborate some reasons for the present state of affairs. If the analysis is correct, there can be little expectation for choice becoming *zeitgeist* in the 1980s. What remains to be seen is whether the 1980s is but one chapter in a longer story.

Acknowledgements

I wish to express my thanks to James Fannelli, Vincent Rogers, John Brubacher, William Boyd and Charles Kerchner, all of whom made helpful suggestions from their own distinctive perspectives.

Notes

1. Subsequent polling data shows support dropping below 50%.

2. Over the past several years I have worked in a variety of ways with the Connecticut affiliate of the Council for American Private Education in their efforts to bring private school concerns to the public consciousness. Much of my thinking results indirectly from meetings with that group and with State of Connecticut public officials on matters of private school concern. The views expressed here, however, are entirely my own.

3. Families have broad latitude to use private schools if they wish. Such schools, however, are entitled to no direct public assistance. The children who attend such schools may be entitled to certain health and welfare services at government expense if such assistance has a clearly secular purpose, does not entangle the state in any way with private school operations, and does not either advance or inhibit religion. The minimal assistance that has been provided never satisfied most proponents of choice.

4. The largest increases in the last decade have been in state general aid and in state and federal special education aid. Neither of these programs helps the private schools. Chapter Two of the Education Consolidation and Improvement Act does provide more aid to private schools than its predecessor categorical programs. But this is a tiny federal program and the only new one in which private schools participate. At both time periods private school aid accounted for well under one percent of all school spending. Private school aids are aids-in-kind.

References

ANDERSON, D. L. (1981) 'Restrictions on public aid to Sectarian schools', *The Educational Forum*, 45 (2), pp. 215–244.

CATTERALL, J. S. (1984) 'Politics and aid to private schools', *Educational Evaluation and Policy Analysis*, 6, (4) pp. 35–40.

CIBULKA, J. G., O'BRIEN, T. J. and ZEWE, D. (1982) *Inner-City Private Elementary Schools: A Study* (Milwaukee: Marquette University Press).

CIBULKA, J. G. (1985) 'Catholic school closings: juxtaposing efficiency and responsiveness', paper presented at the annual meeting of the American Educational Research Association, New Orleans, LA.

CLARK, D. L. (1987) 'High school seniors react to their teachers and their schools', *Phi Delta Kappan* 68 (7), pp. 503–509.

COLEMAN, J. S., HOFFER, T. and KILGORE, S. B. (1982) *High School Achievement: Public, Catholic and Private Schools* (New York: Basic Books).

DOYLE, D. P. and FINN, C. E. Jr. (1984) 'American schools and the future of local control', *The Public Interest*, 77, pp. 77–85.

ERICKSON, D. (1982) 'Disturbing evidence about the ''One Best System'' ', in R.B. Everhart (ed.) *The Public School Monopoly* (Cambridge, MA: Ballinger Publishing Co.).

GALLUP, G. H. (1983) 'The 15th annual Gallup Poll of the public's attitudes toward the public schools', *Phi Delta Kappan*, 65 (1) pp. 33–47.

GARMS, W., GUTHRIE, J. and PIERCE, L. (1978) *The Economics and Financing of Public Education* (Englewood Cliffs: Prentice-Hall).

HICKROD, G. A. B., CHAUDARI, R. B. and HUBBARD, B. C. (1986). *The Decline And Fall Of School Finance Reform In Illinois: A Study of the Politics Of School Finance: 1973 to 1986* (Normal, IL: Center for the Study of Educational Finance, Department of Educational Administration and Foundations, Illinois State University).

JONES, T. H. (1981) 'Federal mandates and the future of public schools', in J. J. Hanus (ed.) *The Nationalization of State Government* (Lexington, MA: Lexington Books).

LINES, P. (1985) *Compulsory Education Laws and their Impact on Public and Private Education With Suggested Statutory Language* (Denver: Education Commission of the States).

MADDOX, R. L. (1986) 'Why vouchers are wrong', *Church And State*, 39, (9), pp. 22–23.

MALEN, B. (1985) 'Tuition tax credits in Minnesota: a historical view of the national precedent', paper presented at the annual meeting of the American Educational Research Association, New Orleans, LA.

NATIONAL ASSESSMENT OF EDUCATIONAL PROGRESS (1981) *Reading And Mathematics Achievement in Public and Private Schools: Is There A Difference?* (Denver: Education Commission of the States) ERIC# 206 682.

REICHLEY, A. J. (1985) *Religion In American Public Life* (Washington DC: Brookings Institution).

SIRKIN, J. R. (1986) 'Governors appear set to propose school reforms', *Education Week*, 5 (25), 5 March, p. 1, 16.

SORAUF, F. J. (1976) *The Wall of Separation* (Princeton: Princeton University Press).

VIADERO, D. (1987) 'Perpich seeks end to school-expense deduction', *Education Week*, (22) 25 February, p. 10.

Legal Citations

Aguilar v. *Felton*. 739 F2nd 48, 1984; 153 LW 5013, 1985.

Committee for Public Education And Religious Liberty v. *Nyquist*. 93 S. Ct 2955, 1973.

Lemmon v. *Kurtzman*, 91 S Ct 2105, 1971.

Meek v. *Pittenger*, 95 S. Ct 1753, 1975.

Mueller v. *Allen*,103 S. Ct 3062; 463 U S 388, 1983.

Wollman v. *Walter*. 97 S. Ct 2593, 1977.

12   *The uncertain future of national education policy: private schools and the federal role*

Bruce S. Cooper
Fordham University and the University of London

Introduction

The setting was the Carl Perkins Hearing Room, the US House of Representatives 10 March 1987. The atmosphere was tense and the stakes were high. Two key witnesses were testifying before the House Subcommittee on Education: the Bishop of Covington, Kentucky, the Most Reverend John A. Hughes, a speaker for Catholic and other religious schools, was at one end of the table; and at the other end Dr Richard R. Green, Superintendent of the Minneapolis public schools, spokesman for the American Association of School Administrators (AASA), the national superintendents' group, as well as other public school associations. Their concern was nothing short of the future of federal aid to education; their topic, the re-authorization of Chapter 1, the nation's largest and most important law for federal support to education.

In past years, Bishop Hughes and Dr Green would have appeared before this subcommittee arm-in-arm, united in advocating a common bill for the continuance of the $3.4 billion program, which had between 1965 and 1985 pumped more than $40 billion of federal aid into the poorest schools, in the poorest neighborhoods, to give remedial help to the neediest, lowest achieving children in reading, writing, and mathematics. Today, however, the two leaders were arguing from conflicting ideological positions and for different programs, signaling a division in the once cohesive lobby for federal aid to education and an apparent collapse of the coalition which had successfully protected Title I/Chapter 1 since 1965.

Bishop Hughes, chair of the Committee on Education of the United State Catholic Conference, spoke first, 'on behalf of 2.8 million children who attend the 9245 elementary and secondary Catholic schools, as well as for the millions of people, parents, and others who support them' (*Testimony on HR 950*, p.1). The Bishop broke ranks with the public school groups when he uttered the unutterable: advocating a kind of limited 'voucher' to parents for the 300,000 or so poor, low achieving children eligible for Chapter 1 services in Catholic and other religious schools, if the public schools were unable to provide services themselves. He stated in his testimony:

> First, we recommend that school districts be allowed to provide a *parental grant* as an option within the Chapter 1 program. This would provide parents of Chapter 1 students alternative methods of obtaining supplemental educational services best suited for their children. The school district could provide such a compensatory education grant equal to the Chapter 1 per pupil expenditure within the district if equitable services could not be provided in any other way. (p. 3, emphasis added).

Though the good bishop was careful not to say the no-no word 'voucher' – he instead used terms such as 'parental grant' and 'compensatory education grant' – reactions from the public school spokesman, Dr Green, and from the Democratic subcommittee chair, Augustus G. ('Gus') Hawkins of California, were swift and sure: Green stated in no uncertain terms that private schools were 'divisive' and should receive no public aid through the parents. Representative Hawkins, leaning back in his chair, high atop the hearing room dias, said that no 'voucher bill' would ever be reported out of 'his committee'. All that HR 950, the bill on the table, was prepared to offer private, parochial school pupils was a $30 million add-on grant to help *public schools districts* with extra capital costs for serving these private school students off the premises of the parochial schools, as the courts now require. In the words of Superintendent Green:

> We are pleased to endorse the new $30 million authorization in Section 117(d) to help local districts pay for the capital expenses they have had to incur in providing services to private school students. We believe this provision will significantly help districts comply with the Supreme Court's *Aguilar* v. *Felton* ruling (Testimony, March 10, 1987, p.3).

So, the schism between public and private school groups had appeared. The stage was now set for a new era in school policy and politics: school faction against school faction. After more than two decades of relative comity and stability, the basic framework of educational politics had changed (Cooper and Poster 1986). The rules of the game, and the coalitions that played by these rules, were severely altered, though contests between advocates of public aid to private, religiously-affiliated schools and those against any public aid to non-public schools were almost as old as the nation itself (Cooper 1985, Levin 1983).

This chapter analyzes the events leading up to this conflict between public and parochial school advocates. Why had the relative calm between 1965 (when President Lyndon B. Johnson signed into law the Elementary and Secondary Education Act, with its all-important Title I, later called Chapter 1) and 1985 been broken? How had the US Supreme Court's ruling on 1 July 1985, in *Aguilar* v. *Felton*, a decision forbidding public school teachers from entering parochial schools to deliver these Chapter 1 services to eligible students, disrupted the relationship between public and private school interest groups? And, based on this new relationship, what is the future of federal aid to education, as illustrated in the 1987 legislation for the re-authorization of Chapter 1: one continuing Chapter 1 as is (as indicated by HR 950) and the other introduced by the Reagan administration, advocating locally-issued, optional vouchers to parents for their eligible, but unserved children in church-related schools.

Background

The politics of conflict resolved

The relationship between private schools and government finance has a long and complex history, one relevant to the future of national education policy in 1987 and beyond. Prior to 1965, public aid to parochial schools had been a major stumbling block to the passage of a law for federal aid to schools. Whenever a federal assistance bill was introduced in the late 1940s through the early 1960s, supporters of private, sectarian schools demanded a fair share of the money for their schools and their children. A coalition against federal aid to parochial schools emerged, comprised of the public school establishment, the civil liberties groups (e.g., Protestants and Other Americans United for the Separation of Church and State, and the American Civil Liberties Union), and the American Jewish Congress (see Eidenberg and Morey 1969: 204).

And 1965, when President Lyndon Johnson introduced the Elementary and Secondary Education Act, was no different. The key spokesperson for the Catholic schools, the Rt. Reverend Frederick G. Hockwalt of the National Catholic Welfare Conference, refused to support the bill unless aid was included for children in his schools. Direct funding would not work: politically it was too divisive; constitutionally it would certainly have violated the First Amendment doctrine of the 'separation of Church and State'. What was President Johnson to do?

The formula worked out in ESEA was a stroke of genius and the well-known Johnsonian 'art of the possible'. He insisted on the following: (1) that parochial school students receive *services*, not funds, under the same guarantees and eligibility requirements as students in public schools; (2) that the concept of 'child benefit' be substituted for direct aid to private schools; and (3) most importantly, that the funds be given totally and directly to the public schools, which would then hire additional public school staff to serve the private schools. The same approach was used in the 'sharing' of materials, books, audio-visual equipment, in Title II of the same law: these items would be 'owned' by public schools and 'loaned' to private schools which had eligible students. In all, then, the Title I/Chapter 1 law explicitly guaranteed equitable services for all 'entitled' children, in both public and private schools. Without the dual concepts of 'entitlement' whereby all needy children were eligible for services, and 'child benefit', whereby federal resources went to private school children, not private schools, it is very unlikely that the Title 1 program would have been enacted into law.

Once passed, a twenty-year history of co-operation between local school districts and parochial schools emerged. In 97% of the cases, eligible Title I/Chaper 1 children were served on the premises of their private schools: public school teachers were given a religiously 'neutral' room in the parochial school where they could give remedial help in reading and mathematics to students. It was simple, safe, and convenient – since Chapter 1 children could easily leave their regular classroom (in what often was called a 'pull-out' program) and enter the remedial center for help. Everyone seemed happy: public schools got extra money, extra staff, and primary responsibility for the program in parochial schools; private school students received much-needed help, located in their schools; and private schools received indirect help, via their children's education. Political leaders, too, found a welcome base of support in the Democratic strongholds, the major cities where many Catholic schools, serving poor children, were located. It was no wonder that Chapter 1 was re-authorized so handily between 1965 and 1985 with such strong, unified political support from both political parties and public and private schoold groups.

The Court, Constitution, and conflict

On 1 July, 1985, however, the US Supreme Court, in the *Aguilar* v. *Felton* decision, ruled that the hard-won accommodation between public and private, sectarian sectors was no longer legal. According to a 5–4 decision of the judges, public school teachers could no longer come onto the premises of the parochial school to offer the remedial help, because such involvement was 'excessively entangling'. The Supreme Court found that the Chapter 1 program failed the triparte test of constitutionality created earlier in the *Lemon* v. *Kurtzman* decision. According to *Lemon*, statutes must (1) have 'secular purposes', (2) 'neither advance nor inhibit religion', and (3) not foster 'an excessive government entanglement' [403 US 602, 612–13 (1971)]. But in order for authorities to know that criteria one and two are being met – that the program was neither advancing nor inhibiting religion and was 'secular' in purpose, public official had to monitor and observe the Chapter 1 program. The inspectorial function, then, violated the third test, the 'excessive entanglement' prohibition. To fulfill the first two requirements, they must violate the third, a judicial Catch-22. As reported in the Court decision about New York City schools, public school supervisors

> took specific steps to be sure that its Chapter 1 classes were free of religious content. It instructed its personnel to avoid all involvement with religious activities in the schools to which it was assigned; it directed them to keep contact with private school personnel to a minimum; and most important, it set up a supervisory system involving unannounced classroom visits (*Aguilar*, p.10).

Programmatic fall-out: In the two academic years (1985–86 and 1986–87) since the Court's ruling, school districts have found it difficult to impossible to continue serving Chapter 1 children off the premises of the parochial schools legally, conveniently, economically, and equitably. Recent surveys (US Department of Education 1987) show that the most common form of off-site service is to transport private school children to public schools. This approach has not been favored by many parents and private school leaders – since it is highly disruptive, time-consuming, and inconvenient.

Other attempts by school districts have included using mobile classroom vans which rotate around the district, parked at the curbside of the private school to take on Chapter 1 children in groups of 4 to 8 students. This method is easier for the children (they only have to walk a few yards), but it has proved very expensive (vans cost between $45,000 and $105,000 each per year to rent or buy, operate, maintain, store, insure, and fuel), difficult to move through city traffic, and labor intensive (they require a teacher, guard, and driver, plus a maintenance crew). Parents have complained that the vans show up late, or not at all, tie up traffic, and block access to the schools. (Large city parochial schools may have six to ten of these monsters parked at the doorstep, eliminating virtually all the teachers, parking spots, blocking access to the doors, and confusing delivery trucks, fire trucks, and garbage vans.) One Catholic school administrator mentioned that the 'wrong van' showed up, which did not have the children's workbooks and records – so the teachers had nothing to 'teach with'.

Other districts have tried hooking Chapter 1 schools together electronically, using television or computers. These methods have the advantage of being within the private school, available, and simple; they do pose problems of use, however, since parochial schools must provide the staff and expertise in the building to utilize the technogical forms of Chapter 1 services. Perhaps Chapter 1 children also need a personal approach, not a canned program beamed in from the central board of public education. Problems of software development, use of technology, and where to fit the remedial services into the school program still exist. Only about 8% of the districts are attempting to use technology to overcome the strictures of *Aguilar*.

In all, then, the aftermath of the Court decision has been disasterous for the Chapter 1 remedial program. Attendance has dropped on average from between 27 to 46% in various districts, as parents remove their children or as districts cannot put together a workable program, due, for example, to the inability to purchase enough vans (hence, the request of the federal government in HR 950 for more funds for capital costs).

Legal and political fall-out: Besides the obvious educational difficulties created by the off-site requirement, the *Aguilar* decision now threatens the basic, legal tenets which have supported federal aid to education in the USA for over 20 years. First, the 'child benefit' theory is in question. The Court now holds that children can only benefit from an environment other than the one which their parents have selected, the religious setting, if these pupils are to receive the resources which the government has guaranteed and argued these students need to survive.

For many, leaving the comfort, security, and ethos of their school – for a ride to an alien public school where they are 'outsiders' and seen as 'deprived' – is a significant imposition.

For some religious families, such as the Orthodox Jewish students in the Chapter 1 program, the public school, with its co-educational program, is a violation of beliefs and norms. Hence, the key concept of 'child benefit' has now been significantly modified: it now means that students can only benefit away from their chosen school, effectively killing the tenet for them.

Second, making it impossible for some children to receive their much-needed and legally-prescribed federal services, just because of their choice of school, violates the basic concept of 'entitlement'. Now only public school children are 'entitled' to Title I/Chapter1, because it is conveniently available to them in their schools. Private school children must lose the service or give up school time to attempt to receive remediation. What other groups will be next to loose their entitled rights? Without this stipulation, the basis of federal aid for compensatory education is eroded and threatened, starting with the private school student.

Third, and perhaps most seriously, the Court decision, and its aftermath for the parochial school students of the nation, have threatened the very First Amendment rights of religious freedom which the courts are supposedly protecting. Now, since *Aguilar*, children must give up their religious choice, in order to get the programs their parents want. In effect, the Supreme Court has given greater emphasis to the 'Establishment clause' (the 'separation of Church and State' doctrine) and much less to the 'Free Exercise' portion of the Bill of Rights. For the hundred thousand or so children who are denied Chapter 1 remedial help since the Court decision, one could argue that they have also lost their religious liberty and choice. For they are penalized educationally for exercising a religious conviction: that being in a Catholic, Jewish, or Protestant setting is important to them. They, unlike other children, must now chose beween getting much-needed educational services or exercising religious freedom.

So while the government recognizes the sanctity of religion in other sectors, and provides at public expense chaplains for the armed services, for the US Congress itself (which opens each session with a prayer), for hospitals run by religious foundations, and so forth, the Court has now determined that families will be deprived of useful, equitable educational assistance if they also want a religious experience for their offspring. Thus, in its effort to prevent the government's involvement in the 'Establishment of religion', through federal aid to parochial schools, the Court may be running rough-shod over the other half of the First Amendment, the preservation of 'free exercise' of religion, an irony from a court so intent on the preservation of fundamental liberty in the US.

The political fall-out from *Aguilar* occupies us in the remainder of this chapter. The nature of federal politics of education, now and in the future, will likely witness a return to the past: the era between the second World War and 1965 when ESEA was first legislated. Our analysis will show basically two styles of political behavior: (1) prior to 1965, when school politics was ideological, fiercely divisive, and crippling to the enactment of new legislation; and (2) between 1965 and 1985, when groups buried their ideological differences (though not very deeply, we have discovered), calm and compromise were possible, and an accommodation was carefully accomplished.

The first style, the all-or-nothing conflict so common before 1965 and ESEA, was prevalent as early as 1948 when President Truman pressed for a general aid to education bill in his State of the Union Address and when the Senate in that same year easily passed the bill by a vote of 58 to 15. But the issue of aid to parochial schools emerged with full and divisive force in the House. Representative John Lesinski (Democrat, Michigan) chaired the House Education and Labor Committee and appointed Graham Barden (Democrat, North Carolina) to head the Subcommittee on Education. The so-called Barden bill was significantly different from the Senate version, denying any kind of aid to private and parochial schools. Lesinski, a Catholic, 'vowed that this "anti-Catholic bill" would never clear the full committee... The colloquy between Barden and Lesinski', according to Eidenberg and Morey (1969) 'ignited a religious controversy which had been smoldering for years' (p. 20). Francis Cardinal Spellman, prelate of New York, had even stronger feelings, calling the Barden bill 'a craven crusade of religious prejudice against Catholic children'. When even Mrs Eleanor Roosevelt backed Barden and his law prohibiting federal aid to parochial schools, the Cardinal wondered why this pillar of Democratic principles should 'repeatedly plead causes that are anti-Catholic'.

The presentations in Congress in 1987 have much in common with these earlier conflicts. As we shall see, the bills under consideration divide, rather than unite, the ideological sides in this debate. The key difference, perhaps, is the ultimate irony that the Republican administration is pleading the case for Catholic and Jewish schools, while the Democrats – long thought to be the party of the immigrant, the ethnic poor, and the urban voter – are backing the bill which will, in effect, make it impossible for children in Catholic and Jewish schools to receive the resources they are guaranteed and need. Does this foreshadow a shift in party alliances, with the Democrats speaking for the school establishment (teachers and administrators associations), while the Republicans defend the rights of parochial school families, many of whom are Black, Protestant, White, Catholic and Jewish?

The interest groups

Key to our understanding of the future of federal aid to education is an analysis of the positions of the key actors in the battle for re-authorization. As just discussed, the clarity of purpose and the unity of action which had characterized Chapter 1 and Title I for the last 22 years (since 1965) appear lost. Interest groups now stand in conflict with one another, rather than as valuable allies in a unified effort to gain Congressional re-authorization. Here is an overview of the key lobbying groups: their power, interests, and actions.

Religious school groups

Roman Catholic: Perhaps the group with the most to lose, or gain, in this current battle in Congress are children attending Roman Catholic schools. These pupils receive about 90% of all Chapter 1 services within the non-public school sector, since the Catholic church operates the largest number of private schools for low income students. Their support for Chapter 1/Title I has been strong and constant over the years. The leaders of the Catholic school organizations were relatively successful in (1) pressing bills in Congress which benefit their children; (2) working closely with local school boards in developing high-quality, on-site programs prior to the court ruling: and (3) overcoming the resistence of some key districts and states which have laws and policies against giving aid to non-public school students.

In particular, Catholic lobbyists have successfully obtained clauses in the Chapter 1 laws and re-authorizations which forcefully guarantee equitable services to all low income, low achieving students regardless of their choice of schools. Even HR 950, which is likely unworkable under the 'off-site' requirement of the *Aguilar* decision, has a stipulation in Section 117(a) that expenditures 'for educationally deprived children in private schools shall be equal to expenditures for children enrolled in public schools'. And like earlier versions, this bill has a 'bypass provision' to ensure that the federal government can get funds to private school students, even when this effort is resisted or forbidden by local or state laws and policies.

Following the court decision, the Office of the General Counsel of the US Catholic Conference (USCC), the political arm of the Catholic bishops, has followed the impact of the change on Catholic schools. It has urged its schools to continue pressing for their hard-won rights and equitability. It has counselled patience and co-operation with local authorities in working out various off-site programs. When it became clear, however, that these off-the-premises approaches were failing, there was no clear alternative, other than some form of voucher.

Yet, the USCC has failed to mount a powerful movement to change Chapter 1 after *Aguilar*. In part, the leadership of Catholic education has been ambivalent because no simple, clear alternative presents itself – as expressed in Bishop Hughes's testimony discussed at the opening of this chapter. Besides pressing for a 'parent certificate', the Bishop also supported, in the next paragraph, the expansion of HR 950 by $30 million for capital costs. It appeared that USCC was covering its bets, whether the Democratic or Republic administration's bill was passed. In part, Chapter 1 does not appear to be important enough for the hierarchy of the church to play for keeps. No Msgr Hockwalt, the leader of the Catholics during President Johnson's drafting of ESEA in 1965, has emerged to talk tough to the Congress. After all, HR 950 includes language and provision for private school students – though its method of delivery, via public school staff has proved less than equitable.

Jewish school groups: Another religious group has joined in support of federal aid to education. The Jewish community, long a stalwart in backing aid to public schools alone, has now begun to speak in favor of federal funding of Chapter 1 for children in private, Jewish schools. In part, this turnabout has occurred with the opening of Jewish day schools by all the main branches of American Judaism. The Orthodox community, with by far the largest number of day schools (often called *yeshivas*), receives some $3 million yearly in federal aid to its nearly 5000 needy children in 75 schools. The Conservative Jewish schools have many fewer schools and almost no pupils who qualify for Chapter 1. And even the Reform Jewish community, at its 1986 Biennial meeting of the Union of American Hebrew Congregations, has passed a resolution urging the UAHC to support local Jewish communities in their efforts to open Reform Jewish all-day schools, but only after the resolution renewed the deep commitment of the Jewish community to public schools.

The strongest Jewish advocacy group for Chapter 1 children in Jewish schools is Agudath Israel of America, a political organization representing the interest of the Orthodox community. Agudath Israel stands strongly alongside the USCC and its Catholic children in backing vouchers and other efforts to gain a fair share of federal funds for children in private schools. But unlike the Catholics, the Jewish groups find themselves backing these programs, like Chapter 1, because by Orthodox belief Jewish boys and girls should not go to school together; co-education, a universal quality of public education, is unacceptable to these families. Thus, Agudath Israel backs Jewish education because it is the only alternative. And since these schools accept all Jewish children, regardless of family size and income, the need for government-sponsored services is great.

Like the Catholics, the Jews find the 'off-site' provision of programs less than satisfactory; thus, Agudath Israel stands firmly with the Catholic interest groups in supporting some form of modified family certificate or 'voucher'.

Public school groups

Teachers' unions: Teachers' associations, particularly the National Education Association (NEA), have found any proposal to grant funds to parents, any kind of voucher, an attempt, in the union's eyes, to steal public funds from the much-maligned public schools. Recently, when President Reagan and Secretary of Education William J. Bennett proposed a Chapter 1 voucher, the response from the head of NEA was fast and negative. Mary H. Futtrell, NEA President, proclaimed her organization's opposition to any effort to divert public money to parents:

> Sadly, the current administration has chosen the opposite course: It has abandoned needy children, systematically slashing Chapter 1 funds ... Substituting vouchers for what remains of Chapter 1 signals a further retreat. The intent of the Administration's proposal is not to improve but to impoverish public schools, to weaken the very institutions that have most helped the most needy. Vouchers are a hoax, a guise for funneling public monies to private schools. When this strategy is defended on the grounds that it will unleash the potential of 11 million disadvantaged children, the hoax becomes hypocritical, odious, and cruel. (Futtrell 1986: 14).

Even though public school teachers have been teaching in private schools under Chapter 1 for over 20 years, the idea of continuing this service in some other way, perhaps through some direct form of aid, is now strenuously opposed by the unions.

Administrators' groups: The public school administrators association, such as AASA represented by Dr Green in the opening scenario, have lined up against attempts to fund families of private school students under Chapter 1. The Association of California School Administrators opposes the choice-making of parents inherent in various voucher schemes, arguing that parent choice is 'selfish' concern for the child at the expense of the society:

> Parent choice proceeds from the belief that the purpose of education is to provide individual students with an education. In fact, educating the individual is but a means to the *true end* of education – which is to create a viable social order to which individuals contribute and by which they are sustained. 'Family choice' is, therefore, basically selfish and anti-social in that it focuses on the 'wants' of a single family rather than the 'needs' of society. (ACSA 1979: viii, emphasis added).

One should be weary of people expounding the 'true end' of education. Also, since when is a concern among parents that their children be well-behaved, safe, and effectively educated in reading, writing, reasoning, mathematics, and basic decency a 'selfish and anti-social aim'? After all, what more could a society expect from children than to be knowledgeable, skillful, competent, and respectful young people, even in a private schools, goals which must be a vital concern to all parents and society as well.

Other groups, too, have opposed vouchers and other approaches to privatization in education, even when limited to Chapter 1. It seems clear that 'educators' – teachers, administrators, school boards – feel that they have the most to lose by shifting funds to parents, even when these guaranteed services cannot be delivered to parochial schools except at great cost and inefficiency.

The political parties

Too little attention is payed to the role of partisan groups in determining federal school policies in the USA. Quite clearly, the Democratic Party supports enlarged federal involvement in education, though it reflects the basic concerns of the teachers and administrators, not parochial school parents and leaders. The Republicans came into office under the banner of reduced federal involvement and a disbanded US Department of Education. Yet, in the early years of the Reagan presidency, the administration did much to focus attention on education as a national issue and has presented a number of interesting concepts.

Once Republican policy-makers and groups such as the American Enterprise Institute, CATO, and the Heritage Foundation realized that education was a good outlet for their efforts to privatize education, fund the individual, and press for vouchers, conservatives began to expand their role in education. From *What Works* (US Department of Education 1986) to *Investing in Our Children* (Doyle and Levine 1985), from *Excellence in Education: The States Take Charge* (Doyle and Hartle 1985), to *A Nation Prepared?* (Carnegie Forum 1986), the importance in education of the Republic administration and its beliefs has expanded.

Yet, interestingly, on the Chapter 1 issue the Republican administration seems powerless to press its Chapter 1 voucher. In part, this is the result of the rising power of Democrats in Congress, the weakened state of the president after 'Irangate', the lack of unified lobbying among Catholics and Jews, and the lack of understanding among lawmakers concerning the changing issues in aid to parochial schools.

Some practical politics

The future of Chapter 1, the major compensatory education law, will likely be settled before this volume is published. In fact, Congress appears to be moving rapidly with hearings completed in the House and the Senate now in process (spring 1987). A range of suggestions has been made for restructuring Chapter 1 during re-authorization. At least six options have been considered, as shown in figure 1. They are arranged in a continuum from total privatization, with a national/local voucher for all children in school, to the total 'nationalization' of Chapter 1, wherein parochial school students would be dropped from the federal law – an option favored by many teachers' associations and the groups supporting the total separation of Church and State (e.g., PEARL, National Coalition for Public Education And Religious Liberty, the group responsible for initiating the *Aguilar* v. *Felton* case in the first place). Recently, PEARL has filed another suit which argues that it is unconstitutional for public school districts to 'handle' any funds for parochial school students, which would make Chapter 1 services unavailable under HR 950 to any private school pupils via the public schools (vouchers, anyone?).

These six options for aid to private school students are analyzed below in light of a five-part test: legality, feasibility, practicality, acceptability, and educational advisibility:

1. *Legality under the Constitution*: Is the option going to pass Court muster as non-entangling?
2. *Political feasibility*: Would such a proposal pass Congress and the White House, given current and future political beliefs?
3. *Practicality*: Could local education authorities or other agencies implement such a proposal, given issues of educational quality and efficiency?
4. *Acceptability to parents*: Would families and private school leaders find the plan useful to them?
5. *Educational advisibility*: Would the alternative lead to a quality educational program for children in non-public schools?

Option 1: Total privatization of education

At one extreme on the continuum, the US might overcome the problem of funding non-

Figure 1.   Policy options for the future of Chapter 1

Options	Example	Brief Analysis
Option 1: Total voucherization	New Hampshire, 'Alum Rock' experiment	Unlikely: requires joint action of states, and local government
Option 2: Chapter 1: Manditory local voucher	TEACH bill	Died in committee: strong 'compensatory' and 'privatization' qualities: allows choice among schools and private/public sectors
Option 3: Chapter 1: Local option voucher	(a) Wednesday Group's CHOICE bill (b) Reagan administration's Compensatory Educational Certificates bill, subtitle A	Died last session: parental choice and 'Individualized Instructional Plan' In 100th Congress: strong opposition from Democrats and public education lobby; private school concern about options to locals
Option 4: Chapter 1: By-pass to parents	Vitullo-Martin/Cooper Proposal: already done in by-pass states e.g., Missouri, Virginia	Difficult during Congressional re-authorization; legal questions
Option 5: Chapter 1: Re-authorize with small increase for private school off-site costs	Hawkin's Bill (HR-950)	Status quo: continues off-site approach: strong Democratic/teacher union support; loses parochial school groups
Option 6: Chapter 1: Remove denominational private school students from law	Pre-1965 approach	Strong support from PEARL, some public school groups; not likely

public and public schools by 'going private', through a universal school voucher or tax credits (negative tax credits for the poor). Such a plan would create a large, regional 'market' in education, where parents could select among a variety of public and private schools and the government funds 'would follow the child' to the schoolhouse door.

Such ideas have been around since the 1960s (Jencks 1970). (They actually can be traced back to the 1820s when states funded schools which were sponsored by a variety of local denominational, eleemosynary, and public schools.) New Hampshire in 1974 came close to passing a statewide voucher scheme, whereby all education would be available with a grant from the state. Many communities in the upper tier of New England (Vermont, New Hampshire, and Maine) already allow parents to opt out of their 'local' schools, to any available school of choice, even schools located across state borders in other states.

These total privatization plans (vouchers, tax credits, transfer credits) would likely pass the first test, *constitutionality*. In fact, the US Supreme Court in *Mueller* v. *Allen* ruled that Minnesota's state tuition tax deduction program was legal, since families could apply for tax relief from school costs whether their children attended a public or private school. It was non-entangling since it did not involve public schools administering a denomination program; and it neither 'established' nor 'prohibited' religion, since it was evenhandedly available for a portion of costs to attend either public or private schools.

On the second test, *political feasibility* total privatization fails miserably: there is no chance of passage at the national level at this time. Ever since economist Milton Friedman (1955) proposed the voucherization of education, the idea has raised the deepest enmity of school professionals.

Practicality and *acceptability* seem high, however. Such a plan could easily be implemented, with checks being issued to families of school-age children, through some kind of local voucher authority which could act as a distributor, clearinghouse, and fair advertising agency. The experience of the Alum Rock limited voucher plan (see Rand Corporation 1981, Lines 1985) seems to show that it can be done. Other nations, such as Holland and Denmark, both with official state religions, have given families wider choice at public expense. And public interest in vouchers remains high, with various polls showing that parents would enjoy the chance to choose their children's school. Black parents, for example, prefer choice under a voucher by 64% in favor, 23% against, as indicated in a Gallup Poll in 1983.

The ideas seems to pass most of the criteria: total privatization is likely legal, probably workable, certainly intriguing. Whether it would lead to improve education quality is not known. But politically, such an extreme is a bombshell and has virtually no chance of passing.

Option 6: Drop private school students from the law

The opposite extreme from total privatization through a general school voucher would be to drop private school students from federal aid programs completely (see figure 1). Such a move would please PEARL and other groups which object to any involvement of 'church and state'. Such a strong move would however, run counter to the whole history of Title I/Chapter 1, which depended on support from lawmakers from heavily Catholic and Jewish areas. Such drastic medicine would also radically change the 'entitlement' quality of the compensatory education laws which guaranteed help to children who qualify (poor, low achieving) regardless of what kind of schools they select.

To drop the private school pupils from the major federal aid program would be dramatic indeed. It would mean that the First Amendment concerns about 'entanglement' would completely overpower the right of 'free exercise', though if Chapter 1 remains as is (as under the pending bill, HR 950), the net effect may be the same: parochial school students may be excluded *de facto* since the off-site provision is too inconvenient, costly, and unworkable.

Chapter 1 Vouchers

If total voucherization (total privatization of education) is not possible, and if it is unlikely that private school students will be excluded entirely, what about using Chapter 1 as an opportunity to give parents more choice over what kinds of *remedial* education their offspring might get? The Chapter 1 voucher has a certain appeal; three such bills have been introduced in Congress since the *Aguilar* decision. These plans vary in two important ways: first, these proposed policies differ as to whether they include all Chapter 1-eligible children or just those attending non-public schools. Second, they vary as to whether they are manditory or optional at the local level. Three bills, TEACH, CHOICE, and a Compensatory Education Certificate (CEC) law all created Chapter 1 vouchers. The first, TEACH, required that all Chapter 1 children receive a voucher; CHOICE and the CEC law allowed local districts the option to issue them to nonpublic school families.

Option 2: Manditory voucherization of Chapter 1

The Equity And CHoice Act (TEACH) proposed in 1985 the total voucherization of Chapter 1 and required that local education authorities issue these grants to all Chapter 1-eligible pupils in private schools. Based on the local average expenditure for Chapter 1 in the public schools, ranging from about $400 to $1300 per child per year, these TEACH vouchers would be awarded by the local district to private school families.

Under the principle established in *Aguilar* granting vouchers to parents might likely be legal, since public schools themselves have no direct contact with denominational ones: no supervision is required, other than to see that the grant is in an educational setting. According to TEACH, the voucher could be cashed in three different settings: (1) a public school in same district where the child was currently enrolled: (2) a public school in another school district, allowing children to apply the voucher toward the costs of going to an out-of-district public school: or (3) a private school for use in remedial education or tuition.

In terms of the five-part criteria for evaluating Chapter 1 programs, the manditory Chapter 1 voucher stands much like other privatization measures. It is probably workable, acceptable to many parents, and educationally sound, though until it is tried on a wide scale, it is hard to be precise. But, TEACH is unacceptable politically; it died in the House Education subcommittee in 1985 for most of the same reasons as a general voucher bill would: too threatening to the forces that support the public schools. Constitutionally, TEACH would likely pass a legal test, under the *Mueller* decision, though if the PEARL case now pending were to be decided in PEARL's favor, then the fact that local school districts handled the TEACH voucher money would be 'entangling' and a violation of the 'separation' principle.

The politics of TEACH illustrates the new politics of education in the US. Supporters (though weak) stand up against a powerful array of teachers' unions, civil liberties groups, and other liberal public interests. Perhaps a voluntary Chapter 1 voucher, controlled by the local education authorities, to be discussed next, might be more acceptable.

Option 3: A local option voucher (LOV)

Two more recent bills – one proposed last session by a group of Republican Congressmen called the Wednesday Group, the other introduced in 1987 by the Reagan Administration with a 'compensatory Education certificate' (CEC) – appear to overcome some of the problems of other voucher plans, though its chances of passage seem dim.

The CHOICE Bill: The CHOICE legislation (CHildren's Opportunity [or Option] for Intensive Compensatory Education Act of 1986) has five principles at its heart. First, it targets Chapter 1 services 'on those children who are most in need: educationally disadvantaged low-income students'. Second, it stresses 'comprehensive' and 'effective' services: third, the law would 'significantly increase the participation of parents' in the educative process. Fourth, it expands the service options by including 'special instruction services by a range of public, private elementary and secondary schools and universities'.

Fifth, it assures continued 'enforcement of civil rights laws'. If a locality cannot serve private school students well, it can use 'the issuance of educational vouchers' (Section 555.a) for poor, underachieving school children, much as Chapter 1 has since its inception.

New to CHOICE, however, would be the use of Individualized Instructional Plans (or IIPs), much like children in special education receive. Even private school students are included:

> Representatives of private schools shall be consulted with respect to the development of such a plan if the child is primarily enrolled in a private elementary or secondary school, or if the child is currently receiving special instructional services from a private school through the issuance of an educational voucher. [Sec.556,f.(3)]

Parents would then be invited to participate in setting their children's compensatory education program, whether they attended a public or a private school. Similar to earlier laws, CHOICE allowed a bypass, whereby states that constitutionally prohibit the issuing of vouchers to parochial schools could seek a direct grant from the US Department of Education, as is now the case in Missouri, Oklahoma, and Virginia. As Republican Congressman Thomas Petri, one of the bill's sponsors explains, the proposed law 'offers a variety of alternatives', which assures that 'the spirit of free enterprise and competition is alive and well'.

On the five-part test, CHOICE would likely be acceptable to parents and private schools, would be workable, and does overcome the constitutional problem of having public schools serve private ones. The direct involvement in drawing up the Individualized Instructional Plan may be a legal problem, though PL 94–142 does require direct involvement of parents, private school, and public school (though the private school inclusion in this law is under challenge in some states for its possible illegality). And like TEACH, the CHOICE bill was not successful in Congress and is now dead (see figure 1). It faced the same political difficulties as all the other voucher schemes, whether manditory or local options.

Republican Administration's Compensatory Education Certificates: In March 1987, as Chapter 1 reauthorization began, the Reagan administration introduced its own law in contrast to the Democratic bill HR 950. The administration's law contained an optional, local voucher provision in its American Excellence Act of 1987 (AEA). Much like CHOICE, the AEA law makes a strong point of including children who attended parochial schools, including a Compensatory Education Certificate (CEC). This law, then, allows LEAs to fund local private schools pupils and their families through a grant, as a way around the problems posed by the *Aguilar* decision.

Similar to TEACH, this bill permits families, once they receive their CEC, to use it in their local private or public school, or outside the district in a public school or university program for remediation. In the words of the proposed law

> the Act would authorize and LEA to provide these certificates if it determines that doing so (1) would be more effective in meeting the needs of eligible children than direct services provided by the LEA, or (2) needed to provide services required under Chapter 1.

This bill has several advantages over earlier voucher proposals. It leaves the decision on issuing a CEC to the local school board, thus allowing the district to decide. Some cities, such as New York City, might decide that it is cheaper and easier to give the parents the voucher, rather than to pay exhorbitant amounts for vans, buses, computers hook-ups, costs which come out of both the public school and private school portion in equal proportions ('off the top').

Legally, this kind of grant might be acceptable, since there are no public employees on the premises of the parochial school. It would be workable, sound, and efficient, though politically, as our opening scenario indicates, the bill faces tough going. There are some questions as to whether LEAs would give away these resources, and how parents might use them. But such practical matters pale beside the obvious political problems which this proposal – however interesting and elegant – seems to pose.

Why the Republican Party has not gone out strongly for it, joined by the Catholic and Jewish school leaders, is difficut to say. Obviously, the political consensus around Chapter 1 is disrupted; but no clear avenue has been opened for replacing Chapter 1 services on the premises. Republican lawmakers likely do not want to offend the powerful local public school interests; Catholic and Jewish leaders eem somewhat disorganized and are unwilling to attack Chapter 1 publicly. But, once the bill reaches the floor of the House and Senate, some of the issues may become clearer and opposition to HR 950 (to be discussed next) may emerge.

HR 950: Chapter 1 reauthorization law: House Democrats and moderate Republicans seem to be supporting this bill, entitled the 'Special Educational Needs Act of 1987' the reauthorization of Chapter 1. From a private school perspective, the proposed law is basically a continuation of the program, as is, with the requirement for the range of off-site programs, with a small addition of funds ($30 million) for capital costs associated with the leasing or buying of property, mobile vans, and educatinal radio, television, and computers).

From research already completed (Vitullo-Martin and Cooper 1987), it seems quite clear that HR 950 will not recover the parochial school youngsters who have left the program, either because it was too inconvenient or simply was not available to them locally. The bill, while it acknowledges the problems created by *Aguilar*, fails to respond in an effective way; instead, it gives the local districts more money. This approach is consistent with previous practices in Chapter 1, where public school interest groups are more interested in receiving and controlling the millions of federal dollars. The idea of losing control of even a small portion of the funds is anathema to a system which has become used to federal funding, and will hardly give up. (LEAs would rather spend millions on vans, renovation of buildings, costly transportation, and educationally unsound programs thant give up a penny to private school parents for their children.)

Thus, in terms of our five criteria, HR 950 fulfills the political feasibility, in that it appears to have storng political support from the Democrat-controlled Congress and from the powerful public school lobby. In terms of legality, at this time continuing off-site will pass constitutional concerns. But, on grounds of educational quality, convenience, acceptability, and practicality, we have already seen that moving children off-site is not working. The latest figures from Agudath Israel on its participation rates among children in Jewish schools, for example, show that among the 4403 eligible for service under Chapter 1 in 1987, and 926 (or 21%) are actually being served: 745 children in the 72 mobile vans leased by the boards of education, 81 in neutral sites, and 100 in public schools locations. One wonders, too, about the educational quality of a program that so separates the remedial function under Chapter 1 from the regular education effort of the non-public schools.

Option 4: National bypass provision

As shown in figure 1, part 4, one other approach to the future of federal aid to non-public schools would be to use the provision for bypass in the current or future laws (e.g., HR 950) to allow unserved children in parochial schools to receive the Chapter 1 program. Under such an approach (see Vitullo-Martin and Cooper 1987), the US Secretary of Education could 'invoke bypass' for communities which were not providing equitable services and parents or groups of parents could become the 'third party agent' for direct funding.

This method has already been used in 105 school districts between 1970 and 1986 when LEAs were unwilling or unable (usually because of a state constitutional prohibition against public aid to private schools) to serve parochial school students. The process, as in the past, is being stipulated in the current reauthorization legislation, and could be used imediately in locations where the *Aguilar* decision has made off-premises programs unworkable   or unavailable. It could be extended to the entire nation, since overall the data show a sharp decrease in both the quantity and quality of services for children attending religiously-affiliated schools. It would be legal and would have the effect of voucherizing Chapter 1 without a long and bitter Congressional fight over the issue.

Summary

It seems quite clear that the future of federal aid to education, particularly to denominational schools, is changed and uncertain. The rules of the game have shifted from consensus and co-operation among school interest groups, to open conflict over the nature of future programs. Whereas the US Catholic Conference and Agudath Israel of America had joined the American Association of School Administrators, the National Education Associateon, and the American Federation of Teachers, in supporting a common bill for re-authorizing Chapter 1 since 1965, when the Elementary and Secondary Education Act was drafted, these groups are now divided.

Public school groups want business as usual: a continuation of the current scheme. Private school interests see the unworkability of using the existing approach of having public schools serve private, sectarian students, and want a change. What had been a joint belief in *equity* for all underprivileged, low achieving students under the concepts of 'entitlement' and 'child benefit' has now been transformed to a battle over *choice* and vouchers. What was once a calm, consensual process has become a highly ideological, sometime vitriolic debate, with a superintendent of schools telling a Congressional subcommittee that private schools are of questionable value, as divisive. Sounds like the 'good old days' of anti-Catholic, anti-Jewish, anti-private schools, so common as the public schools were gaining their size, power, and hegemony in the US.

The future of Chapter 1, and by implication, all federal aid to education, revolves around whether one accepts the *status quo* that (1) private schools are adequately being served under the current Chapter 1 formula – letting public schools deliver services to parochial schools; and (2) that a few, very minor adjustments, like a small amount of new funds, will make Chapter 1 work fine as is. Or one may believe that some major restructuring of the program is necessary, along the lines of direct funding to families through a parental certificate or bypass provision.

The extremes

The future of federal aid could take one of two extremes: to restrict federal aid to public schools only, or to attempt broad forms of privatization through family choice and empowerment. Either extreme is highly ideological, divisive, and difficult, though there are strong groups at either end.

The middle way

At the center are basically two competing futures. Either allow LEAs to grant certificates to unserved, eligible families so the parents can buy the guaranteed services; or continue to ask public school staff to provide the services the services through extra funding (the *status quo* with a few extra dollars). It appears at the time of writing this essay that HR 950 has the best chance of passage in the autumn of 1987 or early in 1988.

The only likely means of changing the Chapter 1 program to serve private school students is a strong stand by private school groups, working closely with Republicans who favor privatization and some Democrats who fear a reaction from their largely Catholic and Jewish constituents. But, in the spring of 1987, after the first round of hearings in the House and Senate, little political pressure has been exerted. Funding and serving children in parochial schools is too small an issue right now to bring the legislative process to a halt, as Msgr Frederick G. Hockwalt, spokeperson for the US Catholic Welfare Council, successfully did in 1965, until Congress paid attention to the needs of children in non-public schools. The Catholic associations do not seem to have the will, or the power, right now. Perhaps, privatization and choice, 'Republican issues', have obscured the needs of children in basically Democratic regions: New York City, Philadelphia, Chicago, and so forth.

Whatever future that the nation accepts in 1987–88 for federal aid to education, it seems clear that we have entered a new era, one with less stability, less clarity of policy outcome, and greater risks. Ironically, just as the nation is coming to accept the value of religion and religious education, of the rights of families to chose the kinds of education for their children, and the apparent successes of parochial schools in helping children who suffer from poverty and ignorance, we find the national political system punishing the least privileged simply because they exercise a religious choice in education. While we recognize the remedial needs of these students, that they should and must have this help if they are to *succeed in life*, we may now continue an aid structure which forces them to chose between a religious program or remedial services – a cruel, lose/lose dilemma.

Many Catholic and Orthodox Jewish schools hang on by a thread, charging low tuition to the urban poor, and struggling to stay open. Now, the withdrawal of these 'guaranteed' federal services, either by law or by making them practically inaccessible, may be the last straw for some. Many inner-city denominational schools will likely close in the next few years: they will read the message from Congress that they are not worth saving (that meeting public school interests is more important politically to a nation than funding the children who need the help, wherever they go to school).

Thus, much is at stake: the future of religious rights and liberties, freedom of choice in education, and the relations between government and schools, society and religion. The opportunities are great at this cross-roads, but so are the risks. For at a time when issues are changing and controversial, coalitions unstable and unpredictable, and former allies aligned in opposition to one another, the future of national education policy is truly uncertain.

References

ASSOCIATION OF CALIFORNIA ADMINISTRATORS (1979) *Background Material on the Family Choice Inititaive* (Sacramento: ACSA).

CARNEGIE FORUM ON EDUCATION AND THE ECONOMY (1986) *A Nation Prepared? Teachers for the 21st Century* The Report of the Task on Teaching as a Profession, (New York: Carnegie Corporation).

COOPER, B.S. and POSTER, J. (1986) 'Commentary: Breakdown of a coalition', *Education Week* 21 May, p. 28.

COOPER, B.S. (1985) 'Refighting the private school wars', *Politics of Education Bulletin*, 12, pp. 14–16.

DOYLE, D.P. and COOPER, B.S. (1986) 'Funding the individual? An essay on the future of Chapter 1', paper presented to the National Conference on Alternative Strategies in Compensatory Education, Washington, DC, 18–19 November and forthcoming in a book.

DOYLE, D.P. and HARTLE, T.W. (1985) *Excellence in Education: The States Take Charge* (Washington, DC: The American Enterpise Institute).

DOYLE, D.P. and LEVINE, M. (1985) *Investing in Our Children: Education Relations* (Washington, DC: The American Enterprise Institute).

EIDENBERG, E. and MOREY, R.D. (1969) *An Act of Congress: The Legislative Process and Making of Education Policy* (New York: W.W. Norton).

FRIEDMAN, M. (1955) 'The role of government in education', in R.A. Solo (ed.) *Economics and the Public Interest* (New Brunswick, NJ: Rutgers University Press), pp. 123–153.

FUTTRELL, M.H. (1986) 'Commentary' *Education Week*, 6 January, p. 14.

JENCKS, C. (1970a) *Education Vouchers: A Report on Financing Elementary Education by Grants to Parents* (Cambridge, MA: Center for the Study of Public Policy).

LEVIN, H.M. (1983) 'Educational choice and the pains of democracy', in T. James and H. Levin (eds.), *Public Dollars for Private Schools: The Case of Tuition Tax Credits* (Philadelphia: Temple University Press), pp. 17–38.

LINES, P.M. (1985) *Peaceful Uses for Tuition Vouchers: Looking Back and Looking Forward* (Denver: Education Commission of the States).

RAND CORPORATION (1981) 'The education and human resources council', *A Study of Alternatives in American Education, Vol VII* (Santa Monica, CA: Rand Corporation).

VITULLO-MARTIN, T. and COOPER, B. (1987) *The Separation of Church and Child: The Constitution and Federal Aid to Religious Schools* (Indianapolis: Hudson Institute).

US DEPARTMENT OF EDUCATION (1986) *What Works: Research About Teaching and Learning* (Washington, DC: USDE).

US DEPARTMENT OF EDUCATION. (1987) 'Preliminary findings from the national assessment of Chapter 1 about the participation of private school students', Fast Response Survey System, ECIA Chapter 1, (Washington DC: USDE).

13   The politics of school reform in Tennessee: a view from the classroom

Frances C. Fowler
Anderson County Schools, Tennessee*

In 1973 I accepted a teaching position in Anderson County, Tennessee. By Tennessee standards, this system was well off; in average per pupil local expenditure it ranked among the top 10% in the state. Yet conditions in the elementary school to which I was assigned were inadequate at best. The 40-year-old building had a leaking roof and an erratic heating system. Classroom teachers taught all subjects and had a half-hour planning period each week. We had no secretarial support and ran off our own materials on the ancient ditto machine in the office – when it was working. Several locally developed curriculum guides lay in my closet, but no one suggested I use them. My principal, also a full-time teacher, had no time to evaluate us; we filled out our own evaluation forms and he signed them.

Such was schooling in Tennessee on the eve of the education reform movement. As in most Southern states, it was underfunded, backward, and decentralized. Achievement test scores were low; the dropout rate was high. Then in 1979 Lamar Alexander became governor. One of his goals was to attract industry to Tennessee. However, he soon realized that the state's weak school system handicapped it. Education reform was in the air, so the governor seized the issue in the early 1980s and launched a muti-faceted reform of education in his state.

Because of the nature of some of the reforms and the way in which they were implemented, reform in Tennessee has been marked by bitter conflict. Some of it, particularly the controversy surrounding the Basic Skills First program, has been largely in-house. However, the passage of legislation to set up a Career Ladder provoked a mighty public battle between the administration and the Tennessee Education Association (TEA), to which 80% of the teachers belong. In early 1987, that battle has not yet ended. There is a new governor, but the struggle continues.

In the following chapter, I shall indicate the broad scope of the reforms implemented in Tennessee, but I shall focus on just two – the Basic Skills First and Career Ladder programs. More than the other reforms, these involve the basic issues of control, equity, and excellence. They also raise a fundamental question: is it politically feasible to implement the current conception of educational excellence in a situation where neither adequacy nor equity has been achieved? First, however, it will be necessary to examine the context in which Tennessee's reforms took place. The nature of the conflict can be understood only against the background of school funding and school politics in Tennessee.

---

*The views expressed in this chapter are those of the author, and do not necessarily represent official positions of the Tennessee Education Association.

The context

Tennessee school finance

Tennessee has long been among the poorest states in the US, and in 1980-81 ranked fiftieth in average per pupil expenditure. Funding problems have been compounded by the fact that Tennessee has no income tax and relies heavily on sales and local property taxes. In 1980-81, 13% of Tennessee school funds came from the Federal government, 40% from local governments, and 47% from the state. The percentage of state funding had dropped from 57% in 1947 (State of Tennessee 1982).

At the beginning of the reform movement, Tennessee had a state foundation program and used the weighted pupil method to determine educational need. Included in the foundation program was a required local tax effort, which represented less than 10% of the total local tax effort. In addition, local districts were required to pay a salary supplement of at least $1145 to each certified teacher. This funding method caused wide disparities in educational quality. These differences were increased by a heavy reliance on local option sales taxes and by the fact that Tennessee law permits cities and other entities to withdraw from county school systems and set up their own districts (State of Tennessee 1982). The importance of these differences is suggested by the fact that in 1980, the four wealthiest school districts in the state averaged $1115 in per pupil expenditure, while the fifteen poorest averaged $582. (Achilles *et al.* 1985).

Not surprisingly, the Tennessee Comprehensive Education Study concluded, 'The most important problems confronting Tennessee in funding the public schools are questions of adequacy and equity' (State of Tennessee 1982: 231). This study recommended some changes in funding practices. As a result, in July 1985 the state legislature passed a law regarding the equalization of assessed property values used in calculating local educational effort. This should redress some, but not all, of the inequities in local funding efforts.

Tennessee's political culture

Education in Tennessee is riddled with politics from top to bottom – a situation which is encouraged by governance structures at state and local levels. At the beginning of the reform movement, the head of K-12 education in Tennessee was a commissioner of education who was appointed by the governor and served as a member of his cabinet. The governor also appointed the State Board of Education (SBE), of which he and the commissioner were members; indeed, the commissioner chaired the Board. The SBE was weak and susceptible to political influence. It had no staff and depended administratively on the State Department of Education (SDE) – which the commissioner also headed.

In 1982 the SDE had 459 staff members who worked directly with K-12 education (State of Tennessee 1982). Since SDE employment is not based on civil service examinations, and there is little job security, the SDE is susceptible to influence from above and below. Staff members closely follow policy lines laid down by the commissioner. At the same time, knowing that they might otherwise lose their jobs, they try to maintain good relations with local school districts.

Tennessee has 142 school districts. In them, 110 school boards and 80 superintendents are popularly elected. Both the school board and the superintendent are elected in 70 districts (State of Tennessee 1982). The school system is a major employer in many rural counties; thus political factions seek control of school boards and superintendencies. Because

Tennessee's tenure law provides no job security for non-certified personnel and protects certified personnel only against dismissal, it is possible to run a Tennessee school system as a patronage machine. This situation is, in fact, by no means rare. As a result, the educational establishment in Tennessee is characterized by political distrust. Educators at all levels tend to evaluate new policies from a political standpoint, and they value tenure as an essential protection against political game playing.

Major-policy making actors

The governor: Republican Lamar Alexander became governor in 1979, being sworn into office a few days early because his predecessor had been indicted. Clean-cut Alexander, who had a forthright manner and an attractive young family, benefited from the apparent contrast between himself and other state politicians; his popularity led to his re-election in 1982 by a wide margin. Moreover, Alexander had important connections. He had worked as an aide in the Nixon White House, where he met Chester E. Finn. Finn, a professor at Vanderbilt University during much of Alexander's governorship, became one of his education advisors. Alexander also used his position as governor to make other connections. A leader in the National Governor's Association, he was acquainted with many national figures in the school reform movement. He had excellent connections, and with them the power to reward people by introducing them to important individuals. A brilliant political strategist, Alexander knew how to exploit every aspect of his power.

The legislature: Called the 'General Assembly', both houses of the legislature had Democratic majorities during Alexander's governorship. However, Tennessee Democrats tend to be conservative, so there were few ideological differences between them and the governor. Regarded as sensitive to pressure from interest groups, the General Assembly tended to succumb easily to lobbying. This susceptibility to outside political forces made it the battleground in the war between Alexander and TEA over the Career Ladder.

The TEA: From its headquarters at the foot of Nashville's Capitol Hill, TEA had long been a leader in shaping state education policy. Until the early 1970s the organization was dominated by administrators and worked with other education groups. As late as 1976, Tennessee's education groups were described as following a statewide monolithic pattern. However, the 1978 passage of a professional negotiations law led to a statewide fragmented pattern, with TEA functioning as one education lobby, while another lobby consisted of administrator, school board, and higher education groups (Achilles *et al.* 1985).

From 1977 to 1983 TEA steadily lost membership – a total of 14% in six years. Outside observers interpreted this as a sign of weakness, but internal changes had actually strengthened TEA. Unification with NEA in 1975 had led to the establishment of a statewide network of field representatives. In 1976, TEA's new PACs made their first endorsements. The passage of the negotiations law in 1978 necessitated a statewide training program for local leaders. As a result, by 1983 many school districts in Tennessee had a core of strong teacher leaders whom TEA had initiated into politics. Thus TEA, with 38,434 members, had a high potential for unity and political effectiveness. Later, Alexander would admit that he had underestimated TEA's power (Aldrich 1984).

The Basic Skills First program

Development of Basic Skills First

Basic Skills First (BSF), a state-mandated elementary mathematics and reading curriculum, was the first education reform implemented in Tennessee. It was actually initiated by the administration which preceded Alexander's, but this early version was never widely diffused. During its early years, Alexander's SDE apparently assigned a low priority on the basic skills project. Then in 1981 it moved rapidly to develop and pilot its own program. In June 1981, two committees spent two weeks developing curriculum guides and tests. During the 1981–82 school year, 115 schools piloted BSF, which the governor praised in a January 1982 speech. That year's state budget contained additional funds for BSF and incentives for local education agencies (LEAs) to implement it. By 1982–83, it was in use in 607 schools.

In his January 1983 speech before the Tennessee Press Association, Alexander included BSF as one of the ten points in his Better Schools Program. By the 1985–86 school year, all LEA's were required to implement both the BSF mathematics and reading components or comparable local programs which had been approved by the SDE.

BSF program components

BSF is a minimum competency program based on the mastery learning concept. There is a curriculum guide for both reading and mathematics for each grade, K-8. Each guide contains a sequenced listing of skills, a brief explanation of the content, and suggested activities. Brief, usually multiple-choice, tests are provided for most of the skills; the original program included 788 tests, K-8. The original management system consisted of individual records, class records, and a computer program. In grades 3, 6, and 8 students take state-developed BSF Achievement Tests, which are criterion referenced to BSF. The tests results for individual students are sent to parents and teachers. Each school system receives a school by school analysis of the scores; the SDE also releases district level scores to the media.

In 1986, in response to teachers' complaints about record-keeping, the SDE appointed a new BSF Director. As a result, the mathematics component has been shortened and simplified; a streamlined reading curriculum is to be released in the summer of 1987.

The SDE initiated a BSF Exemplary Schools Program in 1984-85. In order to apply, an LEA must critically evaluate the implementation of BSF in its schools. After studying this evaluation, the SDE sends a team to make an on-site visitation. Schools which are judged exemplary are honored in various ways. In 1984–85, 45 schools were found to be exemplary; in 1985–86, 143 received the award.

Implementation

The SDE seems to have used a research, development, and diffusion model in implementing BSF. However, its failure properly to execute the development and diffusion phases caused the implementation process to be unnecessarily difficult. It is essential to smooth implementation that innovations reach adopters in a practicable form. But, although BSF had been piloted, evaluated, and revised, the program which teachers were asked to use in their classrooms in 1985–86 was virtually unworkable. The curriculum guides were unwieldy; there were far too many tests; and the management system was overly complex. As a result, teachers became frustrated. Many did not fully implement the program.

Nor did the SDE adequately carry out the diffusion phase, which should have included thorough demonstrations of the program to the adopters. In Anderson County, for example, the mathematics component was presented to teachers in a two-hour workshop. The demonstrations of the reading and computer management components were even more deficient. A representative from each school was asked to attend a two-hour workshop, then return to his or her building and explain the program to other teachers. This approach was especially ineffective in relation to the computers; in many schools they were not used because no one knew how to operate them.

Implementation was further complicated by the fact that the SDE, working hard to implement the entire Better Schools Program, was unable to deliver materials to the LEAs on time. In Anderson County, for example, the test booklets did not arrive until late September; the computers finally appeared in January. The net effect of these implementation problems was inevitable; they irritated teachers, created hostile feelings toward the program, and undermined the credibility of the SDE.

Issues surrounding Basic Skills First

Allocation of resources Although some educators complained about the money which LEAs were spending to duplicate BSF materials, by far the most controversial aspect of the program was the amount of teacher time required to run it. In order to understand this issue, one must be aware of the time constraints under which Tennessee's elementary teachers operate. Many spend $7\frac{1}{2}$ hours in their building each day. Moreover, according to a survey which TEA conducted in 1985, 77% of K-3 and 69% or 4–8 teachers had no duty-free lunch period, and 58% did not have even 30 minutes a day to plan. Thus, the addition of BSF record-keeping represented a great burden.

The time problem was raised as early as the fall of 1981 when, in seven meetings held to evaluate the pilot program, administrators complained about the teacher time which BSF required (Roney 1981). In 1984 TEA's Instruction and Professional Development Commission conducted a survey of 300 scientifically selected teachers involved in the BSF program. The overwhelming majority agreed with the statement that BSF record-keeping reduced instructional time. Teachers who participated in the survey were invited to make comments. Of the 116 comments, 99 were negative, and 67% of those were related to time. (TEA 1984)

Equity: BSF has raised three equity issues. Since it contains no remediation for students who fail the tests, many educators have expressed concern about its effect on weak students. This problem has been largely resolved by the Career Ladder program since many of the teachers who work extended contracts are providing remedial summer courses keyed to BSF.

A second equity issue relates to the release of the BSF Achievement Test scores to the media. Every spring sees a rash of newspaper articles with headlines like COUNTY SCHOOLS OUTRANK CITY. Buried deep in the article one can usually find a statement by the city superintendent, explaining that many factors, including social class, affect test scores, and that lower scores do not necessarily imply inferior quality. Still, the impression is created that test scores prove that some school systems are better then others. Both the former chairman of the State Board of Education and the Tennessee Organization of School Superintendents have publicly protested this use of BSF and other test scores.

Finally, because of the nature of the BSF program, implementation has been easier in wealthy school districts than in poor ones, which typically lack aides, teacher planning time, and supplementary materials. BSF places disproportionately heavy demands on the poor systems, absorbing teacher time and ADA money which are already inadequate to their needs. It is therefore not surprising that, according to the minutes of the SBE, in 1985 58% of the BSF Exemplary Schools came from the top quarter of school systems in local per pupil expenditure.

Control: Obviously, BSF represents a shift of the power to plan curriculum from the local to the state level. Administrators involved in the pilot program expressed fears that the SDE was planning to develop a full curriculum and that their own academic freedom was in danger (Roney 1981). Teachers also sensed a loss of control, complaining that they felt like robots and were unable to exercise their professional judgment. Although the time issue was voiced more openly, undoubtedly the loss of control over curriculum lay at the heart of many complaints about BSF.

Evaluation of Basic Skills First

Although implementation has been difficult and many Tennessee educators resent BSF, on balance the program has benefited the children of Tennessee. Of course, most elementary teachers were teaching basic skills before they ever heard of BSF. However, the existence of a state curriculum offers several undeniable advantages. It encourages a uniformity of content which is valuable in this mobile age. It sets clear goals for teachers, students, and parents. It emphasizes for the public the importance of proficiency in mathematics and reading. It has probably improved the instruction of teachers who are weak in task analysis and organization. A state curriculum was long overdue in Tennessee, and it is likely to strengthen education in the state – if it remains in place.

In early 1987, with a new Democratic governor in office and new leadership in the SDE, all the Alexander programs are in doubt, including BSF. However, since BSF has not been a notorious political football, it will probably be retained if its proponents effectively solve two problems. The first, of course, is the amount of teacher time which it absorbs. Hopefully, this problem will be largely solved by the revisions currently underway. The other problem which must be resolved is one of equity. The publication of test scores in the media is probably unavoidable in this era of accountability. But it is demoralizing to educators who work in difficult situations to suggest to the public that a simple comparison of average test scores reveals much about school quality. The solution is not to stop publishing test scores, but to publish a wider range of comparisons: gain scores, scores of systems with similar local expenditures, rankings of schools which work with similar populations, and so forth. Such an approach would be more honest and less distressing to educators who struggle to teach children from meager backgrounds. It would also remove a major complaint about BSF and improve the program's chances of survival.

The Career Ladder program

The Tennessee Comprehensive Education Study (TCES)

In June 1981, the General Assembly initiated a comprehensive study of the state's public schools, from kindergarten through higher education. The goal of the study, the first since 1955, was to develop long range plans for each level of public education. After a year of work, the TCES task force presented a 566-page report containing information on the state's public schools and analyses of their funding, governance structures, and legal foundations. The task force made recommendations for each educational level and proposed that school funding be made more equitable and that governance structures be modified to reduce political influence on the schools. TCES also tentatively endorsed merit pay for teachers and proposed a 'master teacher' plan, under which the principal and teachers in each school would select an experienced teacher to work with new and student teachers (State of Tennessee 1982) The report was presented to the legislature in January 1983.

The Better Schools Program

On 28 January, 1983, Governor Alexander addressed the Tennessee Press Association and a statewide television audience. In his speech the governor presented a ten-point education reform agenda which he called the 'Better Schools Program'. A summary of this agenda follows: items which were eventually implemented are asterisked; items which were recommended in TCES are so indicated.

1. *Basic Skills First (TCES)
2. *Computer Skills Next (partially TCES)
3. Mandatory kindergarten (TCES)
4. *More high school math and science (TCES)
5. *Residential summer schools for gifted juniors and seniors
6. *Redefinition of vocational education curriculum (TCES)
7. Classroom discipline: state-paid teacher liability insurance and *alternate schools
8. Adult job training put under the Board of Regents (TCES)
9. *Centers of Excellence at universities (TCES)
10. *Master Teacher and Principal Programs (partially TCES)

Alexander spent much of his speech elaborating on the Master Teacher Program. Describing the plan as a way to attract talented people to teaching and keep them there, he proposed a four-step career path for Tennessee teachers. Teachers on the second step would receive an incentive pay supplement of $1000 annually; teachers on the third step would receive $2000 ($4000 if they chose to work an eleventh month); and master teachers on the top step would earn $3000 ($5000 for an eleventh and $7000 for a twelfth month). Entrance into the three top levels would be determined by state-trained evaluators from outside the teacher's system.

However, Alexander proposed quotas on the number of teachers to whom the state would pay the top incentives. In any given LEA, the state would fund only 10% of the teachers at the fourth level and 25% at the third. If more of a district's teachers were recommended for the upper levels, the LEA could choose who would receive merit pay. Those not chosen could elect to 'go on the market' and sign contracts to teach for LEAs which had not filled their quotas.

Alexander made it clear that the Master Teacher Plan was central to his reform proposal and that he would veto any tax increase which did not include funding for it. Thus, as in many other states, additional education financing was contingent upon major reform – in this case, upon reform of teacher compensation.

The battle over Master Teacher

Alexander apparently had a well-planned strategy for gaining support to pass his program.

The day after the Better Schools speech, he launched a statewide campaign to sell it to the general public, to influential power actors, and to the education establishment. He toured the state, making 24 public appearances before the middle of February. In the following months he held bean suppers, invited President Reagan and Education Secretary Bell to the state to endorse the plan, and initiated a public relations program. His efforts were successful; in the spring of 1983 a public opinion poll revealed strong public support for his proposal.

Alexander also succeeded in his efforts to win the influential. He already had strong media support. The Chambers of Commerce, the Tennessee Taxpayers Association, the Business Round Table, and the Tennessee Association of Manufacturers also fell in line. Alexander moved early to win over the Democratic leadership of the General Assembly, gaining the support of House Speaker McWherter and other key figures.

The governor was least successful with the education establishment. Only the administrations of the state's universities offered consistent support. The PTA as well as the superintendents' and school boards' organizations gave token support, endorsing the concept but not working actively for any bill. The Tennessee Association for Supervision and Curriculum Development raised questions about the program in an editorial. The few AFT locals in the state opposed it. And TEA went to war over the plan.

At first, however, the leadership of TEA, evidently caught by surprise, seemed to have no strategy. The Board of Directors met with Alexander on 29 January, 1983, and did not take a clearly negative position, although they were quite dubious about the program. However, after close legal study of Alexander's proposal, TEA leaders concluded that the provision for free agent teachers who could move at will about the state, contracting individually with LEAs, would undercut both the tenure and negotiations laws. They were also concerned about the lack of adequate provisions for due process.

During February, TEA leaders conferred for thirteen hours with the governor's representatives but were unable to resolve any major problems. As a result, the Board of Directors voted to oppose the bill. On 3 March, the same day that the administration introduced the Master Teacher Bill, TEA had a rival bill introduced. TEA then launched a broad internal communications campaign, urging teachers to work to defeat the governor's program. 'The efforts of TEA must be massive', it told its members. 'Every teacher must be involved . . . Talking to your legislators and sending letters, petitions, phone calls, and other messages to legislators will help get the job done' (Booth and Cheshier 1983).

Throughout March, both sides lobbied the legislature; in fact, some observers commented that the Master Teacher Bill was the most heavily lobbied piece of legislation they had ever seen. The result, in April, was a victory for TEA; by a 5–4 vote the Senate Education Committee established a committee to study both bills and recommend a teacher improvement plan by February 1984. The battle then shifted to the committee, which met from July to November. The governor won this round; in late November the committee recommended a bill which, from TEA's point of view, resolved few problems.

However, on the eve of the 1984 session of the General Assembly, both Alexander and TEA had to face unpleasant facts. Alexander had the votes to pass a Master Teacher bill; he did not have the votes to pass the tax increase to fund it. TEA leaders realized that they would have to accept some form of merit pay. Both were ready to compromise. A group of legislators and TEA leaders met secretly to work out a compromise bill. Basically, TEA agreed to accept incentive pay, and the administration agreed to withdraw the provisions which undercut tenure and negotiations. TEA then lobbied successfully for enough votes to pass the necessary tax increase. (Cheshier 1987)

The education reform legislation

During the winter of 1984, the General Assembly passed legislation which mandated education reform and raised taxes to fund it. First on the agenda was the Public Education Governance Reform Act of 1984 (PEGRA). PEGRA restructured the State Board of Education, increased its power, and authorized it to employ staff. The governor still appointed the Board, but PEGRA required that its members be confirmed by the legislature. No member could be an elected official or educator; thus it was a lay board, and the governor and commissioner could no longer serve on it. The object of PEGRA was to create an independent Board which could truly establish policy for K-12 education (B. Dalton 1985, Lansford 1984).

The Comprehensive Education Reform Act of 1984 (CERA) set up a five-step career ladder for teachers and a three-step ladder for administrators. The teachers' ladder included a one-year probationary step and a three-year apprentice level. At the end of a satisfactory fourth year, teachers hired after 30 June 1984, would have to apply for Career Ladder I, which carried a $1000 supplement and required passage of a state-approved evaluation. At the end of five years, these teachers could opt for another Level I certificate or apply for Level II. Admission to this level required a passing score on an evaluation administered by a state team. Level II carried a merit stipend of $2000 and a chance to work an extended contract for an additional $2000. At the end of the twelfth year, teachers could apply for Level III, also calling for evaluation by a state team. Entry into Level III earned a $3000 stipend and the chance to work an additional one or two months at $2000 a month. The administrators' ladder was similar, but carried $4000 and $7000 bonuses (French 1984/85).

CERA provided that teachers hired before 1 July 1984 could choose whether or not to enter the program. Tenured teachers were essentially grandfathered into Level I; during 1984–85 they could use one of five methods to enter it; later, they would have to undergo a special, state-approved evaluation. Teachers and administrators with enough experience could elect to apply immediately for the upper levels through evaluation by a state team. In addition to the career ladder bonuses, CERA gave a 10% pay increase to all teachers.

The General Assembly passed a tax increase package which provided a billion dollars to support PEGRA, CERA, and most of the Better Schools Program over the next four years.

Implementation of the Career Ladder

First year: The administration wanted to implement the program during the 1984-85 school year. Therefore, in the spring of 1983 Alexander appointed a committee to develop an evaluation system. It was ready by December. From 21 March to 30 March, the SDE trained 115 teachers as evaluators, and the evaluation instrument was field-tested in April. The program was on line as scheduled, in the fall of 1984. Obviously this was very rapid implementation, and Susan Rosenholz, one of the developers of the evaluation system, resigned in December 1983, partly because she considered the field-testing inadequate for proper validation of the instrument.

Most of the teachers who were eligible to do so entered Level I during 1984–85. In addition, 7743 applied to be evaluated for Levels II and III; however, the SDE was able to process only 3132 teachers and 221 administrators. These individuals underwent a rigorous evaluation by three state evaluators. They were observed three times, had to take the professional skills section of the Tennessee Career Ladder Test, and prepared a portfolio documenting their expertise in planning, teaching strategy, classroom management, evaluation, and leadership. In addition, their principal, three peers, and a group of students filled out questionnaires on their performance. In June 1985, Governor Alexander appeared publicly across the state to announce the names of the successful candidates. Of those evaluated, 35% of the teachers and 67% of the administrators had made the upper levels.

Throughout the first year of implementation, TEA maintained a low profile. Its Board of Directors encouraged members to try for Level I, but refused to take a position on Levels II and III. TEA sponsored workshops to help members prepare for evaluation; these led to a skirmish with the administration over the release of materials which the SDE considered confidential. Otherwise, TEA said little publicly about the new program.

Second year: Based on the first year of implementation, the SDE made some changes. It prepared a new orientation manual for those undergoing evaluation and deleted the portfolio. In the second year, 1760 educators were evaluated for the upper levels, and 83.6% reached them. SDE representatives explained the higher success rate as a result of self-selection process on the part of the candidates (French 1987).

Meanwhile, TEA leaders began to feel pressure from their members to take a more negative stand on the Career Ladder. By the summer of 1985 a faction which advocated repeal of the program had emerged in Middle Tennessee. This movement centered in one small city system and four rural ones; four of these five systems ranked below the state average in teacher salary. This group began to lobby the Board of Directors in July. In the fall, they circulated a petition calling for the repeal of the Career Ladder among teachers in twelve counties; allegedly, 90% signed it. In October they presented their petition at a Board meeting, and several of their leaders made impassioned pleas for repeal. They continued to pressure the Board throughout the year.

Other sources confirmed that teachers had an overwhelmingly negative view of the program. A TEA survey conducted among 1000 scientifically selected members in April 1985 showed that 77% felt that the Career Ladder had a negative effect on morale; 86% felt that it would not work fairly or effectively. By November 1985, when the survey was repeated, these figures had risen to 90% and 94% respectively. Not long after the second TEA survey, the Knox County Task Force on Education – proponents of the program – surveyed 900 Knox County teachers with similar results. Fully 98% disagreed that the Better Schools Program had boosted teacher morale; 97% disagreed that teachers considered the program successful (Levary 1986).

However, the general public and most of the state's political leaders still strongly supported the Career Ladder. Thus TEA faced a difficult dilemma – finding a position which would be politically viable both internally and externally. In February 1986, its Board of Directors adopted a resolution to seek major modifications in or repeal of the program in 1987 if teacher morale did not rise significantly. In the spring TEA's Representative Assembly adopted a similar resolution.

Third year: The SDE divided teacher evaluations into fall and spring cycles and fully evaluated 750 teachers in the fall. Of these, 77% reached Levels II and III. In January 1987, the new Democratic Governor Ned McWherter – who had been endorsed by TEA – dismissed most of the Assistant Commissioners of Education in the SDE, including both the Director of the Career Ladder Program and the person who had administered it in its early stages. In February the new Commissioner of Education began publicly to criticize the program as too complicated and too costly (Levary 1987).

Meanwhile, in an effort to determine members' views, TEA had run its 1000-member survey for the third time and held 'input sessions' across the state. Concluding that morale had not risen significantly, the Board of Directors voted in January 1987 to have a bill introduced into the legislature to modify the program. Although there would still be five steps, the Career Ladder would be entirely optional and no one would have to undergo a state evaluation to enter it. In effect, TEA's proposal retained a Career Ladder facade to please the public, while altering the program significantly to placate teachers.

Issues surrounding the Career Ladder

Control: Virtually all observers on both sides agree that the central issue in the conflict over the Career Ladder was power – specifically, TEA's power to influence education policy. Supporters of Alexander's reforms saw the teachers' organization as a union which was accustomed to a leading role in policy-making. Like most unions its primary concern was member welfare; thus it constantly sought 'more of the same' – higher salaries, more fringe benefits, smaller class size, and more members (Lansford 1984). When the governor and the SDE emerged as important policy-making actors, TEA felt threatened and fought to retain its power (Trusty 1987).

Not surprisingly, TEA leaders interpreted the struggle differently. They perceived the original Master Teacher Plan as a 'union-busting' tactic, for by weakening tenure it would have destroyed teachers' ability to work collectively in state politics. For TEA the conflict with the governor centered on whether or not Tennessee's teachers would continue to function as a group or would become individual entrepreneurs. In short, teacher solidarity was at stake (Cheshier 1987, Winters 1987).

Equity: Traditionally, Tennesseans have understood equity primarily in racial terms: they have largely ignored the more comprehensive issue of social class, even though the Appalachian region of the state includes some of the poorest whites in the nation. A major effect of the Career Ladder has been to heighten awareness of the issue of social class.

As has been noted, the overwhelming majority of teachers consider the program unfair. This perception is based to a great extent on the nature of the evaluation system and on the fact that the same instrument is used to evaluate all regular K-12 classroom teachers in the state. The evaluation system, based on Madeline Hunter's teaching model, rewards elaborate planning, frequent evaluation, use of a variety of teaching media, adaptation to varying ability levels, and pupil time on task. Thus teachers feel that it gives a significant advantage to the teachers who have the most time to plan, the most money for materials, the most paraprofessional assistance, and the most cooperative students. In short, they believe that it favors wealthy districts, secondary teachers, and the teachers of middle class students.

Frankly, little statistical data exists to support teachers' views, though their perceptions have been echoed by some state legislators, one of whom charged that the Career Ladder would lead to 'class warfare'. TEA leaders also share their concern, fearing that over time the program will cause rich systems to get richer and poor ones to get poorer (Cheshier 1987).

According to the administration, socioeconomic data have been gathered and analyzed, revealing no significant differences between the social class of students whose teachers earn merit pay and those whose teachers do not (French 1987). However, these data are not readily available for study, nor have they been disseminated in popular form to teachers. Thus, the belief that the program discriminates on the basis of social class persists.

Allocation of resources: Although the Career Ladder has been criticized for the amount of time it takes for teachers to prepare for evaluation and to complete related paperwork, most critics focus on its cost. In the first year, 29 full-time SDE personnel ran it; in the second and third years it required 39 staff members (State of Tennessee 1986). In addition, several consultants and over a hundred evaluators have been on loan to the SDE from universities and LEAs'. Evaluators travel widely in the state, spending nights in hotels and eating in restaurants. SDE workshops for participants, open houses for prospective candidates, and public relations efforts add to expenses. The estimated cost of evaluating a single teacher varies greatly. Those who administer the program say that the average is $1600–$1800 (M. Dalton 1987), but the new Commissioner of Education has publicly stated that the evaluation of a single person costs $5000 (Levary 1987). Regardless of the exact figure, rank-and-file educators find it hard to accept such expenses in a state which ranks close to the bottom in virtually every category of educational expenditure.

Political exploitation: TEA and Alexander's other political opponents have frequently accused him of developing the Career Ladder and rushing to implement it in order to gain national political prominence. According to these critics, polls showed that education was an emerging issue and that Alexander was weak in this area. Since merit pay was popular with the public, the SDE and Chester Finn developed the original Master Teacher program and Bailey, Deardourff and Associates, a Washington-based political consultation agency, packaged it (Bryant 1983). Alexander's supporters have steadily denied these charges; they argue that concern for the state's economic future motivated the governor.

Evaluation of the Career Ladder

It is obvious that Tennessee's Career Ladder has been plagued by many of the problems historically associated with merit pay in education – low morale, divisiveness, complexity, and high administrative costs. Therefore, this evaluation will focus instead on other ways that the program has affected education and the politics of education in Tennessee.

Undeniably, the passage of CERA made possible the injection of large amounts of money into public education. Teachers' salaries have gone up, a number of new curriculum components have been introduced, and the state has begun to fund some planning time for elementary teachers, aides, and duty-free lunch (McElrath and Howard 1985). In addition, the Career Ladder has focused attention on evaluation and staff development – two areas in which education in Tennessee has been weak. Though many have criticized the SDE's rather rigid approach to both subjects, educators who have been through evaluation or participated in SDE workshops will probably retain a sense of the importance of professional development. Extended contract activities by Level II and III teachers have provided remedial and enrichment programs for many students. Finally, the conflict around the program has led to extensive media coverage, underscoring for the general public the seriousness of the educational enterprise.

The implementation of the Career Ladder has also restructured the political environment in which future educational policy will be shaped. The conflict around CERA generated considerable power, and all the major policy-making actors gained from it. For the first time in recent history, Tennessee had an activist SDE. By developing and implementing the Career Ladder, Alexander's SDE gained an unusual degree of visibility both within the profession and in the media. With a new governor in office, the SDE may fall back into its earlier pattern; however, a precedent has been established and a role model exists. Thus one long range effect of the Career Ladder may be the strengthening of the SDE.

The new State Board of Education, created by PEGRA, took office in 1984. At first it followed the SDE, but as the conflict around CERA escalated, the Board became increasingly independent. It began to gather its own data and to question some SDE positions. At times it acted as a mediator between the SDE and TEA. Some predict that the emergence of a strong state board may be the most important of the 1984 reforms (B. Dalton 1985).

TEA also gained power from the struggle. The organization's membership has climbed steadily since 1984, with an overall gain of more than 6% in three years. Moreover, TEA leaders believe that the conflict caused a widespread politicization of the teaching force. They have been able to channel this development into increased political activity. First, the 1986 Representative Assembly reorganized T-PACE – TEA's political action arm – greatly expanding both its financial resources and its membership. Next, TEA leaders encouraged teachers to work in the 1986 elections by linking dissatisfaction with education reform to political action. For example, in a campaign handbook distributed across the state, TEA made the connection clear: 'We face critical issues:...education reform...academic freedom...career ladders...Reaching goals means reaching goals through politics – practical politics.' (T-PACE 1986: 1) Unprecedented numbers of teachers worked in the 1986 campaigns; TEA's endorsed gubernatorial candidate and 98 of its 101 endorsed legislative candidates won. Thus, TEA anticipates an expanded role in policy-making (Cheshier 1987, Winters 1987).

TEA leaders are naturally pleased about these developments, but they shadow the future of Alexander's education reforms. Indeed, in early 1987, the future of the Career Ladder itself was in doubt; however, education and politics in Tennessee will long reflect the impact of the program and the conflict which it caused.

Conclusion

Tennessee's experience with education reform raises several interesting questions. Perhaps the most interesting is whether the implementation of educational excellence, as conceived by today's reformers, is politically feasible where neither educational adequacy nor educational equity has been attained. Tennessee's experience suggests that this question must be answered in the negative; it also suggests why.

First, however, the currently popular concept of educational excellence must be explored. For today's reformers, excellence in education means the mastery of academic skills, especially the 'basics'. Teachers can best teach these skills by following a carefully planned and sequenced curriculum, evaluating students frequently, and maintaining detailed progress records. Strict accountability and competition motivate both students and teachers to achieve at high levels. Thus, students should know their test scores, and the average scores of individual schools and districts should be publicized. Teachers, too, should be scored and placed in a hierarchy based on their performance. Outstanding schools, systems, and teachers should be rewarded with publicity, money, and other honors. As educators emulate exemplary practice elsewhere, they will become increasingly excellent.

The reformers' emphasis on academic excellence is commendable, but their concept implies the use of much teacher and administrator time. It takes time to plan, develop supplementary materials, and chart test results. It also takes time to evaluate teachers properly. But because of inadequate funding, time is a resource which is in very short supply in Tennessee schools. As a result, the reform movement placed the state's educators in a difficult dilemma; they could do the extra work on their own time, or they could do it while students completed 'busy work', or they could merely pretend to do it. No doubt most educators used a judicious blend of these methods, but none of them was professionally gratifying. Thus morale dropped.

Simultaneously, teachers observed the implementation of a merit pay system designed to reward them for outstanding performance. However, according to Frederick Herzberg's motivation-hygiene theory, recognition and advancement motivate only when 'hygienic' needs like adequate salary and good working conditions have been met. (Frase *et al.* 1982) Tennessee's history of inadequate school funding meant that most teachers' 'hygienic' needs were far from satisfied. Thus, they considered merit pay an unnecessary luxury. This perception also contributed to the drop in morale.

Finally, according to the reformers' conception of excellence, competition should motivate teachers to achieve. However, competition is motivating only when the competitors have roughly equal advantages – a principle which is well recognized in athletics. In a state marked by gross inequities in school funding, teachers are hardly motivated to achieve when they learn that the highest paid systems have many Level III teachers, or that a wealthy suburban school has high test scores. On the contrary, they are motivated to compare working conditions. Again, their morale drops.

In Tennessee, frustration and low morale led to the politicization of the teaching force because the state had a strong, responsive teachers' union. In a different situation teacher frustration would no doubt have found other outlets: burn-out, disinvestment, token compliance, or the quiet sabotage of the programs. However, in any situation teacher co-operation is absolutely essential to the successful implementation of education reform. The future of Governor Alexander's reforms is in doubt today precisely because he failed to gain that co-operation; he failed to gain it because his reforms were not feasible in Tennessee.

Equity and excellence are commonly presented as contradictory educational goals. However, Tennessee's experience with education reform suggests that a quite different relationship exists between them. It suggests that equity and adequacy provide the indispensable foundation for educational excellence. The establishment of equity is especially important if a competitive, hierarchical conception of excellence is to be implemented. However, in states like Tennessee, it would probably be difficult to implement even an egalitarian form of excellence without seriously addressing the issue of adequacy first. *For ultimately, teachers must implement education reforms.* And teachers consider calls to excellence ludicrous as long as they are moonlighting to feed their families, placing wastebaskets under leaks whenever it rains, and cancelling tests because their school's ancient copying machine is in the repair shop again.

Tennessee's experience with educational reform suggests that there are no short cuts to meaningful and lasting educational reform. Reformers must first solve the problems they inherited from the past before they can expect to build a viable future. Equity and adequacy are the prerequisites of excellence.

References

ACHILLES, C.M., LANSFORD, Z. and PAYNE, W.H. (1985) 'Tennessee educational reform: gubernatorial advocacy', in V.D. Mueller and M.P. McKeown (eds.) *The Fiscal, Legal, and Political Aspects of State Reform of Elementary and Secondary Education* (Cambridge, MA: Ballinger Publishing Company).

ALDRICH, H. (1984) 'The day the PTA stayed home', *The Washington Monthly*, 16 (5), pp. 47–54.

BOOTH, J. and CHESHIER, C.C. (1983) 'To the TEA membership', *TEA News*, 14 (9), p. 2.

BRYANT, G. (1983) 'Is Master Teacher really TEA "buster"?' *TEA News*, 14 (13), p. 5.

CHESHIER, C.C. (1987) Personal interview.

DALTON, B.W. (1985) 'State Board of Education: coming into its own', *Tennessee Teacher*, 53, (2), pp. 8–13.

DALTON, M. (1987) Personal interview.

FRASE, L.E., HETZEL, R.W. and GRANT, R.T. (1982) 'Merit pay: a research-based alternative in Tucson', *Phi Delta Kappan*, 64 (4), pp. 266–269.

FRENCH, R.L. (1984/85) 'Dispelling the myths about Tennessee's Career Ladder program', *Educational Leadership*, 42 (4), pp. 9–14.

FRENCH, R.L. (1987) Personal interview.

LANSFORD, Z. (1984) 'A study of conflict related to the development of the Comprehensive Education Reform Act of 1984', unpublished doctoral dissertation University of Tennessee, Knoxville.

LEVARY, M. (1986) 'Few teachers back Career Ladder, survey says', *The Knoxville News-Sentinel*, 25 February, p. A2.

LEVARY, M. (1987) 'Career Ladder too complicated, costly, state education chief says', *The Knoxville News-Sentinel*, 13 February, p. A9.

MCELRATH, R.L. and Howard, M.R. (1985) 'Better Schools plus one', *Tennessee Education*, 15 (1–2) pp. 16–19.

RONEY, R.K. (1981) 'Report of TABS II implementation team feedback sessions', unpublished manuscript University of Tennessee, Knoxville.

STATE OF TENNESSEE (1982) *The Tennessee Comprehensive Education Study (TCES)* (Nashville, TN: State of Tennessee).

STATE OF TENNESSEE (1986) *The Budget 1986/87* (Nashville, TN: State of Tennessee).

TENNESSEE EDUCATION ASSOCIATION (1984) 'Teachers unhappy about BSF time', *TEA News*, 15 (14), p. 13.

T-PACE (1986) *Victory '86* (Nashville, TN: T-PACE).

TRUSTY, F. (1987) Personal interview.

WINTERS, J. (1987) Personal interview.

14   *The politics of Texas school reform*

Linda M. McNeil
Rice University

The politics of Texas school reform[1]

For decades, Texas public schools have been almost self-caricatures in their reputation for low per-pupil expenditures, state-adopted texts and the forum the adoption hearings provide to right-wing objectors to literature and science curricula, generous outlays for football teams and marching bands, and low teacher pay. When statewide reforms attempted to shift priorities away from these legendary weaknesses, it is somehow not surprising that even the reforms should play to stereotype: the choice of a billionaire to chair the blue ribbon advisory commission, ungrammatical pronouncements by legislators bent on testing teachers for basic literacy skills, galvanized resistance by football coaches faced with enforcing 'No Pass/No Play' rules on their players. The Texas role in the national educational reform movement seems on the surface to be too unique a parody on educational reform to be instructive to the national debates. But school reform in Texas, despite its theatrics, is not an aberrant case.

Within the policies which, taken together, are seen as educational reform in Texas converge political pressures which are playing themselves out in many other states. Some of the legislated reforms in Texas are very close to policies being advocated for national implementation by the current Secretary of Education. It is not yet time to write a history of Texas school reforms in the 1980s; policies are being contested, revised, amended. At this writing a governor not party to the earlier legislation is advocating shifting earnings from teacher retirement funds to prison construction. The theatrics have not yet played themselves out, the many conflicts are far from resolution. Even without a sense of closure to these policy debates, the on-going Texas story serves as a prototype of two central features of this school reform movement: the first, and most important, is the relation of educational reform to economic restructuring. The Texas economy was still thriving when a reform-minded governor took office; as the price of oil dropped, so did the resources for school improvement. Yet the unstable economy inspired reconsideration of the role of public schooling in the economy. One Texas school reform policy which has national import is the idea that public education should somehow be responsible for economic recovery. In this particular state, economic chaos gave rise to thought that schools should create certainties, should test and be held accountable to standardized measures; yet the same educational commissions and legislative packages demanded that public schools somehow provide the imaginative, intellectual 'capital' needed for a high-technology future. Behind the economic improvement rhetoric were built models of accountability anachronistic to the economic future the reformers articulate. Examining the relation between economic restructuring and educational restructuring in Texas may provide an analytical focus for questioning links in other states between perceived economic ills and expected educational remedies; the success of educational reform in economic recovery may well depend on the model of education employed. In Texas, the model for school reform has been an industrial management model anachronistic to the rhetoric of highly technological and inventive economic futures.

The Texas case also brings into the open the critical need to look beyond the 'lightning rod' issues of educational reform. In Texas, No Pass/No Play and teacher testing became the public battlegrounds on which competing educational interests fought for their claims on educational quality. While teachers complained that literacy tests for them were demeaning, reformers assured the public that minimum standards were being raised to rid the classroom of illiterate teachers. Coaches descended on the state capital in grief and anger to protest linking performance in competitive sports to students' passing grades, while the governor and billionaire Ross Perot basked in the knowledge that only a reform which really made a difference would have generated so much heated opposition.

While these debates were filling the evening newscasts and becoming in the public mind synonymous with 'school reform', the significant policy changes were occurring out of sight: authority over curriculum, teacher assessment, funding, attendance, athletic participation, and teacher discretion in a host of areas were all shifting from the local school boards and district offices (and classrooms) to the Texas Education Agency in Austin. Both these shifts in authority and control and the linking of educational reform to economic restructuring place Texas in the mainstream of *philosophies* of school reform in the 1980s. Because the Texas reforms have anticipated some national reforms and have been so publicly debated, they offer a unique opportunity for policy-makers to see in action the conflicts behind the reforms, the unanticipated consequences of some of these reforms, and the need to see reforms in their historical and economic contexts. Because Texans little bother to disguise or moderate the political and economic rationales behind their public policies, what may remain hidden in linking educational policy to the economic and political power structures in other states is more fully visible in Texas. To see the contested policies in Texas, and the overt and hidden shifts in control which accompany them, is to have a window on the kinds of power relations becoming imbedded or contested in other states, whose more sedate politics or more established bureaucratic agencies may tend to make them less visible.

This study of statewide reform policies began as a classroom study of magnet high schools and their curricula.[1] For several years, I have been studying the internal tensions within American public schools, especially as their traditional purposes – education and social control – come into conflict. Extended studies of high school classrooms and administrative policies have demonstrated that this tension lies behind much of what turns up as symptoms of low educational quality (L. McNeil 1986). When the social control purposes (behavior controls, credentialing, outcomes assessments) overwhelm the educational purposes in a school, there is a tendency of teachers to withdraw into a false efficiency model in which they go through the rituals of teaching, but without bringing their personal and professional knowledge into the classroom. In effect, like craftspeople shifted to assembly-line production, they become deskilled; that is, their rich personal knowledge of their subject comes to be split off from the trivialized, packaged knowledge they present to their students. When the tension in a school is resolved in favor of the educational purposes of the school, teachers have much less tendency to participate in their own deskilling; there is much greater likelihood that they will draw on their broadest range of knowledge and will be more successful in engaging their students in learning.

The Midwestern schools where these patterns came to light were schools that seemed on the surface to be 'working'; they had no serious problems, yet neither did they offer alternative models to the traditionally organized American high school, where order-keeping and credentialing of masses of students are held in tension with the attempts to educate individuals.

One set of schools in the Southwest offered a chance to observe teachers in a setting organized specifically in support of academic specialty and quality. These were the magnet high schools, established to help desegregate the schools in a large urban district by offering academically specialized programs of such high quality that students of the three dominant racial groups in the city would be drawn out of their neighborhood schools and into these de-segregated schools. The first few months of the study were spent in gathering exciting data on classroom interactions and curricula in these settings where school organization supported, rather than conflicted with, educative purposes. Teachers were not deskilled, teaching by rote to disengaged students, presenting a watered-down content neither took seriously; rather, they were actively engaged in bringing their liveliest curiosities and pro-fessional knowledge of subject matter and of student learning into the classroom. Most of the teachers had created their courses and many had helped create the specialized curricula at their schools; they worked as professionals and their students responded by taking school seriously.

Not even half-way into these classroom observations, teachers began to hear the rumblings of 'school reform'. Over the course of the research, teachers in these highly specialized schools saw discretion over content, teacher assessment, student assessment and the pacing of their courses shift from their classrooms and their school, to the agencies em-powered by the legislature to 'reform' Texas schools. Out of the spotlight of No Pass/No Play, the best teachers in the state saw 'reforms' threaten their ability to develop meaningful teaching styles and substantive curricula as authority over schooling become more and more distant. Their deskilling took the form of centralized district level outcomes tests and centralized state-level assessments of teachers' classroom behaviors (L. McNeil 1987b). The effects of these shifts in curricula, on students and on teachers is the subject of a larger work (McNeil 1988 forthcoming). The politics of Texas school reform takes on significance for that study because the political debates and dramatic media coverage address so few of the effects of the reforms on such teachers as those in the magnet school study. The Texas political issues take on significance nationally because they are becoming a role model for 'reforming' schools, a role model built on symptoms of educational problems rather than complex institutional factors producing those symptoms.

In the magnet school study, one appeal of the magnet schools is their staying power in a state known for top-down management. Texas has for years been at the extreme end of the spectrum in its top-down organization of schools. This top-down management begins at the state level with its famous state adoption lists for textbooks and continues into school buildings, where teachers teach on the basis of a letter of appointment, rather than a bargained contract. While some teachers do belong to unions, collective bargaining by public employees is not allowed and public employee strikes are illegal. The Texas Education Agency acts under the force of law from the legislature; it mandates rather than advises. The large size of the state and its unequal distribution of resources, rather than collective local resistance by teachers or communities, are the chief impediments to a tightly organized, uniform state schools system.

While several pieces of legislation and numerous efforts by local school boards and building-level staff have addressed the need for public school reform, the key to Texas' role in the national educational reform movement is state legislation that still goes by its House number, 'House Bill 72'. House Bill (HB) 72 is a complex piece of education legislation passed in 1984. Many of its components became policy effective soon after passage; others were referred to state agencies and local school boards for implementation and are still not fully operational. Resistance to the bill has come from many quarters. Clearly, the story of this 'reform' legislation is not yet over. Some of the facts are known; others are not yet fully understood; still others are under internal revision. The November 1986 gubernatorial election changed the people and parties in power in the state. The new administrations's attempts to dramatically change policies derived form HB 72 make any definitive analysis premature.

What can be done now, however, is to begin to frame an analytical perspective on the current state reform movements, using Texas and its contested legislation as a case study in reform policies. The combination of unique historical factors and economic conditions which produced HB 72 (and much of its opposition) exemplify the dependence of educational policy on the broader historical circumstances. Yet the uniqueness of these external factors in Texas has contributed a model of centralized control over schools which is advocated in Washington and surfacing in many state legislatures where such centralization has not been historically prevalent.

The discussion which follows will first provide a description of this legislation, which is being both contested and emulated, and its basis in the particular history of the state at the time of passage. Second, the discussion will trace out the implications for various constituencies of the legislation. Finally, the political nature of Texas school reform will be used to help frame questions significant to the cultural content of schools, the relationship of education to the state, and the relationship between education and economic goals.

Something for everyone

Ernest Boyer (1983) and John Goodlad (1983), in their contributions to the current reform debates, have said that in American high schools 'we want it all'. That could have been the motto of the drafters of the Texas HB 72, in the 1984 legislative session called to pass school reform legislation. Gubernatorial candidate Mark White, a Democrat who cares deeply about education and about the work experiences of teachers, was genuinely concerned with the uneven quality of education in the state where he had been serving as attorney general. He faced a close race with Bill Clements, the extremely conservative Republican millionaire oilman he wished to unseat. One of White's campaign promises was to raise teacher salaries more than 20%; his promise paid off in teacher votes and in the votes of supporters of improved schools. Once in office, however, he was unable to persuade the legislature to pass such a pay increase; many legislators believed teachers were generally not qualified for the higher pay increase. To get the pay increse, White had to promise that there would be quality control, that the taxpayers would be receiving benefits from their expenditures. White's strategy was to put together a comprehensive education reform bill which would provide benefits for as many constituents of education as possible; the teacher pay increase would be one of many features of a broad-sweeping legislative reform for Texas education. The result of White's concern was HB 72; meant to upgrade education and directly help teachers, it has drawn more heated opposition from teachers than any legislation in recent memory. The distance between its intent and it reception is only one of its many ironies.

Ross Perot, a millionaire who made his fortunes in computers rather than ranches and oil, also cared about education. To lend the support of the business community to expected tax increases, Perot chaired a task force charged with drafting a blueprint for reforming Texas schools (Select Committee on Public Education 1984a, b). Although no other state is known to have had such a wealthy and illustrious planner of reforms, Texas was different only in degree, not in kind, from the economic competition rhetoric typical of the alarms sounded in *A Nation at Risk* (National Commission on Excellence in Education 1983) and given at least acknowledgement, if not central status, in all the other major reform reports. To bring Texas schools, and the Texas economy, to a competitive level, Perot's commission considered aspects of schooling ranging from funding to attendance, from athletics to teacher pay, from class size and school day hours to mandatory kindergarten.

The first responsibility was to the teachers. White had promised teachers a significant pay raise. The most obvious benefit of the bill would have to be higher pay for teachers. The Perot commission agreed and the final bill reflected this priority. Second, ostensibly also for teachers, was a career ladder system of merit so that those who performed to higher standards would be appropriately rewarded.

While such a proposal was likely to gain teachers' support, it would not necessarily be popular with voters once they had calculated the expense of using state funds to raise the guaranteed minimums of teacher pay across the state as well as increased local school taxes.

Going against greater expenditures for this and other components of school reform was the long-standing marginality of education to public policy in Texas. Unlike many Midwestern and East Coast states where education had been long valued and made accessible to wide sectors of the population, with higher education being linked correspondingly to greater economic and political power, Texas had traditionally viewed education beyond the primary level as something of a luxury. The economic successes of the state, unlike those states whose economies were driven in part by highly skilled labor, complex mastery of international economics by management, or the production of 'knowledge capital', were based in Texas largely on the presence of fairly easily exploited natural resources. From agriculture and then oil had arisen an economy, so the myth goes, on hard work, luck and land (or what lies beneath it). Many of the state's most powerful corporate owners, oilmen and politicians have traditionally been proud of their relative lack of formal education. Sociology of Texas knowledge would have to study the relations between *savvy and power* rather than *knowledge and power*, in their formal senses. Neither intellectual nor credentialed knowledge has been seen as crucial to economic development in this entrepreneurial state.

In addition, the state has a very poor history of supporting public goods of any kind. It has consistently ranked in the bottom tier of states on almost all measures of payment for public goods, including those which include the channeling of federal funds to residents and communities.[2] The entrepreneurial presumption is that you take care of yourself and your own; if you are not successful right now, either your luck may turn any day, or you're not working hard enough. It is critical for the current educational reform movement in this state to note that even in times of great wealth, individual prosperity and a bulging state treasury, Texas did not spend on public goods (mass transit, parks, health care, pollution control, schools) amounts proportionate to its wealth.

Teacher pay is generally regarded as public employee pay rather than as an investment in a public good, therefore. One way to defuse the reluctance to pay for higher teachers' salaries was to have business leaders heavily represented on the committee. They could forcefully argue that business and industry in this state, whose agriculture faced strong international competition and whose oil reserves had been severely depleted, would become more and more dependent on 'human capital' and 'knowledge capital'. As the state's economy shifted to a high-technology focus, higher educational standards would become an imperative from a private enterprise, not a public goods, perspective.

The second way to elicit support for teacher pay was to promise more benefits for the costs. The parallels to the social efficiency movements of the 1910s and 1920s here are startling: in that era (Callahan 1967) burgeoning secondary school populations, and a history of corruption and patronage in the running of many big city school systems, made business leaders decide to take control of public education. They ran for school boards, promising to increase productivity and efficiency in schools; they bypassed the teaching profession, inviting efficiency experts like Frederick W. Taylor to come from industrial efficiency jobs to redesign secondary schools to resemble the factory. From this era schools derive ability group tracking, standardized tests (testing the factory's 'raw material'), the superintendent as businessman and teacher as hired worker in the credential machine. Schoolmen (and they were men) reasoned that the public would be willing to pay if the public could see tightly managed organizations and measurable results. The accounting practices of industrial production came into widespread use in schools.

In Texas, the promises of productivity to taxpayers came in the form of trade-offs within the reform legislation. Teachers were promised an increase in base pay, with the state making up the difference between poor districts' salary scales for teachers and the state-specified minimums.[3]

In return, the tax-paying public was promised several qualifiers: that teachers would be worth the extra pay, first as entering teachers and later as practicing professionals. Quality control for entering teachers was to be in the form of a test to be taken by all teachers requesting certification and by all currently practicing teachers wishing to retain their teaching certificates. As will be discussed below, this test became a lightning rod issue which alienated teachers far more than the promise of greater pay attracted them.

Second, for the benefit of both taxpayers and teachers, the law would institute a career ladder program by which teachers could be evaluated and rewarded along dimensions other than years of seniority. For the taxpayer the promise would be that no teacher would get merit pay raises who did not earn them; teachers, in turn, would see that extra effort does not go unnoticed. A central component of this career ladder merit system was to be a systematic, regular assessment of the classroom performance of all teachers. Previously, only probationary teachers were typically evaluated more than once each year. In some districts, career teachers were observed and assessed only in alternating years over a two- or three-year cycle. For teachers the benefits of being observed and assessed were to be that they would experience less isolation and more potential to have their work seen and rewarded. For administrators and taxpayers, there would be the move from intuitive (and political) assessments to 'fair', 'objective', 'rational' ones. Teachers would receive at the beginning of the school year a copy of the state-mandated teacher assessment criteria and behaviors against which they would be judged. They and their administrators would both have greater certainty about what their evaluation was supposed to accomplish.

Other benefits for teachers, and for education in general, were to be new attendance laws. The most famous, or infamous, was the No Pass/No Play provision. To counter teachers' frustrations that their students were missing class for pep rallies and athletic games, especially in rural areas on Thursdays and Fridays, athletes would be held to strict grade requirements before being allowed to play in sports during each six-week grading period. The provision not only gave teachers more leverage over class attendance and student activities, especially in varsity athletics (traditionally seen as the domain of coaches and alumnae, not teachers); it sent the message to parents and students that the educative purposes of schooling are to be taken seriously: teachers are to be supported.

The attraction of these portion of the law for the business community were both stated and implied: education was to be valued. Even if it cost more, there would be quality control checks to make sure productivity matched investment. There would be testing and assessing of teachers and more testing of students. Teachers would be tested on the 'professional knowledge' (e.g., 'Which of the following are characteristics of a standardized test?') and on basic literacy. Stricter attendance policies and enforcement would accrue to local districts not only, it was hoped, in increased graduation rates, but in more per-pupil dollars from the state, paid on the basis of actual pupil attendance.

Other provisions of HB 72 dealt with issues of school finance and the role of the state agency. The state agency, for example, was empowered to design (or contract the design of) the 'instruments' for testing teachers and to codify the new attendance policies. 'Guidelines' of implementation were to be developed by various offices within the Texas Education Agency.

One of the most popular provisions of the law for those who worry about the quality of education in such a huge and diverse state was the clause moving toward greater equalization of funding. Texas had not had a history of universally bad public schools; instead, the state had generally assumed that the reputation for educational quality would reside with a few select high schools in wealthy neighbourhoods or oil-rich towns. If Bellaire High School in Houston, or the high schools of the oil town of Midland, for example, turned out Merit Scholars and 'good students', there would emerge leaders for business and the universities and the professions; many other, poorer neighborhoods were written off as not having 'good schools'. Litigation in the 1970s had attempted more than once to redress the maldistribution of tax dollars across school districts on the grounds that local property taxes should not be the primary sources of school funding in a state with such enormous gaps between rich and poor. These lawsuits largely failed, but the vast inequities did not go away; HB 72 took a step in the right direction by mandating a new formula for the distribution of state education funds to local districts. The provision was helpful enough to please legislators representing extremely poor, often minority, districts, but not so radical as to alienate those representatives of the affluent districts which would lose funds once the formula went into effect.

HB 72 looked like a popular law, a genuine attempt to build a coalition in favour of greater spending on public education: an attempt to provide something for all the constituents of public education, teachers, parents, business people, legislators, the state agency (greatly increasing its power), school boards (giving them the role of assessing teachers at the local level, while being able to blame state agencies for designing the assessment instruments), children (mandatory kindergarten, longer school days and years), and so on.

Lightning rods and loss of faith

The lightning rod issues, those which drew the greatest and most public opposition were the teacher tests and No Pass/No Play. Both pitted school personnel against each other and against the state agency. Both figured strongly in Mark White's governor's eventual loss in his very close gubernatorial contest with Bill Clements.

The No Pass/No Play rule is not very radical: students must be passing all their subjects at any six weeks grading period in order to play in a sport or other major activity (band, cheerleading and the like) during the following six weeks. It is seen as a reform aimed at supporting teachers of academic subjects whose leverage over their students during a sports season is often much less than that of the coach. Small towns especially construct a sense of community and special identity around the successes of the football teams. Poor and minority students often envision sports as their ticket to college scholarships and perhaps even professional teams. Interscholastic sports so dominate some smalltown schools (and apparently some suburban ones) that for all practical purposes classes have been dismissed at noon on Friday so that students can travel (spectators as well as athletes) to out-of-town games. While coaches were less vocal publicly in their opposition to the tighter attendance rules in HB 72 (six unexcused absences equal a failure in the course for the term, regardless of the student's grades), they were furious about the grade requirement for players.

Of all the oppositions to provisions of HB 72, it was the coaches' that was best organized, best disseminated around the state, and most frequently heard in formal hearings. Coaches managed to have extensive media coverage of star players, band members, drill team members and cheerleaders whose tears were flowing over exclusion from participation based on failing grades. Some high schools had to cancel games because of insufficient players; other cancelled marching band performances at games. In their small towns coaches became political leaders on state school reform overnight; their professional association sent spokespersons to legislative and agency hearings to protest this rule. Most argued within the spirit of 'school reform', that rather than hurt academic performance, sports participation increased motivation for students who might otherwise see no reason to attend school. The coaches were able, thereby, to appear to buy into the school improvement rhetoric without giving up their intense opposition to No Pass/No Play. While this has generally been viewed as a conflict between athletic and academic interests, it is critical also as another manifestation within this legislation that discretion and authority were passing from the local to the state level. The locus of power over this issue was at last as important as the rule itself. Coaches exerted far more clout than many political observers imagined possible and are credited with helping, at least in a small way, stir up enough opposition to Mark White that Bill Clements, who promised to amend the rule, was elected.

The other lightning rod issue became the testing of teachers. Although most Texas teachers have held 'permanent', 'lifetime' certificates (according to the language printed on the certificate), HB 72 required that to remain certified, all previously certified teachers would have to take the Texas Examination of Current Administrators and Teachers (TECAT), a pencil-and-paper test of basic grammar, professional knowledge and a writing sample. Because the commission, legislature and governor had used the promise of competence to legitimate higher expenditures for teacher pay, the legislation had to provide for a way of measuring teacher competence. The idea of competence, translated into statewide terms, quickly became an issue of basic literacy. Did Texas teachers know the basic skills they were supposed to be teaching to children? An objective test of basic literacy and simple information about classroom practice would satisfy two objectives: it would not be so threatening to teachers that they would balk at taking it (as would, say, the equivalent of the Advanced Placement examination seniors take in the teachers' subject fields), but at the same time it would provide some assurance that no illiterate teacher could 'hide' within the system. A standardized test seemed the best and least expensive way to approach a problem many in the public and in the legislature saw as teachers' blame for low educational quality. Teachers immediately grasped that the trade-off between pay raises and quality control could work against them. The quality of their teaching was not to be considered as a basis for re-certification: certification would rest solely on performance on a standardized test. Because so much of the rhetoric of the reform movement was couched in the language of blaming teachers, teachers were not irrational to fear the test and its consequences. Older teachers, minority teachers, and many teachers who had studied at underfunded, small colleges most feared that they were to be judged against a test aimed at people whose education mirrored greater privilege. While most teachers agreed that illiterate and incompetent teachers have no place in schools, they did not agree that the test would capture this incompetence, nor that all who failed would in fact be incompetent. The abstract fears and ambiguities which arose during the months the test was being prepared turned the teachers against the very governor (Mark White) who saw these reforms in their interests. Law suits were filed by individuals, unions and teacher groups. Some teachers retired early rather than face failing the test; some schools offered cram courses for teachers who needed to review their writing and professional literature (or to hone their test-taking skills).

Those in government and business supporting the test saw it as a marker of basic literacy, of absolute minimum standards for teachers. Common sense often had it that the fears of teachers must themselves be indicators of teacher incompetence; if they were competent, they would have nothing to fear. For teachers, those arguments held little weight; it was the presumption that teachers were the ones in schools that needed reforming that most galled them. And they were equally offended because with their careers, their livelihoods, at stake, the quality of their day-to-day *teaching* was held to be of less importance in re-certification than a test score from a commercial testing firm from out-of-state.

Over 97% of the teachers taking the TECAT passed; their fears of losing jobs because of the test were unfounded. But their fears of losing a voice in their teaching were right on target. Consoling words from the governor ('I knew our teachers could do it') were not enough to compensate for months of uncertainty, for the lack of input into policies that might help their teaching, for the lack of public credibility that built as sample questions appeared in newspapers alongside interviews with worried teachers. Teachers never became as articulate and unified in their reasons for opposing the test as the coaches were over No Pass/No Play. Their public voicing of fears, rather than of positive alternatives, planted in the public mind (and certainly in state agency rhetoric) that teachers do need 'improving', that they need tighter controls from management, that they need more supervision over their teaching. (It is interesting that with so much of the school reform rhetoric aimed at helping economic recovery, no teacher groups noted the cash drain out-of-state in the creation of this test. Dr James Popham of IOX Assessment Associates in California held the contract to develop the test[4]; in a time of great debate over money for teacher pay raises, the contract cost was almost $5,000,000 to develop, administer, and score the test. In addition, the Texas Education Agency subsidized the appropriation with over $200,000 of its own staff time. An independent economic analysis of the test production, preparation courses (many of which aimed at test-taking skills rather than the substance of reading or grammar or pedagogy), personal time and outlay costs by administrators and teachers yielded a conservative estimate of more than $78,000,000. The TEA noted the public cost estimates to be credible (Shepard and Kreitzer 1987). For a test that changed few staffing patterns, had little lasting impact on teachers' reading and writing skills, and no discernible impact on their teaching except to cut into lesson planning time, the financial costs are staggering. The costs of status and confidence and public esteem for teachers will have even longer lasting effects. The strategy to build consensus through an apparently rational objective process only exacerbated divisiveness.

There is much more to be said about teacher tests as instruments for certification and re-certification. What is significant in this case is that the symbolic politics which merged quality control with increased costs backfired dramatically. Not only did teachers alienate their public by failing to explain their opposition, by failing to articulate that these tests lowered standards rather than raise them, they failed to gain credibility as a voice in educational policy. Because the vocal resistance to state-level reforms tended to come from coaches, who favored lenient attendance and grading policies at the expense of academics, the governor and others in policy positions felt they had truly set in motion policies that would up-grade education. On the other hand, because the governor failed to listen to those teacher groups that did try to speak out, because he saw teacher responses as irrational fears rather than pedagogical concerns, he miscounted his votes. Although no one will know just how individual teachers voted, they did not support him as a group and he lost his re-election bid in 1986 by a small margin.

Lasting ironies and hidden controls

The lightning-rod issues of No Pass/No Play and teacher testing were responses to the sense
that in Texas education was out of control. Both of these policies attracted vehement opposition because they attempted to bring under 'control' conditions of schooling (athletic
dominance of academics, allegedly illiterate teachers) which traditionally local administrative
practices had failed over many years to correct. The Texas reforms generally are characterized
by a controlling reaction to anything perceived as a problem and by a shift of the controls to a
level removed from the classroom. For example, there was no sustained debate over the value
of *student* assessments of teacher or teachers' personal assessments of their work as relevant to
a teacher's re-certification. The mentality of reform was that 'we need to do something
about (or to) those teachers'. Such controls over teacher practice can be contested because
they are so public, so overt. As one high-level curriculum supervisor stated, 'Everytime they
try to improve schools, they end up just adding more controls.' So long as such controls are
new, they remain problematic and debatable. Over time, however, overt controls tend to
become imbedded in the structure and taken for granted once they are in place. The Texas
school reforms demonstrate how the imbedding of controls can occur and point to the
complicated relationship between the economic goals of school reform and the tendency to
solve educational problems by adding controls and undermining teacher authority. In the
case of Texas, the model of school reform embodies the controls reminiscent of a time, and an
economic circumstance, long past, ironically helping to lock Texas into a position far short of
the high-technology economy that reformers hoped would develop alongside 'reformed'
schools.

     If one purpose of bureaucratic rules is to gain control over uncertain environments (K.
McNeil 1978), the bureaucrats in the teacher assessment division of the state agency followed
the textbook on bureaucratic controls. The uncertain environment they faced included great
geographic, economic and cultural diversity across school districts; the politics and personalities and favoritisms in local areas; the varying levels of professionalism among both
teachers to be assessed and administrators carrying out assessments.

     The swelling of opposition and alienation in the ranks of teachers did not subside after
the initial administering of the TECAT. The trivial questions and classroom management
slant to its pedagogical topics surfaced again, this time in the state's new 'instrument' for
teacher assessment. A part of the quality control promised in exchange for higher school
taxes for teacher pay was a state-wide check-list for administrative oversight of teacher
quality (TEA 1986). The political and personal uncertainties of teacher evaluations were to be
made 'rational' and 'objective' by placing in the hands of administrators and teachers a list of
behaviors thought to be typical of productive, effective teachers. Teachers' ratings on these
classroom behaviors would provide the basis of their eligibility for mobility up the career
ladder and thereby for merit pay increases. The previous state-required assessment tools had
had such notorious sections as 'uses praise words', followed by a list of about 100 acceptable
'praise words' for teachers to use with children in their classes. This and other weaknesses
created such resistance by teachers, and such unwieldy paperwork for administrators, that
the agency was compelled to begin anew.

     The new instrument is a marvel of bureaucratic precision. Modeled after the activity
analysis model of factory assembly-line pacing, the tasks of the teacher are reduced to 55
generic *behaviors*. These are intended to pertain to all teaching situations, all courses, all grade
levels. Derived primarily from the language of classroom management and cognitive psych-
ology (as applied in its least intellectual form for this purpose), the list enumerates such
teacher behaviors as varying activities and waiting appropriately for student responses to

teacher-asked questions. The 'objective' measures include just three choices of rating by the observer: satisfactory, unsatisfactory (stated on the form like the 'needs improvement' boxes on children's report cards) and the elusive 'EQ', which means exceptional qualities.

Leaving little to chance, those in charge of implementation (as so charged by the very general language of the legislation) developed detailed instructions about the frequency of these assessments, the level of personnel who may conduct assessments, and the necessary training workshop hours the evaluators must have before doing the classroom visits. Two administrators (or an administrator and an experienced teacher) visit each teacher. The primary administrator's assessment is to count 60%; the other observer's portion of the rating counts 60%. The number of visits to a teacher each year is currently being contested and will probably be revised. Teachers see the assessment instrument as ignoring their personal style. They especially object that nowhere in the assessment is there a space for a teacher to explain *why* she or he chose that particular approach to the lesson. In press conferences, the state commissioner of education defused teachers' criticisms of this assessment device as typical of any system that 'needs to have the bugs worked out of it'. He anticipates fine-tuning the 'instrument' and the training of the assessors so that the procedure works smoothly after the initial year. Such deflection carries with it the message that to be against a generic evaluation is to be against improved teaching.

If the assessments went into the personnel file for only rare future reference, or if they became the basis for constructive peer discussions about improving classroom teaching, most of the teachers interviewed in the magnet study, and in several other schools, would not object to being rated by an observer. In fact, however, the entire career ladder system of merit pay is contingent upon the standardized assessments. Teachers must not only attain a certain level of ratings but must maintain those over, say, three consecutive years, before career ladder increments will result. In a non-union state, this makes the teacher entirely vulnerable to the politics, professional knowledge and personalities administering the test. Although supposedly standardized and objective, the instruction book (which all teachers received by the beginning of the last school year) has only one or two sentences guiding assessors (and observed teachers) in designating *EQ* status to their work. Some administrators use Exceptional Quality to mean exceptional as compared to other teachers; others use it to indicate a teacher went beyond his/her own usual norm. Some administrators use this designation liberally; others reserve its use for truly extraordinary teaching; still others consider budget implications of teacher salaries increases and allocate EQs sparingly. No teacher can know in advance whether an administrator will reward (or even recognize) a particularly insightful question or explanation to a student in a given subject.

Although the effect of such an assessment model is the subject of a separate paper (McNeil 1987a), it must be noted here that most teachers feel that to perform well on the 55 item check list in a 40-minute class period often comes closer to a song-and-dance routine than to teaching. If only a few items on the check list are applicable to a given day's lesson, the teacher is forced to forfeit a high rating or alter teaching style for that day of observation, even at the expense of divorcing the lesson from its content and/or the students. The instrument thus deskills the teacher, artificially separating a teacher's knowledge of pedagogy from overt behaviors.

For an assessment to be fair, it must be uniformly managed and administered. The reason for the checklist is to maintain objectivity in what would become political and irrational. Of course, the checklist itself is highly subjective in its creation and is variably applied. For example, one 20-year teacher stated that her biggest objection to the new assessment is that nowhere does it ask for her explanation, for her *why*. There is also no way of checking off attending to a particular student's need in an assessment that assumes the teacher addresses an aggregate class with the teacher at its center. The assessment instrument, ostensibly neutral, also omits variations in teaching style which accompany subject-matter considerations. Students and their needs are notably missing as well.

The assessment mechanism is one more area where Texas teachers participated in a trade-off, gaining a system of merit pay in exchange for an assessment system which is to be generic to all subjects, grades and students. These trade-offs at first seem fair and reasonable, especially if they result in new revenues, supported by the economic establishment without whose support, in this non-public-goods state, increased financial support for schools would be unlikely.

The Faustian component of the agreement is that within a linkage between controls and benefits, *the controls can remain in place even after the resources for the benefits disappear.* This is essential to understand in the current push for a national test for teachers and a national set of tests for students. The current vision is that such tests will not revert to the lowest common denominator because they will include multidimensional 'performances' and multi-dimensional criteria. Such non-computer-graded assessments are very expensive. Once the *tests and their criteria* have been legitimated as the province of the government (or, in this case, the state), or of a national board to be somehow ratified by state certifications, the locus of control for these matters will be out of the hands of local people. And if the resources to support their highest level of expertise should disappear, or shrink in competition with other necessary public expenditures, the controls themselves, the tests and the 'instrument' will persist. Evaluation will have been nationalized at great cost to professional teachers.

This ratcheting effect raises controls each time resources are needed (for example, higher teacher pay); yet it is very difficult to lower the degree or level of control if the resources are taken away. Texas is already demonstrating this ratcheting effect. Governor Mark White and the Ross Perot Commission laid the plans for the complicated package of costs and controls at a time when the state finances were much stronger. The checklists for teacher performance were tolerated because they were thought to be the only politically expedient route to higher pay.

The Texas economy is now in shambles, with no clear end of the decline in sight. The price of oil is extremely low; agriculture is suffering; and the wealth built on those two is collapsing, especially in real estate. The new governor, Bill Clements, no friend to education, is suggesting that the career ladder pay increments due for the next year may have to be postponed. The standardized assessments will of course remain in place. Teachers will have had their professional role reduced to items in a list of 'behaviors' with nothing to show for it. Governor Clements has made several public statements about the career ladder. At first, he indicated that the state treasury could not possibly honor the commitments to higher teacher pay. There was not enough money budgeted to cover all the salary increases for all who might up-grade their career-ladder status. The Governor explained that since there was not enough money for the *teachers*, the surplus should be invested back into the creation of the *assessment instruments*. In other words, assessments were to continue even though one's career ladder step could not be taken. The testing and consulting firms, the administrators who travel to workshops on teacher assessment – all these would reap the benefits of the 'not enough for teacher pay raises' fund. Even more cynical is the governor's later suggestion that education money be switched to prison contruction.

Because it is more complicated and because teachers are not all gathered on assessment days, ready to be photographed by the news media, as they were on TECAT test days, the teacher assessments have not become the volatile public issue that accompanied the teacher testing. However, as the management-based assessment continues in place, it is possible that it becomes taken for granted. Its controls could become imbedded in the structure of administrator-teacher relations; the absence of substantive content and pedagogy, or allowance for teacher style and student differences, could become as routine as student report cards. In such an instance, the hollowness of the assessment categories could become a secondary problem; the first being the necessity of linking resources to controls, in which the controls come to serve only controlling purposes rather than educative ones.

The ratcheting effect of controls linked to benefits brings us back to the original consideration behind Texas school reforms: the economic impetus to assure that schooling will contribute to economic recovery. The choice of Perot to lead the blue ribbon advisory commission and the timing of the reforms grew not only out of a weakening of the traditional economic base in the state, but from a perception that future economic strength would come more from high technology industries than from oil and gas, the future wealth would build much more slowly than the get-rich-quick days of booming oil and real estate, and that the increase in high technology and service industries would necessitate expansion of the 'human capital' side of the economic equation. Citizens would need sophisticated education to create and manage the complex commercial and technological enterprises that would make Texas competitive in world markets. The reputation of public education in the state was not only woefully inadequate as a base for economic restructuring toward high-technology industries, it also was a barrier to relocation by well educated scientists, engineers and managers the state needed to attract if it were to lure industries to the state from other places. The intense push for reforms came not from parents and children, nor from educators, but from the business sector seeking highly educated, highly skilled employees and managers.

Yet the interrelations between economic structures and school policy are not all so simple as Ross Perot's advisory role in shaping an economic rationale for school reform. Once the legislation was passed and its general enabling language operationalized by the state agencies, the rationalizing processes of bureaucracy attempted to neutralize and depoliticize the reform process. This eroded the potential to debate the schools' appropriate role in support of the economic *status quo*, or new directions for highly technological economic development, or empowerment of a generation of students cut out of expectations of economic participation except as clients and modest consumers. None of these can be debated to any effect once the abstract philosophy is transformed by bureaucratic procedure into 'rational' processes such as longer school days or checklists for teacher behaviors. To redress a long history of inequitable funding across districts, the state shifts funds according to a complicated formula from a richer tax base to a poorer one. To ease the political fall-out from this transfer of wealth, there is a parallel policy to publish by district and school the student scores on standardized tests of basic skills. Only a political few from poorer communities will link the scores to inadequate funding and see them as a chance to press for more generous redistribution formulas. For most, the test scores will confirm in the minds of parents in wealthy and middle class schools that they have chosen 'good schools' for their children. Neither the test scores, nor the redistribution policy itself, nor the teacher assessment instruments tells us what the children of poor neighbourhoods need to help them learn. The 'rational' measurements do not give us a clue as to whether teachers have the resources they need for their students. The rational processes define 'in' certain measurable indicators and, by omission or reduction to checklists, define 'out' many other links between school, child and economic futures. The crisis climate in which the legislation was drafted passes to a time of operationalizing that is based on aggregate models of accountability. The language of educational quality bypasses substantive discussion of the content of a public education equal to economic and technological revolutions and takes on instead the language of short-term accounting. Those accounting measures, and the expense needed to maintain them, will likely remain in place after the sense of crisis is past and well before attention to the substance of educational quality is addressed.

The historical precedents for this model of economic-based school reform are clear. The policies themselves are straight out of the past. That a futuristic vision of school reform should recapitulate the school reforms from the early days of factories is full of ironies. Borrowed so closely from the social efficiency model that some of the language and many of the practices could be interchanged with those of Bobbitt and Charters and their 1920s cohort, most of the 1980s Texas school reforms threaten to undermine even the very economic basis for education they are purported to advance (Callahan 1967). To see a high tech future, especially in entrepreneurial terms, and to tie education reform to it, should be a call for curriculum aimed at the highest knowledge in every field. It should call for risk-taking, experimentation, visionary possibilities and open-ended instructional purpose. The model of school reform should be based on highly skilled, highly professional teachers, not teachers deskilled by checklists of generic classroom behaviors.

The anachronism operates on several levels. First, the economic rhetoric which made the costs of reforms palatable to the business community was based on a model from 60 years before. To justify secondary school expenses during rapid industrialism, social efficiency reformers organized schools aroung top-down management with tight management controls based on assumptions of low-skilled teachers and students in need of being processed into stratified, pre-determined jobs. The models of accountability – in the 1980s visible in TECAT scores and generic assessments of teachers as well as publication of aggregate student scores on standardized tests – emphasize short-term, predictable outcomes, also borrowed from the input-output model of earlier industrial production. Such a model has no way to account for the education that encourages the creative minds and highly skilled intellects implied by the rhetoric of an education for a new economic era. One may imagine that the elites who had to be brought reluctantly into paying for Texas school reform envision a few entrepreneurs like themselves in charge of even high-technology industry, with the mass of workers as deskilled or as narrowly skilled as an assembly line worker or the Third World workers currently hired to produce the inventions of a few creative minds. While such may be the result, this counters the rhetoric of this elite in their criticisms of schools as turning out people who can't think, who can't handle higher math, who know little science, who won't take risks, who lack the mental discipline of the Japanese, who will soon be out-of-date in a more complicated world. The language of an economic imperative for educated people is not a language being imposed by critics of the reforms; it is the language of the reformers and as such must be reconciled somehow with the deskilling aspects these new reforms are likely to produce.

Role model for research and policy

Because of its caricatured reputation as a feudal economy with hostility to public goods, Texas could be written off as expected to bungle this latest attempt at education reform. These reforms must be taken seriously, however, if for no other reason than the fact that they are being taken seriously as role models in many other states. Seeing widely publicized reforms implemented in such education-poor states as Texas and Tennessee has given political leverage to those in other states to follow suit. So far, most of the critiques of Texas reforms have centered on inappropriate costs (such as for the TECAT), inadequacy of redistribution of funds to poorer districts, effects of No Pass/No Play rules on athlete drop-out rates or grades. It is now time to take a longer look at the larger issues underlying school reform as we try to learn from the Texas case before proceeding to parallel reforms (such as student outcomes testing) at the national level. Two of those larger issues arise out of the examples discussed here. The first is the role of the state as provider of education. The second is the relationship between the substance of education and the effects of legislated reforms.

Critical scholars have developed a comprehensive body of scholarship on the relationship of education to the nature of the state (Apple 1982). Very often the scholarship discusses the 'intervention' of government in education. Yet in the US the issue is not the role of the state in education, but the role of public education as a part of the state. Schools are a part of the state's role in the distribution of public goods. In entrepreneurial states like Texas, the public goods function of the state has been of less importance historically than the role of the state as intervenor on behalf of property and wealth. In the 1920s these two functions merged when industry began to shift the cost of training, sorting and credentialing workers to the public, especially to public high schools. Expanding public secondary education was built on a coalition of social reformers wanting to extend education to the masses and industrialists needing to rationalize the processes of production (including the intake of 'human capital') as productivity went through periods of rapid expansion.

By having Ross Perot chair the advisory commission on school reform, and by writing the language of those advisories and related legislation in terms of the central role of economic recovery and restructuring, Mark White reiterated the need for a public coalition to fund schools, given the absence of public consensus on the worth of education. The tension between these two roles for the state in education is unavoidable in a state which has much catching up to do in education, but declining resources with which to build. Public education as a public good becomes vital in a state whose wild west mythology is contradicted by its urbanity and international culture. Three of the ten largest cities in the US are in Texas. In addition to native-born Anglos, Hispanics and Blacks, the state has received documented immigrants and refugees and undocumented ones from the Middle East, Mexico, Central America, Southwest Asia, the Caribbean – all in the last ten years. The Houston public school children represent over 100 home languages.

Any critique of the role of the state in shaping education to the needs of economic elites and high-tech industries needs to be in dialogue with the view of the state in a democracy as the primary instrument of public goods. While we despair over the tightly controlling nature of many recent centralized reforms in education, we would despair equally over a defaulting of the state in its obligations to support and extend public education, to help make it accessible to all. At the federal level is an administration wanting to privatize public goods, from selling railroads and the Federal Housing Authority to private owners, to the deregulation of industries. That administration's analog for education is public vouchers to be used at private schools.

Neither this privatization nor the tightening of state-level controls provides a persuasive model for school reform. Many other states are accepting the system as given and are merely tinkering around the margins, setting up a few rungs on career ladders or holding teacher workshops or adding interim-year standardized tests for students. The extremes of the Texas model may serve one purpose: perhaps by negative example of those policies most deskilling, most short-sighted, this state reinforces a graphic call for real reform, for reform that will ground teaching and learning in the needs children have to live in their own time, not repeat the metaphors of education that are long out of sync with reality.

The persistence of top-down management as a means of quality control, or symbolic quality control, is humbling. A biography of Georgia O'Keeffe (Lisle 1980) chronicles the painter's year teaching public school art in Amarillo, Texas. Her required state-adopted textbook would require the children to do 'art' as a sort of copy-book exercise, replicating the affected drawings in the book. Ms O'Keeffe had studied just enough art that she knew she wanted the children to draw what they saw, and more than that, what they felt about what they were seeing. She informed the textbook commission that she would not teach from the adopted book. While she was away, the legislature passed a law requiring the use of textbooks chosen by the state commission.

> Law or no law, Georgia had taken a principled stand and she stubbornly refused to obey. A tense, lengthy struggle between Georgia O'Keeffe and the state of Texas ensued – but when the school year ended, the books had not been bought. (p. 65)

She lost the fight but managed to prolong it until too much of the school year had passed to justify purchasing texts. Perhaps the world owes to Texas's top-down management of curriculum the credit for sending a great artist out of the classroom and into the profession of painter, in which she could affirm the link between painting and experience.

The year of Georgia O'Keeffe's textbook dispute was 1913. Perhaps someone at the commission was glad to see her leave teaching, a teacher who after all did not perform up to the minimum 'standards'. Today politicians and bureaucrats who look at teacher exit figures assume those are the teachers who were afraid of failing the TECAT. They have no rational measure that indicates the number of leavers who want some integrity between what they know and the ways they are permitted, and evaluated, to teach. The politics and false economies of Texas's centralized management of education have been entrenched at least since the novice teacher days of Georgia O'Keeffe. Perhaps it is time to re-examine the role of the state in education and of education as a part of the public goods of the state. Taken seriously, the rhetoric of tying education to a restructuring of the economy would demand a creativity, a spirit of innovation and risk that is not typical of the reforms so far established.

A second function the Texas reforms can play in the national reform debate is to raise to awareness the apparent neutrality of reforms that distance the management of schools from the practice of teachers. Standardizing teacher assessment, limiting recertification to a single test score, evaluating teaching as overt behaviors all tend toward aggregate measures that are devoid of meaning. After all the pressure, expense, conflict, dread and optimism accompanying each of these reforms, we have little sense of the quality of what is taught, the substance of what is learned. My own research in a number of high schools has shown that when the educative purposes of schools are subordinated to the order-keeping, management purposes of schools, teachers begin to ritualize their teaching in an attempt to create some efficiency and authority in a controlling, but rarely supportive, environment (McNeil 1986). Course content processed through ritualistic lists and worksheets loses its credibility for students; it becomes 'school knowledge' too artificially organized and simplified to ring true to students' personal curiosities. As teachers and students bracket their personal knowledge in the exchange of school knowledge, both become disengaged, less motivated and committed. Ironically, principals and school reformers often see this disengagement as a reason to tighten controls, to increase paperwork for teachers and behavior rules for students. A cycle of lowering expectations is kept in motion by the failure to see causes that lie behind the symptoms of poor educational quality.

The magnet school study (McNeil 1988 forthcoming) has shown this same tendency to develop as the most controlling of the Texas reforms were put into place. Teachers who had previously opened their rich store of knowledge to students and brought students into the use of books and community resources to make their own discoveries, found themselves self-consciously altering their teaching styles to have a 'catchy opener' or satisfactory praise word in the presence of evaluators; they found themselves having to prepare their students for simplified standardized district competency tests while at the same time trying to preserve the authenticity of the more complicated approaches to the subject as they had been teaching before.

The centralized, minimum standards had the purpose of raising the level of the worst teaching; in many schools, they have had possibly more effect on the upper level of quality (and on the morale of the best teachers) than on raising minimums. This kind of unintended consequence (and it is impossible to believe any of the reformers wanted these effects from their well-intended policies) must be addressed before other states, and especially the federal government, institute minimum standards of content or teacher performance. Curriculum researchers and teachers must give serious attention to the substance of what is taught and to the effects of centralized reforms on the quality of that substance.

Uncertainty is at the heart of all real teaching. We never know exactly what to teach, how to teach, or what our students will make of our teaching. The recent Texas reforms, sometimes in the name of cost-effectiveness and sometimes in the name of equity districts and populations, have attempted to eliminate the uncertainties. The Texas reforms may enlighten other states if they bring to light the futility of trying to sacrifice personal educative experiences for the sake of ease in accounting. Education will be truly reformed when it can be a public good in its diversity, not in artificial uniformities.

Acknowledgements

A slightly different version of this paper was presented at the Politics of Education Special Interest Group symposium at the Annual Meeting of the American Educational Research Association, Washington, DC, April 1987.

Notes

1. 'Structuring excellence: the potential for district-level intervention', a grant from the National Institute of Education (now OERI), US Department of Education; Linda M. McNeil project director and principal investigator. This ethnographic study of urban magnet high schools consisted of extensive classroom observations, interviews with students and school staff and organizational analysis in selected courses in specialized desegregation high schools in a single urban school district in the Southwest. The central research question was whether magnet schools exemplify organizational structures which enhance the educative purpose of schools rather than exist in tension with them (as is more typical of traditional American high schools). Primarily a study of curriculum and the engagement of teachers and students in the development of personal knowledge or in the exchange of 'school knowledge', across a set of magnet high schools chosen for their organizational variation, the study expanded to include state-level policy as HB 72 and district implementations of the 1982 curriculum reform act began to influence teacher practice. This research is to be reported in a book tentatively entitled *Co-opting the Curriculum* (1988 forthcoming) and the report to NIE/OERI, summer 1987.

2. According to a *New York Times* article (12 April 1987), a Texas welfare family gets about 8% of the average earnings of a similar family not on welfare; in Massachusetts the percentage is closer to 23%. Similarly, a family receiving welfare payments of about $220 in Texas would receive $700–$800 in Massachusetts. In some Texas counties, according to press reports, school teachers who are their family's only wage earners and who have children, qualify for welfare or food stamps.

3. Some teachers learned only after their enthusiastic support for HB 72 that the state contribution to teacher salaries was targeted strictly to raise the minimum allowable teacher salaries, not to raise salary bases across-the-board throughout the state. Teachers in the major cities were frequently already paid well above the state minimums; their districts would not receive additional state funds for raises. One suburban district in the Houston area recognized the sense of betrayal among teachers who expected state-contributions to their salaries and decided to raise their districts' salaries out of local funds in order to have teacher pay follow teacher expectations of this reform package.

4. The connection of James Popham and the instructional objectives exchange, with its history of dissemination of behavioral objectives and curriculum aimed at testable outcomes, has not been the focus of any of the public debate; one reason is that this mechanistic paradigm is largely unknown to the public and not necess-

arily understood as being different from other forms of multiple-choice testing. Another is that most of the follow-up studies have looked at such immediate effects as teacher retirements, minority teacher pass rates and the like. Many teachers express confusion about the origins of these tests, and know little about whether they are drafted by TEA staff in Austin or are commercially produced. They are fairly sure there has been little teacher influence on the tests and they know that to enroll, one must write a check to an Iowa address. This contractual relationship should be thoroughly investigated not only because of the drain of scarce funds from the state, but for the tendency of school reformers in the 1980s to look around for available assessment instruments and then to build program toward them, rather than trying to figure out what is significant about learning and how it should be viewed. See L. McNeil (1987 a) for a discussion of the decision in one district to use a very minimal basic skills test format for the city-wide proficiency tests of course content. In that particular district, the curriculum staff in the central office were then asked to write course objectives and outlines according to the specifications of the test rather than to what they felt students should know. Reaching for a relatively inexpensive, standardized test rather than agonizing over curriculum, then over how it should be taught and how learning should be evaluated, is probably typical as state legislative committees on education rush to approve school reforms and show quick results for any costs that rise.

References

APPLE, M.W. (1982) *Education and Power* (Boston and London: Routledge and Kegan Paul).

BOYER, E. (1983) *High School: A Report on Secondary Education in America*. The Carnegie Foundation (New York and London: Harper and Row).

CALLAHAN, R. (1967) *Education and the Cult of Efficiency* (Chicago: University of Chicago Press).

GOODLAD, J. (1983) *A Place Called School* (New York: McGraw-Hill).

LISLE, L. (1980) *Portrait of an Artist: A Biography of Georgia O'Keefe* (New York: Washington Square Press).

McNEIL, K.E. (1978) 'Understanding organizational power: the weberian legacy', *Administrative Science Quarterly*, March, 23(1), pp. 65–90.

McNEIL, L.M. (1986) *Contradictions of Control: School Structure and School Knowledge* (New York and London: Routledge and Kegan Paul/Methuen).

McNEIL, L.M. (1987 a) 'The co-optation of the curriculum', paper presented at the Annual Meeting of the American Educational Research Association, Washington, DC.

McNEIL, L.M. (1987 b) 'Exit, voice and community: magnet teachers responses to standardization', *Educational Policy* 1 (1), pp. 93–113..

McNEIL, L.M. (1987 forthcoming) *Co-opting the Curriculum* (working title). Monograph reporting the research on magnet high schools. See note 1.

NATIONAL COMMISSION ON EXCELLENCE IN EDUCATION (1983) *A Nation at Risk* (Washington, DC: US Government Printing Office).

PLANK, D.N. (1986) 'The ayes of Texas: rhetoric, reality and school reform', *Politics of Education Bulletin*, 13,(2), pp. 13–16.

SELECT COMMITTEE ON PUBLIC EDUCATION (1984 a) *First Draft of Recommendations*. Mimeograph (Austin, TX: State of Texas).

SELECT COMMITTEE ON PUBLIC EDUCATION (1984 b) *Recommendations*. Mimeograph (Austin, TX: State of Texas).

SHEPARD, L.A. and KREITZER, A.E. (1987) 'The Texas teacher test', paper presented at the Annual Meeting of the American Educational Research Association, Washington, DC.

TEXAS EDUCATION AGENCY (1986/87) *Teacher Appraisal System: Teacher Orientation Manual* (Austin, TX: TEA).

15   *The politics of educational choice in Minnesota*

Tim L. Mazzoni
University of Minnesota

Purpose and perspective

No American state has had more experience with educational choice policy than Minnesota. 'There are now on [its] books', writes Hoffman (1985: 2370), 'versions of the two main elements of the national choice platform – a tuition tax subsidy and a variation on the voucher concept.' Indeed, Minnesota offers a unique vantage point from which to examine educational choice issues in state legislative politics. To undertake such an analysis is the purpose of this chapter. The results of the analysis here illuminate the way in which three kinds of politics – the politics of confrontation, finesse, and collaboration – influence the policy-making process and the chances for policy innovation.

Specifically, the intent of the chapter is to examine policy-making on four issues. Two have produced legislation – tuition tax deductions and post-secondary options. Two have not – education vouchers and open enrollment.[1] The four issues will be examined in terms of six propositions or expectations based upon previous research and theory. First, educational choice will be understood by participants to be a redistributive issue,one which transfers values so that winning by some stakeholders entails losing by others. Second, being a zero-sum game, educational choice will be hard to initiate – and impossible to enact – in legislative subsystems, with their institutionalized access groups, distributive bargaining, and incremental policy outcomes. Third, choice proposals will originate outside these subsystems and be promoted by challenging movements, groups, and entrepreneurs. Fourth, these innovations will be resisted by established stakeholders, especially those whose interests and ideals are most at risk. Fifth, decision-making will be characterized by the politics of broad-based participation, ideological confrontation, and non-incremental as well as incremental outcomes. Sixth, policies ultimately will be determined by the power of challenging versus established coalition.[2]

Educational choice politics on four issues

Issue 1: Tuition tax deductions

Educational choice initiatives in one guise or another have been before Minnesota lawmakers for decades. For most of that time, tax concessions for private school patrons have been the principal issue contested under the rubric: 'freedom of choice'.[3] Enactments began in 1955 when the Legislature approved an income tax deduction for tuition and transportation expenses.[4] Despite a previous history of controversy and its precedent-setting character, the deduction was passed quietly, with apparently no organized opposition nor any media coverage. Malen's (1985: 4–9) analysis reveals that this innovation slipped through as a non-issue. One lawmaker she interviewed stated bluntly: 'I voted for it, but I didn't know it was there.' Another acknowledged: 'It passed without our knowing it.' And an observer recalled that 'some [legislators] were shocked; others just accepted it . . . People don't like to admit they had been duped.'

Tax deductions had been eased through the Minnesota Senate as a free-standing bill. Maneuvering, primarily a deal to cap the deduction at $200 per student, placed it on the 'calendar of ordinary matters', a mechanism intended for the processing of routine enactments. Positioned in this manner, the initiative was approved by the Senate without debate. Since no deduction legislation had come through the House, bill authors and committee leaders attached the measure to an omnibus tax bill that had been passed by that body. The tactic was to insulate the proposal. Said a legislator: 'I did not want to argue it on the House floor as a new bill because people disagreed with it vehemently . . . It made sense to package it with another bill.'

The final element in the decision equation was the logjam that marked the hectic closing of the '55 session, a 'pandemonium' that enabled a handful of top lawmakers to exert decisive influence in the frenzied rush to legislative judgment. The policy-making process, as summed up by Malen(1985: 8–9), was one where 'a few officials who reportedly believed in non-public aids and represented sizeable Catholic communities, a few officials who held stategic committee and chamber posts, utilized ambiguous language, institutional procedures, and privately negotiated agreements to contain an explosive issue, camouflage a policy precedent, and secure a decision outcome which legitimated the principle of tuition tax concessions for private school parents.'

Once passed, the tax deduction statute received little attention as a policy question until the 1970s. By this time two private school groups, the Minnesota Catholic Conference (MCC), representing six dioceses, and the Citizens for Educational Freedom (CEF), the state chapter of a national lobbying organization, had joined forces. MCC efforts on behalf of a 'fair bus bill' had not produced legislation. It made sense to ally with the CEF (a group that the MCC had helped to promote) and to recast private school advocacy as a citizen – not a church – issue. The approach was successful in 1969 in obtaining transportation aid, and the MCC-CEF continued to employ it.

In marked contrast to 1955, the tuition tax credit of 1971 was enacted amidst much interest group-lobbying. Indeed, the press reported lawmakers as claiming that 'no other issue has been lobbied as heavily this session' (Howell 1971: 1) and as pointing to 'crushing political pressure' as the chief factor in the bill's passage (Franklin 1971: 1). The MCC-CEF alliance had mobilized a potent issue constituency to buttress its lobbying campaigns. This constituency, consisting mainly of parents organized through the church structure, was a disciplined political presence in many legislative districts. It could be called upon to contact lawmakers with insistent pleas and, if necessary, with threats of electoral retribution. There was a 'lot of pressure', state officials conceded, 'to vote the right way'. The clout of grass-roots activism, and the willingness and capacity of the MCC-CEF to sustain its advocacy, became the principal source of influence for the private school lobby.

Though the credit law was struck down by the state supreme court in 1974, the MCC-CEF persisted. The fundamental issue for the alliance was that 'parents had the prior right and responsibility to make choices at the elementary and secondary level, and not suffer economic discrimination when they made that choice'. Besides arguments rooted in such mainstream symbols as freedom, rights, and equity – symbols that could activate constituents as well as justify claims – other contentions were advanced. Aiding private schools was portrayed as a state benefit ('if we had to absorb all those [private school kids] we'd be bankrupt'), as a generator of options, and, increasingly in the 1980s, as strengthening a competitive system to motivate improvements in the 'faltering' public schools.

Whether arguments did much more than convince the already convinced – and fire them with zeal – is open to debate. One legislator echoed a common view: 'There is not a damn thing that anyone will say that will change a thing . . . Arguments are irrelevant.' Power, however, was not irrelevant. The deduction limits, with much MCC-CEF urging, were revised upward in 1976 and in 1984. The main political force behind these increases, extending Malen's (1985: 9) conclusion – her four case studies of issue politics were confined to the 1955–1981 period – was the 'relative power of a well organized, politically active, intensely committed, single-issue interest group alliance'.

Yet the power of the MCC-CEF alliance should not be overstated. The basic legislation had been on the books since 1955, and it had been written as a 'facially neutral' statute, one available to all school parents, a construction that broadened appeal and turned back legal challenge. (Its constitutionality was upheld in 1983 by the US Supreme Court in Mueller v. Allen.) Nor was the lost tax revenue, a few million dollars per year, at all large by state standards. The issue, too, had become popular; lawmakers with large private school constituencies embraced it as their own. And state revenue surpluses of the 1970s made it almost fiscally painless to be politically responsive to private school interests.

The minimal resistance of public school groups also made it easier for the MCC-CEF. Though denouncing tax concessions, these groups, noted a veteran observer, 'never really went after the issue'. Certainly they had the resources to have mounted a massive countervailing force. The Minnesota Education Association (MEA), the Minnesota Federation of Teachers (MFT), and the Minnesota School Boards Association (MSBA) were reputed to be among the most influential lobbies in St Paul. The teacher unions, in particular, had the members, money, and organization to heighten the electoral sensitivities of any lawmaker. Yet union political clout was not invested in fighting tax deductions. (The most spirited opposition came in court from the Minnesota Civil Liberties Union).

The weakness of the K-12 groups as a counter lobby had many sources. First, the original statute had been legislated in a manner that left them without access to decision-making. It is not clear that they knew what was occurring until confronted by a *fait accompli*. Second, the distributional politics of deduction increases involved relatively few dollars, stakes that were not of a magnitude to push aside other priorities. Third, the K-12 groups, like any lobbyist pursuing multiple objectives, needed multiple friends, some of whom were likely to be lost if the groups entered into 'acrimonious combat' on the deduction issue. Fourth, lawmakers could be counted upon to contain the concessions, and the courts until 1983 held forth the hope of throwing out the statute. Finally, the lobby itself was split, with the major cleavage aligning teachers against school boards and administrators. This cleavage cut deep, deeper than could be overcome for coalitional purposes by the threat of 'peanuts' tax deductions.

Not only were the public school groups distracted and divided, they were up against a politically capable alliance. The MCC-CEF had their bills carried by legislators who had a record of support for *public* education. Party balance was sought. The issue never was one between Democratic-Farmer-Labor (DFL) lawmakers and Independent-Republican (IR) lawmakers. Initiatives were defined as tax questions. They were routed to the tax committees and not to the education committees, the latter arenas being where the K-12 groups – an integral part of subsystem politics – could have exercised substantial veto power. Instead, this lobby, typically found itself 'outmaneuvered by a smaller alliance, clear on its organzational priorities and its political strategies' (Malen 1985: 27).

Issue 2: Education vouchers

Vouchers were advocated by private school groups, notably by the CEF, in the 1970s. Their bills, however, met with little success (one did pass the House in 1973), and by the end of the decade they appeared to be a dead issue. The CEF could not even obtain a hearing on its demonstration grant proposal. It was not until the early 1980s that the voucher idea re-emerged on the state policy agenda, and when it did the political dynamics of the issue changed. Choice advocacy extended beyond private school interests; it acquired a wider constituency and a more credible claim to legislative attention.

It was a public policy and civic research organization, the Citizens League, that triggered policy discussion of vouchers with a 1982 report on 'rebuilding' Minnesota schools. In neither membership (some 3000 'public-spirited Twin Cities citizens') nor re-sources was the League the typical – and ineffectual – good government organization. True, it did not have political clout. Yet it did have potent resources, ranging from a sensitive issue antenna and policy-relevant information, to organizational credibility and staff continuity, to member access to public and private influentials. Citizen League reports, each developed with staff assistance by committees of member volunteers, had for three decades shaped agenda setting on Minnesota issues, including those in K-12 education (Wilhelm 1984).

During the late 1970s, the League had undertaken a reappraisal of its own strategies, culminating in an *Issues of the '80s* report. In this pathsetting document, informed both by internal discussion and by broader intellectual currents, the League moved from a govern-mental approach to a consumer approach for reforming public services. Problems were identified as being rooted in governmental monopoly and calcified bureaucracy; solutions, it was asserted, were to be found in marketplace competition and user choice. Not surprisingly, given the new orientation, when the Citizens League turned in the 1980s to school reform, it asked the study committee to 'explore the strategic potential of the concept of "choices" ' (Citizens League 1982: 43). In its report, the League recommended three structural changes: deregulation, decentralization, and choice. The last proposed that students be able to select any public school and 'on a regulated basis . . . educational services be purchased from private vendors' (p. 35).

The choice recommendation rapidly became the focal issue in the Citizens League report. Two members of its Board of Directors were disturbed enough to append dissents, both rejecting the capacity of vouchers to expand equity for poor, disadvantaged, and minority students. Partly to blunt the charge of elitism, the League-sponsored bill confined the voucher plan to low-income families. Such a plan, it was contended, allowed low-income parents 'the same freedom to choose schools wealthy and middle-class parents now enjoy'. Along with the equity argument, proponents maintained that vouchers would foster alterna-tive learning opportunities, build parent commitment to education, and enhance productivity through competition. That vouchers would supply funding to private schools was softpedaled – or treated as incidental to the necessity of expanding choice and reforming schools. Voucher critics, of course, took precisely the opposite tact, stressing the 'windfall' that would go to private schools, funds which they branded as an unconstitutional, punitive, and debilitating diversion of money from the public schools.

In the 1983 legislative session, the low-income voucher bill was introduced by a DFL lawmaker, Representative John Brandl, an economist at the Hubert Humphrey Institute. Using the 'Brandl bill' as the vehicle, the Citizen League was able to attract media reporting, to enlist supporters from the proposal's 'natural constituency', and to organize proponents when they testified at hearings. The League co-operated with Public School Incentives (PSI), a non-profit corporation that had been formed in 1981 to 'create alternatives in public school education'. The League also worked closely with several individual choice advocates who had acquired independent influence on the issue. Particularly visible, besides Brandl, were Ted Kolderie, a former League Executive Director and Senior Fellow at the Humphrey Institute, and Joe Nathan, a St Paul educator, author of *Free to Teach* (1983), and – with the support of a foundation grant – an omnipresent policy entrepreneur for *PSI*'s many change alternatives.

The Citizens League co-ordinated some activities with the CEF and the MCC. But no lobbying coalition was forged. There were, to be sure, overlapping concerns. The CEF continued to seek demonstration vouchers, while the MCC had begun to hold workshops to proclaim the merits of 'family-power through family choice'. Still, 'the League's perspective', observed a staffer, 'did not entirely match the private and parochial school concern.' The League prided itself on standing for 'good schools . . . not pro-private schools or pro-public schools'. League officials saw the CEF bill as too limited and worried about it being melded through compromise with their own proposal. As for the MCC, it took a decidedly cautious stance, not wanting to commit significant resources until sure that vouchers would receive serious consideration, that its patrons understood the issue, and that the philosophy of Catholic schools would be respected. Perceiving big stakes in voucher funding, the MCC had an obvious interest in the issue. Yet the organization remained wary and did little beyond testifying for the League bill. As assessed by one lawmaker, 'the full power of the sectarian lobby was certainly not brought to bear on Citizen League positions'; in the same vein, a legislative staffer added, 'There was not even a mildly energetic lobbying effort by the MCC-CEF' (Wilhelm 1985: II, 261).

When it came to enactment, the League and its allies could generate little movement in the Legislature. Education vouchers, even in a modified and regulated form – and with influential proponents – remained politically weak. The poor were a difficult constituency to arouse, and opinion leaders were split on the equity claims of vouchers. The issue was a divisive one within the broader public. Key committee chairs in the Legislature expressed reservations or resistance. DFL Governor Rudy Perpich, an ardent public school booster, privately communicated his distaste. The Commissioner of Education, Ruth Randall – a Perpich appointee – publicly testified against the measures. (Randall did express support for expanded choice within the public school system.) The K-12 groups were unified in their opposition; they prepared to go all out to block voucher bills. In 1984, a new anti-voucher (and anti-tax deduction) organization came into being, the Minnesota Friends of Public Education. Having influential policy advocates among its Directors, along with individuals linked to the K-12 groups, the Friends opposed all 'tax diversions' to private schools.

Though not prompting legislation (Minnesota's school reform laws in 1983 and 1984 consisted of incremental initiatives), the League and its allies did have agenda-setting impact. They had set forth an ideological alternative and justifying rationale. They had made the issue the topic of policy discussion, the inspiration for countermobilization, and the anticipated source of new bills. They had reconfigured the climate of advocacy so that the voucher idea became treated by both friend and foe as a serious one. They had succeeded, within the context of a national 'excellence' movement, in shaping the parameters of debate so that educational choice could be found attractive by other reformers as a response to the demand for improved school quality.

This agenda-setting impact was revealed in late 1984 when the influential Minnesota Business Partnership – a lobbying organization representing the CEOs of the state's largest private corporations – issued its 'Minnesota Plan' for comprehensive K-12 reform. The report was prepared by a California consulting firm, Berman-Weiler Associates (1984), after lengthy study. Their recommendations may not have been well linked to Minnesota data, as critics charged, but they certainly were well linked to the advocacy climate in the state. 'Stipends' for 11th and 12th graders to attend any state-approved public or private program were among the many proposed changes. The presentation of the 'Minnesota Plan'; its mid-November endorsement by the Business Partnership; strategy meetings with the League, Kolderie, Nathan and other restructuring proponents; and, in turn, their informal discussions with top executive branch officials and staffers, were the confluence of events that propelled Governor Perpich to 'the front of the train' on school reform policy-making. And with the entry, energy, and ebullience of the Governor, the political dynamics of the choice issue changed once again.

Issue 3: The defeat of open enrollment

In early 1985, educational choice was suddenly and dramatically given pre-eminent status on the policy agenda by Minnesota's popular chief executive, Rudy Perpich. Stimulated by the Partnership report – yet adopting only portions of it – the Governor's Office launched a campaign for school district open enrollment. Their 'Access to Excellence' plan gave educational choice a primacy not envisioned in the Partnership report'; open enrollment was proclaimed to be the centerpiece, the essential wedge to leverage reform into Minnesota public schools. Perpich wanted 'all Minnesota families [to] be able to select [statewide] the public school their children wish to attend', beginning in 1986–87 with 11th and 12th graders. Nor was this Perpich's only choice proposal. He also advocated the expansion of existing programs permitting high school students to attend post-secondary institutions.

Perpich's agenda setting not only elevated salience but also transformed meaning. The Governor proclaimed that educational choice was about open enrollment and not about vouchers, confining the state-aided competitive market to public school students and institutions. Perpich's insistence on *public* school choice redefined the issue for state lawmakers and lobbying groups. It established a line of political cleavage unlike that which had formed on earlier voucher proposals. Other policy actors had to rethink their positions. Some pro-voucher groups (e.g., the Citizens League and Business Partnership) lined up behind public school choice. Some voucher opponents also sided with Perpich (e.g., the Education Commissioner, secondary principals organization, and PTA). But other voucher opponents sided against him (e.g., the school board, superintendent, and teacher groups). A few voucher opponents declared neutrality (the elementary principals organization) or were internally divided (the Minnesota Friends of Public Education). While private school groups could praise the choice principle, they thought it had been unfairly restricted in the Perpich definition. These groups were either on the sidelines, or they lobbied for the CEF's demonstration district voucher bill during the '85 session.

Open enrollment thus injected a new issue into Minnesota politics. Admittedly, there were issue participants who interpreted the public-private distinction as superficial or transitory. They argued that enactment of the governor's proposal would establish a precedent – a 'foot in the door' – that would extend inexorably to private school inclusion. Some intimated that public school choice was no more than a stalking horse for non-public school aid. Other detractors proclaimed the choice thrust to be but a minor part of a privatization agenda for all public services. But advocates denied the motive and the prospect. Governor Perpich's plan, a staffer insisted, had 'nothing to do with a conservative . . . federal agenda . . . [it] is not at all connected with tuition tax credits or with vouchers. The roots are in a more progressive agenda' (Hoffman 1985: 2371). Perpich and other proponents argued that increasing student choice of public schools would reduce student exit to private schools.

This, for example, was the position of Van Mueller, a former PTA President, who maintained that 'if choice exist [s] in the public sector, people won't need to turn to private schools' (Hoffman 1985: 2370). And Mueller, it should be noted, had taken PTA opposition to the tax deduction law all the way to the US Supreme Court.

While recasting political alignments, open enrollment prompted policy rhetoric that did echo some themes of prior debates. Advocates contended that choice would expand both equity, by giving students access to programs outside their resident district, and excellence, by employing competition to spur schools to implement change and to upgrade performance. Research, it was claimed, showed the benefits of expanded choice for students, parents, and educators. It was asserted, too, that families had the democratic right to choose a public school for their children. Opponents responded to these arguments by disparaging open enrollment as untried (no 'track record'), unnecessary (schools performed well), unfair (benefiting upper-income, metropolitan families), and unwise (promoting marketing gimmicks, undercutting co-operation, and devastating small rural schools). Against the rights of parents and students, opponents pitted the rights of education professionals and school boards.

Controversy over Perpich's 'Access to Excellence' plan started in early January when it was unveiled in a special speech to the Citizens League. Shortly thereafter, a task force (mostly educators) was appointed by Commissioner Randall to make procedural recommendations. The initiative met with a frosty reception in the Legislature, where DFLers retained a solid Senate majority but the IRs had taken control by four votes in the House. Immediate flak came from the school boards and administrator associations (MSBA and MASA), and later the teacher unions, notably the MEA, joined the barrage of criticism. (The K-12 groups also were upset by the lack of prior consultation, being informed about the plan just one day before the Perpich speech.) The how of open enrollment was the initial target, especially anticipated problems having to do with athletic transfers, desegregation regulations, transportation costs, and local district planning. Questions, complaints, and accusations – and the need for citizen support – caused the Governor, beginning in February, to tour rural Minnesota high schools to fire up the public about his plan.

Open enrollment was endorsed by the Citizens League, Business Partnership, Secondary School Principals, and PTA, among others. New support groups were formed: Citizens for Better Schools, a grassroots parent-educator lobby, and the Brainpower Compact, which had many prominent business, educational, and political leaders (including Albert Quie and three other ex-governors) among its members. The major Twin City papers ran laudatory editorials and gave headline news treatment to the issue. Commissioner Randall became a visible and vigorous advocate, and the Education Department served as a staff arm for the Governor's Office. The main opposing organizations were the four most influential K-12 groups: MEA, MFT, MSBA, and MASA. Many local officials denounced the proposal. In rural districts, choice often was equated with 'consolidation', school closings, and community disintegration. The open enrollment debate widened to questions of necessity and merit. It became heated, with the escalating fight between Governor Perpich and his 'establishment' antagonists drawing extensive media play.

The Governor's bill was not ready until late February. It contained many specifics – but rejected key restrictions – recommended by the task force. Toward the end of March, credible sponsors in the House and Senate, persuasive hearing testimony, and advocacy by the Governor, Partnership, and other supporters helped open enrollment win impressive first-round committee victories. But by early April this lobbying effort was matched by that of the resistant K-12 groups, board members, and local educators. Legislative leaders also voiced misgivings. And there was no clear groundswell of favorable constituency sentiment.

Proponents had made the issue a public one, but they could not make it a popular one.[5] Nor could they equal the communication and activation networks of their rivals. Open enrollment was amended out of the school aids bill by a 14–13 decision in the House Education Committee and by a close vote in the Senate Finance Committee. It was not revived on the floor or in a House-Senate conference committee.

Governor Perpich was the driving force behind the movement for public school choice. Coming out of nowhere in January, the Perpich-led coalition generated enough legislative thrust by April to put the matter in doubt. The Governor commanded enormous publicity for his K-12 plan, giving it an unusually high profile for an education issue. He co-ordinated through the Governor's Office and Education Department a diverse mix of influential supporters. He recruited respected bill authors. He personally lobbied one-to-one with lawmakers. He traveled the state touting his plan and trying to gain public backing. The governor's activity, by any standard, was extraordinary; and his strategy, whatever its defects, gave Perpich his only chance of a policy breakthrough. Had he relied on the actors and processes of subsystem politics, the choice initiative would have died stillborn in the Legislature.

Open enrollment was a long shot when Governor Perpich took up the cause. His coalition had to transform popular sentiment – or, more exactly, legislator perceptions of that sentiment – so that it was not a constraint on state action but an impetus for school choice. This had to be accomplished in the absence of a crisis (most Minnesotans gave high marks to public education), without an infusion of new funding to buy off losers and offer side payments (prior legislative commitments and tax relief competition left little surplus available for reform outlays), and in a period of economic dislocation in rural and small-town Minnesota (an acute farm depression sharpened rural distrust of any proposal that smacked of big business and metropolitan advantage). With time as a scarce resource, deficiencies in grassroots networks, fears over the future of small districts, and formidable adversaries, it is remarkable not that open enrollment lost but that it came close to winning.

Issue 4: Enactment of the post-secondary option

Governor Perpich's crusade gave open enrollment dominant status as a school reform issue. Yet centrality for public school choice meant marginality for post-secondary choice. This was not a deliberate diversion. Perpich genuinely believed in open enrollment. Yet uproar over that initiative did draw the 'focus and fire' away from other proposals. It fascinated the media and challenged the education groups. It mushroomed into a gigantic public issue. By comparison, the post-secondary references in the Governor's January speech and the brief provisions in his subsequent bill evoked scant controversy. They started and stayed on the periphery of the policy debate.

Post-secondary choice was not, as some opponents later charged, hidden from public view. The key formulation of the option, undertaken by the House Education Aids Division, came early in the process. And legislative decision-making was open and accessible until final conference committee negotiations. Nor was this provision ignored by either opponents or the press. Hearing testimony may have been meager and newspaper articles few, but they were there. Marginality, not secrecy, characterized policy-making. 'While not on center stage', noted one legislator, '[the post-secondary enrollment option] was always in the wings waiting to make its debut.'

Agenda marginality was necessary for the passage of the post-secondary option, but it was not sufficient. Many reform items in 'Access to Excellence' languished in committee;

others were scaled down into incremental adjustments. That this did not happen to the post-secondary section was primarily due to the interest and involvement of one lawmaker, Representative Connie Levi, who as the incoming IR Majority Leader held the second most powerful position (behind the Speaker) in the Minnesota House.

As in previous terms, Connie Levi served on the Education Committee. While she maintained cordial relationships with the K-12 groups, the Majority Leader had grown progressively more dissatisfied with educator responsiveness to one of her favorite programs, a program authorized in 1982 in what became known as the 'Levi Law'. This little noticed legislation – still on the books – allowed arrangements to be worked out between school districts and post-secondary institutions so that secondary students could take courses not available in their districts in these institutions and, as clarified by a 1984 revision, receive both high school and college credits for 'accelerated' or 'advanced' academic courses. Levi had become dismayed that school districts had done little voluntarily to utilize these statutes. She was prepared to press for new legislation that would lodge initiating authority with parents and students – not school districts – for taking advantage of post-secondary courses. It was Perpich's reform emphasis that gave Levi her chance.

The support of the Perpich proposal by the Minnesota Business Partnership – and by former Governor Al Quie – certainly cleared the way for an IR lawmaker to sponsor a DFL governor's plan. Moreover, the Majority Leader was in an enviable bargaining position. Credibility for Perpich was on the line; he needed some sort of victory. For her authorship, and taking the political risks, Levi could retain legislative control of the bill. Connie Levi was a committed advocate for 'expanding options for kids'; and, by most accounts, the Majority Leader fought hard for the Perpich initiative, though she did not like portions of it and never pressed her caucus for a party-line vote. Nonetheless, 'her baby' was the post-secondary option – an option about which Levi was unabashedly and publicly proud.

A 'Choice in Education' article, specifying in one brief section the Post-secondary Enrollment Options Act, cleared the House Education Aids Division by a small margin and was incorporated in the omnibus school aids bill. That measure then went to the full Education Committee. Here – by a single vote – open enrollment was amended out of the bill, with Representative Levi casting her vote on the losing side. Yet her policy defeat was not nearly so great as the Governor's, for the amendment to strike open enrollment deliberately left the post-secondary option untouched. No matter which way the decision went, the Majority Leader would realize her top priority.

Opposition from K-12 groups was the catalyst among the forces that stopped open enrollment. But the same opposition was not forthcoming on post-secondary choice. These organizations did not, in principle, like the option, believing it would siphon money from the K-12 system. Their lobbyists, however, did not do much more than sporadically voice objections, though some group leaders did try to alert and arouse their memberships. Taking on the House Majority Leader promised few and uncertain benefits – and threatened many and certain costs. It did not appear that more than a few hundred high school students would select the college option. Concentrated opposition would consume resources, and the K-12 groups already were lobbying on many fronts. They worried, too, about a House backlash that could unleash pressures for all-inclusive vouchers. Most of all, reportedly, they did not want to alienate Connie Levi.

The 1985 Legislature ended the regular session with work unfinished, the result being a month of conference committee meetings. During this time, post-secondary choice remained a minor issue. Though only in the House bill – in the Senate Finance Committee the option had been removed along with open enrollment – several Senate conferees were sympathetic. The post-secondary 'remnant', so termed by the press, received almost no media comment.

Whatever risk there was to this measure disappeared when, after committee negotiations stalled, Connie Levi stepped in to mediate the impasse. The Majority Leader and the committee co-chair, DFLer Tom Nelson, who had carried the Governor's bill in the Senate, quickly negotiated an agreement. Post-secondary choice was secured; in some respects, it was actually expanded. In final form the law enabled Minnesota public school students in the 11th and 12th grades to have the option of taking any 'non-sectarian' course from the state's public – or eligible private – colleges, universities, or voc-tech institutions, with these students to receive both state financial support and dual academic credit.

Governor Perpich could take some political credit – or blame – for the options statute. He had pushed the choice idea forward and given it momentum. He had set the policy agenda, prepared the initial alternative, sought out a bipartisan ally, and – inadvertently but importantly – diverted lobbying attention. Even so, Connie Levi, more than Rudy Perpich, was the policy architect of post-secondary choice for Minnesota high school students. Taking advantage of agenda marginality, opponent reluctance, and conference committee decision-making, the Majority Leader drew upon her positional resources, lobbying supporters (mainly the Business Partnership), and political experience to expand the post-secondary option (from the Governor's original proposal) and then to shepherd it through the legislative process. Along with being in the right place at the right time, she had the right resources – and the will and skill to use them. She not only coupled solution to problem, she coupled power to opportunity.

The calm of passage did not extend to the implementation of the Post-secondary Enrollment Options Act, for it quickly became engulfed in school district and legislative controversy. Critics charged that state-funded post-secondary options invited 'abuses', disrupted planning, promoted unfair competition (with two-for-one incentives), encouraged inappropriate choices, and drained money from K-12 education. The MFT brought suit in federal court against implementing the Act as it applied to 'religiously affiliated or oriented' institutions. Pre-session legislative hearings, however, brought balance to the public debate between defenders and detractors. And Commissioner Randall committed resources, staff, and determination to see the post-secondary option through its start-up period. The '86 session did witness intense lobbying by the K-12 groups, several seeking to roll back the program. But buoyed by testimony, an eager constituency (participating students personally visited lawmakers), organized supporters (some in education), and powerful bill authors (Levi and Nelson) – and with a comprehensive evaluation being required for the '87 session[6] – the option survived. One noteworthy amendment did modify the dual credit provision. 'Under the new law', reads a Senate summary (1986), 'the state will only reimburse tuition expenses if the student enrolls in the post-secondary course for secondary credit. However, if a student takes a course at a post-secondary institution and after high school graduation decides to attend that institution, the student *must* [also] be given postsecondary credit.'

Expectations, findings and prospects

The politics of confrontation

The conceptual expectations set forth at the beginning of the chapter offered a reasonably good fit for two issues: education vouchers and open enrollment. For vouchers this was hardly surprising, for it is the quintessential redistributive issue in K-12 education, one that threatens, if fully implemented, to disestablish the public schools. Reforming education through voucher funding was potentially the most explosive of Minnesota's choice proposals. It questioned once settled policy assumptions, exposed philosophical differences, and implicated core interests. It became polarized with challenging groups confronting established groups. The controversy in Minnesota was muted, however, because the voucher bills introduced in 1983 and 1984 were confined to low-income families (or to demonstration districts); and, more importantly, they had no realistic chance of passage. Proponents did not even push them to a vote.

Open enrollment did not precipitate the same political conflict as education vouchers; their lines of cleavage overlapped, but did not correspond. Governor Perpich had altered definitions. Issue saliency disappeared for private school groups; yet other voucher enthusiasts plumped for public school choice. Some voucher opponents joined Perpich; others lined up against him. There was much argument over whether the Governor's proposal was the way station to vouchers, and eventual private school aid – or was the road away from them. Not only did the Perpich initiative alter coalitional alignments, it also fissured as well as fused the K-12 lobby. Not all these groups deplored open enrollment, as they did voucher proposals. A few were intrigued by the all-public approach to choice. Still, open enrollment did set off a policy dispute reminiscent of voucher controversies in its intensity, divisiveness, and passion. In part this was because open enrollment was perceived to be a redistributive, nonincremental issue.

Open enrollment implied enrollment and revenue gains for some schools and districts – and losses of these students and funds for other schools and districts. It proposed to redistribute control over pupil assignment from producers to consumers. Nor were kids, dollars, and power the only stakes. Schools, communities, and lifestyles seemed at issue in small-town, rural Minnesota. Ideals were contested along with interests, with endless debate over whether market competition would contribute to – or subtract from – the quality of education. While the emergent symbol was 'excellence' invoked in arguments over whether client choice meant revitalized performance or diminished morale, the 'equity' symbol continued to be widely invoked in arguments over whether client choice meant expanded access or enhanced elitism. In Minnesota, as Siegel and Wilhoit (1986: 8) observe, the 'political tradition automatically treats concerns over equity alongside issues of quality'. The new symbolic politics of excellence had to be grafted to the old symbolic politics of equity. None more readily grasped this imperative than the Governor's Office; none more explicitly symbolized it than Perpich in his 'Access to Excellence' theme.

Open enrollment was defined by many issue partcipants to be nonincremental as well as redistributive. Certainly there was a case to be made – Governor Perpich and Commissioner Randall tried to make it – that the innovation was 'evolutionary not revolutionary'. Yet proponents frequently hailed the proposal as 'bold', 'daring', and 'fundamental'. That open enrollment was a major departure in principle and program was proclaimed more adamantly by opponents; but they preferred adjectives like 'radical' and 'drastic' to characterize the Governor's 'voucher program'. While some participants did downplay the allocative implications of public school choice, the dominant motif portrayed the issue as consequential, if not earthshaking, in its educational, economic, and governance stakes.

In Minnesota, then, public school choice became embroiled in conflict during the 85 session. It is impossible, however, to know how much discord was caused by the perceived impact of the innovation, and how much was caused by the state context and by participant strategies. Open enrollment became intertwined with two other issues salient at the time: consolidation and vouchers. The contentiousness of the first was exacerbated by the presence in Minnesota of many small school districts, acute rural anxieties about district reorganization, and severe economic distress in agricultural and mining regions. The second was made more abrasive by the state's history of private school advocacy for tax concessions and vouchers, and by the propensity of some public school adherents to interpret all choice proposals as but an extension of that advocacy.

As for conflict-inducing strategies, the constituency mobilization approach – led by Minnesota's most commanding figure, the Governor, and employed by both sides – enlarged and dramatized the dispute. Their public fight captivated the media, which both covered and contributed to the conflict. Evocative symbols were exploited to excite partisans, fuel anger, and solidify rigidity. Gestures at compromise were tentative and unsustained; 'ideological bargaining' (Peterson 1976: ch. 2) displaced 'pluralist bargaining'. Resolution came through head-to-head confrontation, with the verdict going, as it usually does, to the side with the biggest and most combat-ready political battalions.

The politics of finesse

While conceptual expectations fit the education voucher and open enrollment issues, this was only partly true for the tax deduction issue, which over the decades has exhibited 'inside maneuver' as well as 'outside mandate' processes (Malen 1985). And it was not true at all for the post-secondary option issue. The original conceptual perspective had constituted, in effect, a wide angle lens that looked beyond the legislative arena to bring challenging groups, constituency networks, and popular pressures into view. Yet the post-secondary issue – and policy innovation on the tax deduction issue – required, it was discovered, just the reverse, a narrow angle lens that cast legislative leaders and their opportunities into sharp relief. New departures on these issues exemplified Kanter's (1983: 221) conclusion that 'radical innovations' are likely to move ahead 'if they are either marginal (appear off-to-the-side issues so they can slip in unnoticed) or idiosyncratic (can be accepted by a few people with power without requiring much additional support)'.

In the 'slipping by' type of innovation, to use Polsby's term (1984: 159), the scope of conflict remains narrow. Outside political mobilization is not encouraged since that increases the visibility and hence the vulnerability of the proposed change. Yet (as demonstrated in the post-secondary case), the process need not be secretive, much less conspiratorial. Obscurity for an initiative can stem from marginal agenda status, a consequence of being subordinated to other, more highly publicized issues. Confrontation politics, thus, can provide the occasion and the opportunity for finesse politics. Controversy-produced diversion, intentional or accidental, functions like concealment (or camouflage, as in the tax deduction case), especially when myriad demands are crowding for attention, time is a pressing constraint, and decision impact is clouded by uncertainty.

Whether the result of concealment, camouflage, or diversion, low visibility creates a 'policy window' (Kingdon 1984) for insiders to initiate – or to reformulate, if already initiated – major legislative change. This may be done openly with some debate and opposition (post-secondary options) or done surreptitiously with no debate and opposition (tax deductions). In either case, when insiders combine positional leverage and political savvy, with opponent miscalculation (post-secondary options) or unawareness (tax deductions), they can maneuver a policy initiative into the final stages of decision making. Here the centralized insulation afforded by conference committees (post-secondary options) or leader-driven logjams (tax deductions) can be seized upon by insiders to obtain enactments, even of statutes like those mandating educational choice that hold great potential for policy disagreement.

The politics of collaboration

Recently, a third approach to educational choice policy-making has emerged in Minnesota, one that began with the creation of a Governor's Discussion Group for the purpose of agenda setting on K-12 reform issues. This forum came into being just after the 85 session and it met regularly into the '87 session. Consisting of several dozen participants, including all key interest group actors, challenging and established – and headed by Commissioner Randall – the Discussion Group was charged with formulating a plan that was both 'visionary' and acceptable. Perpich signaled that he would no longer champion disruptive reforms, no matter what their purported merit; that he would rely on the Group's plan for his 1987 initiatives; and, therefore, that organizations refusing to take a constructive role would have 'missed the boat' on gaining Perpich's endorsement (Kostouros 1986: 5). With the Governor's Discussion Group being declared by the dominant player to be the main game in town, other players had a compelling incentive to stay involved and to seek compromise.

Overcoming sharp disagreements and occasional wrangling – and, reportedly, the near dissolution into competing reports – the Dissussion Group hammered out a consensus on recommendations, including three dealing with educational choice (Governor's Discussion Group 1986; 1987). These asked the Legislature to (1) 'continue testing the existing controlled choice program [the post-secondary option] for 11th and 12th grade students'; (2) 'test a voluntary K-12 pilot choice program with appropriate assessment . . . participating districts [to] be granted financial assistance'; and (3) have all school districts, individually or collectively, provide alternative programs for dropouts or 'at risk' students, with these students being able to attend 'any school district or other public alternative program regardless of the school district of residence'.[7]

While collaboration has apparently redefined open enrollment and post-secondary options to be bargaining issues, ones where compromises can be struck, no such process is occurring on voucher funding or tax deductions. Because they entangle private school aid – and all its divisive beliefs, symbols, and interests – with educational choice, they were excluded from Discussion Group deliberations. Proposals on these issues remain polarizing. The CEF's demonstration voucher bill, for example, continues to be fought by public school groups. And private school groups are battling a proposed deletion of the tuition tax deduction in Governor Perpich's 1987 recommendations for state income tax reform (Viadero 1987:10).[8] On these educational choice issues, confrontation politics, not finesse politics or collaborative politics, is likely to decide legislative outcomes.

Notes

1. This interpretation rests on multiple sources: newspapers, documents, hearing tapes, publications, Ph D dissertations, and 42 in-depth interviews held in 1985 with legislators or staffers (10), executive agency officials (6), and group representatives (26). Unless otherwise indicated, quotations are from these interviews. For the tax deduction issue, the chapter relies on Malen (1985). Earlier accounts of the other issues appear in Mazzoni (1986a; 1986b).

2. The conceptual basis is set forth in Mazzoni (1986a:4–8).

3. As of 1981–1982 some 92,000 students (10.6% of the state's school-age population) were attending private schools; 70% were in Catholic schools (Minnesota Department of Education 1983).

4. Minnesota's deduction is available to *all* school parents. Its principal effect, however, has been to subsidize tuition expenses of private school parents, especially those from upper-income households (see Darling-Hammond *et al.* 1985:x–xi).

5. Two polls taken during the 1985 campaign reported that 60% and 69% of Minnesota adults opposed 11th and 12th grade open enrollment (Dornfeld 1985:6W, Craig and Samaranayaka 1985:18). A 1987 survey

reported that 47% favored and 49% opposed public school choice for high school students (Dornfeld and Tomson 1987:11A).

6. The evaluation, published in January 1987, reported an unduplicated student count of 3523 (some 3% of the eligible students) for 1985–1986. Revenue reductions for participating school districts averaged less than one percent of grade 11 and 12 state foundation revenue. 'In summary', concludes the report, 'the PSEO program is seen as beneficial by both parents and students, problems reported by post-secondary institutions and high school were generally few and minor, and finally the program had little impact on the nature and scope of courses offered by high schools and post-secondary institutions' (Minnesota Department of Education, 1987: ii–viii).

7. The choice proposal for at-risk students in fact was passed by Minnesota's legislature in 1987.

8. 'The Governor's interest', according to a staffer, 'is to have complete conformity with the new federal tax law; it really doesn't have anything to do with whether it's a good deduction or a bad deduction' (Viadero 1987: 10).

References

BERMAN, WEILER, ASSOCIATES (1984) *The Minnesota Plan: The Design of A New Educational System*, (Vol. 1 Berkeley, California: BWA).

CITIZENS LEAGUE (1982) *Rebuilding Education To Make It Work* (Minneapolis: Citizens League).

CRAIG, W.J. and SAMARANAYAKA, K. (1985) *1985 Minnesota Citizen Opinions on Public Education and Educational Policies* (Minneapolis: CURA, University of Minnesota).

DARLING-HAMMOND, L., and NATARAJ KIRBY, S. with SCHLEGEL, P.M. (1985) *Tuition Tax Deduction and Parent School Choice: A Case Study of Minnesota* (Santa Monica, CA: Rand Corporation).

DORNFELD, S. (1985) 'Public schools rate high', *St Paul Pioneer Press and Dispatch*, 3 March, pp. 1A, 6A.

DORNFELD, S. and TOMSON, E. (1987) 'New initiatives in education favored by public', *St Paul Pioneer Press and Dispatch*, 1 March.

FRANKLIN, R. (1971) 'Tax credits for private schools voted', *Minneapolis Tribune*, 15 May.

GOVERNOR'S DISCUSSION GROUP (1986) *Visionary Plan For Governor Rudy Perpich*, 19 December (St Paul: Minnesota Department of Education).

GOVERNOR'S DISCUSSION GROUP (1987) *Addendum to Visionary Statement* 10 February (St Paul: Minnesota Department of Education).

HOFFMAN, E. (1985) 'Educational "choice" debate has shifted from Washington to the state capitols', *National Journal*, 19 October, pp. 2369–2372.

HOWELL, D. (1971) 'Private school tax bill clears legislature', *Minneapolis Star*, 15 May.

KANTER, R. (1983) *The Change Masters* (New York: Simon and Schuster).

KINGDON, J.W. (1984) *Agendas, Alternatives, and Public Policies* (Boston: Little, Brown).

KOSTOUROUS, J. (1986) 'Whose vision is it, anyway?' *City Business*, 31 December, pp. 1, 5.

MALEN, B. (1985) 'Enacting competitive incentives for K-12 education tuition tax concessions in Minnesota', *Journal of Education Finance*, 11 (1), pp. 1–28.

MAZZONI, T.L. (1986a) 'The choice issue in state school reform: the Minnesota experience', presented at the annual meeting of the American Eduactional Research Association, San Francisco.

MAZZONI, T.L. (1986b) 'Slipping by: how post-secondary options for Minnesota high school students were legislated', *CURA Reporter, University of Minnesota*, 16, p. 5.

MINNESOTA DEPARTMENT OF EDUCATION (1983) *Information on Minnesota's Non-public Schools for 1981–1982.* (St Paul: Department of Education).

MINNESOTA DEPARTMENT OF EDUCATION (1987) *Post-secondary Enrollment Options Program Final Report* (St Paul: Department of Education).

MINNESOTA SENATE (1986) *Session Review*, 12, p. 2.

NATHAN, J. (1983) *Free to Teach* (New York: Pilgrim).

PETERSON, P. (1976) *School Politics, Chicago Style* (Chicago: University of Chicago).

POLSBY, N. (1984) *Political Innovation in America* (New Haven: Yale).

SIEGEL, P. and WILHOIT, G. (1986) *Report to the Minnesota Legislature and State Board of Education* (Washington: National Conference of State Legislatures).

WILHELM, P. (1984) 'The involvement and perceived impact of the Citizens League on Minnesota state school policy-making, 1969–1984', unpublished Ph D dissertation, University of Minnesota.

VIADERO, D. (1987) 'Perpich seeks end to school expense deduction', *Education Week*. 25 February, p. 10.

Index